20 Rules for Successful Investing

1. **Saving is a prerequisite to investing.** Unless you have wealthy, benevolent relatives, living within your means and saving money are prerequisites to investing and building wealth.

2. **Know the three best wealth-building investments.** People of all economic means make their money grow in ownership assets — stocks, real estate, and small business — where you share in the success and profitability of the asset.

3. **Be realistic about expected returns.** Over the long term, 9 to 10 percent per year is about right for ownership investments (such as stocks and real estate). If you run a small business, you can earn higher returns and even become a multimillionaire, but years of hard work and insight are required.

4. **Think long term.** Because ownership investments are riskier (more volatile), you must keep a long-term perspective when investing in them. Don't invest money in such investments unless you plan to hold them for a minimum of five years, preferably a decade or longer.

5. **Match the time frame to the investment.** Selecting good investments for yourself involves matching the time frame you have to the riskiness of the investment. For example, for money that you expect to use within the next year, focus on safe investments, such as money market funds. Invest your longer-term money mostly in wealth-building investments.

6. **Diversify.** Diversification is a powerful investment concept that helps you to reduce the risk of holding more aggressive investments. Diversifying simply means that you should hold a variety of investments that don't move in tandem in different market environments. For example, if you invest in stocks, invest worldwide, not just in the U.S. market. You can further diversify by investing in real estate.

7. **Look at the big picture first.** Understand your overall financial situation and how wise investments fit within it. Before you invest, examine your debt obligations, tax situation, ability to fund retirement accounts, and insurance coverage.

8. **Ignore the minutiae.** Don't feel mystified by or feel the need to follow the short-term gyrations of the financial markets. Ultimately, the prices of stocks, bonds, and other financial instruments are determined by supply and demand, which are influenced by thousands of external issues and millions of investors' expectations and fears.

9. **Allocate your assets.** How you divvy up or allocate your money among major investments greatly determines your returns. The younger you are and the more money you earmark for the long term, the greater the percentage you should devote to ownership investments.

10. **Do your homework before you invest.** You work hard for your money, and buying and selling investments costs you money. Investing isn't a field where acting first and asking questions later works well. Never buy an investment based on an advertisement or a salesperson's solicitation of you.

11. **Keep an eye on taxes.** Take advantage of tax-deductible retirement accounts and understand the impact of your tax bracket when investing outside tax-sheltered retirement accounts.

12. **Consider the value of your time and your investing skills and desires.** Investing in stocks and other securities via the best mutual funds and exchange-traded funds is both time-efficient and profitable. Real estate investing and running a small business are the most time-intensive investments.

13. **Where possible, minimize fees.** The more you pay in commissions and management fees on your investments, the greater the drag on your returns. And don't fall prey to the thinking that "you get what you pay for."

14. **Don't expect to beat the market.** If you have the right skills and interest, your ability to do better than the investing averages is greater with real estate and small business than with stock market investing. The large number of full-time, experienced stock market professionals makes it next to impossible for you to choose individual stocks that will consistently beat a relevant market average over an extended time period.

15. **Don't bail when things look bleak.** The hardest time, psychologically, to hold on to your investments is when they're down. Even the best investments go through depressed periods, which is the worst possible time to sell. Don't sell when there's a sale going on; if anything, consider buying more.

16. **Ignore soothsayers and prognosticators.** Predicting the future is nearly impossible. Select and hold good investments for the long term. Don't try to time when to be in or out of a particular investment.

17. **Minimize your trading.** The more you trade, the more likely you are to make mistakes. You also get hit with increased transaction costs and higher taxes (for non-retirement account investments).

18. **Hire advisors carefully.** Before you hire investing help, first educate yourself so you can better evaluate the competence of those you may hire. Beware of conflicts of interest when you consider advisors to hire.

19. **You are what you read and listen to.** Don't pollute your mind with bad investing strategies and philosophies. The quality of what you read and listen to is far more important than the quantity. Find out how to evaluate the quality of what you read and hear.

20. **Your personal life and health are the highest-return, lowest-risk investments.** They're far more important than the size of your financial portfolio.

Praise for Eric Tyson's Best-Selling For Dummies Titles

"Eric Tyson For President!!! Thanks for such a wonderful guide. With a clear, no-nonsense approach to . . . investing for the long haul, Tyson's book says it all without being the least bit long-winded. Pick up a copy today. It'll be your wisest investment ever!!!"
— Jim Beggs, VA

"Eric Tyson is doing something important — namely, helping people at all income levels to take control of their financial futures. This book is a natural outgrowth of Tyson's vision that he has nurtured for years. Like Henry Ford, he wants to make something that was previously accessible only to the wealthy accessible to middle-income Americans."
— James C. Collins, coauthor of the national bestsellers *Built to Last* and *Good to Great*

"The organization of this book is superb! I could go right to the topics of immediate interest and find clearly written and informative material."
— Lorraine Verboort, Beaverton, OR

"Among my favorite financial guides are . . . Eric Tyson's *Personal Finance For Dummies.*"
— Jonathan Clements, *The Wall Street Journal*

"In *Investing For Dummies,* Tyson handily dispatches both the basics . . . and the more complicated."
— Lisa M. Sodders, *The Capital-Journal*

"Smart advice for dummies . . . skip the tomes . . . and buy *Personal Finance For Dummies*, which rewards your candor with advice and comfort."
— Temma Ehrenfeld, *Newsweek*

"You don't have to be a novice to like *Mutual Funds For Dummies.* Despite the book's chatty, informal style, author Eric Tyson clearly has a mastery of his subject. He knows mutual funds, and he knows how to explain them in simple English."
— Steven T. Goldberg, *Kiplinger's Personal Finance* magazine

"Eric Tyson . . . seems the perfect writer for a *For Dummies* book. He doesn't tell you what to do or consider doing without explaining the why's and how's — and the booby traps to avoid — in plain English. . . . It will lead you through the thickets of your own finances as painlessly as I can imagine."
— Clarence Peterson, *Chicago Tribune*

"*Personal Finance For Dummies* is the perfect book for people who feel guilty about inadequately managing their money but are intimidated by all of the publications out there. It's a painless way to learn how to take control."
— Karen Tofte, producer, National Public Radio's *Sound Money*

More Best-Selling For Dummies Titles by Eric Tyson

Personal Finance For Dummies®

Discover the best ways to establish and achieve your financial goals, reduce your spending and taxes, and make wise personal finance decisions. *Wall Street Journal* bestseller with more than 1.5 million copies sold in all editions and winner of the Benjamin Franklin best business book award. Also check out *Personal Finance in Your 20s For Dummies* and *Personal Finance For Seniors For Dummies*.

Mutual Funds For Dummies®

This best-selling guide is now updated to include current fund and portfolio recommendations. Using the practical tips and techniques, you'll design a mutual fund investment plan suited for your income, lifestyle, and risk preferences.

Home Buying For Dummies®

America's #1 real estate book includes coverage of online resources in addition to sound financial advice from Eric Tyson and frontline real estate insights from industry veteran Ray Brown. Also available from America's best-selling real estate team of Tyson and Brown — *House Selling For Dummies* and *Mortgages For Dummies*.

Real Estate Investing For Dummies®

Real estate is a proven wealth-building investment, but many people don't know how to go about making and managing rental property investments. Real estate and property management expert Robert Griswold and Eric Tyson cover the gamut of property investment options, strategies, and techniques.

Small Business For Dummies®

Take control of your future and make the leap from employee to entrepreneur with this enterprising guide. From drafting a business plan to managing costs, you'll profit from expert advice and real-world examples that cover every aspect of building your own business.

Investing

for
dummies®
A Wiley Brand

7th edition

By Eric Tyson, MBA
Bestselling author of Personal Finance For Dummies

Investing For Dummies®, 7th Edition

Published by: **John Wiley & Sons, Inc.,** 111 River Street, Hoboken, NJ 07030-5774, www.wiley.com

Copyright © 2014 by Eric Tyson

Published simultaneously in Canada

No part of this publication may be reproduced, stored in a retrieval system or transmitted in any form or by any means, electronic, mechanical, photocopying, recording, scanning or otherwise, except as permitted under Sections 107 or 108 of the 1976 United States Copyright Act, without the prior written permission of the Publisher. Requests to the Publisher for permission should be addressed to the Permissions Department, John Wiley & Sons, Inc., 111 River Street, Hoboken, NJ 07030, (201) 748-6011, fax (201) 748-6008, or online at http://www.wiley.com/go/permissions.

Trademarks: Wiley, For Dummies, the Dummies Man logo, Dummies.com, Making Everything Easier, and related trade dress are trademarks or registered trademarks of John Wiley & Sons, Inc., and may not be used without written permission. All other trademarks are the property of their respective owners. John Wiley & Sons, Inc., is not associated with any product or vendor mentioned in this book.

For general information on our other products and services, please contact our Customer Care Department within the U.S. at 877-762-2974, outside the U.S. at 317-572-3993, or fax 317-572-4002. For technical support, please visit www.wiley.com/techsupport.

Wiley publishes in a variety of print and electronic formats and by print-on-demand. Some material included with standard print versions of this book may not be included in e-books or in print-on-demand. If this book refers to media such as a CD or DVD that is not included in the version you purchased, you may download this material at http://booksupport.wiley.com. For more information about Wiley products, visit www.wiley.com.

Library of Congress Control Number: 2013958308

ISBN 978-1-119-29334-7 (pbk); ISBN 978-1-119-29620-1 (ebk); ISBN 978-1-119-29619-5 (ebk)

Investing For Dummies, 7th Edition (9781119293347) was previously published as *Investing For Dummies*, 7th Edition (9781118884928). While this version features a new Dummies cover and design, the content is the same as the prior release and should not be considered a new or updated product.

Manufactured in the United States of America

10 9 8 7 6 5 4 3 2 1

Contents at a Glance

Table of Contents

CHAPTER 8: **Mastering Mutual Funds and Exchange-Traded Funds**............................157

Introduction

During the financial crisis of 2008, things got scary. Large Wall Street firms were going under, stock prices were plummeting, and layoffs and unemployment rates were soaring. And all this was happening in the midst of the 2008 presidential election. Talk of another Great Depression was in the air. In fact, polls showed a majority of Americans feared that another depression was actually happening. Housing prices were dropping sharply in most communities, and more and more properties were ending up in foreclosure.

Investing didn't seem so fun anymore. However, even though the downturn was the worst in decades, it had similarities to prior downturns, and people who kept their sense of perspective have enjoyed tremendous returns since the market bottom.

I know from working with people of modest and immodest economic means that the time-tested ways they increase their wealth are by doing the following:

>> Living within their means and systematically saving and investing money, ideally in a tax-favored manner

>> Buying and holding a diversified portfolio of stocks

>> Building their own small business

>> Investing in real estate

This book explains each of these wealth boosters in detail. Equally if not more important, however, is the information I provide to help you understand and choose investments compatible with your personal and financial goals.

About This Book

The best investment vehicles for building wealth — stocks, real estate, and small business — haven't changed. But you still need money to play in the investment world. Like the first edition of *Investing For Dummies*, the seventh edition of this national bestseller includes complete coverage of these wealth-building investments as well as other common investments, such as bonds. Here are the biggest changes in this edition:

>> **I've freshened up the data and examples in this book to provide you the latest insights and analyses.** Having trouble comprehending what "quantitative easing" is and whether the Federal Reserve's ending it will upset the stock market? Confused about how tax law changes should affect your investment strategies? Wondering about using an advisor to invest in funds that only he can access? Seeking a way to invest in stocks without exposing yourself to the tremendous risks experienced during the financial crisis of the late 2000s? Curious about what an exchange-traded fund (ETF) or hedge fund is and whether you should invest in one? Wondering how to use leveraged ETFs to boost your portfolio's return? Weighing whether and where to invest in real estate given current market conditions and the severe downturn in the late 2000s? Wondering what the best ways are to invest globally? Having trouble making sense of various economic indicators and what they mean to your investment strategy? Wanting to invest in a Health Savings Account (HSA) but don't know why, where, or how? You can find the answers to these questions and many more in this edition.

>> **I offer more information on investing resources.** With the continued growth in websites, software, print publications, media outlets, and other sources of investing advice and information, you're probably overwhelmed in choosing among the numerous investing research tools and resources. Equally problematic is figuring out who you can trust — and who you need to ignore. So many pundits and prognosticators claim excellent track records for their past predictions, but who, really, can you believe? I explain how to evaluate the quality of current investment tools and resources, and I provide tips on deciding who to listen to and who to tune out.

To build wealth, you don't need a fancy college or graduate-school degree, and you don't need a rich dad (or mom), biological or adopted! What you do need is a desire to read and practice the many simple yet powerful lessons and strategies in this book.

Seriously, investing intelligently isn't rocket science. By all means, if you're dealing with a complicated, atypical issue, get quality professional help. But educate yourself first. Hiring someone is dangerous if you're financially challenged. If you do decide to hire someone, you'll be much better prepared if you educate yourself. Doing so can also help you focus your questions and assess that person's competence.

Foolish Assumptions

Every book is written with a certain reader in mind, and this book is no different. Here are some assumptions I made about you:

» You may have some investments, but you're looking to develop a full-scale investment plan.

» You'd like to strengthen your portfolio.

» You want to evaluate your investment advisor's advice.

» You have a company-sponsored investment plan, like a 401(k), and you're looking to make some decisions or roll it over into a new plan.

If one or more of these descriptions sound familiar, you've come to the right place.

Icons Used in This Book

Throughout this book, icons help guide you through the maze of suggestions, solutions, and cautions. I hope the following images make your journey through investment strategies smoother.

ERIC'S PICKS

If you see this icon, I'm pointing out companies, products, services, and resources that have proved to be exceptional over the years. These are resources that I would or do use personally or would recommend to my friends and family.

INVESTIGATE

I use this icon to highlight an issue that requires more detective work on your part. Don't worry, though; I prepare you for your work so you don't have to start out as a novice gumshoe.

REMEMBER

I think the name says it all, but this icon indicates something really, really important — don't you forget it!

TECHNICAL STUFF

Skip it or read it; the choice is yours. You'll fill your head with more stuff that may prove valuable as you expand your investing know-how, but you risk overdosing on stuff that you may not need right away.

TIP

This icon denotes strategies that can enable you to build wealth faster and leap over tall obstacles in a single bound.

WARNING

This icon indicates treacherous territory that has made mincemeat out of lesser mortals who have come before you. Skip this point at your own peril.

Beyond the Book

In addition to the material in the print or e-book you're reading right now, this product comes with some access-anywhere goodies on the web. At www.dummies. com/extras/investing, you can find a variety of helpful articles on topics such as ways to evaluate your current investments, tips for investing in real estate, myths about entrepreneurship, and ten common investing mistakes to avoid. To view this book's Cheat Sheet, simply go to www.dummies.com and search for "Investing For Dummies Cheat Sheet" in the Search box.

Where to Go from Here

If you have the time and desire, I encourage you to read this book in its entirety. It provides you with a detailed picture of how to maximize your returns while minimizing your risks through wealth-building investments. But you don't have to read this book cover to cover. If you have a specific question or two that you want to focus on today, or if you want to find some additional information tomorrow, that's not a problem. *Investing For Dummies*, 7th Edition, makes it easy to find answers to specific questions. Just turn to the table of contents to locate the information you need. You can get in and get out, just like that.

If you're the kind of reader who jumps around from topic to topic instead of reading from cover to cover, you'll be pleased to know that this book has a helpful index that points out the pages where investing terms are defined.

1

Investing Fundamentals

Get familiar with the different types of investments you have to choose from, including stocks, bonds, real estate, small business, and funds.

Deepen your understanding of risks and returns so you can make informed investing decisions and react to changes in the market.

Make wise investing decisions that fit with your overall financial situation and goals.

Chapter 1

Exploring Your Investment Choices

I n many parts of the world, life's basic necessities — food, clothing, shelter, and taxes — gobble the entirety of people's meager earnings. Although some Americans do truly struggle for basic necessities, the bigger problem for other Americans is that they consider just about *everything* — eating out, driving new cars, hopping on airplanes for vacation — to be a necessity. I've taken it upon myself (using this book as my tool) to help you recognize that investing — that is, putting your money to work for you — is a necessity. If you want to accomplish important personal and financial goals, such as owning a home, starting your own business, helping your kids through college (and spending more time with them when they're young), retiring comfortably, and so on, you must know how to invest well.

It has been said, and too often quoted, that the only certainties in life are death and taxes. To these two certainties I add one more: being confused by and ignorant about investing. Because investing is a confounding activity, you may be tempted to look with envious eyes at those people in the world who appear to be savvy with money and investing. Remember that everyone starts with the same level of financial knowledge: none! *No one* is born knowing this stuff! The only difference between those who know and those who don't is that those who know have devoted their time and energy to acquiring useful knowledge about the investment world.

Getting Started with Investing

Before I discuss the major investing alternatives in the rest of this chapter, I want to start with something that's quite basic yet important. What exactly do I mean when I say "investing"? Simply stated, *investing* means you have money put away for future use.

You can choose from tens of thousands of stocks, bonds, mutual funds, exchange-traded funds, and other investments. Unfortunately for the novice, and even for the experts who are honest with you, knowing the name of the investment is just the tip of the iceberg. Underneath each of these investments lurks a veritable mountain of details.

REMEMBER

If you wanted to and had the ability to quit your day job, you could make a full-time endeavor out of analyzing economic trends and financial statements and talking to business employees, customers, suppliers, and so on. However, I don't want to scare you away from investing just because some people do it on a full-time basis. Making wise investments need not take a lot of your time. If you know where to get high-quality information and you purchase well-managed investments, you can leave the investment management to the best experts. Then you can do the work that you're best at and have more free time for the things you really enjoy doing.

An important part of making wise investments is knowing when you have enough information to do things well on your own versus when you should hire others. For example, investing in foreign stock markets is generally more difficult to research and understand compared with investing in domestic markets. Thus, when investing overseas, hiring a good money manager, such as through a mutual fund, makes more sense than going to all the time, trouble, and expense of picking your own individual stocks.

I'm here to give you the information you need to make your way through the complex investment world. In the rest of this chapter, I clear a path so you can identify the major investments and understand the strengths and weaknesses of each.

Building Wealth with Ownership Investments

**ERIC'S
PICKS**

If you want your money to grow faster than the rate of inflation over the long term and you don't mind a bit of a roller-coaster ride from time to time in your investments' values, ownership investments are for you. *Ownership investments* are those investments where you own a piece of some company or other asset (such as stock, real estate, or a small business) that has the ability to generate revenue and profits.

Observing how the world's richest have built their wealth is enlightening. Not surprisingly, many of the champions of wealth around the globe gained their fortunes largely through owning a piece (or all) of a successful company that they (or others) built.

In addition to owning their own businesses, many well-to-do people have built their nest eggs by investing in real estate and the stock market. With softening housing prices in many regions in the late 2000s, some folks newer to the real estate world incorrectly believe that real estate is a loser, not a long-term winner. Likewise, the stock market goes through down periods but does well over the long term. (See Chapter 2 for the straight scoop on investment risks and returns.)

And of course, some people come into wealth through an inheritance. Even if your parents are among the rare wealthy ones and you expect them to pass on big bucks to you, you need to know how to invest that money intelligently.

REMEMBER

If you understand and are comfortable with the risks and take sensible steps to *diversify* (you don't put all your investment eggs in the same basket), ownership investments are the key to building wealth. For most folks to accomplish typical longer-term financial goals, such as retiring, the money that they save and invest needs to grow at a healthy clip. If you dump all your money in bank accounts that pay little if any interest, you're likely to fall short of your goals.

Not everyone needs to make his money grow, of course. Suppose that you inherit a significant sum and/or maintain a restrained standard of living and work your whole life simply because you enjoy doing so. In this situation, you may not need to take the risks involved with a potentially faster-growth investment. You may be more comfortable with *safer* investments, such as paying off your mortgage faster than necessary. Chapter 3 helps you think through such issues.

Entering the stock market

Stocks, which are shares of ownership in a company, are an example of an ownership investment. If you want to share in the growth and profits of companies like Apple, you can! You simply buy shares of their stock through a brokerage firm. However, even if Apple makes money in the future, you can't guarantee that the value of its stock will increase.

Some companies today sell their stock directly to investors, allowing you to bypass brokers. You can also invest in stocks via a stock mutual fund (or an exchange-traded fund), where a fund manager decides which individual stocks to include in the fund. I discuss the various methods for buying stocks in Chapter 6.

You don't need an MBA or a PhD to make money in the stock market. If you can practice some simple lessons, such as making regular and systematic investments and investing in proven companies and funds while minimizing your investment expenses and taxes, you should make decent returns in the long term.

However, I don't think you should expect that you can "beat the markets," and you certainly can't beat the best professional money managers at their own, full-time game. This book shows you time-proven, non-gimmicky methods to make your money grow in the stock market as well as in other financial markets. I explain more about stocks and mutual funds in Part 2.

Owning real estate

People of varying economic means build wealth by investing in real estate. Owning and managing real estate is like running a small business. You need to satisfy customers (tenants), manage your costs, keep an eye on the competition, and so on. Some methods of real estate investing require more time than others, but many are proven ways to build wealth.

John, who works for a city government, and his wife, Linda, a computer analyst, have built several million dollars in investment real estate *equity* (the difference between the property's market value and debts owed) over the past three decades. "Our parents owned rental property, and we could see what it could do for you by providing income and building wealth," says John. Investing in real estate also appealed to John and Linda because they didn't know anything about the stock market, so they wanted to stay away from it. The idea of *leverage* — making money with borrowed money — on real estate also appealed to them.

John and Linda bought their first property, a duplex, when their combined income was just $20,000 per year. Every time they moved to a new home, they kept the prior one and converted it to a rental. Now in their 50s, John and Linda own seven pieces of investment real estate and are multimillionaires. "It's like a second retirement, having thousands in monthly income from the real estate," says John.

John readily admits that rental real estate has its hassles. "We haven't enjoyed getting calls in the middle of the night, but now we have a property manager who can help with this when we're not available. It's also sometimes a pain finding new tenants," he says.

Overall, John and Linda figure that they've been well rewarded for the time they spent and the money they invested. The income from John and Linda's rental properties also allows them to live in a nicer home.

WHO WANTS TO INVEST LIKE A MILLIONAIRE?

Having a million dollars isn't nearly as rare as it used to be. In fact, according to the Spectrem Group, a firm that conducts research on wealth, 9 million U.S. households now have at least $1 million in wealth (excluding the value of their primary home). More than 1.1 million households have $5 million or more in wealth.

Interestingly, households with wealth of at least $1 million rarely let financial advisors direct their investments. Only one of ten such households allows advisors to call the shots and make the moves, whereas 30 percent don't use any advisors at all. The remaining 60 percent consult an advisor on an as-needed basis and then make their own moves.

As in past surveys, recent wealth surveys show that affluent investors achieved and built on their wealth with ownership investments, such as their own small businesses, real estate, and stocks.

TIP

Ultimately, to make your money grow much faster than inflation and taxes, you must take some risk. Any investment that has real growth potential also has shrinkage potential! You may not want to take the risk or may not have the stomach for it. In that case, don't despair: I discuss lower-risk investments in this book as well. You can find out about risks and returns in Chapter 2.

Running a small business

I know people who have hit investing home runs by owning or buying businesses. Unlike the part-time nature of investing in the stock market, most people work full time at running their businesses, increasing their chances of doing something big financially with them.

REMEMBER

If you try to invest in individual stocks, by contrast, you're likely to work at it part time, competing against professionals who invest practically around the clock. Even if you devote almost all your time to managing your stock portfolio, you're still a passive bystander in businesses run by others. When you invest in your own small business, you're the boss, for better or worse.

For example, a decade ago, Calvin set out to develop a corporate publishing firm. Because he took the risk of starting his business and has been successful in slowly building it, today, in his 50s, he enjoys a net worth of more than $10 million and can retire if he wants. Even more important to many business owners — and the reason that financially successful entrepreneurs such as Calvin don't call it quits after they've amassed a lot of cash — are the nonfinancial rewards of investing, including the challenge and fulfillment of operating a successful business.

Similarly, Sandra has worked on her own as an interior designer for more than two decades. She previously worked in fashion as a model, and then she worked as a retail store manager. Her first taste of interior design was redesigning rooms at a condominium project. "I knew when I did that first building and turned it into something wonderful and profitable that I loved doing this kind of work," says Sandra. Today, Sandra's firm specializes in the restoration of landmark hotels, and her work has been written up in numerous magazines. "The money is not of primary importance to me," she says. "My work is driven by a passion . . . but obviously it has to be profitable." Sandra has also experienced the fun and enjoyment of designing hotels in many parts of the United States and overseas.

Most small-business owners (myself included) know that the entrepreneurial life isn't a smooth walk through the rose garden — it has its share of thorns. Emotionally and financially, entrepreneurship is sometimes a roller coaster. In addition to the financial rewards, however, small-business owners can enjoy seeing the impact of their work and knowing that it makes a difference. Combined, Calvin's and Sandra's firms created dozens of new jobs.

TIP

Not everyone needs to be sparked by the desire to start her own company to profit from small business. You can share in the economic rewards of the entrepreneurial world through buying an existing business or investing in someone else's budding enterprise. I talk more about evaluating and buying a business in Part 4 of this book.

Generating Income from Lending Investments

Besides ownership investments (which I discuss in the earlier section "Building Wealth with Ownership Investments"), the other major types of investments include those in which you lend your money. Suppose that, like most people, you keep some money in your local bank — most likely in a checking account but perhaps also in a savings account or certificate of deposit (CD). No matter what type of bank account you place your money in, you're lending your money to the bank.

How long and under what conditions you lend money to your bank depends on the specific bank and the account that you use. With a CD, you commit to lend your money to the bank for a specific length of time — perhaps six months or even a year. In return, the bank probably pays you a higher rate of interest than if you put your money in a bank account offering you immediate access to the money. (You may demand termination of the CD early; however, you'll be penalized.)

As I discuss in more detail in Chapter 7, you can also invest your money in bonds, another type of lending investment. When you purchase a bond that has been issued by the government or a company, you agree to lend your money for a pre-determined period of time and receive a particular rate of interest. A bond may pay you 6 percent interest over the next ten years, for example.

An investor's return from lending investments is typically limited to the original investment plus interest payments. If you lend your money to Apple through one of its bonds that matures in, say, ten years, and Apple triples in size over the next decade, you won't share in its growth. Apple's stockholders and employees reap the rewards of the company's success, but as a bondholder, you don't; you simply get interest and the face value of the bond back at maturity.

Many people keep too much of their money in lending investments, thus allowing others to reap the rewards of economic growth. Although lending investments appear safer because you know in advance what return you'll receive, they aren't that safe. The long-term risk of these seemingly safe money investments is that your money will grow too slowly to enable you to accomplish your personal financial goals. In the worst cases, the company or other institution to which you're lending money can go under and stiff you for your loan.

Considering Cash Equivalents

Cash equivalents are any investments that you can quickly convert to cash without cost to you. With most checking accounts, for example, you can write a check or withdraw cash by visiting a teller — either the live or the automated type.

Money market mutual funds are another type of cash equivalent. Investors, both large and small, invest hundreds of billions of dollars in money market mutual funds because the best money market funds historically have produced higher yields than bank savings accounts. (Some online banks offer higher yields, but you must be careful to understand ancillary service fees that can wipe away any yield advantage — see Chapter 7 for more information.) The yield advantage of a money market fund over a savings account almost always widens when interest rates increase because banks move about as fast as molasses on a cold winter day to raise savings account rates.

WARNING

THE DOUBLE WHAMMY OF INFLATION AND TAXES

Bank accounts and bonds that pay a decent return are reassuring to many investors. Earning a small amount of interest sure beats losing some or all of your money in a risky investment.

The problem is that money in a savings account, for example, that pays 3 percent isn't actually yielding you 3 percent. It's not that the bank is lying; it's just that your investment bucket contains some not-so-obvious holes.

The first hole is taxes. When you earn interest, you must pay taxes on it (unless you invest the money in a retirement account, in which case you generally pay the taxes later when you withdraw the money). If you're a moderate-income earner, you end up losing about a third of your interest to taxes. Your 3 percent return is now down to 2 percent.

But the second hole in your investment bucket can be even bigger than taxes: inflation. Although a few products become cheaper over time (computers, for example), most goods and services increase in price. Inflation in the United States has been running about 3 percent per year over the long term. Inflation depresses the purchasing power of your investments' returns. If you subtract the 3 percent "cost" of inflation from the remaining 2 percent after payment of taxes, I'm sorry to say that you've lost 1 percent on your investment.

To recap: For every dollar you invested in the bank a year ago, despite the fact that the bank paid you your 3 pennies of interest, you're left with only 99 cents in real purchasing power for every dollar you had a year ago. In other words, thanks to the inflation and tax holes in your investment bucket, you can buy less with your money now than you could have a year ago, even though you've invested your money for a year.

Why shouldn't you take advantage of a higher yield? Many bank savers sacrifice this yield because they think that money market funds are risky — but they're not. Money market mutual funds generally invest in ultrasafe things such as short-term bank certificates of deposit, U.S. government–issued Treasury bills, and commercial paper (short-term bonds) that the most creditworthy corporations issue.

Another reason people keep too much money in traditional bank accounts is that the local bank branch office makes the cash seem more accessible. Money market mutual funds, however, offer many quick ways to get your cash. You can write a check (most funds stipulate the check must be for at least $250), or you can call the fund and request that it mail or electronically transfer you money.

TIP

Move extra money that's dozing away in your bank savings account into a higher-yielding money market mutual fund. Even if you have just a few thousand dollars, the extra yield more than pays for the cost of this book. If you're in a high tax bracket, you can also use tax-free money market funds. (See Chapter 8 to find out more about money market funds.)

Steering Clear of Futures and Options

Suppose you think that IBM's stock is a good investment. The direction that the management team is taking impresses you, and you like the products and services that the company offers. Profits seem to be on a positive trend. Everything's looking up.

You can go out and buy the stock. Suppose that it's currently trading at around $100 per share. If the price rises to $150 in the next six months, you've made yourself a 50 percent profit ($150 – $100 = $50) on your original $100 investment. (Of course, you have to pay some brokerage fees to buy and then sell the stock.)

But instead of buying the stock outright, you can buy what are known as *call options* on IBM. A call option gives you the right to buy shares of IBM under specified terms from the person who sells you the call option. You may be able to purchase a call option that allows you to exercise your right to buy IBM stock at, say, $120 per share in the next six months. For this privilege, you may pay $6 per share to the seller of that option (and you'll also pay trading commissions).

If IBM's stock price skyrockets to, say, $150 in the next few months, the value of your options that allow you to buy the stock at $120 will be worth a lot — at least $30. You can then simply sell your options, which you bought for $6 in the example, at a huge profit — you've multiplied your money fivefold!

WARNING

Although this talk of fat profits sounds much more exciting than simply buying the stock directly and making far less money from a stock price increase, call options have two big problems:

>> **You could easily lose your entire investment.** If a company's stock price goes nowhere or rises only a little during the six-month period when you hold the call option, the option expires as worthless, and you lose all — that is, 100 percent — of your investment. In fact, in my example, if IBM's stock trades at $120 or less at the time the option expires, the option is worthless.

>> **A call option represents a short-term gamble on a company's stock price — not an investment in the company itself.** In my example, IBM could expand its business and profits greatly in the years and decades ahead, but the value of the call option hinges on the ups and downs of IBM's stock price over a relatively short period of time (the next six months). If the stock market happens to dip in the next six months, IBM may get pulled down as well, despite the company's improving financial health.

Futures are similar to options in that both can be used as gambling instruments. Futures, for example, can deal with the value of commodities such as heating oil, corn, wheat, gold, silver, and pork bellies. Futures have a delivery date that's in the not-too-distant future. (Do you really want bushels of wheat delivered to your home? Or worse yet, pork bellies?) You can place a small down payment — around 10 percent — toward the purchase of futures, thereby greatly leveraging your "investment." If prices fall, you need to put up more money to keep from having your position sold. (*Note:* Futures on financial instruments like stock market indices and interest rates are generally cash settlement rather than physical delivery, and they're an increasingly large part of the market.) My advice: Don't gamble with futures and options.

TECHNICAL STUFF

The only real use that you may (if ever) have for these *derivatives* (so called because their value is "derived" from the price of other securities) is to hedge. Suppose you hold a lot of a stock that has greatly appreciated, and you don't want to sell now because of the tax bite. Perhaps you want to postpone selling the stock until next year because you plan on not working or because you can then benefit from a lower tax rate. You can buy what's called a *put option*, which increases in value when a stock's price falls (because the put option grants its seller the right to sell his stock to the purchaser of the put option at a preset stock price). Thus, if the stock price does fall, the rising put option value offsets some of your losses on the stock you still hold. Using put options allows you to postpone selling your stock without exposing yourself to the risk of a falling stock price.

Passing Up Precious Metals

Over the millennia, gold and silver have served as mediums of exchange or currency because they have some intrinsic value and can't be debased the way that paper currencies can (by printing more money). These precious metals are used in jewelry and manufacturing.

As investments, gold and silver perform well during bouts of inflation. For example, from 1972 to 1980, when inflation zoomed into the double-digit range in the United States and stocks and bonds went into the tank, gold and silver prices skyrocketed more than 500 percent. With precious metals pricing zooming upward again since 2000, some have feared the return of inflation.

WARNING

Over the long term, precious metals are lousy investments. They don't pay any dividends, and their price increases may, at best, just keep up with (not keep ahead of) increases in the cost of living. Although investing in precious metals is better than keeping cash in a piggy bank or stuffing it in a mattress, the long-term investment returns aren't nearly as good as bonds, stocks, and real estate. (I discuss bonds, stocks, and real estate in detail in Parts 2 and 3.) One way to earn better long-term returns is to invest in a mutual fund containing the stocks of gold and precious metals companies (see Chapter 8 for information).

GET RICH WITH GOLD AND OIL?

During the global economic expansion of the mid-2000s, precious metals (such as gold), oil, and other commodities increased significantly in value. The surge in oil prices certainly garnered plenty of headlines when it surged past $100 per barrel. So, too, did the price of gold as it passed $1,000 per ounce in 2008, setting a new all-time high. These prices represented tremendous increases over the past decade, with the price of oil having increased more than 600 percent (from less than $20 per barrel) and gold more than tripling in value (from less than $300 per ounce).

However, despite these seemingly major moves, when you consider increases in the cost of living, oil prices at $100-plus per barrel were just reaching the levels attained in late 1979! And even with gold hitting about $1,920 per ounce in 2011, it was still far from the inflation-adjusted levels it reached nearly three decades earlier. To reach those levels, gold would have to rise to more than $2,450 an ounce!

So although the price increases in gold and oil (as well as some other commodities) were dramatic during the past decade, over the past 30 years, oil and gold increased in value less than the overall low rate of U.S. inflation. So one would hardly have gotten rich investing in oil and gold over the long-term — rather, it would have been more like treading water.

I'd like to make one final and important point here: Over the long term, investing in a stock mutual fund that focuses on companies involved with precious metals (see Chapter 8) has provided far superior returns compared with investing in gold, silver, or other commodities directly.

Counting Out Collectibles

The term *collectibles* is a catchall category for antiques, art, autographs, baseball cards, clocks, coins, comic books, dolls, gems, photographs, rare books, rugs, stamps, vintage wine, writing utensils, and a whole host of other items.

Although connoisseurs of fine art, antiques, and vintage wine wouldn't like to compare their pastime with buying old playing cards or chamber pots, the bottom line is that collectibles are all objects with little intrinsic value. Wine is just a bunch of old mushed-up grapes. A painting is simply a canvas and some paint that at retail would set you back a few bucks. Stamps are small pieces of paper, usually less than an inch square. What about baseball cards? Heck, my childhood friends and I used to stick these between our bike spokes!

I'm not trying to diminish contributions that artists and others make to the world's culture. And I know that some people place a high value on some of these collectibles. But true investments that can make your money grow, such as stocks, real estate, or a small business, are assets that can produce income and profits. Collectibles have little intrinsic value and are thus fully exposed to the whims and speculations of buyers and sellers. (Of course, as history has shown and as I discuss elsewhere in this book, the prices of particular stocks, real estate, and businesses can be subject to the whims and speculations of buyers and sellers, especially in the short term. Over the longer term, however, market prices return to reality and sensible valuations.)

Here are some other major problems with collectibles:

>> **Markups are huge.** The spread between the price that a dealer pays for an object and the price he then sells the same object for is often around 100 percent. Sometimes the difference is even greater, particularly if a dealer is the second or third middleman in the chain of purchase. So at a minimum, your purchase must typically double in value just to get you back to even. And a value may not double for 10 to 20 years or more!

>> **Lots of other costs add up.** If the markups aren't bad enough, some collectibles incur all sorts of other costs. If you buy more-expensive pieces, for example, you may need to have them appraised. You may have to pay storage and insurance costs as well. And unlike the markup, you pay some of these fees year after year of ownership.

>> **You can get stuck with a pig in a poke.** Sometimes you may overpay even more for a collectible because you don't realize some imperfection or inferiority of an item. Worse, you may buy a forgery. Even reputable dealers have been duped by forgeries.

>> **Your pride and joy can deteriorate over time**. Damage from sunlight, humidity, temperatures that are too high or too low, and a whole host of vagaries can ruin the quality of your collectible. Insurance doesn't cover this type of damage or negligence on your part.

>> **The returns stink.** Even if you ignore the substantial costs of buying, holding, and selling, the average returns that investors earn from collectibles rarely keep ahead of inflation, and they're generally inferior to stock market, real estate, and small-business investing. Objective collectible return data are hard to come by. Never, ever trust "data" that dealers or the many collectible trade publications provide.

The best returns that collectible investors reap come from the ability to identify, years in advance, items that will *become* popular. Do you think you can do that? You may be the smartest person in the world, but you should know that most dealers can't tell what's going to rocket to popularity in the coming decades. Dealers make their profits the same way other retailers do: from the spread or markup on the merchandise that they sell. The public and collectors have fickle, quirky tastes that no one can predict. Did you know that Beanie Babies, Furbies, Pet Rocks, or Cabbage Patch Kids were going to be such hits?

REMEMBER

You can find out enough about a specific type of collectible to become a better investor than the average person, but you're going to have to be among the best — perhaps among the top 10 percent of such collectors — to have a shot at earning decent returns. To get to this level of expertise, you need to invest hundreds if not thousands of hours reading, researching, and educating yourself about your specific type of collectible.

Nothing is wrong with spending money on collectibles. Just don't fool yourself into thinking that they're investments. You can sink lots of your money into these non-income-producing, poor-return "investments." At their best as investments, collectibles give the wealthy a way to buy quality stuff that doesn't depreciate.

TIP

If you buy collectibles, here are some tips to keep in mind:

>> **Collect for your love of the collectible, your desire to enjoy it, or your interest in finding out about or mastering a subject.** In other words, don't collect these items because you expect high investment returns, because you probably won't get them.

>> **Keep quality items that you and your family have purchased and hope will be worth something someday.** Keeping these quality items is the simplest way to break into the collectible business. The complete sets of

baseball cards I gathered as a youngster are now (30-plus years later) worth hundreds of dollars to, in one case, $1,000!

» **Buy from the source and cut out the middlemen whenever possible.** In some cases, you may be able to buy directly from the artist. My brother, for example, purchases pottery directly from artists.

» **Check collectibles that are comparable to the one you have your eye on, shop around, and don't be afraid to negotiate.** An effective way to negotiate, after you decide what you like, is to make your offer to the dealer or artist by phone. Because the seller isn't standing right next to you, you don't feel pressure to decide immediately.

» **Get a buyback guarantee.** Ask the dealer (who thinks that the item is such a great investment) for a written guarantee to buy back the item from you, if you opt to sell, for at least the same price you paid or higher within five years.

» **Do your homework.** Use a comprehensive resource, such as the books by Ralph and Terry Kovel or their website at http://www.kovels.com, to buy, sell, maintain, and improve your collectible.

Chapter 2

Weighing Risks and Returns

A woman passes up eating a hamburger at a picnic because she heard that she could contract a deadly *E. coli* infection from eating improperly cooked meat. The next week, that same woman hops in the passenger seat of her friend's old model car that lacks airbags.

I'm not trying to depress or frighten anyone. However, I am trying to make an important point about risk — something that everyone deals with on a daily basis. Risk is in the eye of the beholder. Many people base their perception of risk, in large part, on their experiences and what they've been exposed to. In doing so, they often fret about relatively small risks while overlooking much larger risks.

Sure, a risk of an *E. coli* infection from eating poorly cooked meat exists, so the woman who was leery of eating the hamburger at the picnic had a legitimate concern. However, that same woman got into the friend's car without an airbag and placed herself at far greater risk of dying in that situation than if she had eaten the hamburger. In the United States, more than 35,000 people die in automobile accidents each year.

In the world of investing, most folks worry about certain risks — some of which may make sense and some of which may not — but at the same time they completely overlook or disregard other, more significant risks. In this chapter, I discuss a range of investments and their risks and expected returns.

Evaluating Risks

Everywhere you turn, risks exist; some are just more apparent than others. Many people misunderstand risks. With increased knowledge, you may be able to reduce or conquer some of your fears and make more sensible decisions about reducing risks. For example, some people who fear flying don't understand that statistically, flying is much safer than driving a car. You're approximately 40 times more likely to die in a motor vehicle than in an airplane. But when a plane goes down, it's big news because dozens and sometimes hundreds of people, who weren't engaging in reckless behavior, perish. Meanwhile, the national media seem to pay less attention to the 100 people, on average, who die on the road every day.

Then there's the issue of control. Flying seems more dangerous to some folks because the pilots are in control of the plane, whereas in your car, you can at least be at the steering wheel. Of course, you can't control what happens around you or mechanical problems with the mode of transportation you're using.

This doesn't mean that you shouldn't drive or fly or that you shouldn't drive to the airport. However, you may consider steps you can take to reduce the significant risks you expose yourself to in a car. For example, you can get a car with more safety features, or you can bypass riding with reckless taxi drivers whose cars lack seat belts.

Although some people like to live life to its fullest and take "fun" risks (how else can you explain mountain climbers, parachutists, and bungee jumpers?), most people seek to minimize risk and maximize enjoyment in their lives. But most people also understand that they'd be a lot less happy living a life in which they sought to eliminate all risks, and they likely wouldn't be able to do so anyway.

REMEMBER

Likewise, if you attempt to avoid all the risks involved in investing, you likely won't succeed, and you likely won't be happy with your investment results and lifestyle. In the investment world, some people don't go near stocks or any investment that they perceive to be volatile. As a result, such investors often end up with lousy long-term returns and expose themselves to some high risks that they overlooked, such as the risk of having inflation and taxes erode the purchasing power of their money.

You can't live without taking risks. Risk-free activities or ways of living don't exist. You can minimize but never eliminate risks. Some methods of risk reduction aren't palatable because they reduce your quality of life. Risks are also composed of several factors. In the sections that follow, I discuss the various types of investment risks and go over proven methods you can use to sensibly reduce these risks while not missing out on the upside that growth investments offer.

Market-value risk

Although the stock market can help you build wealth, most people recognize that it can also drop substantially — by 10, 20, or 30 percent (or more) in a relatively short period of time. After peaking in 2000, U.S. stocks, as measured by the large-company S&P 500 index, dropped about 50 percent by 2002. Stocks on the NAS-DAQ, which is heavily weighted toward technology stocks, plunged more than 76 percent from 2000 through 2002!

After a multiyear rebound, stocks peaked in 2007 and then dropped sharply during the "financial crisis" of 2008. From peak to bottom, U.S. and global stocks dropped by 50-plus percent.

In a mere six weeks (from mid-July 1998 to early September 1998), large-company U.S. stocks fell about 20 percent. An index of smaller-company U.S. stocks dropped 33 percent over a slightly longer period of two and a half months.

If you think that the U.S. stock market crash that occurred in the fall of 1987 was a big one (the market plunged 36 percent in a matter of weeks), take a look at Table 2-1, which lists major declines over the past 100-plus years that were all *worse* than the 1987 crash. Note that two of these major declines happened in the 2000s: 2000 to 2002 and 2007 to 2009.

TABLE 2-1 ## Largest U.S. Stock Market Declines*

Period	Size of Fall
1929–1932	89% (ouch!)
2007–2009	55%
1937–1942	52%
1906–1907	49%
1890–1896	47%
1919–1921	47%
1901–1903	46%
1973–1974	45%
1916–1917	40%
2000–2002	39%

*As measured by changes in the Dow Jones Industrial Average

Real estate exhibits similar unruly, annoying tendencies. Although real estate (like stocks) has been a terrific long-term investment, various real estate markets get clobbered from time to time.

U.S. housing prices took a 25 percent tumble from the late 1920s to the mid-1930s. When the oil industry collapsed in the southern United States in the early 1980s, real estate prices took a beating in that area. Later in the 1980s and early 1990s, the northeastern United States became mired in a severe recession, and real estate prices fell by 20-plus percent in many areas. After peaking near 1990, many of the West Coast housing markets, especially those in California, experienced falling prices — dropping 20 percent or more in most areas by the mid-1990s. The Japanese real estate market crash also began around the time of the California market fall. Property prices in Japan collapsed more than 60 percent.

Declining U.S. housing prices in the mid- to late 2000s garnered unprecedented attention. Some folks and pundits acted like it was the worst housing market ever. Foreclosures increased in part because of buyers who financed their home's purchase with risky mortgages (which I recommend against in my books, including this one — see Chapter 12). I must note here that housing market conditions vary by area. For example, some portions of the Pacific Northwest and South actually appreciated during the mid- to late 2000s, while other markets experienced substantial declines.

After reading this section, you may want to keep all your money in the bank — after all, you know you won't lose your money, and you won't have to be a nonstop worrier. No one has lost 20, 40, 60, or 80 percent of his bank-held savings vehicle in a few years since the FDIC came into existence (major losses prior to then did happen, though). But just letting your money sit around would be a mistake.

REMEMBER

If you pass up the stock and real estate markets simply because of the potential market value risk, you miss out on a historic, time-tested method of building substantial wealth. Instead of seeing declines and market corrections as horrible things, view them as potential opportunities or "sales." Try not to give in to the human emotions that often scare people away from buying something that others seem to be shunning.

Later in this chapter, I show you the generous returns that stocks and real estate as well as other investments have historically provided. The following sections suggest some simple things you can do to lower your investing risk and help prevent your portfolio from suffering a huge fall.

Diversify for a gentler ride

If you worry about the health of the U.S. economy, the government, and the dollar, you can reduce your investment risk by investing overseas. Most large U.S. companies do business overseas, so when you invest in larger U.S. company stocks, you get some international investment exposure. You can also invest in international company stocks, ideally via mutual funds and exchange-traded funds (see Chapter 8).

Of course, investing overseas can't totally protect you in the event of a global economic catastrophe. If you worry about the risk of such a calamity, you should probably also worry about a huge meteor crashing into Earth. Maybe there's a way to colonize outer space . . .

TIP

Diversifying your investments can involve more than just your stock portfolio. You can also hold some real estate investments to diversify your investment portfolio. Many real estate markets actually appreciated in the early 2000s while the U.S. stock market was in the doghouse. Conversely, when U.S. real estate entered a multiyear slump in the mid-2000s, stocks performed well during that period. In the late 2000s, stock prices fell sharply while real estate prices in most areas declined, but then stocks came roaring back.

Consider your time horizon

Investors who worry that the stock market may take a dive and take their money down with it need to consider the length of time that they plan to invest. In a one-year period in the stock and bond markets, a wide range of outcomes can occur (as shown in Figure 2-1). History shows that you lose money about once in every three years that you invest in the stock and bond markets. However, stock market investors have made money (sometimes substantial amounts) approximately two-thirds of the time over a one-year period. (Bond investors made money about two-thirds of the time, too, although they made a good deal less on average.)

Although the stock market is more volatile than the bond market in the short term, stock market investors have earned far better long-term returns than bond investors have. (See the "Stock returns" section later in this chapter for details.) Why? Because stock investors bear risks that bond investors don't bear, and they can reasonably expect to be compensated for those risks. Remember, however, that bonds generally outperform a boring old bank account.

REMEMBER

History has shown that the risk of a stock or bond market fall becomes less of a concern the longer that you plan to invest. As Figure 2-2 shows, as the holding period for owning stocks increases from 1 year to 3 years to 5 years to 10 years and then to 20 years, there's a greater likelihood of seeing stocks increase in value. In

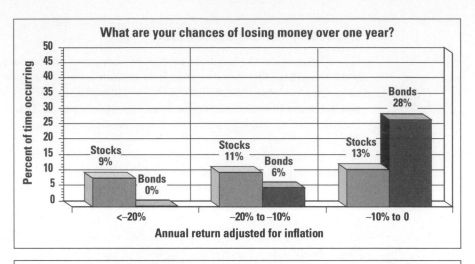

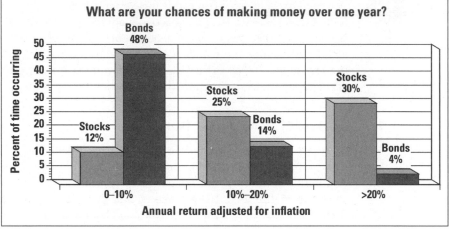

FIGURE 2-1:
What are the odds of making or losing money in the U.S. markets? In a single year, you win far more often (and bigger) with stocks than with bonds.

fact, over any 20-year time span, the U.S. stock market, as measured by the S&P 500 index of larger company stocks, has *never* lost money, even after you subtract the effects of inflation.

Most stock market investors I know are concerned about the risk of losing money. Figure 2-2 clearly shows that the key to minimizing the probability that you'll lose money in stocks is to hold them for the longer term. Don't invest in stocks unless you plan to hold them for at least five years — and preferably a decade or longer. Check out Part 2 of this book for more on using stocks as a long-term investment.

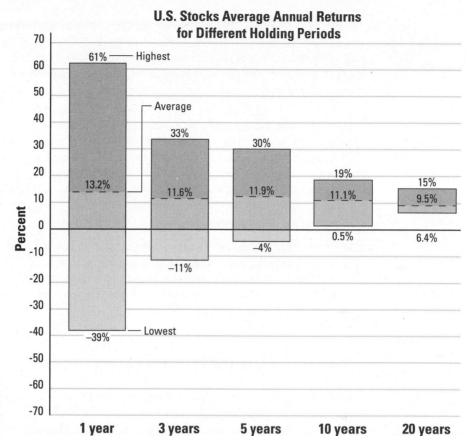

U.S. Stocks Average Annual Returns for Different Holding Periods

Data Source: Standard & Poor's 500 index

© John Wiley & Sons, Inc.

FIGURE 2-2: The longer you hold stocks, the more likely you are to make money.

Pare down holdings in bloated markets

Perhaps you've heard the expression "buy low, sell high." Although I don't believe that you can *time the markets* (that is, predict the most profitable time to buy and sell), spotting a greatly overpriced or underpriced market isn't too difficult. For example, in the second edition of this book, published in 1999, I warned readers about the grossly inflated prices of many Internet and technology stocks (see Chapter 5). Throughout this book, I explain some simple yet powerful methods you can use to measure whether a particular investment market is of fair value, of good value, or overpriced. You should avoid overpriced investments for two important reasons:

>> If and when these overpriced investments fall, they usually fall farther and faster than more fairly priced investments.

>> You should be able to find other investments that offer higher potential returns.

TIP

Ideally, you want to avoid having a lot of your money in markets that appear over-priced (see Chapter 5 for how to spot pricey markets). Practically speaking, avoiding overpriced markets doesn't mean that you should try to sell all your holdings in such markets with the vain hope of buying them back at a much lower price. However, you may benefit from the following strategies:

>> **Invest new money elsewhere.** Focus your investment of new money somewhere other than the overpriced market; put it into investments that offer you better values. As a result, without selling any of your seemingly expensive investments, you make them a smaller portion of your total holdings. If you hold investments outside tax-sheltered retirement accounts, focusing your money elsewhere also allows you to avoid incurring taxes from selling appreciated investments.

>> **If you have to sell, sell the expensive stuff.** If you need to raise money to live on, such as for retirement or for a major purchase, sell the pricier holdings. As long as the taxes aren't too troublesome, it's better to sell high and lock in your profits. Chapter 21 discusses issues to weigh when you contemplate selling an investment.

Individual-investment risk

A downdraft can put an entire investment market on a roller-coaster ride, but healthy markets also have their share of individual losers. For example, from the early 1980s through the late 1990s, the U.S. stock market had one of the greatest appreciating markets in history. You'd never know it, though, if you held one of the great losers of that period.

Consider a company now called Navistar, which has undergone enormous trans-formations in the past two decades. This company used to be called International Harvester and manufactured farm equipment, trucks, and construction and other industrial equipment. Today, Navistar makes mostly trucks.

In late 1983, this company's stock traded at more than $140 per share. It then plunged more than 90 percent over the ensuing decade (as shown in Figure 2-3). Even with a rally in recent years, Navistar stock still trades at less than $50 per share (after dipping below $10 per share). Lest you think that's a big drop, this company's stock traded as high as $455 per share in the late 1970s! If a worker retired from this company in the late 1970s with $200,000 invested in the com-pany stock, the retiree's investment would be worth about $25,000 today! On the other hand, if the retiree had simply swapped his stock at retirement for a diversi-fied portfolio of stocks, which I explain how to build in Part 2, his $200,000 nest egg would've instead grown to more than $4 million!

NAVISTAR INTL (NAV)

FIGURE 2-3:
Even the bull
market of the
1990s wasn't kind
to every
company.

Just as individual stock prices can plummet, so can individual real estate property prices. In California during the 1990s, for example, earthquakes rocked the prices of properties built on landfills. These quakes highlighted the dangers of building on poor soil. In the early 1980s, real estate values in the communities of Times Beach, Missouri, and Love Canal, New York, plunged because of carcinogenic toxic waste contamination. (Ultimately, many property owners in these areas received compensation for their losses from the federal government as well as from some real estate agencies that didn't disclose these known contaminants.)

TIP

Here are some simple steps you can take to lower the risk of individual investments that can upset your goals:

» **Do your homework.** When you purchase real estate, a whole host of inspections can save you from buying a money pit. With stocks, you can examine some measures of value and the company's financial condition and business strategy to reduce your chances of buying into an overpriced company or one on the verge of major problems. Parts 2, 3, and 4 of this book give you information on researching your investment.

» **Diversify.** Investors who seek growth invest in securities such as stocks. Placing significant amounts of your capital in one or a handful of securities is risky, particularly if the stocks are in the same industry or closely related industries. To reduce this risk, purchase stocks in a variety of industries and companies within each industry. (See Part 2 for details.)

» **Hire someone to invest for you.** The best funds (see Chapter 8) offer low-cost, professional management and oversight as well as diversification. Stock funds typically own 25 or more securities in a variety of companies in different industries. In Part 3, I explain how you can invest in real estate in a similar way (that is, by leaving the driving to someone else).

THE LOWDOWN ON LIQUIDITY

The term *liquidity* refers to how long and at what cost it takes to convert an investment into cash. The money in your wallet is considered perfectly liquid — it's already cash.

Suppose that you invested money in a handful of stocks. Although you can't easily sell these stocks on a Saturday night, you can sell most stocks quickly through a broker for a nominal fee any day that the financial markets are open (normal working days). You pay a higher percentage to sell your stocks if you use a high-cost broker or if you have a small amount of stock to sell.

Real estate is generally much less liquid than stock. Preparing your property for sale takes time, and if you want to get fair market value for your property, finding a buyer may take weeks or months. Selling costs (agent commissions, fix-up expenses, and closing costs) can approach 8 to 10 percent of the home's value.

A privately run small business is among the least liquid of the better growth investments that you can make. Selling such a business typically takes longer than selling most real estate.

So that you're not forced to sell one of your investments that you intend to hold for long-term purposes, keep an emergency reserve of three to six months' worth of living expenses in a money market account. Also consider investing some money in highly rated bonds (see Chapter 7), which pay higher than money market yields without the high risk or volatility that comes with the stock market.

Purchasing-power risk

Increases in the cost of living (that is, inflation) can erode the value of your retirement resources and what you can buy with that money — also known as its *purchasing power.* When Teri retired at the age of 60, she was pleased with her retirement income. She was receiving an $800-per-month pension and $1,200 per month from money that she had invested in long-term bonds. Her monthly expenditures amounted to about $1,500, so she was able to save a little money for an occasional trip.

Fast-forward 15 years. Teri still receives $800 per month from her pension, but now she gets only $900 per month of investment income, which comes from some certificates of deposit. Teri bailed out of bonds after she lost sleep over the sometimes roller-coaster-like price movements in the bond market. Her monthly expenditures now amount to approximately $2,400, and she uses some of her investment principal (original investment). She's terrified of outliving her money.

Teri has reason to worry. She has 100 percent of her money invested without protection against increases in the cost of living. Although her income felt comfortable in the beginning of her retirement, it doesn't at age 75, and Teri may easily live another 15 or more years.

The erosion of the purchasing power of your investment dollar can, over longer time periods, be as bad as or worse than the effect of a major market crash. Table 2-2 shows the effective loss in purchasing power of your money at various rates of inflation and over differing time periods.

TABLE 2-2 **Inflation's Corrosive Effect on Your Money's Purchasing Power**

Inflation Rate	10 Years	15 Years	25 Years	40 Years
2%	–18%	–26%	–39%	–55%
4%	–32%	–44%	–62%	–81%
6%	–44%	–58%	–77%	–90%
8%	–54%	–68%	–85%	–95%
10%	–61%	–76%	–91%	–98%

REMEMBER

As a financial counselor, I often saw skittish investors try to keep their money in bonds and money market accounts, thinking they were playing it safe. The risk in this strategy is that your money won't grow enough over the years for you to accomplish your financial goals. In other words, the lower the return you earn, the more you need to save to reach a particular financial goal.

A 40-year-old wanting to accumulate $500,000 by age 65 would need to save $722 per month if she earns a 6 percent average annual return but needs to save only $377 per month if she earns a 10 percent average return per year. Younger investors need to pay the most attention to the risk of generating low returns, but so should younger senior citizens. At the age of 65, seniors need to recognize that a portion of their assets may not be used for a decade or more from the present.

Career risk

REMEMBER

Your ability to earn money is most likely your single biggest asset, or at least one of your biggest assets. Most people achieve what they do in the working world through education and hard work. By education, I'm not simply talking about what one learns in formal schooling. Education is a lifelong process. I've learned far more about business from my own front-line experiences and those of others than I've learned in educational settings. I also read a lot. (In Part 5, I recommend books and other resources that I've found most useful.)

If you don't continually invest in your education, you risk losing your competitive edge. Your skills and perspectives can become dated and obsolete. Although that doesn't mean you should work 80 hours a week and never do anything fun, it does mean that part of your "work" time should involve upgrading your skills.

The best organizations are those that recognize the need for continual knowledge and invest in their workforce through training and career development. Just remember to look at your own career objectives, which may not be the same as your company's.

INFLATION RAGIN' OUTTA CONTROL

You think 6, 8, or 10 percent annual inflation rates are bad? How would you like to live in a country that experienced that rate of inflation in a day? Too much money in circulation chasing after too few goods causes high rates of inflation.

A government that runs amok with the nation's currency and money supply usually causes excessive rates of inflation — dubbed *hyperinflation*. Over the decades and centuries, hyperinflation has wreaked havoc in more than a few countries.

What happened in Germany in the late 1910s and early 1920s demonstrates how bad hyperinflation can get. Consider that during this time period, prices increased nearly one-billionfold! What cost 1 reichsmark (the German currency in those days) at the beginning of this mess eventually cost nearly 1,000,000,000 reichsmarks. People had to cart around so much currency that at times they needed wheelbarrows to haul it! Ultimately, this inflationary burden was too much for the German society, creating a social climate that fueled the rise of the Nazi party and Adolf Hitler.

During the 1990s, a number of countries, especially many that made up the former USSR and others such as Brazil and Lithuania, got themselves into a hyperinflationary mess with inflation rates of several hundred percent per year. In the mid-1980s, Bolivia's yearly inflation rate exceeded 10,000 percent.

Governments often try to slap on price controls to prevent runaway inflation (President Richard Nixon did this in the United States in the 1970s), but the underground economy, known as the *black market,* usually prevails.

Analyzing Returns

When you make investments, you have the potential to make money in a variety of ways. Each type of investment has its own mix of associated risks that you take when you part with your investment dollar and, likewise, offers a different potential rate of return. In the following sections, I cover the returns you can expect with each of the common investing avenues. But first, I walk you through the components of calculating the total return on an investment.

The components of total return

To figure out exactly how much money you've made (or lost) on your investment, you need to calculate the *total return.* To come up with this figure, you need to determine how much money you originally invested and then factor in the other components, such as interest, dividends, and appreciation (or depreciation).

If you've ever had money in a bank account that pays *interest,* you know that the bank pays you a small amount of interest when you allow it to keep your money. The bank then turns around and lends your money to some other person or organization at a much higher rate of interest. The rate of interest is also known as the *yield.* So if a bank tells you that its savings account pays 2 percent interest, the bank may also say that the account yields 2 percent. Banks usually quote interest rates or yields on an annual basis. Interest that you receive is one component of the return you receive on your investment.

If a bank pays monthly interest, the bank also likely quotes a *compounded effective annual yield.* After the first month's interest is credited to your account, that interest starts earning interest as well. So the bank may say that the account pays 2 percent, which compounds to an effective annual yield of 2.04 percent.

When you lend your money directly to a company — which is what you do when you invest in a bond that a corporation issues — you also receive interest. Bonds, as well as stocks (which are shares of ownership in a company), fluctuate in value after they're issued.

When you invest in a company's stock, you hope that the stock increases *(appreciates)* in value. Of course, a stock can also decline, or *depreciate,* in value. This change in market value is part of your return from a stock or bond investment:

$$\frac{\text{Current investment value} - \text{Original investment}}{\text{Original investment}} = \text{Appreciation or depreciation}$$

For example, if one year ago you invested $10,000 in a stock (you bought 1,000 shares at $10 per share) and the investment is now worth $11,000 (each share is worth $11), your investment's appreciation looks like this:

$$\frac{\$11,000 - \$10,000}{\$10,000} = 10\%$$

Stocks can also pay *dividends,* which are the company's sharing of some of its profits with you as a stockholder. Some companies, particularly those that are small or growing rapidly, choose to reinvest all their profits back into the company. (Of course, some companies don't turn a profit, so they don't have anything to pay out!) You need to factor any dividends into your return as well.

Suppose that in the previous example, in addition to your stock appreciating from $10,000 to $11,000, it paid you a dividend of $100 ($1 per share). Here's how you calculate your total return:

$$\frac{(\text{Current investment value} - \text{Original investment}) + \text{Dividends}}{\text{Original investment}} = \text{Total return}$$

You can apply this formula to the example like so:

$$\frac{(\$11,000 - \$10,000) + \$100}{\$10,000} = 11\%$$

After-tax returns

Although you may be happy that your stock has given you an 11 percent return on your invested dollars, remember that unless you held your investment in a tax-sheltered retirement account, you owe taxes on your return. Specifically, the dividends and investment appreciation that you realize upon selling are taxed, although often at relatively low rates. The tax rates on so-called long-term capital gains and stock dividends are lower than the tax rates on other income. In Chapter 3, I discuss the different tax rates that affect your investments and explain how to make tax-wise investment decisions that fit with your overall personal financial situation and goals.

If you've invested in savings accounts, money market accounts, or bonds, you owe Uncle Sam taxes on the interest.

Often, people make investing decisions without considering the tax consequences of their moves. This is a big mistake. What good is making money if the federal and state governments take away a substantial portion of it?

If you're in a moderate tax bracket, taxes on your investment probably run in the neighborhood of 30 percent (federal and state). So if your investment returned 7 percent before taxes, you're left with a return of about 4.9 percent after taxes.

Psychological returns

Profits and tax avoidance can powerfully motivate your investment selections. However, as with other life decisions, you need to consider more than the bottom line. Some people want to have fun with their investments. Of course, they don't want to lose money or sacrifice a lot of potential returns. Fortunately, less expensive ways to have fun do exist!

Psychological rewards compel some investors to choose particular investment vehicles such as individual stocks, real estate, or a small business. Why? Because compared with other investments, such as managed mutual funds, they see these investments as more tangible and, well, more fun.

INVESTIGATE

Be honest with yourself about why you choose the investments that you do. Allowing your ego to get in the way can be dangerous. Do you want to invest in individual stocks because you really believe that you can do better than the best full-time professional money managers? Chances are high that you won't. (See Chapter 6 for details.) Such questions are worth considering as you contemplate which investments you want to make.

Savings and money market account returns

You need to keep your extra cash that awaits investment (or an emergency) in a safe place, preferably one that doesn't get hammered by the sea of changes in the financial markets. By default and for convenience, many people keep their extra cash in a bank savings account. Although the bank offers the U.S. government's backing via the Federal Deposit Insurance Corporation (FDIC), it comes at a price. Most banks pay a low interest rate on their savings accounts. (I discuss banking options, including the sometimes higher-yielding online banks, in Chapter 7.)

Another place to keep your liquid savings is in a money market mutual fund. These are the safest types of mutual funds around and, for all intents and purposes, equal a bank savings account's safety. The best money market funds generally pay higher yields than most bank savings accounts. Unlike a bank, money market mutual funds tell you how much they deduct for the service of managing your money. If you're in a higher tax bracket, tax-free versions of money market funds exist as well. See Chapter 8 for more on money market funds.

TIP

If you don't need immediate access to your money, consider using Treasury bills (T-bills) or bank certificates of deposit (CDs), which are usually issued for terms such as 3, 6, or 12 months. Your money will generally earn more in one of these vehicles than in a bank savings account. (In recent years, the yields on T-bills has been so low that the best FDIC-insured bank savings accounts have higher yields.) Rates vary by institution, so it's essential to shop around. The drawback to T-bills and bank certificates of deposit is that you incur a penalty (with CDs) or a transaction fee (with T–bills) if you withdraw your investment before the term expires (see Chapter 7).

Bond returns

When you buy a bond, you lend your money to the issuer of that bond (borrower), which is generally the federal government or a corporation, for a specific period of time. When you buy a bond, you expect to earn a higher yield than you can with a money market or savings account. You're taking more risk, after all. Companies can and do go bankrupt, in which case you may lose some or all of your investment.

Generally, you can expect to earn a higher yield when you buy bonds that

>> **Are issued for a longer term:** The bond issuer is tying up your money at a fixed rate for a longer period of time.

>> **Have lower credit quality:** The bond issuer may not be able to repay the principal.

Wharton School of Business professor Jeremy Siegel has tracked the performance of bonds and stocks back to 1802. Although you may say that what happened in the 19th century has little relevance to the financial markets and economy of today, the decades since the Great Depression, which most other return data track, are a relatively small slice of time. Figure 2–4 presents the data, so if you'd like to give more emphasis to the recent numbers, you may.

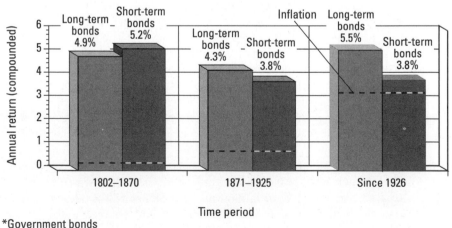

FIGURE 2-4:
A historical view of bond performance: Inflation has eroded bond returns more in recent decades.

*Government bonds

Note that although the rate of inflation has increased since the Great Depression, bond returns haven't increased over the decades. Long-term bonds maintained slightly higher returns in recent years than short-term bonds. The bottom line: Bond investors typically earn about 4 to 5 percent per year.

Stock returns

Investors expect a fair return on their investments. If one investment doesn't offer a seemingly high enough potential rate of return, investors can choose to move their money into other investments that they believe will perform better. Instead of buying a diversified basket of stocks and holding, some investors frequently buy and sell, hoping to cash in on the latest hot investment. This tactic seldom works in the long run.

WARNING

Unfortunately, some of these investors use a rearview mirror when they purchase their stocks, chasing after investments that have recently performed strongly on the assumption (and the hope) that those investments will continue to earn good returns. But chasing after the strongest performing investments can be dangerous if you catch the stock at its peak, ready to begin a downward spiral. You may have heard that the goal of investing is to buy low and sell high. Chasing high-flying investments can lead you to buy high, with the prospect of having to sell low if the stock runs out of steam. Even though stocks as a whole have proved to be a good long-term investment, picking individual stocks is a risky endeavor. See Chapters 5 and 6 for my advice on making sound stock investment decisions.

REMEMBER

A tremendous amount of data exists regarding stock market returns. In fact, in the U.S. markets, data going back more than two centuries document the fact that stocks have been a terrific long-term investment. The long-term returns from stocks that investors have enjoyed, and continue to enjoy, have been remarkably constant from one generation to the next.

Going all the way back to 1802, the U.S. stock market has produced an annual return of 8.3 percent, while inflation has grown at 1.4 percent per year. Thus, after subtracting for inflation, stocks have appreciated about 6.9 percent faster annually than the rate of inflation. The U.S. stock market returns have consistently and substantially beaten the rate of inflation over the years (see Figure 2-5).

Stocks don't exist only in the United States, of course (see Figure 2-6). More than a few U.S. investors seem to forget this fact, as they did especially during the sizzling performance of the U.S. stock market during the late 1990s. As I discuss in the earlier section "Diversify for a gentler ride," one advantage of buying and holding overseas stocks is that they don't always move in tandem with U.S. stocks. As a result, overseas stocks help diversify your portfolio.

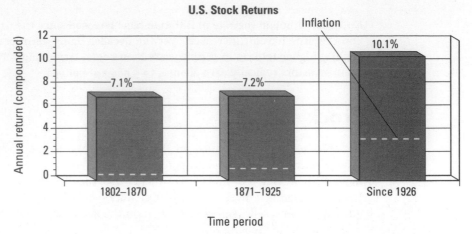

U.S. Stock Returns

Inflation

FIGURE 2-5:
History shows
that stocks have
been a consistent
long-term winner.

© John Wiley & Sons, Inc.

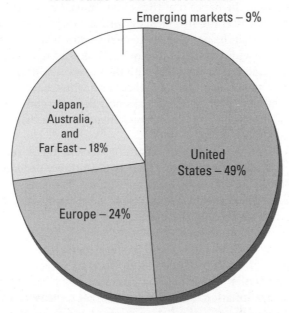

Total Value of Stocks Worldwide

Emerging markets – 9%

Japan,
Australia,
and
Far East – 18%

United
States – 49%

Europe – 24%

FIGURE 2-6:
Plenty of
investing
opportunities
exist outside the
United States.

© John Wiley & Sons, Inc.

In addition to enabling U.S. investors to diversify, investing overseas has proved to be profitable. The investment banking firm Morgan Stanley tracks the performance of stocks in both economically established countries and so-called emerging economies. As the name suggests, countries with *emerging economies* (for example, Brazil, China, India, Malaysia, Mexico, Russia, and Taiwan) are "behind" economically but show high rates of growth and progress.

ARE SMALLER-COMPANY STOCK RETURNS HIGHER?

Stocks are generally classified by the size of the company. Small-company stocks aren't stocks that physically small companies issue; they're simply stocks issued by companies that haven't reached the size of corporate behemoths such as IBM, Wal-Mart, or Coca-Cola. The Standard & Poor's 500 index tracks the performance of 500 large-company stocks in the United States. The Russell 2000 index tracks the performance of 2,000 smaller-company U.S. stocks.

Small-company stocks have outperformed larger-company stocks during the past seven decades. Historically, small-company stocks have produced slightly higher compounded annual returns than large-company stocks. However, nearly all this extra performance is due to just one high-performance time period, from the mid-1970s to the early 1980s. If you eliminate this time period from the data, small stocks have had virtually identical returns to those of larger-company stocks.

Also, be aware that small-company stocks can get hammered in down markets. For example, during the Great Depression, small-company stocks plunged more than 85 percent between 1929 and 1932, while the S&P 500 fell 64 percent. In 1937, small-company stocks plummeted 58 percent, while the S&P 500 fell 35 percent. And in 1969 to 1970, small-company stocks fell 38 percent, while the S&P 500 fell just 5 percent.

Stocks are the best long-term performers, but they have more volatility than bonds and Treasury bills. A balanced portfolio gets you most of the long-term returns of stocks without much of the volatility.

Real estate returns

REMEMBER

Over the years, real estate has proved to be about as lucrative as investing in the stock market. Whenever the U.S. has a real estate downturn, folks question this historic fact (see Chapter 11 for details). However, just as stock prices have down periods, so, too, do real estate markets.

The fact that real estate offers solid long-term returns makes sense because growth in the economy, in jobs, and in population ultimately fuels the demand for real estate.

Consider what has happened to the U.S. population over the past two centuries. In 1800, a mere 5 million people lived within U.S. borders. In 1900, that figure grew to 76.1 million, and today, it's more than 315 million. All these people need places to live, and as long as jobs exist, the income from jobs largely fuels the demand for housing.

Businesses and people have an understandable tendency to cluster in major cities and suburban towns. Although some people commute, most people and businesses locate near major highways, airports, and so on. Thus, real estate prices in and near major metropolises and suburbs generally appreciate the most. Consider the areas of the world that have the most expensive real estate prices: Hong Kong, San Francisco, Los Angeles, New York, and Boston. What these areas have in common are lots of businesses and people and limited land.

Contrast these areas with the many rural parts of the United States where the price of real estate is relatively low because of the abundant supply of buildable land and the relatively lower demand for housing.

Small-business returns

As I discuss in Part 4 of this book, you have several choices for tapping into the exciting potential of the small-business world. If you have the drive and determination, you can start your own small business. Or perhaps you have what it takes to buy an existing small business. If you obtain the necessary capital and skills to assess opportunities and risk, you can invest in someone else's small business.

What potential returns can you get from small business? Small-business owners like me who do something they really enjoy will tell you that the nonfinancial returns can be major! But the financial rewards can be attractive as well.

Every year, *Forbes* magazine publishes a list of the world's wealthiest individuals. Perusing this list shows that most of these people built their wealth by taking a significant ownership stake and starting a small business that became large. These individuals achieved extraordinarily high returns (often in excess of hundreds of percent per year) on the amounts they invested to get their companies off the ground.

You may also achieve potentially high returns from buying and improving an existing small business. As I discuss in Part 4, such small-business investment returns may be a good deal lower than the returns you may gain from starting a business from scratch.

Unlike the stock market, where plenty of historic rate-of-return data exists, data on the success, or lack thereof, that investors have had with investing in small private companies is harder to come by. Smart venture capitalist firms operate a fun and lucrative business: They identify and invest money in smaller startup companies that they hope will grow rapidly and eventually go public. Venture capitalists allow outsiders to invest with them via limited partnerships. To gain entry, you generally need $1 million to invest. (I never said this was an equal-opportunity investment club!)

Venture capitalists, also known as *general partners,* typically skim off 20 percent of the profits and also charge limited partnership investors a hefty 2 to 3 percent annual fee on the amount that they've invested. The return that's left over for the limited partnership investors isn't stupendous. According to Venture Economics, venture funds have averaged comparable annual returns to what stock market investors have earned on average over this same period. The general partners that run venture capital funds make more than the limited partners do.

You can attempt to do what the general partners do in venture capital firms and invest directly in small private companies. But you're likely to be investing in much smaller and simpler companies. Earning venture capitalist returns isn't easy to do. If you think that you're up to the challenge, I explain the best ways to invest in small business in Chapter 15.

Considering Your Goals

How much do you need or want to earn? That may seem like an extraordinarily silly question for me to ask you. Who doesn't want to earn a high return? However, although investing in stocks, real estate, or a small business can produce high long-term returns, investing in these vehicles comes with greater risk, especially over the short term.

Some people can't stomach the risk. Others are at a time in their lives when they can't afford to take great risk. If you're near or in retirement, your portfolio and nerves may not be able to wait a decade for your riskier investments to recover after a major stumble. Perhaps you have sufficient assets to accomplish your financial goals and are concerned with preserving what you do have rather than risking it to grow more wealth.

If you work for a living, odds are that you need and want to make your investments grow at a healthy clip. If your investments grow slowly, you may fall short of your goals of owning a home or retiring or changing careers.

Chapter 3

Getting Your Financial House in Order Before You Invest

B efore you make any great, wealth-building investments, I recommend that you get your financial house in order. Understanding and implementing some simple personal financial management concepts can pay off big for you in the decades ahead.

You want to know how to earn healthy returns on your investments without getting clobbered, right? Who doesn't? Although you generally must accept greater risk to have the potential for earning higher returns (see Chapter 2), in this chapter, I tell you about some high-return, low-risk investments. You have a right to be skeptical about such investments, but don't stop reading this chapter yet. Here, I point out some of the easy-to-tap opportunities for managing your money that you may have overlooked.

Establishing an Emergency Reserve

You never know what life will bring, so having a readily accessible reserve of cash to meet unexpected expenses makes good financial sense. If you have a sister who works on Wall Street as an investment banker or a wealthy and understanding parent, you can use one of them as your emergency reserve. (Although you should ask them how they feel about that before you count on receiving funding from them!) If you don't have a wealthy family member, the ball's in your court to establish a reserve.

SHOULD YOU INVEST EMERGENCY MONEY IN STOCKS?

WARNING

As interest rates drifted lower during the 1990s, keeping emergency money in money market accounts became less and less rewarding. When interest rates were 8 or 10 percent, fewer people questioned the wisdom of an emergency reserve. However, in the late 1990s, which had low money market interest rates and stock market returns of 20 percent per year, more investors balked at the idea of keeping a low-interest stash of cash.

I began seeing articles that suggested you simply keep your emergency reserve in stocks. After all, you can easily sell stocks (especially those of larger companies) any day the financial markets are open. Why not treat yourself to the 20 percent annual returns that stock market investors enjoyed during the 1990s instead of earning a paltry few percent?

At first, that logic sounds great. But as I discuss in Chapter 2, stocks historically have returned about 9 percent per year. In some years — in fact, about one-third of the time — stocks decline in value, sometimes substantially.

Stocks can drop and have dropped 20, 30, or 50 percent or more over relatively short periods of time. Consider what happened to stock prices in the early 2000s and then again in the late 2000s. Suppose that such a drop coincides with an emergency — such as the loss of your job, major medical bills, and so on. Your situation may force you to sell at a loss, perhaps a substantial one.

Here's another reason not to keep emergency money in stocks: If your stocks appreciate and you need to sell some of them for emergency cash, you get stuck paying taxes on your gains.

I suggest that you invest your emergency money in stocks (ideally through well-diversified mutual funds) only if you have a relative or some other resource to tap for money in an emergency. Having a backup resource for money minimizes your need to sell your stock holdings on short notice. As I discuss in Chapter 5, stocks are intended to be a longer-term investment, not an investment that you expect (or need) to sell in the near future.

Make sure you have quick access to at least three months' to as much as six months' worth of living expenses. Keep this emergency money in a savings account (see Chapter 7) or a money market fund (see Chapter 8). You may also be able to borrow against your employer-based retirement account or against your home equity should you find yourself in a bind, but these options are much less desirable.

If you don't have a financial safety net, you may be forced into selling an investment that you've worked hard for. And selling some investments, such as real estate, costs big money (because of transaction costs, taxes, and so on).

Consider the case of Warren, who owned his home and rented an investment property in the Pacific Northwest. He felt, and appeared to be, financially successful. But then Warren lost his job, accumulated sizable medical expenses, and had to sell his investment property to come up with cash for living expenses. Warren didn't have enough equity in his home to borrow. He didn't have other sources — a wealthy relative, for example — to borrow from, either, so he was stuck selling his investment property. Warren wasn't able to purchase another investment property and missed out on the large appreciation the property earned over the subsequent two decades. Between the costs of selling and taxes, getting rid of the investment property cost Warren about 15 percent of its sales price. Ouch!

Evaluating Your Debts

Yes, paying down debts is boring, but it makes your investment decisions less difficult. Rather than spending so much of your time investigating specific investments, paying off your debts (if you have them and your cash coming in exceeds the cash going out) may be your best high-return, low-risk investment. Consider the interest rate you pay and your investing alternatives to determine which debts you should pay off.

Conquering consumer debt

Borrowing via credit cards, auto loans, and the like is an expensive way to borrow. Banks and other lenders charge higher interest rates for consumer debt than for debt for investments, such as real estate and business. The reason: Consumer loans are the riskiest type of loan for a lender.

TIP

Many folks have credit card or other consumer debt, such as an auto loan, that costs 8, 10, 12, or perhaps as much as 18-plus percent per year in interest (some credit cards whack you with interest rates exceeding 20 percent if you make a late payment). Reducing and eventually eliminating this debt with your savings is like putting your money in an investment with a guaranteed *tax-free* return equal to the rate that you pay on your debt.

For example, if you have outstanding credit card debt at 15 percent interest, paying off that debt is the same as putting your money to work in an investment with a guaranteed 15 percent tax-free annual return. Because the interest on consumer debt isn't tax-deductible, you need to earn more than 15 percent by investing your money elsewhere in order to net 15 percent after paying taxes. Earning such high investing returns is highly unlikely, and in order to earn those returns, you'd be forced to take great risk.

Consumer debt is hazardous to your long-term financial health (not to mention damaging to your credit score and future ability to borrow for a home or other wise investments) because it encourages you to borrow against your future earnings. I often hear people say things like "I can't afford to buy most new cars for cash — look at how expensive they are!" That's true, new cars *are* expensive, so you need to set your sights lower and buy a good used car that you *can* afford. You can then invest the money that you'd otherwise spend on your auto loan.

INVESTIGATE

Using consumer debt may make sense if you're financing a business. If you don't have home equity, personal loans (through a credit card or auto loan) may actually be your lowest-cost source of small-business financing. (See Chapter 14 for details.)

Mitigating your mortgage

Paying off your mortgage more quickly is an "investment" for your spare cash that may make sense for your financial situation. However, the wisdom of making this financial move isn't as clear as paying off high-interest consumer debt; mortgage interest rates are generally lower, and the interest is typically tax-deductible.

When used properly, debt can help you accomplish your goals — such as buying a home or starting a business — and make you money in the long run. Borrowing to buy a home generally makes sense. Over the long term, homes generally appreciate in value.

If your financial situation has changed or improved since you first needed to borrow mortgage money, reconsider how much mortgage debt you need or want. Even if your income hasn't escalated or you haven't inherited vast wealth, your frugality may allow you to pay down some of your debt sooner than the lender requires. Whether paying down your debt sooner makes sense for you depends on a number of factors, including your other investment options and goals.

Consider your investment opportunities

INVESTIGATE

When evaluating whether to pay down your mortgage faster, compare your mortgage interest rate with your investments' rates of return (which I define in Chapter 2). Suppose you have a fixed-rate mortgage with an interest rate of 5 percent. If you decide to make investments instead of paying down your mortgage more quickly, your investments need to produce an average annual rate of return, before taxes, of about 5 percent to come out ahead financially. (Technically, this comparison should be done on an after-tax basis, but the outcome is unlikely to change.)

Besides lacking the money to do so (the most common reason), other good reasons *not* to pay off your mortgage any quicker than necessary include the following:

>> **You instead contribute to your retirement accounts, such as a 401(k), an IRA, or a Keogh plan (especially if your employer offers matching money).** Paying off your mortgage faster has no tax benefit. By contrast, putting additional money into a retirement plan can immediately reduce your federal and state income tax burdens. The more years you have until retirement, the greater the benefit you receive if you invest in your retirement accounts. Thanks to the compounding of your retirement account investments without the drain of taxes, you can actually earn a lower rate of return on your investments than you pay on your mortgage and still come out ahead. (I discuss the various retirement accounts in detail in the section "Funding Your Retirement Accounts" later in this chapter.)

>> **You're willing to invest in growth-oriented, volatile investments, such as stocks and real estate.** To have a reasonable chance of earning a greater return on your investments than it costs you to borrow on your mortgage, you must be aggressive with your investments. As I discuss in Chapter 2, stocks and real estate have produced annual average rates of return of about 8 to 9 percent. You can earn even more by creating your own small business or by investing in others' businesses. Paying down a mortgage ties up more of your capital and thus reduces your ability to make other attractive investments. To more aggressive investors, paying off the house seems downright boring — the financial equivalent of watching paint dry.

WARNING

You have no guarantee of earning high returns from growth-type investments, which can easily drop 20 percent or more in value over a year or two.

>> **Paying down the mortgage depletes your emergency reserves.** Psychologically, some people feel uncomfortable paying off debt more quickly if it diminishes their savings and investments. You probably don't want to pay down your debt if doing so depletes your financial safety cushion. Make sure that you have access — through a money market fund or other sources (a family member, for example) — to at least three months' worth of living expenses (as I explain in the earlier section "Establishing an Emergency Reserve").

REMEMBER

Don't be tripped up by the misconception that somehow a real estate market downturn, such as the one that most areas experienced in the mid- to late 2000s, will harm you more if you pay down your mortgage. Your home is worth what it's worth — its value has *nothing* to do with your debt load. Unless you're willing to walk away from your home and send the keys to the bank (also known as *default*, which damages your credit report and score), you suffer the full effect of a price decline, regardless of your mortgage size, if real estate prices drop.

Don't get hung up on mortgage tax deductions

Although it's true that mortgage interest is usually tax-deductible, don't forget that you must also pay taxes on investment profits generated outside of retirement accounts (if you do forget, you're sure to end up in trouble with the IRS). You can purchase tax-free investments like municipal bonds (see Chapter 7), but over the long haul, such bonds and other types of lending investments (bank savings accounts, CDs, and other bonds) are unlikely to earn a rate of return that's higher than the cost of your mortgage.

And don't assume that those mortgage interest deductions are that great. Just for being a living, breathing human being, you automatically qualify for the so-called "standard deduction" on your federal tax return. In 2014, this standard deduction was worth $6,200 for single filers and $12,400 for married couples filing jointly. If you have no mortgage interest deductions — or have fewer than you used to — you may not be missing out on as much of a write-off as you think. (Plus, it's a joy having one less schedule to complete on your tax return!)

Establishing Your Financial Goals

You may have just one purpose for investing money, or you may desire to invest money for several different purposes simultaneously. Either way, you should establish your financial goals before you begin investing. Otherwise, you won't know how much to save.

For example, when I was in my 20s, I put away some money for retirement, but I also saved a stash so I could hit the eject button from my job in management consulting. I knew that I wanted to pursue an entrepreneurial path and that in the early years of starting my own business, I couldn't count on an income as stable or as large as the one I made from consulting.

I invested my two pots of money — one for retirement and the other for my small-business cushion — quite differently. As I discuss in the section "Choosing the Right Investment Mix" later in this chapter, you can take more risk with the "longer-term" money, so I invested the bulk of my retirement nest egg in stock mutual funds. With the money I saved for the startup of my small business, I took an entirely different track. I had no desire to put this money in risky stocks — what if the market plummeted just as I was ready to leave the security of my full-time job? Thus, I kept this money safely invested in a money market fund that had a decent yield but didn't fluctuate in value.

Tracking your savings rate

In order to accomplish your financial goals (and some personal goals), you need to save money, and you also need to know your savings rate. Your *savings rate* is the percentage of your past year's income that you saved and didn't spend. Without even doing the calculations, you may already know that your rate of savings is low, nonexistent, or negative and that you need to save more.

REMEMBER

Part of being a smart investor involves figuring out how much you need to save to reach your goals. Not knowing what you want to do a decade or more from now is perfectly normal — after all, your goals and needs evolve over the years. But that doesn't mean you should just throw your hands in the air and not make an effort to see where you stand today and think about where you want to be in the future.

An important benefit of knowing your savings rate is that you can better assess how much risk you need to take to accomplish your goals. Seeing the amount that you need to save to achieve your dreams may encourage you to take more risk with your investments.

During your working years, if you consistently save about 10 percent of your annual income, you're probably saving enough to meet your goals (unless you want to retire at a relatively young age). On average, most people need about 75 percent of their pre-retirement income throughout retirement to maintain their standard of living.

If you're one of the many people who don't save enough, you need to do some homework. To save more, you need to reduce your spending, increase your income, or both. For most people, reducing spending is the more feasible way to save.

INVESTIGATE

To reduce your spending, first figure out where your money goes. You may have some general idea, but you need to have facts. Get out your checking account history, examine your online bill-paying records, and review your credit card bills and any other documentation that shows your spending history. Tally up how much you spend on dining out, operating your car(s), paying your taxes, and everything else. After you have this information, you can begin to prioritize and make the necessary trade-offs to reduce your spending and increase your savings rate. Earning more income may help boost your savings rate as well. Perhaps you can get a higher-paying job or increase the number of hours that you work. But if you already work a lot, reining in your spending is usually better for your emotional and economic well-being.

If you don't know how to evaluate and reduce your spending or haven't thought about your retirement goals, looked into what you can expect from Social Security, or calculated how much you should save for retirement, now's the time to do so. Pick up the latest edition of my book *Personal Finance For Dummies* (Wiley) to find out all the necessary details for retirement planning and much more. (If you're age 50 or over, check out *Personal Finance For Seniors For Dummies,* which I coauthored with retirement expert Bob Carlson.)

Determining your investment tastes

Many good investing choices exist: You can invest in real estate, the stock market, mutual funds, exchange-traded funds, or your own or someone else's small business. Or you can pay down mortgage debt more quickly. What makes sense for you depends on your goals as well as your personal preferences. If you detest risk-taking and volatile investments, paying down your mortgage, as recommended earlier in this chapter, may make better sense than investing in the stock market.

To determine your general investment tastes, think about how you would deal with an investment that plunges 20 percent, 40 percent, or more in a few years or less. Some aggressive investments can fall fast. (See Chapter 2 for examples.) You shouldn't go into the stock market, real estate, or small-business investment arena if such a drop is likely to cause you to sell low or make you a miserable, anxious wreck. If you haven't tried riskier investments yet, you may want to experiment a bit to see how you feel with your money invested in them.

TIP

A simple way to mask the risk of volatile investments is to *diversify* your portfolio — that is, to put your money into different investments. Not watching prices too closely helps, too — that's one of the reasons real estate investors are less likely to bail out when the property market declines. Stock market investors, unfortunately, can get daily and even minute-by-minute price updates. Add that fact to the quick phone call or click of your computer mouse that it takes to dump a stock in a flash, and you have all the ingredients for short-sighted investing — and potential financial disaster.

INVESTING AS A COUPLE

You've probably learned over the years how challenging it is just for you to navigate the investment maze and make sound investing decisions. When you have to consider someone else, dealing with these issues becomes doubly hard given the typically different money personalities and emotions that come into play.

In most couples with whom I've worked as a financial counselor, usually one person takes primary responsibility for managing the household finances, including investments. As with most marital issues, the couples that do the best job with their investments are those who communicate well, plan ahead, and compromise.

Here are a couple of examples to illustrate my point. Martha and Alex scheduled meetings with each other every three to six months to discuss financial issues. With investments, Martha came prepared with a list of ideas, and Alex would listen and explain what he liked or disliked about each option. Alex would lean toward more aggressive, growth-oriented investments, whereas Martha preferred conservative, less volatile investments. Inevitably, they would compromise and develop a diversified portfolio that was moderately aggressive. Martha and Alex worked as a team, discussed options, compromised, and made decisions they were both comfortable with. Ideas that made one of them very uncomfortable were nixed.

Henry and Melissa didn't do so well. The only times they managed to discuss investments were in heated arguments. Melissa often criticized what Henry was doing with their money. Henry got defensive and criticized Melissa for other issues. Much of their money lay dormant in a low-interest bank account, and they did little long-term planning and decision making. Melissa and Henry saw each other as adversaries, argued and criticized rather than discussed, and were plagued with inaction because they couldn't agree and compromise. They needed a motivation to change their behavior toward each other and some counseling (or a few advice guides for couples) to make progress with investing their money.

Aren't your long-term financial health and marital harmony important? Don't allow your problems to fester! Remember what the famous psychologist Dr. Phil McGraw says about problems and making changes: "You can't change what you don't acknowledge." I couldn't agree more with this assessment when it comes to money problems, including investing issues.

In my work as a financial counselor, one of the most valuable and difficult things I did for couples stuck in unproductive patterns of behavior was to help them get the issue out on the table. For these couples, the biggest step was making an appointment to discuss their financial management. Once they did, I could get them to explain their different points of view and then offer compromises.

Funding Your Retirement Accounts

Saving money is difficult for most people. Don't make a tough job impossible by forsaking the tax benefits that come from investing through most retirement accounts.

Gaining tax benefits

Retirement accounts should be called "tax-reduction accounts" — if they were, more people would be more motivated to contribute to them. Contributions to these plans are generally deductible for both your federal and state income taxes. Suppose that you pay about 35 percent between federal and state income taxes on your last dollars of income. (See the section "Figuring your tax bracket" later in this chapter.) With most of the retirement accounts that I describe in this chapter, you can save yourself about $350 in taxes for every $1,000 that you contribute in the year that you make your contribution.

After your money is in a retirement account, any interest, dividends, and appreciation grow inside the account without taxation. With most retirement accounts, you defer taxes on all the accumulating gains and profits until you withdraw your money down the road, which you can do without penalty after age 59½. In the meantime, more of your money works for you over a long period of time. In some cases, such as with the Roth IRAs described later in this chapter, withdrawals are tax-free, too.

The good old U.S. government now provides a tax credit for lower-income earners who contribute up to $2,000 into retirement accounts. The maximum credit of 50 percent applies to the first $2,000 contributed for single taxpayers with an adjusted gross income (AGI) of no more than $18,000 and married couples filing jointly with an AGI of $36,000 or less (these income ranges are for tax year 2014). Singles with an AGI of between $18,000 and $19,500 and married couples with an AGI between $36,000 and $39,000 are eligible for a 20 percent tax credit. Single taxpayers with an AGI of more than $19,500 but no more than $30,000 and married couples with an AGI between $39,000 and $60,000 can get a 10 percent tax credit. This credit is claimed on IRS Form 8880, "Credit for Qualified Retirement Savings Contributions."

Starting your savings sooner

WARNING

A common mistake that many investors make is neglecting to take advantage of retirement accounts because of their enthusiasm to spend or invest in non-retirement accounts. Not investing in tax-sheltered retirement accounts can cost you hundreds, perhaps thousands, of dollars per year in lost tax savings. Add up that loss over the many years that you work and save, and not taking advantage of these tax-reduction accounts can easily cost you tens of thousands to hundreds of thousands of dollars in the long term. Ouch!

To take advantage of retirement savings plans and the tax savings that accompany them, you must first spend less than you earn. Only then can you afford to contribute to these retirement savings plans (unless you already happen to have a stash of cash from previous savings or inheritance).

REMEMBER

The sooner you start to save, the less painful it is each year to save enough to reach your goals. Why? Because your contributions have more years to compound.

Each decade you delay saving approximately doubles the percentage of your earnings that you need to save to meet your goals. For example, if saving 5 percent per year in your early 20s gets you to your retirement goal, waiting until your 30s to start may mean socking away 10 percent to reach that same goal; waiting until your 40s, 20 percent. Beyond that, the numbers get truly daunting.

If you enjoy spending money and living for today, you should be more motivated to start saving sooner. The longer that you wait to save, the more you ultimately need to save and, therefore, the less you can spend today!

Checking out retirement account options

If you earn employment income (or receive alimony), you have options for putting money away in a retirement account that compounds without taxation until you withdraw the money. In most cases, your contributions to these retirement accounts are tax-deductible.

Company-based plans

If you work for a for-profit company, you may have access to a *401(k)* plan, which typically allows you to save up to $17,500 per year (for tax year 2014). Many nonprofit organizations offer *403(b)* plans to their employees. As with a 401(k), your contributions to a 403(b) plan are deductible on both your federal and state taxes in the year that you make them. Nonprofit employees can generally contribute up to 20 percent or $17,500 of their salaries, whichever is less. In addition to the upfront and ongoing tax benefits of these retirement savings plans, some employers match your contributions.

Older employees (defined as being at least age 50) can contribute even more into these company-based plans — up to $23,000 in 2014. Of course, the challenge for many people is to reduce their spending enough to be able to sock away these kinds of contributions.

If you're self-employed, you can establish your own retirement savings plans for yourself and any employees that you have. In fact, with all types of self-employment retirement plans, business owners need to cover their employees as well. *Simplified employee pension individual retirement accounts* (SEP-IRA) and *Keogh plans* allow you to sock away about 20 percent of your self-employment income (business revenue minus expenses), up to an annual maximum of $52,000 (for tax year 2014). Each year, *you* decide the amount you want to contribute — no minimums exist (unless you do a Money Purchase Pension Plan type of Keogh).

REMEMBER

Keogh plans require a bit more paperwork to set up and administer than SEP-IRAs. Unlike SEP-IRAs, Keogh plans allow *vesting schedules* that require employees to remain with the company a number of years before they earn the right to their retirement account balances. (If you're an employee in a small business, you *can't* establish your own SEP-IRA or Keogh — that's up to your employer.) Many plans also allow business owners to exclude employees from receiving contributions until they complete a year or two of service.

If an employee leaves prior to being fully vested, his unvested balance reverts to the remaining Keogh plan participants. Keogh plans also allow for *Social Security integration,* which effectively allows those in the company who earn high incomes (usually the owners) to receive larger-percentage contributions for their accounts than the less highly compensated employees. The logic behind this idea is that Social Security taxes and benefits top out after you earn $117,000 (for tax year 2014). Social Security integration allows higher-income earners to make up for this ceiling.

Owners of small businesses shouldn't deter themselves from doing a retirement plan because employees may receive contributions, too. If business owners take the time to educate employees about the value and importance of these plans in saving for the future and reducing taxes, they'll see it as a rightful part of their total compensation package.

IRAs

If you work for a company that doesn't offer a retirement savings plan, or if you've exhausted contributing to your company's plan, consider an *individual retirement account* (IRA). Anyone with employment income (or who receives alimony) may contribute up to $5,500 each year to an IRA (or the amount of your employment or alimony income if it's less than $5,500 in a year). If you're a nonworking spouse, you're eligible to put up to $5,500 per year into a spousal IRA. Those age 50 and older can put away up to $6,500 per year (effective in 2014).

Your contributions to an IRA may or may not be tax-deductible. For tax year 2014, if you're single and your adjusted gross income is $60,000 or less for the year, you can deduct your full IRA contribution. If you're married and you file your taxes jointly, you're entitled to a full IRA deduction if your AGI is $96,000 per year or less.

TIP

If you can't deduct your contribution to a standard IRA account, consider making a contribution to a nondeductible IRA account called the *Roth IRA*. Single taxpayers with an AGI less than $114,000 and joint filers with an AGI less than $181,000 can contribute up to $5,500 per year to a Roth IRA. Those age 50 and older can contribute $6,500. Although the contribution isn't deductible, earnings inside the account are shielded from taxes, and, unlike a standard IRA, qualified withdrawals from the account are free from income tax.

Annuities

If you've contributed all you're legally allowed to contribute to your IRA accounts and still want to put away more money for retirement, consider annuities. *Annuities* are contracts that insurance companies back. If you, the *annuity holder* (investor), should die during the so-called *accumulation phase* (that is, prior to receiving payments from the annuity), your designated beneficiary is guaranteed reimbursement of the amount of your original investment.

Annuities, like IRAs, allow your capital to grow and compound tax deferred. You defer taxes until you withdraw the money. However, unlike an IRA that has an annual contribution limit of a few thousand dollars, you can deposit as much as you want in any year to an annuity — even millions of dollars, if you've got it! However, as with a Roth IRA, you get no upfront tax deduction for your contributions.

REMEMBER

Because annuity contributions aren't tax-deductible, and because annuities carry higher annual operating fees to pay for the small amount of insurance that comes with them, consider contributing to one only after you've fully exhausted your other retirement account investing options. Because of their higher annual expenses, annuities generally make sense only if you have 15 or more years to wait until you need the money.

Choosing retirement account investments

When you establish a retirement account, you may not realize that the retirement account is simply a shell or shield that keeps the federal, state, and local governments from taxing your investment earnings each year. You still must choose which investments you want to hold inside your retirement account shell.

You may invest your IRA or self-employed plan retirement account (SEP-IRAs, Keoghs) money into stocks, bonds, mutual funds, exchange-traded funds, and even bank accounts. Mutual funds (offered in most employer-based plans), which I cover in detail in Chapter 8, are an ideal choice because they offer diversification and professional management. After you decide which financial institution you want to invest through, simply obtain and complete the appropriate paperwork for establishing the specific type of account you want. (Go to the later section "Choosing the Right Investment Mix" for more information.)

Taming Your Taxes in Non-Retirement Accounts

When you invest outside of tax-sheltered retirement accounts, the profits and distributions on your money are subject to taxation. So the non-retirement account investments that make sense for you depend (at least partly) on your tax situation.

REMEMBER

If you have money to invest, or if you're considering selling current investments that you hold, taxes should factor into your decision. But tax considerations alone shouldn't dictate how and where you invest your money. You should also weigh investment choices, your desire and the necessity to take risk, personal likes and dislikes, and the number of years you plan to hold the investment (see the section "Choosing the Right Investment Mix," later in the chapter, for more information on these other factors).

Figuring your tax bracket

You may not know it, but the government charges you different tax rates for different parts of your annual income. You pay less tax on the *first* dollars of your earnings and more tax on the *last* dollars of your earnings. For example, if you're single and your taxable income totaled $50,000 during 2014, you paid federal tax at the rate of 10 percent on the first $9,075, 15 percent on the taxable income above $9,075 up to $36,900, and 25 percent on income above $36,900 up to $50,000.

Your *marginal tax rate* is the rate of tax that you pay on your *last*, or so-called *highest*, dollars of income. In the example of a single person with taxable income of $50,000, that person's federal marginal tax rate is 25 percent. In other words, he effectively pays a 25 percent federal tax on his last dollars of income — those dollars earned between $36,900 and $50,000. (Don't forget to factor in the state income taxes that most states assess.)

TIP

Knowing your marginal tax rate allows you to quickly calculate the following:

>> Any additional taxes that you would pay on additional income

>> The amount of taxes that you save if you contribute more money into retirement accounts or reduce your taxable income (for example, if you choose investments that produce tax-free income)

Table 3-1 shows the federal income tax rates for singles and for married households that file jointly.

TABLE 3-1   **2014 Federal Income Tax Rates**

Singles Taxable Income	Married Filing Jointly Taxable Income	Federal Tax Rate
Less than $9,075	Less than $18,150	10%
$9,075 to $36,900	$18,150 to $73,800	15%
$36,900 to $89,350	$73,800 to $148,850	25%
$89,350 to $186,350	$148,850 to $226,850	28%
$186,350 to $405,100	$226,850 to $405,100	33%
$405,100 to $406,750	$405,100 to $457,600	35%
More than $406,750	More than $457,600	39.6%

Knowing what's taxed and when to worry

Interest you receive from bank accounts and corporate bonds is generally taxable. U.S. Treasury bonds pay interest that's state-tax-free. Municipal bonds, which state and local governments issue, pay interest that's federal-tax-free and also state-tax-free to residents in the state where the bond is issued. (I discuss bonds in Chapter 7.)

Taxation on your *capital gains,* which is the *profit* (sales minus purchase price) on an investment, works under a unique system. Investments held less than one year generate *short-term capital gains,* which are taxed at your normal marginal rate. Profits from investments that you hold longer than 12 months are *long-term capital gains.* These long-term gains cap at 20 percent, which is the rate that applies only for those in the highest federal income tax bracket of 39.6 percent. The long-term capital gains tax rate is just 15 percent for everyone else, except for those in the two lowest income tax brackets of 10 and 15 percent. For these folks, the long-term capital gains tax rate is 0 percent.

Use these strategies to reduce the taxes you pay on investments that are exposed to taxation:

>> **Opt for tax-free money markets and bonds.** If you're in a high enough tax bracket, you may find that you come out ahead with tax-free investments. Tax-free investments yield less than comparable investments that produce taxable earnings, but because of the tax differences, the earnings from tax-free investments *can* end up being greater than what taxable investments leave you with. In order to compare properly, subtract what you'll pay in federal as well as state taxes from the taxable investment to see which investment nets you more.

>> **Invest in tax-friendly stock funds.** Mutual and exchange-traded funds that tend to trade less tend to produce lower capital gains distributions. For funds held outside tax-sheltered retirement accounts, this reduced trading effectively increases an investor's total rate of return. *Index funds* are mutual funds that invest in a relatively static portfolio of securities, such as stocks and bonds (this is also true of some exchange-traded funds). They don't attempt to beat the market. Rather, they invest in the securities to mirror or match the performance of an underlying index, such as the Standard & Poor's 500 (which I discuss in Chapter 5). Although index funds can't beat the market, the typical actively managed fund doesn't, either, and index funds have several advantages over actively managed funds. See Chapter 8 to find out more about tax-friendly stock mutual funds, which include some non-index funds, and exchange-traded funds.

>> **Invest in small business and real estate.** The growth in value of business and real estate assets isn't taxed until you sell the asset. Even then, with investment real estate, you often can roll over the gain into another property as long as you comply with tax laws. However, the current income that small business and real estate assets produce is taxed as ordinary income.

Short-term capital gains (investments held one year or less) are taxed at your ordinary income tax rate. This is another reason you shouldn't trade your investments quickly (within 12 months).

Choosing the Right Investment Mix

Diversifying your investments helps buffer your portfolio from being sunk by one or two poor performers. In the following sections, I explain how to mix up a great recipe of investments.

Considering your age

When you're younger and have more years until you plan to use your money, you should keep larger amounts of your long-term investment money in *growth* (ownership) vehicles, such as stocks, real estate, and small business. As I discuss in Chapter 2, the attraction of these types of investments is the potential to really grow your money. The risk: The value of your portfolio can fall from time to time.

The younger you are, the more time your investments have to recover from a bad fall. In this respect, investments are a bit like people. If a 30-year-old and an 80-year-old both fall on a concrete sidewalk, odds are higher that the younger person will fully recover and the older person may not. Such falls sometimes disable older people.

TIP

A long-held guiding principle says to subtract your age from 110 and invest the resulting number as a percentage of money to place in growth (ownership) investments. So if you're 35 years old:

$$110 - 35 = 75 \text{ percent of your investment money can be in growth investments}$$

If you want to be more aggressive, subtract your age from 120:

$$120 - 35 = 85 \text{ percent of your investment money can be in growth investments}$$

Note that even retired people should still have a healthy chunk of their investment dollars in growth vehicles like stocks. A 70-year-old person may want to totally avoid risk, but doing so is generally a mistake. Such a person can live another two or three decades. If you live longer than anticipated, you can run out of money if it doesn't continue to grow.

REMEMBER

These tips are only general guidelines and apply to money that you invest for the long term (ideally for ten years or more). For money that you need to use in the shorter term, such as within the next several years, more-aggressive growth investments aren't appropriate. See Chapters 7 and 8 for short-term investment ideas.

Making the most of your investment options

No hard-and-fast rules dictate how to allocate the percentage that you've earmarked for growth among specific investments like stocks and real estate. Part of how you decide to allocate your investments depends on the types of investments that you want to focus on. As I discuss in Chapter 5, diversifying in stocks worldwide can be prudent as well as profitable.

Here are some general guidelines to keep in mind:

>> **Take advantage of your retirement accounts.** Unless you need accessible money for shorter-term non-retirement goals, why pass up the free extra returns from the tax benefits of retirement accounts?

>> **Don't pile your money into investments that have gained lots of attention.** Many investors make this mistake, especially those who lack a thought-out plan to buy stocks. In Chapter 5, I provide numerous illustrations of the perils of buying attention-grabbing stocks.

>> **Have the courage to be a contrarian.** No one likes to feel that he is jumping on board a sinking ship or supporting a losing cause. However, just as in shopping for something at retail stores, the best time to buy something of quality is when its price is reduced.

>> **Diversify.** As I discuss in Chapter 2, the values of different investments don't move in tandem. So when you invest in growth investments, such as stocks or real estate, your portfolio's value will have a smoother ride if you diversify properly.

>> **Invest more in what you know.** Over the years, I've met successful investors who have built substantial wealth without spending gobs of their free time researching, selecting, and monitoring investments. Some investors, for example, concentrate more on real estate because that's what they best understand and feel comfortable with. Others put more money in stocks for the same reason. No one-size-fits-all code exists for successful investors. Just be careful that you don't put all your investing eggs in the same basket (for example, don't load up on stocks in the same industry that you believe you know a lot about).

>> **Don't invest in too many different things.** Diversification is good to a point. But if you purchase so many investments that you can't perform a basic annual review of all of them (for example, reading the annual report from your mutual fund), you have too many investments.

>> **Be more aggressive with investments inside retirement accounts.** When you hit your retirement years, you'll probably begin to live off your non-retirement account investments first. Allowing your retirement accounts to continue growing can generally save you tax dollars. Therefore, you should be relatively less aggressive with investments outside of retirement accounts because that money may be invested for a shorter time period.

Easing into risk: Dollar cost averaging

Dollar cost averaging (DCA) is the practice of investing a regular amount of money at set time intervals, such as monthly or quarterly, into volatile investments, such as stocks and stock mutual funds. If you've ever had money deducted from your paycheck and invested it into a retirement savings plan investment account that holds stocks and bonds, you've done DCA.

TIP

Most people invest a portion of their employment compensation as they earn it, but if you have extra cash sitting around, you can choose to invest that money in one fell swoop or to invest it gradually via DCA. The biggest appeal of gradually feeding money into the market via DCA is that you don't dump all your money into a potentially overheated investment just before a major drop. Thus, DCA helps shy investors psychologically ease into riskier investments.

DCA is made to order for skittish investors with large lump sums of money sitting in safe investments like CDs or savings accounts. For example, using DCA, an investor with $100,000 to invest in stock funds can feed her money into investments gradually — say, at the rate of $12,500 or so quarterly over two years — instead of investing her entire $100,000 in stocks at once and possibly buying all of her shares at or near a market peak. Most large investment companies, especially mutual funds, allow investors to establish automatic investment plans so the DCA occurs without an investor's ongoing involvement.

Of course, like any risk-reducing investment strategy, DCA has drawbacks. If growth investments appreciate (as they're supposed to), a DCA investor misses out on earning higher returns on his money awaiting investment. Finance professors Richard E. Williams and Peter W. Bacon found that approximately two-thirds of the time, a lump-sum U.S. stock market investor earned higher first-year returns than an investor who fed the money in monthly over the first year.

However, knowing that you'll probably be ahead most of the time if you dump a lump sum into the stock market is little solace if you happen to invest just before a major plunge in prices. In the fall of 1987, the U.S. stock market, as measured by the Dow Jones Industrial Average, plummeted 36 percent, and from late 2007 to early 2009, the market shed 55 percent of its value.

So investors who fear that stocks are due for such a major correction should practice DCA, right? Well, not so fast. Apprehensive investors who shun lump-sum investments and use DCA are more likely to stop the DCA investment process if prices plunge, thereby defeating the benefit of doing DCA during a declining market.

So what's an investor with a lump sum of money to do?

>> **First, weigh the significance of the lump sum to you.** Although $100,000 is a big chunk of most people's net worth, It's only 10 percent if your net worth is $1,000,000. It's not worth a millionaire's time to use DCA for $100,000. If the cash that you have to invest is less than a quarter of your net worth, you may not want to bother with DCA.

>> **Second, consider how aggressively you invest (or invested) your money.** For example, if you aggressively invested your money through an employer's retirement plan that you roll over, don't waste your time on DCA.

DCA makes sense for investors with a large chunk of their net worth in cash who want to minimize the risk of transferring that cash to riskier investments, such as stocks. If you fancy yourself a market prognosticator, you can also assess the current valuation of stocks. Thinking that stocks are pricey (and thus riper for a fall) increases the appeal of DCA.

TIP

If you use DCA too quickly, you may not give the market sufficient time for a correction to unfold, during and after which some of the DCA purchases may take place. If you practice DCA over too long of a period of time, you may miss a major upswing in stock prices. I suggest using DCA over one to two years to strike a balance.

As for the times of the year that you should use DCA, mutual fund and exchange-traded fund investors should use DCA early in each calendar quarter because funds that make taxable distributions tend to do so late in the quarter.

Your money that awaits investment in DCA should have a suitable parking place. Select a high-yielding money market fund that's appropriate for your tax situation.

REMEMBER

One last critical point: When you use DCA, establish an automatic investment plan so you're less likely to chicken out. And for the more courageous, you may want to try an alternative strategy to DCA — *value averaging,* which allows you to invest more if prices are falling and invest less if prices are rising.

Suppose, for example, that you want to value-average $500 per quarter into an aggressive stock mutual fund. After your first quarterly $500 investment, the fund drops 10 percent, reducing your account balance to $450. Value averaging suggests that you invest $500 the next quarter plus another $50 to make up the shortfall. (Conversely, if the fund value had increased to $550 after your first investment, you would invest only $450 in the second round.) Increasing the amount that you invest requires confidence when prices fall, but doing so magnifies your returns when prices ultimately turn around.

Treading Carefully When Investing for College

WARNING

Many well-intentioned parents want to save for their children's future educational expenses. The mistake they often make, however, is putting money in accounts in their child's name (in so-called *custodial accounts*) or saving outside of retirement accounts in general.

The more money you accumulate outside tax-sheltered retirement accounts, the less assistance you're likely to qualify for from federal and state financial aid sources. Don't make the additional error of assuming that financial aid is only for the poor. Many middle-income and even some modestly affluent families qualify for some aid, which can include grants and loans available, even if you're not deemed financially needy.

Under the current financial needs analysis that most colleges use in awarding financial aid, the value of your retirement plan is *not* considered an asset. Money that you save *outside* of retirement accounts, including money in the child's name, is counted as an asset and reduces eligibility for financial aid.

Also, be aware that your family's assets, for purposes of financial aid determination, also generally include equity in real estate and businesses that you own. Although the federal financial aid analysis no longer counts equity in your primary residence as an asset, many private (independent) schools continue to ask parents for this information when they make their own financial aid determinations. Thus, paying down your home mortgage more quickly instead of funding retirement accounts can harm you financially. You may end up with less financial aid and pay more in taxes.

TIP

Don't forgo contributing to your own retirement savings plan(s) in order to save money in a non-retirement account for your children's college expenses. When you do, you pay higher taxes both on your current income and on the interest and growth of this money. In addition to paying higher taxes, you're expected to contribute more to your child's educational expenses (because you'll receive less financial aid).

If you plan to apply for financial aid, it's a good idea to save non-retirement account money in your name rather than in your child's name (as a custodial account). Colleges expect a greater percentage of money in your child's name (35 percent) to be used for college costs than money in your name (6 percent). Remember, though, that from the standpoint of getting financial aid, you're better off saving inside retirement accounts.

However, if you're affluent enough that you expect to pay for your cherub's full educational costs without applying for financial aid, you can save a bit on taxes if you invest through custodial accounts. Prior to your child's reaching age 19, the first $2,000 of interest and dividend income is taxed at your child's income tax rate rather than yours. After age 19 (for full-time students, it's those under the age of 24), *all* income that the investments in your child's name generate is taxed at your child's rate.

Education Savings Accounts

WARNING

Be careful about funding an Education Savings Account (ESA), a relatively new savings vehicle. In theory, an ESA sounds like a great place to park some college savings. You can make nondeductible contributions of up to $2,000 per child per year, and investment earnings and account withdrawals are free of tax as long as you use the funds to pay for elementary and secondary school or college costs. However, funding an ESA can undermine your child's ability to qualify for financial aid. It's best to keep the parents as the owners of such an account for financial aid purposes, but be forewarned that some schools may treat money in an ESA as a student's asset.

Section 529 plans

Also known as *qualified state tuition plans*, Section 529 plans offer a tax-advantaged way to save and invest more than $100,000 per child toward college costs (some states allow upward of $300,000 per student). After you contribute to one of these state-based accounts, the invested funds grow without taxation. Withdrawals are also tax-free so long as the funds are used to pay for qualifying higher educational costs (which include college, graduate school, and certain additional expenses of special-needs students). The schools need not be in the same state as the state administering the Section 529 plan.

REMEMBER

As I discuss in the preceding section dealing with Education Savings Accounts, Section 529 plan balances can harm your child's financial aid chances. Thus, such accounts make the most sense for affluent families who are sure that they won't qualify for any type of financial aid. If you do opt for an ESA and intend to apply for financial aid, you should be the owner of the accounts (not your child) to maximize qualifying for financial aid.

Allocating college investments

If you keep up to 80 percent of your investment money in stocks (diversified worldwide) with the remainder in bonds when your child is young, you can maximize the money's growth potential without taking extraordinary risk. As your child makes his way through the later years of elementary school, you need to begin to make the mix more conservative — scale back the stock percentage to 50 or 60 percent. Finally, in the years just before your child enters college, whittle the stock portion down to no more than 20 percent or so.

HOW TO PAY FOR COLLEGE

If you keep stashing away money in retirement accounts, it's reasonable for you to wonder how you'll actually pay for education expenses when the momentous occasion arises. Even if you have some liquid assets that can be directed to your child's college bill, you will, in all likelihood, need to borrow some money. Only the affluent can truly afford to pay for college with cash.

One good source of money is your home's equity. You can borrow against your home at a relatively low interest rate, and the interest is generally tax-deductible. Some company retirement plans — 401(k)s, for example — allow borrowing as well.

A plethora of financial aid programs allow you to borrow at reasonable interest rates. The Unsubsidized Stafford Loans and Parent Loans for Undergraduate Students (PLUS), for example, are available, even when your family isn't deemed financially needy. In addition to loans, a number of grant programs are available through schools and the government as well as through independent sources.

Complete the Free Application for Federal Student Aid (FAFSA) to apply for the federal government programs. Grants available through state government programs may require a separate application. Specific colleges and other private organizations, including employers, banks, credit unions, and community groups, also offer grants and scholarships.

Many scholarships and grants don't require any work on your part — simply apply for such financial aid through your college. However, you may need to seek out other programs as well. Check directories and databases at your local library, your kid's school counseling department, and college financial aid offices. Also try local organizations, churches, employers, and so on, because you have a better chance of getting scholarship money through these avenues than through countrywide scholarship and grant databases.

Your child can also work and save money during high school and college for school. In fact, if your child qualifies for financial aid, she's generally expected to contribute a certain amount to education costs from employment (both during the school year and summer breaks) and from savings. Besides giving your gangly teen a stake in her own future, this training encourages sound personal financial management down the road.

Diversified mutual funds (which invest in stocks in the United States and internationally) and bonds are ideal vehicles to use when you invest for college. Be sure to choose funds that fit your tax situation if you invest your funds in non-retirement accounts. See Chapter 8 for more information.

Protecting Your Assets

You may be at risk of making a catastrophic investing mistake: not protecting your assets properly due to a lack of various insurance coverages. Manny, a successful entrepreneur, made this exact error. Starting from scratch, he built up a successful million-dollar business. He invested a lot of his own personal money and sweat into building the business over 15 years.

One day, catastrophe struck: An explosion ripped through his building, and the ensuing fire destroyed virtually all the firm's equipment and inventory, none of which was insured. The explosion also seriously injured several workers, including Manny, who didn't carry disability insurance. Ultimately, Manny had to file for bankruptcy.

Decisions regarding what amount of insurance you need to carry are, to some extent, a matter of your desire and ability to accept financial risk. But some risks aren't worth taking. Don't overestimate your ability to predict what accidents and other bad luck may befall you.

Here's what you need in order to protect yourself and your assets:

>> **Major medical health insurance:** I'm not talking about one of those policies that pays $100 a day if you need to go into the hospital, or cancer insurance, or that $5,000 medical expense rider on your auto insurance policy. I know it's unpleasant to consider, but you need a policy that pays for all types of major illnesses and major medical expenditures. The health insurance arena is undergoing major upheaval due to the Affordable Care Act (Obamacare), which among other things is implementing tax penalties for folks without health insurance. See Chapter 14 for more information.

Consider taking a health plan with a high deductible, which can minimize your premiums. Also consider channeling extra money into a Health Savings Account (HSA), which provides tremendous tax breaks. As with a retirement account, contributions provide an upfront tax break, and money can grow over the years in an HSA without taxation. You can also tap HSA funds without penalty or taxation for a wide range of current health expenses.

» **Adequate liability insurance on your home and car to guard your assets against lawsuits:** You should have at least enough liability insurance to protect your *net worth* (assets minus your liabilities/debts) or, ideally, twice your net worth. If you run your own business, get insurance for your business assets if they're substantial, such as in Manny's case. Also consider professional liability insurance to protect against a lawsuit. You may also want to consider incorporating your business (which I discuss more in Chapter 14).

» **Long-term disability insurance:** What would you (and your family) do to replace your income if a major disability prevented you from working? Even if you don't have dependents, odds are that *you* are dependent on you. Most large employers offer group plans that have good benefits and are much less expensive than coverage you'd buy on your own. Also, check with your professional association for a competitive group plan.

» **Life insurance, if others are dependent on your income:** If you're single or your loved ones can live without your income, skip life insurance. If you need coverage, buy term insurance that, like your auto and home insurance, is pure insurance protection. The amount of term insurance you need to buy largely depends on how much of your income you want to replace.

» **Estate planning:** At a minimum, most people need a simple will to delineate to whom they'd like to leave all their worldly possessions. If you hold significant assets outside retirement accounts, you may also benefit from establishing a living trust, which keeps your money from filtering through the hands of probate lawyers. Living wills and medical powers of attorney are useful to have in case you're ever in a medically incapacitated situation. If you have substantial assets, doing more involved estate planning is wise to minimize estate taxes and ensure the orderly passing of your assets to your heirs.

In my experience as a financial counselor, I've seen that although many people lack particular types of insurance, others possess unnecessary policies. Many people also keep very low deductibles. Remember to insure against potential losses that would be financially catastrophic for you — don't waste your money to protect against smaller losses. (See the latest edition of my book *Personal Finance For Dummies*, published by Wiley, to discover the right and wrong ways to buy insurance, what to look for in policies, and where to get good policies.)

2

Stocks, Bonds, and Wall Street

Chapter 4

The Workings of Stock and Bond Markets

To buy and enjoy using a computer or cellphone, you don't need to know the intricacies of how it's put together and how it works. The same holds true for investing in stocks and bonds. However, spending some time understanding how and why the financial markets function may make you more comfortable with investing and make you a better investor.

In this chapter, I explain the ways that companies raise capital, and I give you a brief primer on financial markets and economics so you can understand and be comfortable with investing in the financial markets.

How Companies Raise Money through the Financial Markets

All businesses start small — whether they begin in a garage, a spare bedroom, or a rented office. As companies begin to grow, they often need more money (known as *capital* in the financial world) to expand and afford their growing needs, such as hiring more employees, buying computer systems, and purchasing other equipment. Many smaller companies rely on banks to lend them money, but growing and successful firms have other options, too, in the financial markets. Companies can choose between two major money-raising options when they go into the financial markets: issuing stocks and issuing bonds.

Deciding whether to issue stocks or bonds

A world of difference exists between the two major types of securities, both from the perspective of the investor and from that of the issuing company:

>> **Bonds are loans that a company must pay back.** Instead of borrowing money from a bank, many companies elect to sell *bonds,* which are IOUs to investors. The primary disadvantage of issuing bonds compared with issuing stock, from a company's perspective, is that the company must repay this money with interest. On the other hand, the business doesn't have to relinquish ownership when it borrows money. Companies are also more likely to issue bonds if the stock market is depressed, meaning that companies can't fetch as much for their stock.

>> **Stocks are shares of ownership in a company.** Some companies choose to issue stock to raise money. Unlike bonds, the money that the company raises through a stock offering isn't paid back, because it's not a loan. When the investing public buys stock, these outside investors continue to hold and trade it. (Although companies occasionally buy their own stock back, usually because they think it's a good investment, they're under no obligation to do so.)

Issuing stock allows a company's founders and owners to sell some of their relatively illiquid private stock and reap the rewards of their successful company. Many growing companies also favor stock offerings because they don't want the cash drain that comes from paying loans (bonds) back.

Although many company owners like to take their companies public (issuing stock) to cash in on their stake of the company, not all owners want to go public, and not all who do go public are happy that they did. One of the numerous drawbacks of establishing your company as public includes the burdensome financial reporting requirements, such as publishing quarterly earnings statements and annual reports. Not only do these documents take lots of time and money to produce, but they can also reveal competitive secrets. Some companies also harm their long-term planning ability because of the pressure and focus on short-term corporate performance that comes with being a public company.

Ultimately, companies seek to raise capital in the lowest-cost way they can, so they elect to sell stocks or bonds based on what the finance folks tell them is the best option. For example, if the stock market is booming and new stock can sell at a premium price, companies opt to sell more stock. Also, some companies prefer to avoid debt because they don't like carrying it.

REMEMBER

From your perspective as a potential investor, you can usually make more money in stocks than bonds, but stocks are generally more volatile in the short term (see Chapter 2).

Taking a company public: Understanding IPOs

Suppose that The Capitalist Company (TCC) wants to issue stock for the first time, which is called an *initial public offering* (IPO). If TCC decides to go public, the company's management team works with *investment bankers,* who help companies decide when and at what price to sell stock and then help actually sell (distribute) the new shares to investors willing to purchase them.

Now suppose that based upon their analysis of the value of TCC, the investment bankers believe that TCC can raise $20 million by issuing stock that represents a particular portion of the company. When a company issues stock, the price per share that the stock is sold for is somewhat arbitrary. The amount that a prospective investor will pay for a particular portion of the company's stock should depend on the company's profits and future growth prospects. Companies that produce higher levels of profits and grow faster can generally command a higher sales price for a given portion of the company.

Consider the following ways that investment bankers can structure the IPO for TCC:

Price of Stock	Number of Shares Issued
$5	4 million shares
$10	2 million shares
$20	1 million shares

In fact, TCC can raise $20 million in an infinite number of ways, thanks to varying stock prices. If the company wants to issue the stock at a higher price, the company sells fewer shares.

REMEMBER

A stock's price per share by itself is meaningless in evaluating whether to buy a stock. Ultimately, the amount that investors will pay for a company's stock should depend greatly on the company's growth and profitability prospects. To determine the price-earnings ratio of a particular company's stock, you take the price per share of the company's stock and divide it by the company's earnings per share.

$$\frac{\text{The value of a company's stock}}{\text{relative to (divided by) its earnings}} = \text{its } \textit{price-earnings ratio}$$

In the case of TCC, suppose that its stock is currently valued in the marketplace at $30 per share and that it earned $2 per share in the past year, which produces a price-earnings ratio of 15. Here are the numbers:

$$\frac{\$30 \text{ per share}}{\$2 \text{ per share}} = 15$$

In Chapter 5, I talk more about price-earnings ratios and the factors that influence stock prices.

Understanding Financial Markets and Economics

Tens of thousands of books, millions of articles, and enough PhD dissertations to pack a major landfill explore the topics of how the financial markets and economy will perform in the years ahead. You can spend the rest of your life reading all this stuff, and you still won't get through it. In the following sections, I explain what you need to know about how the factors that influence the financial markets and economy work so you can make informed investing decisions.

Driving stock prices through earnings

The goal of most companies is to make money, or earnings (also called *profits*). *Earnings* result from the difference between what a company takes in *(revenue)* and what it spends *(costs)*. I say *most* companies because some organizations' primary purpose is not to maximize profits. Nonprofit organizations, such as colleges and universities, are a good example. But even nonprofits can't thrive without a steady money flow.

Companies that trade publicly on the stock exchanges seek to maximize their profit — that's what their shareholders want. Higher profits generally make stock prices rise. Most private companies seek to maximize their profits as well, but they retain much more latitude to pursue other goals.

REMEMBER

Among the major ways that successful companies increase profits are by doing the following:

>> **Building better mousetraps:** Some companies develop or promote an invention or innovation that better meets customer needs. For example, many consumers welcomed the invention of the digital camera, which eliminated the need for costly and time-consuming development of film. The digital camera also made transferring and working with pictures much easier.

>> **Opening new markets to your products:** Many successful U.S.-based companies, for example, have been stampeding into foreign countries to sell their products. Although some product adaptation is usually required to sell overseas, selling an already proven and developed product or service to new markets generally increases a company's chances for success.

>> **Being in related businesses:** Consider the hugely successful Walt Disney Company, which was started in the 1920s as a small studio that made cartoons. Over the years, it expanded into many new but related businesses, such as theme parks and resorts, movie studios, radio and television programs, toys and children's books, and video games.

>> **Building a brand name:** In blind taste tests, popular sodas and many well-known beers rate comparably to many generic colas and beers that are far cheaper. Yet some consumers fork over more of their hard-earned loot because of the name and packaging. Companies build brand names largely through advertising and other promotions. (*For Dummies* is a brand name, but *For Dummies* books cost about the same as lower-quality and smaller books on similar subjects!)

>> **Managing costs and prices:** Smart companies control costs. Lowering the cost of manufacturing their products or providing their services allows companies to offer their products and services more cheaply. Managing costs may help fatten the bottom line (profit). Sometimes, though, companies try to cut too many corners, and their cost-cutting ways come back to haunt them in the form of dissatisfied customers — or even lawsuits based on a faulty or dangerous product.

>> **Watching the competition:** Successful companies don't follow the herd, but they do keep an eye on what the competition is up to. If lots of competitors target one part of the market, some companies target a less-pursued segment that, if they can capture it, may produce higher profits thanks to reduced competition.

Weighing whether markets are efficient

Companies generally seek to maximize profits and maintain a healthy financial condition. Ultimately, the financial markets judge the worth of a company's stock or bond. Trying to predict what happens to the stock and bond markets and to individual securities consumes many a market prognosticator.

In the 1960s, to the chagrin of some market soothsayers, academic scholars developed a theory called the *efficient market hypothesis.* This theory basically maintains the following logic: Lots of investors collect and analyze all sorts of information about companies and their securities. If investors think that a security, such as a stock, is overpriced, they sell it or don't buy it. Conversely, if many investors believe that a security is underpriced, they buy it or hold what they already own. Because of the competition among all these investors, the price that a security trades at generally reflects what many (supposedly informed) people think it's worth.

Therefore, the efficient market theory implies that trading in and out of securities and the overall market in an attempt to be in the right stocks at the right time is a futile endeavor. Buying or selling a security because of "new" news is also fruitless because the stock price adjusts so quickly to this news that investors can't profit by acting on it. As Burton Malkiel so eloquently said in his classic book *A Random Walk Down Wall Street,* this theory, "Taken to its logical extreme . . . means that a blindfolded monkey throwing darts at a newspaper's financial pages could select a portfolio that would do just as well as one carefully selected by the experts." Malkiel added, "Financial analysts in pin-striped suits don't like being compared with bare-assed apes."

Some money managers have beaten the market averages. In fact, beating the market over a year or three years isn't difficult, but few can beat the market over a decade or more. Efficient market supporters argue that some of those who beat the markets, even over a ten-year period, do so because of luck. Consider that if you flip a coin five times, on some occasions you get five consecutive heads. This coincidence actually happens, on average, once every 32 times you do five coin-flip sequences because of random luck, not skill. Consistently identifying in advance which coin flipper will get five consecutive heads isn't possible.

Strict believers in the efficient market hypothesis say that it's equally impossible to identify the best money managers in advance. Some money managers, such as those who manage mutual funds, possess publicly available track records. Inspecting those track records (and understanding the level of risk taken for the achieved returns) and doing other common-sense things, such as investing in funds that have lower expenses, improve your odds of performing a bit better than the market.

Various investment markets differ in how efficient they are. *Efficiency* means that the current price of an investment accurately reflects its true value. Although the stock market is reasonably efficient, many consider the bond market to be even more efficient. The real estate market is less efficient because properties are unique, and sometimes less competition and access to information exist. If you can locate a seller who really needs to sell, you may be able to buy property at a sizeable discount from what it's really worth. Small business is also less efficient. Entrepreneurs with innovative ideas and approaches can sometimes earn enormous returns.

Moving the market: Interest rates, inflation, and the Federal Reserve

For decades, economists, investment managers, and other (often self-anointed) gurus have attempted to understand the course of interest rates, inflation, and the monetary policies set forth by the Federal Reserve. Millions of investors follow these economic factors. Why? Because interest rates, inflation, and the Federal Reserve's monetary policies seem to move the financial markets and the economy.

Realizing that high interest rates are generally bad

Many businesses borrow money to expand. People like you and me, who are affectionately referred to as *consumers*, also borrow money to finance home and auto purchases and education.

Interest rate increases tend to slow the economy. Businesses scale back on expansion plans, and some debt-laden businesses can't afford high interest rates and go under. Most individuals possess limited budgets as well and have to scale back some purchases because of higher interest rates. For example, higher interest rates translate into higher mortgage payments for home buyers.

If high interest rates choke business expansion and consumer spending, economic growth slows or the economy shrinks — and possibly ends up in a recession. The most common definition of a *recession* is two consecutive quarters (six months) of contracting economic activity.

The stock market usually develops a case of the queasies as corporate profits shrink. High interest rates may depress investors' appetites for stocks as the yields increase on certificates of deposit (CDs), Treasury bills, and other bonds.

Higher interest rates actually make some people happy. If you locked in a fixed-rate mortgage on your home or on a business loan, your loan looks much better than if you had a variable-rate mortgage. Some retirees and others who live off the interest income on their investments are happy with interest rate increases as well. Consider back in the early 1980s, for example, when a retiree received $10,000 per year in interest for each $100,000 that he invested in certificates of deposit that paid 10 percent.

Fast-forward to the early 2000s: A retiree purchasing the same CDs saw interest income slashed by about 70 percent, because rates on the CDs were just 3 percent. So for every $100,000 invested, only $3,000 in interest income was paid.

If you try to live off the income that your investments produce, a 70 percent drop in that income is likely to cramp your lifestyle. So higher interest rates are better if you're living off your investment income, right? Not necessarily.

Discovering the inflation and interest rate connection

Consider what happened to interest rates in the late 1970s and early 1980s. After the United States successfully emerged from a terrible recession in the mid-1970s, the economy seemed to be on the right track. But within just a few years, the economy was in turmoil again. The annual increase in the cost of living (known as the *rate of inflation*) burst through 10 percent on its way to 14 percent. Interest rates, which are what bondholders receive when they lend their money to corporations and governments, followed inflation skyward.

REMEMBER

Inflation and interest rates usually move in tandem. The primary driver of interest rates is the rate of inflation. Interest rates were much higher in the 1980s because the United States had double-digit inflation. If the cost of living increases at the rate of 10 percent per year, why would you, as an investor, lend your money (which is what you do when you purchase a bond or CD) at 5 percent? Interest rates were so much higher in the early 1980s because you or I would never do such a thing.

In recent years, interest rates have been low. Therefore, the rate of interest that investors can earn lending their money has dropped accordingly. Although low interest rates reduce the interest income that comes in, the corresponding low rate of inflation doesn't devour the purchasing power of your principal balance. That's why lower interest rates aren't necessarily worse and higher interest rates aren't necessarily better as you try to live off your investment income.

So what's an investor to do when he's living off the income he receives from his investments but doesn't receive enough because of low interest rates? Some retirees have woken up to the risk of keeping all or too much of their money in short-term CD and bond investments. (Review the sections in Chapter 3 dealing with asset allocation and investment mix.) A simple but psychologically difficult solution is to use up some of your principal to supplement your interest and dividend income. Using up your principal to supplement your income is what effectively happens anyway when inflation is higher — the purchasing power of your principal erodes more quickly. You may also find that you haven't saved enough money to meet your desired standard of living — that's why you should consider your retirement goals well before retiring (see Chapter 3).

Exploring the role of the Federal Reserve

When the chairman of the Federal Reserve Board speaks (currently it's Janet Yellen; before her, it was Ben Bernanke), an extraordinary number of people listen. Most financial market watchers and the media want to know what the Federal Reserve has decided to do about *monetary policy.* The Federal Reserve is the central bank of the United States. The Federal Reserve Board comprises the 12 presidents from the respective Federal Reserve district banks and the 7 Federal Reserve governors, including the chairman who conducts the Federal Open Market Committee meetings behind closed doors eight times a year.

What exactly is the Fed (as it's known), and what does it do? The *Federal Reserve* sets monetary policy. In other words, the Fed influences interest-rate levels and the amount of money or currency in circulation, known as the *money supply,* in an attempt to maintain a stable rate of inflation and growth in the U.S. economy.

Buying money is no different from buying lettuce, computers, or sneakers. All these products and goods cost you dollars when you buy them. The cost of money is the interest rate that you must pay to borrow it. And the cost or interest rate of money is determined by many factors that ultimately influence the supply of and demand for money.

The Fed, from time to time and in different ways, attempts to influence the supply of and demand for money and the cost of money. To this end, the Fed raises or lowers short-term interest rates, primarily by buying and selling U.S. Treasury bills on the open market. Through this trading activity, known as *open market operations,* the Fed is able to target the Federal funds rate — the rate at which banks borrow from one another overnight.

The senior officials at the Fed readily admit that the economy is quite complex and affected by many things, so it's difficult to predict where the economy is heading. If forecasting and influencing markets are such difficult undertakings, why does the Fed exist? Well, the Fed officials believe that they can have a positive influence in creating a healthy overall economic environment — one in which inflation is low and growth proceeds at a modest pace.

Over the years, the Fed has come under attack for various reasons. Various pundits have accused former Fed Chairman Alan Greenspan of causing speculative bubbles (see Chapter 5), such as the boom in technology stock prices in the late 1990s or in housing in the early 2000s. Some economists have argued that the Federal Reserve has, at times, goosed the economy by loosening up on the money supply, which leads to a growth spurt in the economy and a booming stock market, just in time to make El Presidente look good prior to an election. Conveniently, the consequences of inflation take longer to show up — they're not evident until after the election. In recent years, others have questioned the Fed's ability to largely do what it wants without accountability.

Many factors influence the course of stock prices. Never, ever make a trade or investment based on what someone at the Federal Reserve says or what someone in the media or some market pundit reads into the Fed chairman's comments. You need to make your investment plans based on your needs and goals, not what the Fed does or doesn't do.

What the heck is "quantitative easing"?

During and after the 2008 financial crisis, many pundits interviewed on financial cable television programs and website pontificators used the Federal Reserve as a punching bag, blaming the Fed for various economic problems, including the 2008 financial crisis. Despite the rebounding economy and stock market, some of the critics got even more vocal in blasting the Fed's quantitative easing program begun late in 2010.

More often than not, these critics, who typically and erroneously claim to have predicted the 2008 crisis, have an agenda to appear smarter than everyone else, including the Fed. Some of these pseudo-experts are precious metals hucksters and thus like to claim that the Fed is going to cause hyperinflation that will impoverish you unless you buy gold, silver, and the like.

In one popular video that has millions of YouTube views, the author claims the following using goofy cartoonish characters:

>> The Fed is printing a ton of money to implement quantitative easing (QE).

>> QE is being done to stop deflation (falling prices), but the Fed is too dumb to realize that consumer prices are rising, not falling.

>> The Fed has been wrong about everything the past 20 years.

>> Fed Chairman Ben Bernanke is unqualified for his job because he has no business experience, has no policy experience, and has never held an elected office. He is a fool who's been wrong about everything during his tenure in

office and has already blown up the American economy and is now working on blowing up the world economy.

>> The government is stupidly buying Treasuries from Goldman Sachs at grossly inflated prices (rather than buying Treasuries from the Treasury department). Goldman Sachs is ripping off the American people.

Although it's stunning in and of itself that this video has been watched millions of times in a short time period, even more amazing and disturbing is how many mainstream media and other websites and outlets have promoted and recommended the video, making little if any effort to fact-check and reality-check its contents. I do so to set the record straight and to advance your understanding of what quantitative easing really is and why the Fed is doing it. Let's go through the video's main assertions point by point:

>> The Fed is not printing a ton of money (expanding the money supply) to implement QE. Retail money market assets and bank deposits could increase, for example, if individuals decided to hold more cash. Demand for these highly liquid assets can come from folks around the world, so increased demand for the U.S. dollar during times of stress can lead to the growth of M2 (the leading measure of the money supply). Changes in money supply are complicated.

>> The Fed is well aware that there's inflation right now but has been concerned that the rate has been quite low by historic standards and that there were signs of accelerating deflation during the severe recession.

>> If the Fed had been wrong about everything the past 20 years, our economy would be in a shambles and our stock market wouldn't have appreciated more than 500 percent over that period. Yes, the U.S. has a somewhat elevated unemployment rate, but that's due to various factors, notably current tax policy.

>> Bernanke was well-qualified for his job.

>> The Fed is buying Treasuries from banks at competitive prices and is doing so to encourage more bank lending. Saying that the Fed is directing this buying solely to Goldman Sachs is absurd. The Fed conducts such Treasury open market operations through an approved list of 18 primary dealers, and Goldman is one of the 18 dealers operating in a highly competitive environment. Goldman-bashing has been going on for a long time.

Interestingly, I haven't seen much questioning of the background and agenda of the person behind this fact-challenged YouTube video, who in some articles is referred to as a "30-year-old real estate manager." He has no discernible background or expertise in the subject matter discussed in the video, which helps explain why nearly every statement in the video is wrong.

In various speeches and selected interviews, Fed Chairman Bernanke has explained QE. Here's one fairly plain English explanation that Bernanke gave during the height of the credit crisis (*Note:* "Central bank" means the Federal Reserve):

> Quantitative easing can be thought of as an expansion of the central bank's balance sheet with no intentional change in its composition. That is, the central bank undertakes more open market operations with the objective of expanding bank reserve balances, which the banking system should then use to make new loans and buy additional securities. However, when credit spreads are very wide, as they are at present, and the credit markets are quite dysfunctional, it becomes less likely that new loans and additional securities purchases will result from increasing bank reserve balances.
>
> In contrast, credit easing focuses on the mix of loans and securities that the central bank holds as assets on its balance sheet as a means to reduce credit spreads and improve the functioning of private credit markets. The ultimate objective is improvement in the credit conditions faced by households and businesses. In this respect, the Federal Reserve has focused on improving functioning in the credit markets that are severely disrupted and that are key sources of funding for financial firms, nonfinancial firms, and households.

Chapter 5

Building Wealth with Stocks

S ome people liken investing in the stock market to gambling. A real casino structures its games — such as slot machines, blackjack, and roulette — so that in aggregate, the casino owners siphon off a major chunk (40 percent) of the money that people gamble with. The vast majority of casino patrons lose money, in some cases all of it. The few who leave with more money than they came with are usually people who are lucky and are smart enough to quit while they're ahead.

I can understand why some individual investors feel that the stock market resembles legalized gambling. Fortunately, the stock market isn't a casino — it's far from it. Shares of stock, which represent portions of ownership in companies, offer a way for people of modest and wealthy means, and everybody in between, to invest in companies and build wealth. History shows that long-term investors can win in the stock market because it appreciates over the years. That said, some people who remain active in the market over many years manage to lose some money because of easily avoidable mistakes, which I can keep you from making in the future. This chapter gets you up to speed on successful stock market investing.

Taking Stock of How You Make Money

REMEMBER

When you purchase a share of a company's stock, you can profit from your ownership in two ways:

>> **Dividends:** Most stocks pay dividends. Companies generally make some profits during the year. Some high-growth companies reinvest most or all of their profits right back into the business. Many companies, however, pay out some of their profits to shareholders in the form of quarterly *dividends*.

>> **Appreciation:** When the price per share of your stock rises to a level greater than you originally paid for it, you make money. This profit, however, is only on paper until you sell the stock, at which time you realize a *capital gain*. (Such gains realized over periods longer than one year are taxed at the lower long-term capital gains tax rate; see Chapter 3.) Of course, the stock price per share can fall below what you originally paid as well (in which case you have a loss on paper unless you realize that loss by selling).

If you add together dividends and appreciation, you arrive at your total return. Stocks differ in the dimensions of these possible returns, particularly with respect to dividends.

Defining "The Market"

You invest in stocks to share in the rewards of capitalistic economies. When you invest in stocks, you do so through the stock market. What is the stock market? Everybody talks about "The Market" the same way they do the largest city nearby ("The City"):

The Market is down 137 points today.

With The Market hitting new highs, isn't now a bad time to invest?

The Market seems ready for a fall.

When people talk about The Market, they're usually referring to the U.S. stock market. Even more specifically, they're usually speaking about the *Dow Jones Industrial Average,* created by Charles Dow and Eddie Jones, which is a widely watched index or measure of the performance of the U.S. stock market. Dow and Jones, two reporters in their 30s, started publishing a paper that you may have heard of — *The Wall Street Journal* — in 1889. Like the modern-day version, the 19th-century *Wall Street Journal* reported current financial news. Dow and Jones also compiled stock prices of larger, important companies and created and calculated indexes to track the performance of the U.S. stock market.

The Dow Jones Industrial Average ("the Dow") market index tracks the performance of 30 large companies that are headquartered in the United States. The Dow 30 includes companies such as telecommunications giant Verizon Communications; airplane manufacturer Boeing; beverage maker Coca-Cola; oil giant Exxon Mobil; technology behemoths IBM, Intel, and Microsoft; drug makers Merck and Pfizer; fast-food king McDonald's; and retailers Home Depot and Wal-Mart.

Some criticize the Dow index for encompassing so few companies and for a lack of diversity. The 30 stocks that make up the Dow aren't the 30 largest or the 30 best companies in America. They just so happen to be the 30 companies that senior staff members at *The Wall Street Journal* think reflect the diversity of the economy in the United States (although utility and transportation stocks are excluded and tracked in other Dow indexes). The 30 stocks in the Dow change over time as companies merge, decline, and rise in importance.

Looking at major stock market indexes

Just as New York City isn't the only city to visit or live in, the 30 stocks in the Dow Jones Industrial Average are far from representative of all the different types of stocks that you can invest in. Here are some other important market indexes and the types of stocks they track:

TECHNICAL STUFF

>> **Standard & Poor's (S&P) 500:** Like the Dow Jones Industrial Average, the S&P 500 tracks the price of 500 larger-company U.S. stocks. These 500 big companies account for more than 70 percent of the total market value of the tens of thousands of stocks traded in the United States. Thus, the S&P 500 is a much broader and more representative index of the larger-company stocks in the United States than the Dow Jones Industrial Average is.

Unlike the Dow index, which is primarily calculated by adding the current share price of each of its component stocks, the S&P 500 index is calculated by adding the total market value (capitalization) of its component stocks.

- » **Russell 2000:** This index tracks the market value of 2,000 smaller U.S. company stocks of various industries. Although small-company stocks tend to move in tandem with larger-company stocks over the longer term, it's not unusual for one to rise or fall more than the other or for one index to fall while the other rises in a given year. For example, in 2001, the Russell 2000 actually rose 2.5 percent while the S&P 500 fell 11.9 percent. In 2007, the Russell 2000 lost 1.6 percent versus a gain of 5.5 percent for the S&P 500. Be aware that smaller-company stocks tend to be more volatile. (I discuss the risks and returns in more detail in Chapter 2.)

- » **Wilshire 5000:** Despite its name, the Wilshire 5000 index actually tracks the prices of more than 5,000 stocks of U.S. companies of all sizes — small, medium, and large. Thus, many consider this index the broadest and most representative of the overall U.S. stock market.

- » **MSCI EAFE:** Stocks don't exist only in the United States. MSCI's EAFE index tracks the prices of stocks in the other major developed countries of the world. *EAFE* stands for Europe, Australasia, and Far East.

- » **MSCI Emerging Markets:** This index follows the value of stocks in the less economically developed but "emerging" countries, such as Brazil, China, Russia, Taiwan, India, South Africa, Chile, Mexico, and so on. These stock markets tend to be more volatile than those in established economies. During good economic times, emerging markets usually reward investors with higher returns, but stocks can fall farther and faster than stocks in developed markets.

WARNING

Conspicuously absent from this list of major stock market indexes is the NASDAQ index. With the boom in technology stock prices in the late 1990s, CNBC and other financial media started broadcasting movements in the technology-laden NASDAQ index, thereby increasing investor interest and the frenzy surrounding technology stocks. (See the section titled "The Internet and technology bubble" later in this chapter.) I'm not a fan of sector (industry) specific investing, because it undermines diversification and places you in the role of a professional money manager in having to determine when and how much to invest in specific industry groups. I suggest ignoring the NASDAQ as well as other industry-concentrated indexes.

Counting reasons to use indexes

Indexes serve several purposes. First, they can quickly give you an idea of how particular types of stocks perform in comparison with other types of stocks. In 1998, for example, the S&P 500 was up 28.6 percent, whereas the small-company Russell 2000 index was down 2.5 percent. That same year, the MSCI foreign stock EAFE index rose 20.3 percent. In 2001, by contrast, the S&P 500 fell 11.9 percent, and the EAFE foreign stock index had an even worse year, falling 21.4 percent. In 2013, the S&P 500 surged 29.7 percent while the foreign EAFE index returned 18 percent.

BULL AND BEAR MARKETS

If you read magazines or newspapers or listen to people talk about the stock market, you often hear references to bull markets and bear markets. You may know which term means a good market and which term means a bad market for investors, but you may not know where these silly terms come from.

It's hard to find agreement on the origin of these terms, but my favorite description comes from Robert Claiborne's *Loose Cannons and Red Herrings — A Book of Lost Metaphors* (W. W. Norton & Company). The term *bear,* according to Claiborne, originates from a proverb that mocks a man who "sells the bearskin before catching the bear." Here's the connection to the stock market: When dealers in the stock market thought that the market had become too pricey and speculative, these dealers sold stock that they hadn't yet "caught" (bought). These dealers were labeled "bearskin jobbers" and, later, "bears."

The practice that these bearish dealers engaged in is referred to as *short selling.* They hoped that when they ultimately bought the stock that they had first sold, they could buy it back at a lower price. Their profit was the difference between the price that they originally sold it for and the price they later bought it for. Short selling is simply investing in reverse: You sell first and buy back later. The worst situation for a bear is when prices go up and he must buy back the stock at a high price. As Claiborne quoted, "He who sells what isn't his'n / Must buy it back or go to prison."

The bulls, according to Claiborne, are those who work the "other side" of the street. Bulls buy stocks with the hope and expectation that they will rise in value. Ben Travato, a man whom Claiborne describes as one prone to inventing colorful but often inaccurate etymologies, said that bulls toss stocks up in the air with their horns.

An alternative explanation for these terms comes from research that economic and investment strategist Don Luskin shared with me. He says that the terms were in use in the early 1700s in the financial markets in England and that they derive from the staged fights between wild animals that were offered as cruel public amusements at the time. When bulls were pitted against bears, the bull fought with an upward motion of its horns; the bear fought with a downward motion of its paws.

Indexes also allow you to compare or benchmark the performance of your stock market investments. If you invest primarily in large-company U.S. stocks, for example, you should compare the overall return of the stocks in your portfolio to a comparable index — in this case, the S&P 500. (As I discuss in Chapter 8, index mutual funds, which invest to match a major stock market index, offer a cost-effective, proven way to build wealth by investing in stocks.)

You may also hear about some other types of more narrowly focused indexes, including those that track the performance of stocks in particular industries, such as advertising, banking, computers, pharmaceuticals, restaurants, semiconductors, textiles, and utilities. Other indexes cover the stock markets of other countries, such as the United Kingdom, Germany, France, Canada, and Hong Kong.

WARNING

Focusing your investments in the stocks of just one or two industries or smaller countries is dangerous due to the lack of diversification and your lack of expertise in making the difficult decision about what to invest in and when. Thus, I suggest that you ignore these narrower indexes. Many companies, largely out of desire for publicity, develop their own indexes. If the news media report on these indexes, the index developer obtains free advertising. (In Chapter 8, I discuss investing strategies, such as those that focus on value stocks or growth stocks, which also have market indexes.)

Stock-Buying Methods

When you invest in stocks, many (perhaps too many) choices exist. Besides the tens of thousands of stocks from which you can select, you also can invest in mutual funds, exchange-traded funds (ETFs), or hedge funds, or you can have a stockbroker select for you.

Buying stocks via mutual funds and exchange-traded funds

If you're busy and suffer no delusions about your expertise, you'll love the best stock mutual funds. Investing in stocks through mutual funds can be as simple as dialing a toll-free phone number or logging on to a fund company's website, completing some application forms, and zapping it some money.

Mutual funds take money invested by people like you and me and pool it in a single investment portfolio in securities, such as stocks and bonds. The portfolio is then professionally managed. Stock mutual funds, as the name suggests, invest primarily or exclusively in stocks (some stock funds sometimes invest a bit in other stuff, such as bonds).

Exchange-traded funds (ETFs) are the new kid on the block, certainly in comparison to mutual funds. ETFs are in many ways similar to mutual funds, specifically index funds (see Chapter 8), except that they trade on a stock exchange. One potential attraction is that some ETFs offer investors the potential for even lower operating expenses than comparable mutual funds and may be tax–friendlier. I expand on ETFs and explain which ones to consider using in Chapter 8.

REMEMBER

Stock funds include many advantages:

>> **Diversification:** Buying individual stocks on your own is relatively costly unless you buy reasonable chunks (100 shares or so) of each stock. But in order to buy 100 shares each in, say, a dozen companies' stocks to ensure diversification, you need about $60,000 if the stocks that you buy average $50 per share.

>> **Professional management:** Even if you have big bucks to invest, mutual funds offer something that you can't deliver: professional, full-time management. Mutual fund managers peruse a company's financial statements and otherwise track and analyze its business strategy and market position. The best managers put in long hours and possess lots of expertise and experience in the field. (If you've been misled into believing that with minimal effort you can rack up market-beating returns by selecting your own stocks, please be sure to read the rest of this chapter.)

Look at it this way: Mutual funds are a huge time-saver. On your next day off, would you rather sit in front of your computer and do some research on semiconductor and toilet paper manufacturers, or would you rather enjoy dinner or a movie with family and friends? (The answer to that question depends on who your family and friends are!)

>> **Low costs — if you pick 'em right:** To convince you that funds aren't a good way for you to invest, those with a vested interest, such as stock-picking newsletter pundits, may point out the high fees that some funds charge. An element of truth rings here: Some funds are expensive, charging you a couple percent or more per year in operating expenses on top of hefty sales commissions.

But just as you wouldn't want to invest in a fund that a novice with no track record manages, why would you want to invest in a high-cost fund? Contrary to the "You get what you pay for" notion often trumpeted by those trying to sell you something at an inflated price, some of the best managers are the cheapest to hire. Through a *no-load* (commission-free) mutual fund, you can hire a professional, full-time money manager to invest $10,000 for a mere $20 to $100 per year. Some index funds and exchange-traded funds charge even less.

REMEMBER

As with all investments, mutual funds have some drawbacks. Consider the following:

>> **The issue of control is a problem for some investors.** If you like being in control, sending your investment dollars to a seemingly black-box process where others decide when and in what to invest your money may unnerve you. However, you need to be more concerned about the potential blunders that you may make investing in individual stocks of your own choosing or, even worse, those stocks pitched to you by a broker.

>> **Taxes are a concern when you invest in mutual funds outside of retirement accounts.** Because the fund manager decides when to sell specific stock holdings, some funds may produce relatively high levels of taxable distributions. Fear not — simply select tax-friendly funds if taxes concern you.

In Chapter 8, I discuss investing in the best mutual and exchange-traded funds that offer a high-quality, time- and cost-efficient way to invest in stocks worldwide.

Using hedge funds

Like mutual funds, *hedge funds* are a managed investment vehicle. In other words, an investment management team researches and manages the funds' portfolio. However, hedge funds are oriented to affluent investors and typically charge steep fees — a 1.0 to 1.5 percent annual management fee plus a 20 percent cut of the annual fund returns.

No proof exists that hedge funds as a group perform better than mutual funds. In fact, the objective studies that I've reviewed show inferior hedge fund returns, which makes sense. Those high hedge fund fees depress their returns. Notwithstanding the small number of hedge funds that have produced better long-term returns, too many affluent folks invest in hedge funds due to the fund's hyped marketing and the badge of exclusivity they offer.

Selecting individual stocks yourself

More than a few investing books suggest and enthusiastically encourage people to do their own stock picking. However, the vast majority of investors are better off *not* picking their own stocks, in my observations and experience.

I've long been an advocate of educating yourself and taking responsibility for your own financial affairs, but taking responsibility for your finances doesn't mean that you should do *everything* yourself. Table 5-1 includes some thoughts to consider about choosing your own stocks.

TABLE 5-1   **Why You're Buying Your Own Stocks**

Good Reasons to Pick Your Own Stocks	Bad Reasons to Pick Your Own Stocks
You enjoy the challenge.	You think you can beat the best money managers. (If you can, you're in the wrong profession!)
You want to learn more about business.	You want more control over your investments, which you think may happen if you understand the companies that you invest in.
You possess a substantial amount of money to invest.	You think that mutual funds are for people who aren't smart enough to choose their own stocks.
You're a buy-and-hold investor.	You're attracted to the ability to trade your stocks anytime you want.

Some popular investing books try to convince investors that they can do a *better* job than the professionals at picking their own stocks. Amateur investors, however, need to devote a lot of study to become proficient at stock selection. Many professional investors work 80 hours a week at investing, but you're unlikely to be willing to spend that much time on it. Don't let the popularity of those do-it-yourself stock-picking books lead you astray.

REMEMBER

Choosing a stock isn't as simple as visiting a restaurant chain (or buying a pair of shoes or an iGadget), liking it, buying its stock, and then sitting back and getting rich watching your stock zoom to the moon.

If you invest in stocks, I think you know by now that guarantees don't exist. But as in many of life's endeavors, you can buy individual stocks in good and not-so-good ways. So if you want to select your own individual stocks, check out Chapter 6, where I explain how to best research and trade them.

Spotting the Right Times to Buy and Sell

After you know about the different types of stock markets and ways to invest in stocks, you may wonder how you can build wealth with stocks and not lose your shirt. Nobody wants to buy stocks before a big drop.

As I discuss in Chapter 4, the stock market is reasonably efficient. A company's stock price normally reflects many smart people's assessments as to what is a fair price. Thus, it's not realistic for an investor to expect to discover a system for how to "buy low and sell high." Some professional investors may be able to spot good times to buy and sell particular stocks, but consistently doing so is enormously difficult.

The simplest and best way to make money in the stock market is to consistently and regularly feed new money into building a diversified and larger portfolio. If the market drops, you can use your new investment dollars to buy more shares. The danger of trying to time the market is that you may be "out" of the market when it appreciates greatly and "in" the market when it plummets.

Calculating price-earnings ratios

Suppose I tell you that the stock for Liz's Distinctive Jewelry sells for $50 per share and that another stock in the same industry, The Jazzy Jeweler, sells for $100. Which would you rather buy?

If you answer, "I don't have a clue because you didn't give me enough information," go to the head of the class! On its own, the price per share of stock is meaningless. Although The Jazzy Jeweler sells for twice as much per share, its profits may also be twice as much per share — in which case The Jazzy Jeweler stock price may not be out of line given its profitability.

The level of a company's stock price relative to its earnings or profits per share helps you calibrate how expensively, cheaply, or fairly a stock price is valued.

$$\frac{\text{Stock Price Per Share}}{\text{Annual Earnings Per Share}} = \text{Price-earnings (P/E) ratio}$$

Over the long term, stock prices and corporate profits tend to move in sync, like good dance partners. The *price-earnings ratio*, or P/E ratio (say, "P E" — the slash isn't pronounced), compares the level of stock prices to the level of corporate profits, giving you a good sense of the stock's value. Over shorter periods of time, investors' emotions as well as fundamentals move stocks, but over longer terms, fundamentals possess a far greater influence on stock prices.

P/E ratios can be calculated for individual stocks as well as entire stock indexes, portfolios, or funds.

Over the past 100-plus years, the P/E ratio of U.S. stocks has averaged around 15. During times of low inflation, the ratio tends to be higher — in the high teens to low 20s. As I cautioned in the second edition of this book, published in 1999, the P/E ratio for U.S. stocks got into the 30s, well above historic norms even for a period of low inflation. Thus, the down market that began in 2000 wasn't surprising, especially given the fall in corporate profits that put even more pressure on stock prices.

Just because U.S. stocks have historically averaged P/E ratios of about 15 doesn't mean that every individual stock will trade at such a P/E. Here's why: Suppose that you have a choice between investing in two companies, Superb Software and

Tortoise Technologies. Say both companies' stocks sell at a P/E of 15. If Superb Software's business and profits grow 40 percent per year and Tortoise's business and profits remain flat, which would you buy?

Because both stocks trade at a P/E of 15, Superb Software appears to be the better buy. Even if Superb's stock continues to sell at 15 times its earnings, its stock price should increase 40 percent per year as its profits increase. Faster-growing companies usually command higher price-earnings ratios.

REMEMBER

Just because a stock price or an entire stock market seems to be at a high price level doesn't necessarily mean that the stock or market is overpriced. Always compare the price of a stock to that company's profits per share or the overall market's price level to the overall corporate profits. The price-earnings ratio captures this comparison. Faster-growing and more-profitable companies generally sell for a premium — they have higher P/E ratios. Also remember that future earnings, which are difficult to predict, influence stock prices more than current earnings, which are old news.

Citing times of speculative excess

Because the financial markets move on the financial realities of the economy as well as on people's expectations and emotions (particularly fear and greed), you shouldn't try to time the markets. Knowing when to buy and sell is much harder than you think.

WARNING

Be careful that you don't get sucked into investing lots of your money in aggressive investments that seem to be in a hyped state. Many people don't become aware of an investment until it receives lots of attention. By the time everyone else talks about an investment, it's often nearing or at its peak.

In the sections that follow, I walk you through some of the biggest speculative bubbles. Although some of these examples are from prior decades and even centuries, I chose these examples because I find that they best teach the warning signs and dangers of speculative fever times.

The Internet and technology bubble

Note: This first section is excerpted from the second edition of this book, published in 1999, which turned out to be just one year before the tech bubble actually burst.

In the mid-1990s, a number of Internet-based companies launched initial public offerings of stock. (I discuss IPOs in Chapter 4.) Most of the early Internet company stock offerings failed to really catch fire. By the late 1990s, however, some of these stocks began meteoric rises.

The bigger-name Internet stocks included companies such as Internet service provider America Online, Internet auctioneer eBay, and Internet portal Yahoo!. As with the leading new consumer product manufacturers of the 1920s that I discuss in the section "The 1920s consumer spending binge," later in this chapter, many of the leading Internet company stocks skyrocketed. Please note that the absolute stock price per share of the leading Internet companies in the late 1990s was meaningless. The P/E ratio is what mattered. Valuing the Internet stocks based upon earnings posed a challenge because many of these Internet companies were losing money or just beginning to make money. Some Wall Street analysts, therefore, valued Internet stocks based upon revenue and not profits.

Valuing a stock based upon revenue and not profits can be highly dangerous. Revenues don't necessarily translate into high profits or any profits at all.

Now, some of these Internet companies may go on to become some of the great companies and stocks of future decades. However, consider this perspective from veteran money manager David Dreman: "The Internet stocks are getting hundredfold more attention from investors than, say, a Ford Motor in chat rooms online and elsewhere. People are fascinated with the Internet — many individual investors have accounts on margin. Back in the early 1900s, there were hundreds of auto manufacturers, and it was hard to know who the long-term survivors would be. The current leaders won't probably be long-term winners."

Internet stocks aren't the only stocks being swept to excessive prices relative to their earnings at the dawn of the new millennium. Various traditional retailers announced the opening of Internet sites to sell their goods, and within days, their stock prices doubled or tripled. Also, leading name-brand technology companies, such as Dell Computer, Cisco Systems, Lucent, and PeopleSoft, traded at P/E ratios in excess of 100. Investment brokerage firm Charles Schwab, which expanded to offer Internet services, saw its stock price balloon to push its P/E ratio over 100. As during the 1960s and 1920s, name-brand growth companies soared to high P/E valuations. For example, coffee purveyor Starbucks at times had a P/E near 100.

What I find troubling about investors piling in to the leading, name-brand stocks, especially in Internet and technology-related fields, is that many of these investors don't even know what a price-earnings ratio is and why it's important. Before you invest in any individual stock, no matter how great a company you think it is, you need to understand the company's line of business, strategies, competitors, financial statements, and price-earnings ratio versus the competition, among many other issues. Selecting and monitoring good companies take lots of research, time, and discipline.

Also, remember that if a company taps in to a product line or way of doing business that proves highly successful, that company's success invites lots of competition. So you need to understand the barriers to entry that a leading company has erected and how difficult or easy it is for competitors to join the fray. Also, be wary of analysts' predictions about earnings and stock prices. As more and more investment banking analysts initiated coverage of Internet companies and issued buy ratings on said stocks, investors bought more shares. Analysts, who are too optimistic (as shown in numerous independent studies), have a conflict of interest because the investment banks that they work for seek to cultivate the business (new stock and bond issues) of the companies that they purport to rate and analyze. The analysts who say, "buy, buy, buy all the current market leaders" are the same analysts who generate much new business for their investment banks and get the lucrative job offers and multimillion-dollar annual salaries.

WARNING

Simply buying today's rising and analyst-recommended stocks often leads to future disappointment. If the company's growth slows or the profits don't materialize as expected, the underlying stock price can nosedive. This happened to investors who piled in to the stock of computer disk-drive maker Iomega back in early 1996. After a spectacular rise to about $27½ per share, the company fell on tough times. Iomega stock subsequently plunged to less than $3 per share. In 2008, it was acquired by EMC for less than $4 per share.

Presstek, a company that uses computer technology for direct imaging systems, rose from less than $10 per share in mid-1994 to nearly $100 per share just two years later — another example of supposed can't-lose technology that crashed and burned. As was the case with Iomega, herds of novice investors jumped on the Presstek bandwagon simply because they believed that the stock price would keep rising. By 1999, less than three years after hitting nearly $100 per share, the stock price plunged more than 90 percent to about $5 per share. It's been recently trading under $1 per share.

ATC Communications, which was similar to Iomega and glowingly recommended by the Motley Fool website, plunged by more than 80 percent in a matter of months before the Fools recommended selling.

The Japanese stock market juggernaut

Lest you think that the United States cornered the market on manias, overseas examples abound. A rather extraordinary mania happened not so long ago in the Japanese stock market.

After Japan's crushing defeat in World War II, its economy was in shambles. Two major cities — Hiroshima and Nagasaki — were destroyed, and more than 200,000 people died from atomic bombs.

Out of the rubble, Japan emerged a strengthened nation that became an economic powerhouse. Over the course of 22 years, from 1967 to 1989, Japanese stock prices rose thirtyfold (an amazing 3,000 percent) as the economy boomed. From 1983 to 1989 alone, Japanese stocks soared more than 500 percent.

In terms of the U.S. dollar, the Japanese stock market rise was all the more stunning, because the dollar lost value versus Japan's currency, the yen. The dollar lost about 65 percent of its value during the big run-up in Japanese stocks. In dollar terms, the Japanese stock market rose an astonishing 8,300 percent from 1967 to 1989.

WARNING

Many people considered investing in Japanese stocks close to a sure thing. Increasing numbers of people became full-time stock market investors in Japan. Many of these folks were actually speculators who relied heavily on borrowed funds. As the Japanese real estate market boomed in tandem with the stock market, real estate investors borrowed from their winnings to invest in stocks and vice versa.

Borrowing heavily was easy to do; Japan's banks were awash in cash, and it was cheap to borrow. Established investors could make property purchases with no money down. Cash abounded from real estate as the price of land in Tokyo soared 500 percent from 1985 to 1990. Despite the fact that Japan has only 1/25th as much land as the United States, Japan's total land values at the close of the 1980s were four times that of all the land in the United States!

Speculators also used futures and options (discussed in Chapter 1) to gamble on higher short-term Japanese stock market prices. (Interestingly, Japan doesn't allow selling short.)

Price-earnings ratios? Forget about it. To justify the high prices that they paid for stocks, Japanese market speculators pointed out that the real estate that many companies owned was zooming to the moon and making companies more valuable.

Price-earnings ratios on the Japanese market soared during the early 1980s and ballooned to more than 60 times earnings by 1987. As I point out elsewhere in this chapter, such lofty P/E ratios were sometimes awarded to select individual stocks in the United States. But the *entire* Japanese stock market, which included many mediocre and not-so-hot companies, possessed P/E ratios of 60-plus!

When Japan's Nippon Telegraph and Telephone went public in February 1987, it met such frenzied enthusiasm that its stock price was soon bid up to a stratospheric 300-plus price-earnings ratio. At the close of 1989, Japan's stock market, for the first time in history, unseated the U.S. stock market in total market value of all stocks. And this feat happened despite the fact that the total output of the Japanese economy was less than half that of the U.S. economy.

Even some U.S. observers began to lose sight of the big picture and added to the rationalizations for the high levels of Japanese stocks. After all, it was reasoned, Japanese companies and executives were a tightly knit and closed circle, investing heavily in the stocks of other companies that they did business with. The supply of stock for outside buyers was thus limited as companies sat on their shares.

Corporate stock ownership went further, though, as stock prices were sometimes manipulated. Speculators gobbled up the bulk of outstanding shares of small companies and traded shares back and forth with others whom they partnered with to drive up prices. Company pension plans began to place all (as in 100 percent) of their employees' retirement money in stocks with the expectation that stock prices would always keep going up.

The collapse of the Japanese stock market was swift. After peaking at the end of 1989, the Tokyo market fell nearly 50 percent in the first nine months of 1990 alone. By the middle of 1992, Japanese stocks had dropped nearly 65 percent — a decline that the U.S. market hasn't experienced since the Great Depression. Prices then stagnated during the rest of the 1990s and then fell again in the 2000s until 2008, putting it at a level that was more than 80 percent lower than the peak reached nearly two decades prior. Japanese investors who borrowed lost everything. The total loss in stock market value was about $3 trillion, about the size of the entire Japanese annual output.

Several factors finally led to the pricing of the Japanese stock market bubble. Japanese monetary authorities tightened credit as inflation started to creep upward and concern increased over real estate market speculation. As interest rates began to rise, investors soon realized that they could earn 15 times more interest from a safe bond versus the paltry yield on stocks.

As interest rates rose and credit tightened, speculators were squeezed first. Real estate and stock market speculators began to sell their investments to pay off mounting debts. Higher interest rates, less-available credit, and the already grossly inflated prices greatly limited the pool of potential stock buyers. The falling stock and real estate markets fed off each other. Investor losses in one market triggered more selling and price drops in the other. The real estate price drop was equally severe, registering 50 to 60 percent or more in most parts of Japan after the late 1980s.

The 1960s weren't just about rock 'n' roll

The U.S. stock market mirrored the climate of the country during this decade of change and upheaval. The stock market experienced both good years and bad years, but overall it gained.

During the 1960s, consumer product companies' stocks were quite popular and were bid up to stratospheric valuations. When I say "stratospheric valuations," I mean that some stock prices were high relative to the company's earnings — my old friend, the price-earnings (P/E) ratio. Investors had seen such stock prices rise for many years and thought that the good times would never end.

Take the case of Avon Products, which sells cosmetics door-to-door, primarily with an army of women. During the late 1960s, Avon's stock regularly sold at a P/E of 50 to 70 times earnings. (Remember, the market average is about 15.) After trading as high as $140 per share in the early 1970s, Avon's stock took more than two decades to return to that high level. Remember that during this time period the overall U.S. stock market rose more than tenfold!

When a stock such as Avon's sells at such a high multiple of earnings, two factors can lead to a bloodletting:

>> The company's profits might continue to grow, but investors may decide that the stock isn't such a great long-term investment after all and not worth, say, a P/E of 60. Consider that if investors decide it's worth only a P/E of 30 (still a hefty P/E), the stock price would drop 50 percent to cut the P/E in half.

>> The second shoe that can drop is the company's profits or earnings. If profits fall, say, 20 percent, as Avon's did during the 1974–75 recession, the stock price will fall 20 percent, even if it continues to sell for 60 times its earnings. But when earnings drop, investors' willingness to pay an inflated P/E plummets along with the earnings. So when Avon's profits finally did drop, the P/E that investors were willing to pay plunged to 9. Thus, in less than two years, Avon's stock price dropped nearly 87 percent!

Avon wasn't alone in its stock price soaring to a rather high multiple of its earnings in the 1960s and early 1970s. Well-known companies such as Black & Decker (which has since merged into Stanley Works), Eastman Kodak (which later declared bankruptcy), and Kmart (which used to be called S.S. Kresge in those days and was later merged into Sears Holdings) sold for 60 to as much as 100 times earnings. Many other well-known and smaller companies sold at similar and even more outrageous premiums to earnings.

The 1920s consumer spending binge

The Dow Jones Industrial Average soared nearly 500 percent in a mere eight years, from 1921 to 1929, allowing for one of the best bull market runs for the U.S. stock market. The country and investors had good reason for economic optimism. New devices — telephones, cars, radios, and all sorts of electric appliances — were making their way into the mass market. The stock price of RCA, the radio manufacturer, for example, ballooned 5,700 percent during this eight-year stretch.

Speculation in the stock market moved from Wall Street to Main Street. Investors during the 1920s were able to borrow lots of money to buy stock through *margin borrowing.* You can still margin borrow today — for every dollar that you put up, you may borrow an additional dollar to buy stock. At times during the 1920s, investors could borrow up to nine dollars for every dollar that they had in hand. The amount of margin loans outstanding swelled from $1 billion in the early 1920s to more than $8 billion in 1929. When the market plunged, *margin calls* (which require putting up more money due to declining stock values) forced margin borrowers to sell their stock, thus exacerbating the decline.

The steep run-up in stock prices was also due in part to market manipulation. Investment pools used to buy and sell stocks among one another, thus generating high trading volume in a stock, which made it appear that interest in the stock was great. Also, writers who dispensed enthusiastic prognostications about said stock were in cahoots with pool operators. (Reforms later passed by the Securities and Exchange Commission addressed these problems.)

Not only were members of the public largely enthusiastic, but so, too, were the supposed experts. After a small decline in September 1929, economist Irving Fisher said in mid-October, "Stock prices have reached what looks like a permanently high plateau." High? Yes! Permanent plateau? Investors wish!

On October 25, 1929, just days before all heck began breaking loose, President Herbert Hoover said, "The fundamental business of the country . . . is on a sound and prosperous basis." Days later, multimillionaire oil tycoon John D. Rockefeller said, "Believing that fundamental conditions of the country are sound . . . my son and I have for some days been purchasing sound common stocks."

By December of that same year, the stock market had dropped by more than 35 percent. General Electric President Owen D. Young said at that time, "Those who voluntarily sell stocks at current prices are extremely foolish." Well, actually not. By the time the crash had run its course, the market had plunged 89 percent in value in less than three years.

The economy went into a tailspin. Unemployment soared to more than 25 percent of the labor force. Companies entered this period with excess inventories, which mushroomed further when people slashed their spending. High overseas tariffs stifled American exports. Thousands of banks failed, because early bank failures triggered "runs" on other banks. (No FDIC insurance existed in those days.)

REMEMBER

Psychologically, it's easier for many people to buy stocks *after* they've had a huge increase in price. Just as you shouldn't attempt to drive your car looking solely through your rearview mirror, basing investments solely on past performance usually leads novice investors into overpriced investments. If many people talk about the stunning rise in the market and new investors pile in based on the expectation of hefty profits, tread carefully.

MANIAS IN PRIOR CENTURIES

I could fill an entire book with modern-day stock market manias. But bear with me as I roll back the clocks a few centuries to observe other market manias, the first being England's so-called South Seas bubble of 1719. South Seas wasn't the kind of company that would've met today's socially responsible investors' needs. Initially, the South Seas Company focused on the African slave trade, but too many slaves died in transit, so it wasn't a lucrative business.

If you think government corruption is a problem today, consider what politicians of those days did without the scrutiny of a widely read press. King George backed the South Seas Company and acted as its governor. Politicos in Parliament bought tons of stock in the South Seas Company and even rammed through Parliament a provision that allowed investors to buy stock on borrowed money. The stock of the South Seas Company soared from about £120 to more than £1,000 in just the first six months of 1720.

After such an enormous run-up, insiders realized that the stock price was greatly inflated and quietly bailed. Citizens fell all over themselves to get into this surefire moneymaker. Other seafaring companies pursued the South Seas trade business, so the greedy politicians passed a law that stated that only government-approved companies could pursue trade. The stocks of these other companies tumbled, and investor losses led to a chain reaction that prompted selling of the South Seas Company stock, which plunged more than 80 percent by the autumn of that same year.

England wasn't the only European country that was swept up in an investment mania. Probably the most famous mania of them all was the tulip bulb (yes, those flowers that you can plant in your own home garden). A botany professor introduced tulips into Holland from Turkey in the late 1500s. Residents allowed a fascination with these bulbs to turn into an investment feeding frenzy.

At their speculative peak, the price of a single tulip bulb was the equivalent of more than $10,000 in today's dollars. Many people sold their land holdings to buy more. Documented cases show that people traded a bulb for a dozen acres of land! Laborers cut back on their work to invest. Eventually, tulip bulb prices came crashing back to earth. A trip to your local nursery shows you what a bulb sells for today.

I'm not saying that you need to sell your current stock holdings if you see an investment market getting frothy and speculative. As long as you diversify your stocks worldwide and hold other investments, such as real estate and bonds, the stocks that you hold in one market need to be only a fraction of your total holdings. Timing the markets is difficult: You can never know how high is high and when it's time to sell and then know how low is low and when it's time to buy. And if you sell non-retirement account investments at a profit, you end up sacrificing a lot of the profit to federal and state taxes.

Buying more when stocks are "on sale"

Along with speculative buying frenzies come valleys of pessimism when stock prices are falling sharply. Having the courage to buy when stock prices are "on sale" can pay big returns.

In the early 1970s, interest rates and inflation escalated. Oil prices shot up as an oil embargo choked off supplies, and Americans had to wait in long lines for gas. Gold prices soared, and the U.S. dollar plunged in value on foreign currency markets.

If the economic problems weren't enough to make most everyone gloomy, the U.S. political system hit an all-time low during this period as well. Vice President Spiro Agnew resigned in disgrace under a cloud of tax-evasion charges. Then Watergate led to President Richard Nixon's August 1974 resignation, the first presidential resignation in the nation's history.

When all was sold and done, the Dow Jones Industrial Average plummeted more than 45 percent from early 1973 until late 1974. Among the stocks that fell the hardest were those that were most popular and selling at extreme multiples of earnings in the late 1960s and early 1970s. (See the section "The 1960s weren't just about rock 'n' roll," earlier in this chapter.)

Take a gander at Table 5-2 to see the drops in some well-known companies and see how cheaply these stocks were valued relative to corporate profits (look at the P/E ratios) after the worst market drop since the Great Depression.

TABLE 5-2   **Stock Bargains in the Mid-1970s**

Company	Industry	Stock Price Fall from Peak	1974 P/E
Abbott Laboratories	Drugs	66%	8
H&R Block	Tax preparation	83%	6
Chemical Bank	Banking	64%	4
Coca-Cola	Beverages	70%	12

(continued)

TABLE 5-2 *(continued)*

Company	Industry	Stock Price Fall from Peak	1974 P/E
Disney	Entertainment	75%	11
Dun & Bradstreet	Business information	68%	9
General Dynamics	Military	81%	3
Hilton Hotels	Hotels	87%	4
Humana	Hospitals	91%	3
Intel	Semiconductors	76%	6
Kimberly-Clark	Consumer products	63%	4
McGraw-Hill	Publishing	90%	4
Mobil	Oil	60%	3
PepsiCo	Beverages	67%	8
Pitney Bowes	Postage meters	84%	6
PPG Industries	Glass	60%	4
Quaker Oats	Packaged food	76%	6
Rite Aid	Drugstores	95%	4
Scientific-Atlanta	Communications equipment	82%	4
Sprint	Telephone	67%	7

Those who were too terrified to buy stocks in the mid-1970s actually had time to get on board and take advantage of the buying opportunities. The stock market did have a powerful rally and, from its 1974 low, rose nearly 80 percent over the next two years. But over the next half dozen years, the market backpedaled, losing much of its gains.

In the late 1970s and early 1980s, inflation continued to escalate well into double digits. Corporate profits declined further, and unemployment rose higher than in the 1974 recession. Although some stocks dropped, others simply treaded water and went sideways for years after major declines in the mid-1970s. As some companies' profits increased, P/E bargains abounded (as shown in Table 5-3).

TABLE 5-3   # More Stock Bargains in the Late 1970s and Early 1980s

Company	Industry	Stock Price Fall from Peak	P/E Late 70s/Early 80s
Anheuser-Busch	Beer	75%	8
Campbell Soup	Canned foods	36%	6
Coca-Cola	Beverages	61%	8
Colgate-Palmolive	Personal care	69%	6
General Electric	Consumer/industrial products	44%	7
General Mills	Food	44%	6
Gillette	Shaving products	74%	5
McDonald's	Fast food	46%	9
MMM	Consumer/industrial products	50%	8
Pacific Gas & Electric	Utility	52%	6
J.C. Penney	Department stores	80%	6
Procter & Gamble	Consumer products	46%	8
Rubbermaid	Rubber products	60%	7
Sara Lee	Food	60%	5
Schering Plough	Drugs	71%	7
Wells Fargo	Banking	50%	3
Whirlpool	Household appliances	63%	5

During the 2008 financial crisis, panic (and talk of another Great Depression) was in the air and stock prices dropped sharply. Peak to trough, global stock prices plunged 50-plus percent. While some companies went under (and garnered lots of news headlines), those firms were few in number and were the exception rather than the norm. Many terrific companies weathered the storm, and their stock could be scooped up by investors with cash and courage at attractive prices and valuations.

REMEMBER

When bad news and pessimism abound and the stock market has dropped, it's actually a much safer and better time to buy stocks. You may even consider shifting some of your money out of your safer investments, such as bonds, and invest more aggressively in stocks. Investors feel during these times that prices can drop further, but if you buy and hold for the long term, you'll be amply rewarded. Most of the stocks listed in the preceding several pages have appreciated 500 to 2,500-plus percent in the subsequent decades.

Avoiding Problematic Stock-Buying Practices

WARNING

You may be curious about ways to buy individual stocks, but note that if the methods you're curious about appear in the following sections, it's because I *don't* recommend using them. You can greatly increase your chances of success and earn higher returns if you avoid the commonly made stock-investing mistakes that I present next.

Beware of broker conflicts of interest

Some investors make the mistake of investing in individual stocks through a broker who earns a living from commissions. The standard pitch from these firms and their brokers is that they maintain research departments that monitor and report on stocks. Their brokers, using this research, tell you when to buy, sell, or hold. Sounds good in theory, but this system has significant problems.

WARNING

Many brokerage firms happen to be in another business that creates enormous conflicts of interest in producing objective company reviews. These investment firms also solicit companies to help them sell new stock and bond issues. To gain this business, the brokerage firms need to demonstrate enthusiasm and optimism for the company's future prospects.

Brokerage analysts who, with the best of intentions, write negative reports about a company find their careers hindered in a variety of ways. Some firms fire such analysts. Companies that the analysts criticize exclude those analysts from analyst meetings about the company. So most analysts who know what's good for their careers and their brokerage firms don't write disapproving reports (but some do take chances).

Although investment insiders know that analysts are pressured to be overly optimistic, historically it's been hard to find a smoking gun to prove that this pressuring is indeed occurring, and few people are willing to talk on the record about it. One firm was caught encouraging its analysts via a memo not to say negative things about companies. As uncovered by *Wall Street Journal* reporter Michael Siconolfi, Morgan Stanley's head of new stock issues stated in a memo that the firm's policy should include "no negative comments about [its] clients." The memo also stated that any analyst's changes in a stock's rating or investment opinion "which might be viewed negatively" by the firm's clients had to be cleared through the company's corporate finance department head.

Various studies of the brokerage firm's stock ratings have conclusively demonstrated that from a predictive perspective, most of its research is barely worth the cost of the paper that it's printed on. In Chapter 6, I recommend independent research reports worth perusing. In Chapter 9, I cover the important issues that you need to consider when you select a good broker.

Don't short-term trade or try to time the market

Unfortunately (for themselves), some investors track their stock investments closely and believe that they need to sell after short holding periods — months, weeks, or even days. With the growth of Internet and computerized trading, such shortsightedness has taken a turn for the worse as more investors now engage in a foolish process known as *day trading*, where they buy and sell a stock within the same day!

WARNING

If you hold a stock only for a few hours or a few months, you're not investing; you're gambling. Specifically, the numerous drawbacks that I see to short–term trading include the following:

>> **Higher trading costs:** Although the commission that you pay to trade stocks has declined greatly in recent years, especially through online trading (which I discuss in Chapter 9), the more you trade, the more of your investment dollars go into a broker's wallet. Commissions are like taxes — once paid, those dollars are forever gone, and your return is reduced. Similarly, the spread between the price you pay to purchase a stock and the price you would receive to sell the same stock (known as the *bid-ask spread*) can be a significant drag on your investment return.

>> **More taxes (and tax headaches):** When you invest outside of tax-sheltered retirement accounts, you must report on your annual income tax return every time that you buy and then sell a stock. After you make a profit, you must part with a good portion of it through the federal and state capital gains tax that you owe from the sale of your stock. If you sell a stock within one year of buying it, the IRS and most state tax authorities consider your profit short-term, and you owe a much higher rate of tax than if you hold your stock for more than a year. Holding your stock for more than a year qualifies you for the favorable long-term capital gains tax rate (a topic that I discuss in Chapter 21). The return that you keep (after taxes) is more important than the return that you make (before taxes).

>> **Lower returns:** If stocks increase in value over time, long-term buy-and-hold investors enjoy the fruits of the stock's appreciation. However, if you jump in and out of stocks, your money spends a good deal of time *not* invested in stocks. The overall level of stock prices in general and individual stocks in particular sometimes rises sharply during short periods of time.

Thus, short-term traders inevitably miss some stock run-ups. The best professional investors I know don't engage in short-term trading for this reason (as well as because of the increased transaction costs and taxes that such trading inevitably generates).

>> **Lost opportunities:** Most of the short-term traders I've met over the years spend inordinate amounts of time researching and monitoring their investments. During the late 1990s, I began to hear of more and more people who quit their jobs so they could manage their investment portfolios full time! Some of the firms that sell day-trading seminars tell you that you can make a living trading stocks. Your time is clearly worth something. Put your valuable time into working a little more on building your own business or career instead of wasting all those extra hours each day and week watching your investments like a hawk, which hampers rather than enhances your returns.

>> **Poorer relationships:** Time is your most precious commodity. In addition to the financial opportunities that you lose when you indulge in unproductive trading, you need to consider the personal consequences as well. Like drinking, smoking, and gambling, short-term trading is an addictive behavior. Spouses of day traders and other short-term traders report unhappiness over how much more time and attention their mates spend on their investments than on their families. And what about the lack of attention that day traders and short-term traders give other relatives and friends? (See the sidebar "Recognizing an investment gambling problem" in this chapter to help determine whether you or a loved one has a gambling addiction.)

How a given stock performs in the next few hours, days, weeks, or even months may have little to do with the underlying financial health and vitality of the company's business. In addition to short-term swings in investor emotions, unpredictable events (such as the emergence of a new technology or competitor, analyst predictions, changes in government regulation, and so on) push stocks one way or another in the short term.

All these reasons should convince you to avoid engaging in day trading or *market timing* (trying to jump in and out of particular investments based on current news and other factors). Be skeptical of any market prognosticator who claims to be able to time the markets and boasts of numerous past correct calls and market-beating returns.

REMEMBER

As I say throughout this part of the book, stocks are intended to be long-term holdings. You shouldn't buy stocks if you don't plan to hold them for at least five years or more — and preferably seven to ten. When stocks suffer a setback, it may take months or even years for them to come back.

RECOGNIZING AN INVESTMENT GAMBLING PROBLEM

Some gamblers spend their time at the racetrack, and you can find others in casinos. Increasingly, though, you can find gamblers at their personal computers, tracking and trading stocks.

More investors than ever are myopically focused on stocks' short-term price movements. Several factors contribute to this troubling activity: the continued growth of the Internet, the increased responsibility more folks have in managing their own retirement investments, and increased media coverage (including cable stock market channels). Also, companies touting themselves as educational institutions suck legions of novice investors into dangerous practices. Masquerading under such pompous names as institutes or academies, these firms purport to teach you how to get rich by day-trading stocks. Perhaps you have heard their seminar or training ads on the radio or have seen them on stock market cable television channels or on the Internet. All you have to do is part with several thousand dollars for the training, and then you're home free. But the only people getting rich are the owners of such seminar companies.

The nonprofit organization Gamblers Anonymous developed the following 20 questions to help you figure out whether you or someone you know is a compulsive gambler who needs help. According to Gamblers Anonymous, compulsive gamblers typically answer yes to seven or more of these questions:

1. Did you ever lose time from work or school due to gambling?

2. Has gambling ever made your home life unhappy?

3. Did gambling affect your reputation?

4. Have you ever felt remorse after gambling?

5. Did you ever gamble to get money with which to pay debts or otherwise solve financial difficulties?

6. Did gambling cause a decrease in your ambition or efficiency?

7. After losing, did you feel you must return as soon as possible and win back your losses?

8. After a win, did you have a strong urge to return and win more?

9. Did you often gamble until your last dollar was gone?

(continued)

(continued)

10. Did you ever borrow money to finance your gambling?

11. Have you ever sold anything to finance gambling?

12. Were you reluctant to use "gambling money" for normal expenditures?

13. Did gambling make you careless of the welfare of your family?

14. Did you ever gamble longer than you had planned?

15. Have you ever gambled to escape worry or trouble?

16. Have you ever committed, or considered committing, an illegal act to finance gambling?

17. Did gambling cause you to have difficulty in sleeping?

18. Do arguments, disappointments, or frustrations create within you an urge to gamble?

19. Did you ever have an urge to celebrate any good fortune by a few hours of gambling?

20. Have you ever considered self-destruction as a result of your gambling?

Be wary of gurus

It's tempting to wish that you could consult a guru who could foresee an impending major decline and get you out of an investment before it tanks. Believe me when I say that plenty of these pundits are talking up such supposed prowess. The financial crisis of 2008 brought an avalanche of prognosticators out of the woodwork claiming that if you had been listening to them, you could have not only sidestepped losses but also made money.

WARNING

From having researched many such claims (see the "Guru Watch" section of my website, www.erictyson.com), I can tell you that nearly all these folks significantly misrepresented their past predictions and recommendations. And the very, very few who made some halfway decent predictions in the recent short term had poor or unremarkable longer-term track records.

As you develop your plans for an investment portfolio, be sure to take a level of risk and aggressiveness with which you're comfortable. Remember that no pundit has a working crystal ball that can tell you what's going to happen with the economy and financial markets in the future.

Shun penny stocks

Even worse than buying stocks through a broker whose compensation depends on what you buy and how often you trade is purchasing penny stocks through brokers who specialize in such stocks. Tens of thousands of smaller-company stocks trade on the over-the-counter market. Some of these companies are quite small and sport low prices per share that range from pennies to several dollars, hence the name *penny stocks.*

Here's how penny-stock brokers typically work: Many of these firms purchase prospect lists of people who have demonstrated a propensity for buying other lousy investments by phone. Brokers are taught to first introduce themselves by phone and then call back shortly thereafter with a tremendous sense of urgency about a great opportunity to get in on the "ground floor" of a small but soon-to-be stellar company. Not all these companies and stocks have terrible prospects, but many do.

WARNING

The biggest problem with buying penny stocks through such brokers is that they're grossly overpriced. Just as you don't make good investment returns by purchasing jewelry that's marked up 100 percent, you don't have a fighting chance to make decent money on penny stocks that the broker may flog with similar markups. The individual broker who cons you into "investing" in such cheap stocks gains a big commission, which is why he continues to call you with "opportunities" until you send him a check. Many brokers in this business who possess records of securities violations also possess an ability to sell, so they have no problem gaining employment with other penny-stock peddlers.

A number of penny-stock brokerage firms are known for engaging in manipulation of stock prices. They drive up prices of selected shares to suck in gullible investors and then leave the public holding the bag. These firms may also encourage companies to issue new overpriced stock that their brokers can then sell to folks.

The Keys to Stock Market Success

REMEMBER

Anybody, no matter what her educational background, IQ, occupation, income, or assets, can make solid returns through stock investments. Over long periods of time, based on historic performance, you can expect to earn an average of about 9 percent per year total return by investing in stocks.

TIP

To maximize your chances of stock market investment success, do the following:

>> **Don't try to time the markets.** Anticipating where the stock market and specific stocks are heading is next to impossible, especially over the short term. Economic factors, which are influenced by thousands of elements as well as human emotions, determine stock market prices. Be a regular buyer of stocks with new savings. As I discuss earlier in this chapter, consider buying more stocks when they're on sale and market pessimism is running high. Don't make the mistake of bailing out when the market is down!

>> **Diversify your investments.** Invest in the stocks of different-sized companies in varying industries around the world. When assessing your investments' performance, examine your whole portfolio at least once a year and calculate your total return after expenses and trading fees.

>> **Keep trading costs, management fees, and commissions to a minimum.** These costs represent a big drain on your returns. If you invest through an individual broker or a financial advisor who earns a living on commissions, odds are that you're paying more than you need to be. And you're likely receiving biased advice, too.

>> **Pay attention to taxes.** Like commissions and fees, federal and state taxes are a major investment "expense" that you can minimize. Contribute most of your money to your tax-advantaged retirement accounts. You can invest your money outside of retirement accounts, but keep an eye on taxes (see Chapter 3). Calculate your annual returns on an *after*-tax basis.

>> **Don't overestimate your ability to pick the big-winning stocks.** One of the best ways to invest in stocks is through mutual funds (see Chapter 8), which allow you to use an experienced, full-time money manager at a low cost to perform all the investing grunt work for you.

Chapter 6

Investigating and Purchasing Individual Stocks

This chapter provides a crash course in researching individual companies and their stocks. Be sure you consider your reasons for taking this approach before you head down the path of picking and choosing your own stocks. If you haven't already done so, take a look at Chapter 5 to better understand the process of purchasing stocks on your own.

If you decide to tackle the task of researching your own stocks, you don't have to worry about finding enough information: The problem to worry about is information overload. You can literally spend hundreds of hours researching and reading information on one company alone. Therefore, you need to focus on where you can get the best bang for your buck and time.

Building on Others' Research

If you were going to build a house, you probably wouldn't try to do it on your own. Instead, you'd likely find some sort of kit or a set of plans drawn up by people who have built many houses. You can do the same when picking individual stocks. In the following sections, I highlight useful resources that allow you to hit the ground running when you're trying to pick the best stocks. In addition to the resources I cover here, check out Part 5 for other useful resources for researching individual stocks.

Discovering the Value Line Investment Survey

ERIC'S PICKS

Value Line is an investment research company. Value Line's securities analysts have been tracking and researching stocks since the Great Depression. Their analysis and recommendation track record is quite good, and their analysts are beholden to no one. Many professional money managers use the *Value Line Investment Survey*, a Value Line weekly newsletter, as a reference because of its comprehensiveness.

The beauty of Value Line's service is that it condenses the key information and statistics about a stock (and the company behind the stock) to a single page. Suppose you're interested in investing in Starbucks, the retail coffeehouse operator. You've seen all its stores, and you figure that if you're going to shell out more than $3 for a cup of its flavored hot water, you may as well participate in the profits and growth of the company. You look up the recent stock price (I explain how to do so later in this chapter if you don't know how) and see that it's about $75 per share.

Take a look at the important elements of the *Value Line Investment Survey* page for Starbucks in Figure 6-1.

REMEMBER

The information in Value Line's reports is in no way insider information. Look at these reports the same way that you review a history book: They provide useful background information that can keep you from repeating common mistakes.

1. Business

This section of the report describes the business(es) that Starbucks participates in. You can see that Starbucks is the largest retailer of specialty coffee in the world. Although 88 percent of the company's sales come from retail, note that 12 percent come from other avenues — such as mail-order, online, and supermarket sales. You also find details about joint ventures, such as Starbucks' partnerships with Pepsi and Dreyer's to develop and sell bottled coffee drinks and ice creams, respectively. This section also shows you that the senior executives and directors of the company own a sizeable stake (3.3 percent) of the stock; seeing that these folks have a financial stake in the success of the company and stock is a good thing.

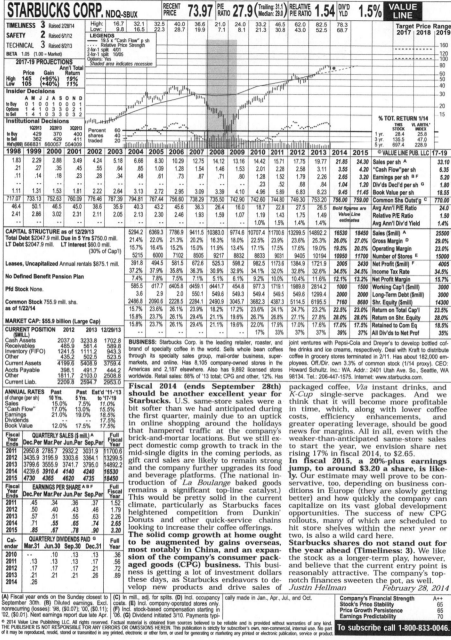

FIGURE 6-1:
*Value Line
Investment Survey*
report on
Starbucks.

2. Analyst assessment

A securities analyst (in this case, Justin Hellman) follows each *Value Line Investment Survey* stock. An analyst focuses on specific industries and follows a few dozen stocks. This section of the Value Line report provides the analyst's summary and commentary of the company's current situation and future plans.

3. Value Line's ratings

The *Value Line Investment Survey* provides a numerical ranking for each stock's Timeliness (expected performance) over the next year. One is highest and 5 is lowest, but only about 5 percent of all stocks receive these extreme ratings. A 2 rating is above average and a 4 rating is below average; about one-sixth of the ranked stocks receive each of these ratings. All remaining stocks — a little more than half of the total ranked — get the average 3 rating.

The Safety rating works the same way as the Timeliness rating, with 1 representing the best and least volatile stocks and the most financially stable companies. Five is the worst Safety ranking; it denotes the most volatile stocks and least financially stable companies.

Starbucks' current ratings are 3 for Timeliness, which is average, and 2 for Safety, which is above average. I've never been a fan of predictions and short-term thinking. (One year is a very short period of time for the stock market.) However, historically, Value Line's ranking system has held one of the best overall track records according to the *Hulbert Financial Digest,* which tracks the actual performance of investment newsletter recommendations. Even so, you shouldn't necessarily run out and buy a particular stock because of its high ranking. Just keep in mind that higher-ranked stocks within the *Value Line Investment Survey* have historically outperformed those without such ratings.

4. Stock price performance

The graph in Figure 6-1 shows you the stock price's performance over the past decade or so. The highest and lowest points of the line on the graph indicate the high and low stock prices for each month. At the top of the graph, you see the year's high and low prices. Starbucks stock has risen significantly since the company first issued stock in 1992, but Starbucks certainly has experienced some down periods. (The small box in the lower-right corner of the graph shows you the total return that an investor in this stock earned over the previous one, three, and five years and compares those returns to the average stock. The graph in Figure 6-1 shows you that Starbucks declined significantly from 2006 through 2008 but has since rebounded smartly.)

The graph also shows how the price of the stock moves with changes in the company's *cash flow* (money coming in minus money going out). The solid line in the

Starbucks graph represents 19.5 times the company's cash flow. Over time, just as stock prices tend to track corporate profits, so, too, should they generally follow cash flow. Cash flow is an important measure of a company's financial success and health — it's different from *net profits*, which the company reports for tax purposes. For example, the tax laws allow companies to take a tax deduction each year for the *depreciation* (devaluation) of the company's equipment and other assets. Although depreciation is good because it helps lower a company's tax bill, subtracting it from the company's revenue gives an untrue picture of the company's cash flow. Thus, in calculating a company's cash flow, you don't subtract depreciation from revenue.

5. Historic financials

This section shows you 12 to 18 years of financial information on the company (in the case of Starbucks, you get information going back to just 1998). The two most helpful pieces of information in this section are

>> **Book value per share:** This number indicates the value of the company's assets, including equipment, manufacturing plants, and real estate, minus any liabilities. Book value gives somewhat of a handle on the amount that the company can sell for if it has a "going-out-of-business sale." I say *somewhat* because the value of some assets on a company's books isn't correct. For example, some companies own real estate, bought long ago, that is worth far more than the company's current financial statements indicate. Conversely, some manufacturers with equipment find that if they have to dump some equipment in a hurry, they need to sell the equipment at a discount to entice a buyer.

The book value of a bank, for example, can mislead you if the bank makes loans that won't be paid back, and the bank's financial statements don't document this fact. All these complications with book value are one of the reasons full-time, professional money managers exist. (If you want to delve more into a company's book value, you need to look at other financial statements, such as the company's annual report, which I discuss in the section "Understanding Annual Reports" later in this chapter.)

>> **Market share:** For some companies (not Starbucks), the *Value Line Investment Survey* also provides another useful number in this section of the report: the *market share,* which indicates the portions of the industry that the company has captured in a given year. A sustained decline in a company's market share is a dangerous sign that may indicate its customers are leaving for other companies that presumably offer better products at lower prices. But a decline in market share doesn't necessarily mean that you should avoid investing in a particular company. You can produce big returns if you identify companies that reposition and strengthen their product offerings to reverse a market share decrease.

6. P/E ratio

This section tells you that Starbucks sells at a P/E (price-to-earnings ratio) of 27.9 because of its recent stock price and earnings. This particular P/E is higher than that of the overall market. (You can see that Starbucks' P/E is 1.54 times that of the overall market.) To understand the importance of P/E in evaluating a stock, see Chapter 5.

7. Capital structure

This section summarizes the amount of outstanding stocks and bonds that the company possesses. Remember that when a company issues these securities, it receives *capital* (money). The most useful number to examine in this section is the company's debt. If a company accumulates a lot of debt, the burden of interest payments can create a real drag on profits. If profits stay down for too long, debt can even push some companies into bankruptcy.

Figure 6-1 shows you that Starbucks has an outstanding debt of $2,048 million. But how do you know if this is a lot, a little, or just the right amount of debt?

Possessing a larger cushion to cover debt is more important when the company's business is volatile. You can calculate *total interest coverage,* which compares a company's annual profits to the yearly interest payments on its total debt. This number tells you the number of years that the company's most recent annual profits can cover interest on all the company's debt.

For example, if a company has a total interest coverage of 4.5x, the company's most recent yearly profits can cover the interest payments on all debt for about 4½ years. Starbucks' most recent annual profits of $1,722 million dwarf its interest payments of $60 million by a factor of more than 28 to 1. Warning signs for total interest coverage numbers include a steep decline in this number over time and profits that cover less than one year's worth of interest.

8. Current position

This section provides a quick look at how the company's *current assets* (assets that the company can convert into cash within a year relatively easily) compare with its *current liabilities* (debts due within the year). Trouble may be brewing if a company's current liabilities exceed or are approaching its current assets.

TECHNICAL STUFF

Some financial analysts calculate the quick ratio. The *quick ratio* ignores inventory when comparing current assets to current liabilities. A company may have to dump inventory at a relatively low price if it needs to raise cash quickly. Thus, some analysts argue, you need to ignore inventory as a current asset.

9. Annual rates

This nifty section can save wear and tear on your calculator. The good folks at Value Line calculate rates of growth (or shrinkage) on important financial indicators, such as *sales* (revenues) and *earnings* (profits) over the past five and ten years. This section also lists Value Line's projections for the next five years.

WARNING

Projections can prove highly unreliable, even from a research firm as good as Value Line. In most cases, the projections assume that the company will continue as it has in the most recent couple years.

10. Quarterly financials

For the most recent years, the *Value Line Investment Survey* shows you an even more detailed quarterly breakout of sales and profits, which may disclose changes that annual totals mask. In this section of the report, you can also see the seasonality of some businesses. Starbucks, for example, tends to have its slowest quarter in the winter (quarter ending March 31). This trend makes sense if you figure that many of the customers who frequent Starbucks' coffee shops do so as they walk around town, which people tend to do less of on blustery winter days.

Considering independent brokerage research

If you're going to invest in individual stocks, you need a brokerage account. In addition to offering low trading fees, the best brokerage firms allow you to easily tap into useful research, especially through the firm's website, that you can use to assist you with your investing decisions.

Because discount brokers aren't in the investment banking business of working with companies to sell new issues of stock, discount brokers have a level of objectivity in their research reports that traditional brokers (ones like Merrill Lynch, Morgan Stanley, and so on) too often lack. Some discount brokers, such as Charles Schwab, produce their own research reports, but most discount brokers simply provide reports from independent third parties. See Chapter 9 for how to select a top-notch brokerage firm.

Examining successful money managers' stock picks

TIP

To make money in stocks, you certainly don't need an original idea. In fact, it makes sense to examine what the best money managers are buying for their portfolios. Don't worry; I'm not suggesting that you invade their privacy or ask rude questions!

Mutual fund managers, for example, are required to disclose at least twice a year what stocks they hold in their portfolio. You can call the best fund companies and ask them to send their most recent semiannual reports that detail their stock holdings, or you can view those reports on many fund companies' websites. (See Chapter 8 for more information on the best stock mutual funds.)

Through its website, Morningstar (www.morningstar.com) allows you to see which mutual funds hold large portions of a given stock that you may be researching and what the success or lack thereof is of the funds that are buying a given stock.

Finally, you can follow what investment legend Warren Buffett is buying through his holding company, Berkshire Hathaway. If you'd like to review Berkshire's complete corporate filings on your own, visit the Securities and Exchange Commission website at www.sec.gov.

Reviewing financial publications and websites

Many publications and websites cover the world of stocks. But you have to be careful. Just because certain columnists or publications advocate particular stocks or investing strategies doesn't mean you'll achieve success by following their advice.

TIP

The following publications offer useful columns and commentary, sometimes written by professional money managers, on individual stocks: *Barron's, Bloomberg Business Week, Forbes, Kiplinger's,* and *The Wall Street Journal.* In addition, hundreds of websites are devoted to stock picking. I name my favorite investing sites in Chapter 19.

Understanding Annual Reports

After you review the *Value Line Investment Survey* page on a company and want to dig further into financial documents, the next step is to ask yourself why. Why do you want to torture yourself so?

After successfully completing one of the better MBA programs (Stanford's), taking more than my fair share of accounting and finance courses, and then living and working in the real world, I've gotten to know investment managers and financial analysts who research companies. Although some financial documents aren't that difficult to read (I show you how in this section), interpreting what they mean in respect to a company's future isn't easy.

REMEMBER

All publicly traded companies must annually file certain financial documents. Consider reviewing these documents to enhance your understanding of a company's businesses and strategies rather than for the predictive value that you may hope they provide.

The first of such useful documents that companies produce is the *annual report.* This yearly report provides standardized financial statements as well as management's discussion about how the company has performed and how it plans to improve its performance in the future. If you're a bit of the skeptical sort, as I am, you may think, "Aren't the company's officials going to make everything sound rosy and wonderful?"

To a certain extent, yes, but not as badly as you may think, especially at companies that adhere to sound accounting principles and good old-fashioned ethics. First, a large portion of annual reports include the company's financial statements, which an accounting firm must audit. However, audits don't mean that companies and their accounting firms can't (often legally) structure the company's books to make them look rosier than they really are. And some companies have pulled the wool over the eyes of their auditors, who then become unwitting accomplices in producing false financial figures.

WARNING

You've surely heard of the accounting scandals at companies such as Enron and WorldCom. These companies manipulated their financial books, with the blessing of supposedly blue-chip corporate auditors, to mislead investors into believing that the companies were more profitable than they really were. (Identifying trouble *before* other investors do is a skill that many professional investors haven't mastered. If you can identify trouble early, go manage other people's money!)

Also keep in mind that more than a few companies have been sued for misleading shareholders with inflated forecasts or lack of disclosure of problems. Responsible companies try to present a balanced and, of course, hopeful perspective in their annual reports. Most companies' annual reports are also written by non-techno geeks, so you have a decent chance of understanding them.

The following sections walk you through the three main elements of the standard annual report: financial and business highlights, the balance sheet, and the income statement.

Financial and business highlights

The first section of most annual reports presents a description of a company's recent financial highlights and business strategies. You can use this information to find out about the businesses that the company is in and where the company is heading. For example, in Figure 6-1, the *Value Line Investment Survey* report mentions that Starbucks is also in the specialty sales business. Starbucks' annual report can provide more detail about that specialty sales business.

Okay, enough about the coffee business; it's time to expose you to another industry. T. Rowe Price is a publicly traded investment management company that offers some good mutual funds.

Balance sheet

You can find a company's hard-core financials in the back portion of most annual reports. (You can find many of these same numbers in *Value Line Investment Survey* reports, but you get more specific details in the company's annual report.) All annual reports contain a *balance sheet,* which is a snapshot summary of all the company's *assets* (what the company owns) and *liabilities* (what the company owes). The balance sheet covers the company's assets and liabilities from the beginning of the year to the last day of the company's year-end, which is typically December 31. Some companies use a fiscal year that ends at other times of the year.

A company's balance sheet resembles a personal balance sheet. The entries, of course, look a little different because you likely don't own things like manufacturing equipment. Figure 6-2 shows a typical corporate balance sheet.

CONSOLIDATED BALANCE SHEETS

(in millions, except share data)

December 31,	2012	2013
Assets		
Cash and cash equivalents	$ 879.1	$ 1,398.0
Accounts receivable and accrued revenue	353.9	398.8
Investments in sponsored funds	1,140.1	1,611.9
Debt securities held by savings bank subsidiary	136.0	—
Other investments	304.7	313.6
Property and equipment	561.0	572.9
Goodwill	665.7	665.7
Other assets	162.3	72.2
Total assets	**$ 4,202.8**	**$ 5,033.1**
Liabilities and Stockholders' Equity		
Liabilities		
Accounts payable and accrued expenses	$ 89.7	$ 103.9
Accrued compensation and related costs	90.8	72.4
Income taxes payable	21.5	38.7
Customer deposits at savings bank subsidiary	154.7	—
Total liabilities	**356.7**	**215.0**
Commitments and contingent liabilities		
Stockholders' equity		
Preferred stock, undesignated, $.20 par value— authorized and unissued 20,000,000 shares	—	—
Common stock, $.20 par value—authorized 750,000,000; issued 257,018,000 shares in 2012 and 262,073,000 shares in 2013	51.4	52.4
Additional capital in excess of par value	631.0	894.6
Retained earnings	3,031.8	3,682.8
Accumulated other comprehensive income	131.9	188.3
Total stockholders' equity	**3,846.1**	**4,818.1**
Total liabilities and stockholders' equity	**$ 4,202.8**	**$ 5,033.1**

SOURCE: T. Rowe Price Associates, Inc. 2013 Annual Report

FIGURE 6-2: The balance sheet from a T. Rowe Price annual report.

Assets

The assets section of the balance sheet lists the following items that a company holds or owns that are of significant value:

INVESTIGATE

>> **Cash:** I suspect that you know what cash is. Lest you think that stacks of green bills sit around in corporate vaults, rest assured that companies invest this money to earn interest. Explanatory notes often follow the balance sheet to explain certain items in more detail.

>> **Accounts receivable:** This item represents money that is owed to the company, such as customer invoices that haven't been paid yet.

As companies grow, their accounts receivable usually do, too. Watch out for cases where the receivables grow faster than the sales (revenue). This growth may indicate that the company is having problems with its products' quality or pricing. Unhappy customers pay more slowly or demand bigger price discounts.

>> **Investments:** In addition to cash, some companies may invest in other securities, such as bonds and stocks. Just as with your own personal situation, companies usually invest money that they don't expect to use in the near future.

>> **Property and equipment:** All companies need equipment to run their businesses. This equipment can include office furniture, computers, real estate they own, and manufacturing machinery that companies use to make their products. Equipment becomes less valuable over time, so a company must consider this depreciation as a cost of doing business each year. Therefore, if a company ceases buying new equipment, this entry on the balance sheet gradually decreases because the company continues to subtract the depreciation from the value of the equipment.

>> **Goodwill:** One of the assets that doesn't show up on most companies' balance sheets is their *goodwill.* Companies work hard through advertising, product development, and service to attract and retain customers and to build *name-brand recognition.*

Companies can't put a value on the goodwill that they've generated, but when they purchase (acquire) another firm, some of the purchase price is considered goodwill. Specifically, if a company is acquired for $100 million but has a *net worth* (assets minus liabilities) of just $50 million, the extra $50 million goes to goodwill. The goodwill then becomes an asset on the acquiring company's balance sheet.

>> **Other assets:** This catch-all category may include some stuff that can make your eyes glaze over. For example, companies keep a different set of books for tax purposes (yes, this is legal). Not surprisingly, companies do so because the IRS allows, in some cases, more deductions than what the company is

required to show from an accounting standpoint on their financial statements. (If you were a company, wouldn't you want your shareholders, but not the IRS, to see gobs of profits?) Companies treat tax deferment as an asset until the IRS receives more of its share down the road.

INVESTIGATE

Manufacturing and retail companies also track and report *inventory* (the product that hasn't yet been sold) as an asset. Generally speaking, as a business grows, so does its inventory. If inventory grows more quickly than revenue, such growth may be a warning sign. This growth can indicate that customers are scaling back purchases and that the company miscalculated and overproduced. It can also be a leading indicator of an obsolete or inferior product offering.

Liabilities

This section of the balance sheet summarizes all the money that a company owes to other entities:

>> **Accounts payable:** When a company places orders to purchase things for its business, it sometimes has a lag between receiving a bill and paying it; the money owed is called *accounts payable.* As with inventory and accounts receivable, accounts payable generally increase with a company's increasing revenue.

INVESTIGATE

If accounts payable increase faster than revenue, the company may have a problem. On the other hand, that increase can also be a sign of good financial management. The longer you take to pay your bills, the longer you have the money in your pocket working for you.

>> **Accrued compensation:** This line tallies money that the company must someday pay its employees. For example, many larger firms maintain pension plans. These plans promise workers who retire with at least five years of service a monthly income check in retirement. Thus, the company must reserve this money that it owes and list it as a liability or debt that it must someday pay.

>> **Income taxes payable:** Companies are in business to make a profit, and as they earn those profits, they need to reserve a portion to pay income taxes. As I explain in the preceding section, some of the taxes that the company owes can be the result of accounting differences between the company's financial statements and those filed with the IRS.

>> **Dividends payable:** Not all companies pay dividends (see Chapter 4) to their shareholders. But those companies that do pay dividends typically declare the dividend several weeks in advance of when they actually owe the dividend. During this interim period, the company lists the not-yet-paid dividends as a liability.

Stockholders' equity

The difference between a company's assets and liabilities is known as *stockholders' equity*. Stockholders' equity is what makes balance sheets always balance.

TECHNICAL
STUFF

When companies issue stock, they receive cash, which they then list as an asset. Companies divide stock proceeds between *par value* and *capital in excess of par value*. In the case of T. Rowe Price (see Figure 6-2), the par value is $0.20 per share. Par values are arcane — and largely meaningless.

Income statement

The other big financial statement in an annual report is the income statement (see Figure 6-3 for a T. Rowe Price income statement). I discuss the elements of a corporate income statement next.

CONSOLIDATED STATEMENTS OF INCOME

(in millions, except earnings per share)

Year ended December 31,	2011	2012	2013
Revenues			
Investment advisory fees	$ 2,349.0	$ 2,592.0	$ 3,022.6
Administrative fees	321.2	332.6	343.7
Distribution and servicing fees	74.6	96.1	117.2
Net revenue of savings bank subsidiary	2.3	1.8	.7
Net revenues	**2,747.1**	**3,022.5**	**3,484.2**
Operating Expenses			
Compensation and related costs	969.8	1,047.6	1,156.9
Advertising and promotion	90.8	89.8	88.7
Distribution and servicing costs	74.6	96.1	117.2
Depreciation and amortization of property and equipment	72.0	80.9	90.6
Occupancy and facility costs	115.0	124.7	135.8
Other operating expenses	198.0	219.1	257.6
Total operating expenses	**1,520.2**	**1,658.2**	**1,846.8**
Net Operating Income	**1,226.9**	**1,364.3**	**1,637.4**
Non-operating investment income	23.7	70.8	63.0
Income before income taxes	1,250.6	1,435.1	1,700.4
Provision for income taxes	477.4	551.5	652.7
Net income	**$ 773.2**	**$ 883.6**	**$ 1,047.7**
Earnings Per Share on Common Stock			
Basic	$ 3.01	$ 3.47	$ 4.02
Diluted	$ 2.92	$ 3.36	$ 3.90

SOURCE: T. Rowe Price Associates, Inc. 2013 Annual Report

FIGURE 6-3:
A T. Rowe Price income statement.

Revenue

Revenue is simply the money that a company receives from its customers as compensation for its products or services. Just as you can earn income from your job(s) as well as from investments and other sources, a company can make money from a variety of sources. In the case of mutual fund provider T. Rowe Price, the firm collects fees (investment advisory and administrative) for the mutual fund investments that it manages on behalf of its customers as well as privately managed money for wealthy individuals and institutions. The company also receives income from its own money that it has invested.

Ideally, you want to see a steady or accelerating rate of growth in a company's revenue. If a company's revenue grows more slowly, you need to inquire why. Is it because of poor service or product performance, better competitor offerings, ineffective marketing, or all the above?

For companies with multiple divisions or product lines, the annual report may detail the revenue of each product line in a later section. If it doesn't, check out some of the other financial statements that I recommend in the next section, "Exploring Other Useful Corporate Reports." Examine what spurs or holds back the company's overall growth and which different businesses the company operates in. Look for businesses that were acquired but don't really fit with the company's other business units as a red flag. Large companies that have experienced stalled revenue growth sometimes try to enter new businesses through acquisition but then don't manage them well because they don't understand the keys to their success.

When researching retail stores, such as restaurant chains (for example, McDonald's) or clothing stores (for example, The Gap), examine the revenue changes that come from opening new locations versus the changes at existing locations, sometimes referred to as *same stores.* Be concerned if you find that a company's revenue growth comes from opening new locations rather than growth at existing locations. This situation may indicate that opening more locations is masking weakness in the company's business.

Expenses

Just as personal income taxes and housing, food, and clothing expenses gobble up much of your personal income, company expenses use up much, and sometimes all, of a company's revenue.

Even healthy, growing businesses can get into trouble if their expenses grow faster than their revenues. Well-managed companies stay on top of their expenses during good and bad times. Unfortunately, it's easy for companies to get sloppy during good times.

It's particularly useful to examine each category of expenses relative to (in other words, as a percentage of) the company's revenue to see which ones grow or shrink. As a well-managed and financially healthy company grows, expenses as a percentage of revenue should decrease. In turn, profits as a percentage of revenue increase.

T. Rowe Price's total operating expenses relative to total revenues have decreased, while profits (net operating income) relative to total revenues have increased. Not all expense categories necessarily decrease.

Net income calculations

The net result of expenses that increase more slowly than revenues is a fatter bottom line. Sometimes companies experience one-time events, such as the sale of a division, which can change profits temporarily. Companies usually list these one-time events in the section under expenses.

I encourage you to review the company's statement of cash flows included in its annual report. Cash can flow into and out of a company from normal business operations, investment activities, and financing activities. Sometimes a company may report higher profits but actually be facing decreased cash flow from operations, for example, if its customers are getting slower with paying bills (which could indicate that its customers are having financial problems or that they're unhappy with the product or service being provided).

Earnings per share

Last but not least, and of great importance to shareholders, is the calculation of earnings per share. Higher profits per share generally help fuel a higher stock price, and declining profits feed falling stock prices. Remember, though, that smart financial market participants are looking ahead, so if you run out to buy stock in a company that's reporting higher profits, those higher profits are old news and likely have already been priced into the company's current market value.

Exploring Other Useful Corporate Reports

In addition to annual reports, companies produce other financial statements, such as 10-Ks, 10-Qs, and proxies, that you may want to peruse. You can generally obtain these reports from the companies' websites, from the companies' investor relations departments, or from the Securities and Exchange Commission website, www.sec.gov (see Chapter 19 for more on this site).

FUNDAMENTAL VERSUS TECHNICAL ANALYSIS

Throughout this chapter and Chapter 5, I talk a lot about the financial statements and analysis of a company — balance sheets, revenues, expenses, earnings, price-earnings ratios, and so on. Analyzing financial statements and making investing decisions based on them is known as *fundamental analysis.*

Another school of stock market analysis, known as *technical analysis,* involves examining chart patterns, volume of trading in a stock, and all sorts of indicators that have little, if anything, to do with the underlying stock.

Technical analysts say things like, "Stock XYZ has a major support area at $20 per share" and "Stock ABC has broken out above $30 per share." I suggest that you ignore this school of thinking. In fact, ignoring the technical analysts will likely increase your stock market profits. Why? Because technical analysis thinking encourages a trader's, not an investor's, mindset.

Many technical analysts work for brokerage firms and write daily, weekly, or monthly assessments of the entire stock market and some individual stocks. Recommendations and advice change over time, and the result is that you trade more. Not coincidentally, these brokerage firms make more money the more you trade! Investment newsletter writers are the other big advocates of this Ouija-board approach to investment management. Again, it's a great approach for the newsletter writers who hook you on a $200-per-year newsletter.

10-Ks

10-Ks are expanded versions of the annual report. Most investment professionals read the 10-K rather than the annual report because the 10-K contains additional data and information, especially for a company's various divisions and product lines. Also, 10-Ks contain little of the verbal hype that you find in most annual reports. In fact, the 10-K is probably one of the most objective reports that a company publishes. If you're not intimidated by annual reports or if you want more company meat, read the 10-Ks from the companies you want to check out.

10-Qs

10-Qs provide information similar to the 10-K but on a quarterly basis. 10-Qs are worth your time if you like to read reasonably detailed discussions by management of the latest business and financial developments at a certain company.

However, I recommend leaving the research to Value Line's analysts (see the earlier section "Discovering the Value Line Investment Survey").

The financial data in 10-Qs is unaudited and not of great use for the long-term investor. But if you want to watch your investments like a hawk and try to be among the first to detect indications of financial problems (easier said than done), this report is required reading.

WARNING

Some companies go back to restate their quarterly financials. Remember that the accountants haven't fully approved these interim numbers. Companies may take their financial lumps in one quarter to get problems behind them, so one bad quarter doesn't necessarily indicate a harmful long-term trend.

Proxies

The final corporate document that you may want to review is the annual *proxy statement*, which companies send out to their shareholders in advance of their annual meeting. The proxy statement contains some of the more important financial information and discussions that you can find in the 10-K. It also contains information on other corporate matters, such as the election of the board of directors. (*Directors* — who are usually corporate executives, lawyers, accountants, and other knowledgeable luminaries — serve as sounding boards, counselors, and sometimes overseers to the management team of a company.)

The proxy statement becomes much more important when a company faces a takeover or some other controversial corporate matter, such as the election of an alternative board of directors. As a shareholder, you get to vote on proposed board members and on select other corporate issues, which you can read about in the proxy statement.

The proxy statement tells you who serves on the board of directors as well as how much they and the executives of the company are paid. At annual meetings, where the board of directors discusses proxy statements, shareholders sometimes get angry and ask why the executives are paid so much when the company's stock price and business underperform.

Getting Ready to Invest in Stocks

There's always a chorus of self-anointed gurus saying that you can make fat profits if you pick your own stocks.

Unless you're extraordinarily lucky or unusually gifted at analyzing company and investor behavior, you won't earn above-average returns if you select your own stocks.

Keep the amount that you dedicate to individual stock investments to a minimum — ideally, no more than 20 percent of your invested dollars. I encourage you to do such investing for the educational value and enjoyment that you derive from it, not because you smugly think you're as skilled as the best professional money managers. (If you want to find out more about analyzing companies, read the chapters in Part 4 on small business as well as the chapters in Part 5 on investing resources.)

Understanding stock prices

Just about every major financial and news site on the Internet offers stock quotes for free as a lure to get you to visit the site. To view a stock price quote online, all you need is the security's trading symbol (which you obtain by using the stock symbol look-up feature universally offered with online quote services). Most major newspapers print a listing of the prior day's stock prices. Daily business papers, such as *The Wall Street Journal* and *Investor's Business Daily,* also publish stock prices daily.

Cable business channels, such as Bloomberg, CNBC, and Fox Business, have stock quotes streaming across the bottom of the screen. You can stop by a local brokerage office and see the current stock quotes whizzing by on a long, narrow screen on a wall. Many brokerage firms also maintain publicly accessible terminals (that look a lot like personal computers) on which you can obtain current quotes.

The following table is a typical example of the kinds of information that you can find in daily price quotes in papers and online; the quotes in this table are for the information technology giant International Business Machines (also known as Big Blue or IBM). After the name of the company, you see the trading symbol, IBM, which is the code that you and brokers use to look up the price on computer-based quotation systems.

International Business Machines (IBM)	
52-wk range	172.19 – 211.98
Last trade	4:00 pm EST (196.47)
Change	+1.36 (+0.70%)
Day's range	194.35 – 196.86
Open	194.38

International Business Machines (IBM)	
Volume	4,211,284
P/E ratio	13.4
Mkt cap	198.4B
Div/Shr	3.80
Yield	2.00%

Here's a breakdown of what the information in this table means:

>> **52-week range:** These two numbers indicate the low ($172.19) and high ($211.98) trading prices for IBM during the past 52 weeks.

>> **Last trade:** This line indicates the most recent price that the stock traded at (you can see that this IBM quote was from 4:00 p.m. Eastern Standard Time, which is when the New York Stock Exchange closes for the day).

>> **Change:** This entry indicates how that price differs from the previous day's close. In this case, you can see that the stock was up 1.36 points (0.70 percent) from the prior day's close.

>> **Day's range:** These two numbers are the lowest and highest prices that the stock traded at during the day.

>> **Open:** This line tells you the trade price at the market's open.

>> **Volume:** This number indicates the number of shares that traded through this point in the trading day. (To conserve space, many newspapers indicate the volume in hundreds of shares — in other words, you must add two zeros to the end of the number to arrive at the actual number of shares.)

>> **The P/E ratio:** As I explain in Chapters 4 and 5, the P/E ratio measures the price of IBM's stock relative to the company's earnings or profits.

>> **Market capitalization (mkt cap):** This number tells you the current market value of all of IBM's stock, which in this case is $198.4 billion. You calculate this value by multiplying the current price per share by the total number of shares outstanding. (See Chapter 8 for an explanation of so-called market caps as they apply to stocks and stock funds.)

>> **Dividends/share (div/shr):** This number shows you the current dividend (in this case, $3.80 per share), which the company pays yearly to shareholders. Most companies actually pay out one-quarter of their total annual dividend every three months.

>> **Yield:** This number indicates the effective percentage yield that the stock's dividend produces. To calculate the effective yield, divide the dividend by the current stock price. Thus, IBM shareholders can expect to receive a dividend worth about 2.0 percent of the current stock price.

Now you know how to read stock quotes!

Purchasing stock "direct" from companies

Numerous companies sell their stock directly to the public. Proponents of these direct stock purchase plans say that you can invest in stocks without paying any commissions. Well, the commission-free spiel isn't quite true, and investing in such plans poses other challenges.

If you want to purchase directly from Home Depot, for example, you need a minimum initial investment of $500. Buying stock "direct" isn't free; in the case of Home Depot, for example, you have to pay a $5 enrollment fee. Although that may not sound like much on a $500 investment, $5 represents 1 percent of your investment. For subsequent purchases, you pay 5 percent up to a maximum of $2.50 per purchase plus 5 cents per share.

If you want to sell your shares, you have to pay a fee to do that, too — $10 plus 15 cents per share. Overall, these fees compare to what you would pay to buy stock through a discount broker (see Chapter 9 for details). In some cases, these fees are actually higher! For example, you can reinvest dividends at no cost through many discount brokers.

Some direct stock purchase plans entail even more hassle and cost than the type I just discussed. With other plans, you must buy your initial shares through a broker and then transfer your shares to the issuing company in order to buy more! Also, you can't pursue most direct stock purchase plans within retirement accounts.

WARNING

Every time you want to set up a stock purchase plan with a company, you must request and complete the company's application forms. If you go through the headache of doing so, say, a dozen times, you're rewarded with a dozen statements on a regular basis from each individual company. Frankly, because of this drawback alone, I prefer to buy stock through a discount brokerage account that allows centralized purchasing and holding of various stocks as well as consolidated tax-reporting statements.

Placing your trade through a broker

Unless you decide to buy stock directly, you generally need a broker. As I explain in Chapter 9, discount brokers are the best way to go — they take your orders and charge far less than conventional brokerage firms, which generally pay their brokers on commission.

After you decide which discount broker you want to use (again, I provide all the info you need to make this decision in Chapter 9), request (by phone or via the Internet) an account application package for the type of account that you desire (non-retirement, IRA, Keogh, and so on). Complete the forms (call the firm's toll-free number or visit a branch office if you get stuck) and mail or take them back to the discounter.

When you're ready to place your order, simply call the discount broker and explain what you want to do (or use your touch-tone phone or computer to place your order). You have two options:

>> **Market order:** I recommend placing what's known as a *market order.* Such an order instructs your broker to buy you the amount of stock that you desire (100 shares, for example) at the current and best (lowest) price available. With securities in which there's little trading or generally volatile price movements, market orders are a bit riskier. As a result, you may want to instead consider a limit order.

>> **Limit order:** Alternatively, you can try to buy a desired stock at a specific price. For example, you can place a purchase order at $32.50 per share when the stock's last trade was $33 per share. This type of order is known as a *limit order* and is good until you cancel it. I don't recommend that you try this tactic, because it requires you to hope and gamble that the stock drops a little before it rises. If the stock simply rises from its current price of $33 per share or drops to $32.55 before it makes a big move higher, you may kick yourself. If you think that the stock is a good buy for the long haul, go buy it with a market order. If you don't think it's a good buy, don't buy it.

TIP

One final word of advice: Try to buy stock in good-size chunks, such as 100 shares. Otherwise, commissions gobble a large percentage of the small dollar amount that you invest. If you don't have enough money to build a diversified portfolio all at once, don't sweat it. Diversify over time. Purchase a chunk of one stock after you have enough money accumulated and then wait to buy the next stock until you've saved another chunk to invest.

Chapter 7

Exploring Bonds and Other Lending Investments

L ending investments are those in which you lend your money to an organization, such as a bank, company, or government, which typically pays you a set or fixed rate of interest. *Ownership investments,* by contrast, provide partial ownership of a company or some other asset, such as real estate, that has the ability to generate revenue and potential profits.

Lending investments aren't the best choice if you really want to make your money grow. However, even the most aggressive investors should consider placing some of their money into lending investments. The following table shows when such investments do and don't make sense.

Consider Lending Investments If . . .	Consider Ownership Investments When . . .
You need current income.	You don't need or want much current income.
You expect to sell within five years.	You're investing for the long term (seven to ten-plus years).

(continued)

(continued)

Consider Lending Investments If . . .	Consider Ownership Investments When . . .
Investment volatility makes you a wreck, or you just want to cushion some of the volatility of your other riskier investments.	You don't mind or can ignore significant ups and downs.
You don't need to make your money grow after inflation and taxes.	You need more growth to reach your goals.

Lending investments are everywhere — through banks, credit unions, brokerage firms, insurance companies, and mutual fund companies. Lending investments that you may have heard of include bank accounts (savings and certificates of deposit), Treasury bills and other bonds, bond mutual funds (and now exchange-traded bond funds), mortgages, and guaranteed-investment contracts.

In this chapter, I walk you through these investments, explain what's good and bad about each, and discuss situations in which you could consider using (or not using) them. I also tell you what to look for — and look out for — when comparing lending investments.

Banks: Considering the Cost of Feeling Secure

Putting your money in a bank may make you feel safe for a variety of reasons. If you're like most people, your first investing experience was at your neighborhood bank, where you established checking and savings accounts.

Part of the comfort of keeping money in the bank stems from the fact that the bank is where your parents may have first steered you financially. Also, at a local branch, often within walking distance of your home or office, you find vaults, security-monitoring cameras, and barriers in front of the tellers. Most of these things shouldn't make you feel safer about leaving your money with the bank, however — they're needed because of bank robberies!

TIP

Bank branches cost a lot of money to operate. Guess where that money comes from. From bank depositors, of course! These operating costs are one of the reasons the interest rates that banks pay often pale in comparison to some of the similarly secure alternatives I discuss in this chapter.

Facing the realities of bank insurance

Some people are consoled by the Federal Deposit Insurance Corporation (FDIC) insurance that comes with bank accounts. It's true that if your bank fails, your account is insured by the U.S. government up to $250,000. So what? Every Treasury bond is issued and backed by the federal government — the same debt-laden organization that stands behind the FDIC. Plenty of other equally safe lending investments yield higher returns than bank accounts.

WARNING

Just because the federal government stands behind the banking FDIC system doesn't mean that your money is 100 percent safe in the event of a bank failure. Although you're insured for $250,000 in a bank, if the bank crashes, you may wait quite a while to get your money back — and you may get less interest than you thought you would. Banks fail and will continue to fail. During the 1980s and early 1990s, and again in the late 2000s, hundreds of insured banks and savings and loans failed annually. (Between the early 1990s and late 2000s, only a handful of banks failed annually.)

Any investment that involves lending your money to someone else or to some organization, including putting your money in a bank or buying a Treasury bond that the federal government issues, carries risk. Although I'm not a doomsayer, any student of history knows that governments and civilizations fail.

Online banking: More for you?

With the continued growth of the online world, you can find more and more banking options online. Of particular appeal are higher-interest online savings accounts. The best of them do pay higher interest rates than their brick-and-mortar peers and money market funds.

Online banks don't generally have any or many retail branches; they conduct most of their business over the Internet and through the mail. By lowering the costs of doing business, the best online banks may offer better account terms, such as paying you higher interest rates on your account balances. Online banks can also offer better terms on loans.

Online banking is convenient, too. It's generally available 24/7. You can usually conduct most transactions more quickly on the Internet, and by banking online, you save the bank money, which enables the bank to offer you better deals.

WARNING

Here's the issue that I have with online banks: With many online accounts, you face fees and hassles to actually access your money. Also, if you're looking to park a major chunk of money for a long time, you can do better, for example, with safe bond funds.

Technology allows you to do more and more banking online. But remember to protect yourself and your money. You need to put on your detective hat when investigating online banks and be ready to do some searching for the best and safest deals. Never pick a bank simply because you saw one of their ads or because you know a coworker who uses that bank. These sections tell you what you need to do to evaluate an online bank and how to make the most of banking online.

Evaluating FDIC coverage

So what do you look for in an online bank? First you need to select a bank that participates in the U.S. government-operated Federal Deposit Insurance Corporation (FDIC) program. Otherwise, if the online bank you chose fails, your money isn't protected. The FDIC covers your deposits at each bank up to $250,000.

INVESTIGATE

To see whether a bank is covered, never simply take the bank's word for it or accept the bank's display of the FDIC logo on its website or in its offices as proof. Instead, go to the FDIC's BankFind page (http://research.fdic.gov/bankfind) to search the database of FDIC-insured institutions. You can search by bank name, city, state, or zip code of the bank. For an insured bank, you can see the date it became insured, its insurance certificate number, the main office location for the bank (and branches), its primary government regulator, and other links to detailed information about the bank. In the event that your bank doesn't appear on the FDIC list yet claims FDIC coverage, contact the FDIC at 877-275-3342.

WARNING

Beware that some online banks are able to offer higher interest rates because they're based overseas and don't participate in the FDIC program. Participating banks in the FDIC program must pay insurance premiums into the FDIC fund, which, of course, adds to a bank's costs.

Other online bank issues to investigate

INVESTIGATE

In addition to ensuring that a bank is covered by the FDIC, you should get answers to the following questions:

>> **What's the bank's reputation for its services?** Reputation isn't an easy thing to investigate, but at a minimum, you can conduct an Internet search of the bank's name along with the word "complaints" or "problems" and examine the results.

>> **How accessible and knowledgeable are the customer service people at the bank?** You want to be able to speak with a helpful person when you need assistance. Look for a phone number on the online bank's website and call it to see how much trouble you have reaching a live person. Ask the customer service representatives questions (including the following) to determine how knowledgeable and service-oriented they are.

>> **What are the processes and options for withdrawing your money?** This issue is important to discuss with the bank's customer service people because you want convenient, low-cost access to your money. For example, if a bank lacks ATMs, what does the bank charge you for using other ATMs?

>> **What are the fees for particular services?** You can typically find this information on the bank's website in a section titled "account terms" or "disclosures." Also, look for the "Truth in Savings Disclosure," which answers relevant account questions in a standardized format.

Being wary of the certificate of deposit (CD)

Other than savings accounts, banks also sell *certificates of deposit* (CDs). CDs are an often overused bank investment — investors use them by default, often without researching their pros and cons. The attraction is that you may get a higher rate of return on a CD than on a bank savings or money market account. And unlike a bond (which I discuss in the "Why Bother with Bonds?" section later in this chapter), a CD's principal value doesn't fluctuate. CDs also give you the peace of mind afforded by the government's FDIC insurance program.

The reason that CDs pay higher interest rates than savings accounts is that you commit to tie up your money for a period of time, such as 6, 12, or 24 months. The bank pays you 1 to 2 percent and then turns around and lends your money to others through credit cards, auto loans, real estate loans, business loans, and so on. The bank then charges those borrowers an interest rate of 10 percent or more. Not a bad business!

When you tie up your money in a CD and later decide you want it back before the CD matures, a hefty penalty (typically about six months' interest) is shaved from your return. With other lending investments, such as bonds and bond mutual funds, you can access your money without penalty and generally at little or no cost.

In addition to penalties for early withdrawal, CDs yield less than a high-quality bond with a comparable maturity (for example, two, five, or ten years). Often, the yield difference is 1 percent or more, especially if you don't shop around and simply buy CDs from the local bank where you keep your checking account.

High-tax-bracket investors who purchase CDs outside of their retirement accounts should be aware of a final and perhaps fatal flaw of CDs: The interest on CDs is fully taxable at the federal and state levels. Bonds, by contrast, are available (if you desire) in tax-free (federal and/or state) versions.

You can earn higher returns and have better access to your money when it's in bonds than you can when it's in CDs. Bonds make especially good sense when you're in a higher tax bracket and would benefit from tax-free income in a non-retirement account. CDs make the most sense when you know, for example, that you can invest your money for one year, after which you need the money for some purchase that you expect to make. Just make sure that you shop around to get the best interest rate. If having the U.S. government insurance gives you peace of mind, also take a look at Treasury bonds, which I discuss later in this chapter. Treasury bonds (also known as *Treasuries*) tend to pay more interest than many CDs.

Swapping your savings account for a money market fund

Because bank accounts generally pay pretty crummy interest rates, you need to think long and hard about keeping your spare cash in the bank.

You can, if you so choose, keep your checking account at your local bank. But you don't have to. I don't, because I use a money market fund that offers unlimited check writing at a mutual fund company. I also don't keep my extra savings in the bank.

Instead of relying on the bank as a place to keep your extra savings, try *money market funds,* which are a type of mutual fund that doesn't focus on bonds or stocks. Money market funds offer a higher-yielding alternative to bank savings and bank money market deposit accounts.

Money market funds, which are offered by mutual fund companies (see Chapter 8), are unique among mutual funds because they don't fluctuate in value and because they maintain a fixed $1-per-share price. As with a bank savings account, your principal investment in a money market fund doesn't change in value. If you invest your money in a money market fund, it earns *dividends* (which are just another name for the interest you'd receive in a bank account).

Money market fund advantages

The best money market mutual funds offer the following benefits over traditional bank savings accounts:

>> **They provide higher yields.** The best money market mutual funds historically have paid higher yields because they don't have the high overhead that banks do. The most efficient mutual fund companies (I discuss them in Chapter 8) don't have scads of branch offices. (Here's an exception to the higher-yields rule: The extended period of ultra-low interest rates following the severe recession of 2008 took away the yield advantage of money funds.)

Banks can get away with paying lower yields because they know that many depositors believe that the FDIC insurance that comes with a bank savings account makes it safer than a money market mutual fund. Also, the FDIC insurance is an expense that banks ultimately pass on to their customers.

>> **They come in a variety of tax-free versions.** So if you're in a high tax bracket (see Chapter 3), tax-free money market funds offer you something that bank accounts don't.

Another useful feature of money market mutual funds is the ability they provide you to write checks, without charge, against your account. Most mutual fund companies require that the checks that you write be for larger amounts — typically at least $250. They don't want you using these accounts to pay all your small household bills, because checks cost money to process.

However, a few money market funds (such as those that brokerage cash management accounts at firms like Charles Schwab, TD Ameritrade, Vanguard, and Fidelity) allow you to write checks for any amount and can completely replace a bank checking account. Do keep in mind that some brokerage firms hit you with service fees if you don't have enough assets with them or don't have regular monthly electronic transfers, such as through direct deposit of your paycheck or money transfer from your bank account. With these types of money market funds, you can leave your bank altogether because these brokerage accounts often come with debit cards that you can use at bank ATMs for a nominal fee.

TIP

Money market funds are a good place to keep your emergency cash reserve of at least three to six months' living expenses. They're also a great place to keep money awaiting investment elsewhere in the near future. If you're saving money for a home that you expect to purchase soon (in the next year or so), a money market fund can be a safe place to accumulate and grow the down payment. You don't want to risk placing such money in the stock market, because the market can plunge in a relatively short period of time.

Just as you can use a money market fund for your personal purposes, you also can open a money market fund for your business. I have one for my business. You can use this account to deposit checks that you receive from customers, to hold excess funds, and to pay bills via the check-writing feature.

Money market fund disadvantages (if you'd really call them that)

Higher yields, tax-free alternatives, and check writing — money market funds almost sound too good to be true. What's the catch? Good money market funds really don't have a catch, but you need to know about one difference between bank accounts and money market mutual funds: Money market funds aren't insured (however, they were for a one-year period during the 2008–2009 financial crisis).

As I discuss earlier in this chapter, bank accounts come with FDIC insurance that protects your deposited money up to $250,000. So if a bank fails because it lends too much money to people and companies that go bankrupt or abscond with the funds, you should get your money back from the FDIC.

The lack of FDIC insurance on a money market fund shouldn't trouble you. Mutual fund companies can't fail, because they have a dollar invested in securities for every dollar that you deposit in their money market funds. By contrast, banks are required to have available just a portion, such as 10 to 12 cents, for every dollar that you hand over to them (the exact amount depends on the type of deposit).

REMEMBER

A money market fund's investments can decline slightly in value, which can cause the money market fund's share price to fall below a dollar. Cases have occurred where money market funds bought some bad investments (this happened more during the 2008–2009 financial crisis). However, in nearly every case, the parent company running the money market fund infused cash into the affected fund, thus enabling it to maintain the $1-per-share price.

The only money market funds that did "break the buck" didn't take in money from people like you or me; in one case, the fund was run by a bunch of small banks for themselves. This money market fund made some poor investments. The share price of the fund declined by 6 percent, and the fund owners decided to disband the fund; they didn't bail it out, because they would have been repaying themselves. In another case, a money market fund that took in money from institutions declined by 3 percent.

TIP

Stick with bigger mutual fund companies if you're worried about the lack of FDIC insurance (or consider an online bank savings account with FDIC and reasonable fees). These companies have the financial wherewithal and the largest incentive to save a foundering money market fund. Fortunately, the bigger fund companies have the best money market funds anyway. You can find more details about money market funds in Chapter 8.

Why Bother with Bonds?

Conservative investors prefer bonds (that is, conservative when it comes to taking risk, not when professing their political orientation). Otherwise-aggressive investors who seek diversification or investments for shorter-term financial goals also prefer bonds. The reason? Bonds offer higher yields than bank accounts, usually without the volatility of the stock market.

Bonds are similar to CDs, except that bonds are securities that trade in the market with a fluctuating value. For example, you can purchase a bond, scheduled to mature five years from now, that a company such as the retailing behemoth Wal-Mart issues. A Wal-Mart five-year bond may pay you 5.25 percent interest. The company sends you interest payments on the bond for five years. And as long as Wal-Mart doesn't have a financial catastrophe, the company returns your original investment to you after the five years is up. So in effect, you're loaning your money to Wal-Mart (instead of to the bank when you deposit money in a bank account).

WARNING

The worst that can happen to your bond investment is that the business goes into a tailspin and the company ends up in financial ruin — also known as bankruptcy. If the company does go bankrupt, you may lose all your original investment and miss out on the remaining interest payments you were supposed to receive.

But bonds that high-quality companies issue are quite safe — they rarely default. Besides, you don't have to invest all your money earmarked for bonds in just one or two bonds. If you own bonds in many companies (which you can easily do through a bond mutual fund or exchange-traded fund) and one bond unexpectedly takes a hit, it affects only a small portion of your portfolio. And unlike CDs, you can generally sell your bonds anytime you want at minimal cost. (Selling and buying most bond mutual funds costs nothing, as I explain in Chapter 8.)

REMEMBER

Bond investors accept the risk of default because bonds generally pay you more than bank savings accounts and money market mutual funds. But there's a catch. As I discuss later in this chapter, bonds are riskier than money market funds and savings accounts because their value can fall if interest rates rise. Plus you're forgoing the security of FDIC insurance (which bank accounts have). However, bonds tend to be more stable in value than stocks. (I cover the risks and returns of bonds and stocks in Chapter 2.)

Investing in bonds is a time-honored way to earn a better rate of return on money that you don't plan to use within the next couple of years or more. As with stocks, bonds can generally be sold any day that the financial markets are open. Because their value fluctuates, though, you're more likely to lose money if you're forced to sell your bonds sooner rather than later. In the short term, if the bond market happens to fall and you need to sell, you could lose money. In the longer term, as is the case with stocks, you're far less likely to lose money.

WARNING

Don't put your emergency cash reserve into bonds — that's what a money market fund or bank savings account is for. And don't put too much of your longer-term investment money into bonds, either. As I explain in Chapter 2, bonds are generally inferior investments for making your money grow. Growth-oriented investments, such as stocks, real estate, and your own business, hold the greatest potential to build wealth.

Here are some common situations in which investing in bonds can make sense:

>> **You're looking to make a major purchase.** This purchase should be one that won't happen for at least two years, such as buying a home or some other major expenditure. Shorter-term bonds may work for you as a higher-yielding and slightly riskier alternative to money market funds.

>> **You want to diversify your portfolio.** Bonds don't move in tandem with the performance of other types of investments, such as stocks. In fact, in a terrible economic environment (such as during the Great Depression in the early 1930s or the financial crisis of 2008), bonds may appreciate in value while riskier investments such as stocks plunge.

>> **You're interested in long-term investments.** You may invest some of your money in bonds as part of a longer-term investment strategy, such as for retirement. You should have an overall plan for how you want to invest your money, sometimes referred to as an *asset allocation strategy* (see Chapter 8). Aggressive, younger investors should keep less of their retirement money in bonds than older folks who are nearing retirement.

>> **You need income-producing investments.** If you're retired or not working much, bonds can be useful because they're better at producing current income than many other investments.

Assessing the Different Types of Bonds

Bonds differ from one another according to a number of factors — length (number of years) to maturity, credit quality, and the entities that issue the bonds (the latter of which has tax implications that you need to be aware of). After you have a handle on these issues, you're ready to consider investing in individual bonds and bond mutual funds.

Unfortunately, due to shady marketing practices by some investing companies and salespeople who sell bonds, you can have your work cut out for you while trying to get a handle on what many bonds really are and how they differ from their peers. But don't worry. In the following sections, I help you wade through the muddy waters.

Determining when you get your money back: Maturity matters

REMEMBER

Maturity simply means the time at which the bond promises to pay back your principal — next year, in 7 years, in 15 years, and so on. A bond's maturity gives you a good (although far-from-perfect) sense of how volatile a bond may be if interest rates change. If interest rates fall, bond prices rise; if interest rates rise, bond prices fall. Longer-term bonds drop more in price when the overall level of interest rates rises.

Suppose you're considering investing in two bonds that the same organization issues, and both yield 7 percent. The bonds differ from one another only in when they'll mature: One is a 2-year bond; the other is a 20-year bond. If interest rates were to rise just 1 percent (from 7 percent to 8 percent), the 2-year bond may decline about 2 percent in value, whereas the 20-year bond could fall approximately five times as much — 10 percent.

If you hold a bond until it matures, you get your principal back, unless the issuer defaults. In the meantime, however, if interest rates rise, bond prices fall. The reason is simple: If the bond that you hold is issued at, say, 7 percent, and interest rates on similar bonds rise to 8 percent, no one (unless they don't know any better) wants to purchase your 7-percent bond. The value of your bond has to decrease enough so that it effectively yields 8 percent.

Bonds are generally classified by the length of time until maturity:

>> Short-term bonds mature in the next few years.

>> Intermediate-term bonds come due within three to ten years.

>> Long-term bonds mature in more than 10 years, generally up to 30 years.

TECHNICAL STUFF

Although rare, a number of companies issue 100-year bonds! A number of railroads did, as did Coca-Cola, Disney, IBM, the New York Port Authority, and the government of China! Such bonds are quite dangerous to purchase, especially if they're issued during a period of relatively low interest rates.

Most of the time, longer-term bonds pay higher yields than short-term bonds. You can look at a chart of the current yield of similar bonds plotted against when they mature — such a chart is known as a *yield curve.* Most of the time, this curve slopes upward. Investors generally demand a higher rate of interest for taking the risk of holding longer-term bonds. (To see the current yield curve, visit my website at www.erictyson.com.)

Weighing the likelihood of default

In addition to being issued for various lengths of time, bonds differ from one another in the creditworthiness of the issuer. To minimize investing in bonds that default, purchase highly rated bonds. Credit-rating agencies such as Moody's, Standard & Poor's, and Fitch rate the credit quality and likelihood of default of bonds.

The *credit rating* of a bond depends on the issuer's ability to pay back its debt. Bond credit ratings are usually done on some sort of a letter-grade scale where, for example, AAA is the highest rating and ratings descend through AA and A, followed by BBB, BB, B, CCC, CC, C, and so on. Here's the lowdown on the ratings:

>> **AAA- and AA-rated bonds** are considered *high-grade* or *high-credit quality bonds.* Such bonds possess little chance — a fraction of 1 percent — of default.

>> **A- and BBB-rated bonds** are considered *investment-grade* or *general-quality bonds.*

>> **BB- or lower-rated bonds** are known as *junk bonds* (or by their marketed name, *high-yield bonds*). Junk bonds, also known as *non-investment grade bonds,* are more likely to default — perhaps as many as a couple of percent per year actually default.

Why would any sane investor buy a bond with a low credit rating? He or she may purchase one of these bonds because issuers pay a higher interest rate on lower-quality bonds to attract investors. The lower a bond's credit rating and quality, the higher the yield you can and should expect from such a bond. Poorer-quality bonds, though, aren't for the faint of heart, because they're generally more volatile in value.

WARNING

I don't recommend buying individual junk bonds — consider investing in these only through a well-run junk-bond fund.

Examining the issuers (and tax implications)

Besides varying in credit ratings and maturity, bonds also differ from one another according to the type of organization that issues them — in other words, what kind of organization you lend your money to. The following sections go over the major options and tell you when each option may make sense for you.

Treasury bonds

Treasuries are IOUs from the U.S. government. The types of Treasury bonds include Treasury *bills* (which mature within a year), Treasury *notes* (which mature between one and ten years), and Treasury *bonds* (which mature in more than ten years). These distinctions and delineations are arbitrary — you don't need to know them for an exam.

Treasuries pay interest that's state-tax-free but federally taxable. Thus, they make sense if you want to avoid a high state-income-tax bracket but not a high federal-income-tax bracket. However, most people in a high state-income-tax bracket also happen to be in a high federal-income-tax bracket. Such high-tax-bracket investors may be better off in municipal bonds (explained in the next section), which are both federal- and state-income-tax-free (in their state of issuance).

TIP

The best use of Treasuries is in place of bank CDs. If you feel secure with the federal government insurance (which is limited to $250,000) that a bank CD provides, check out a Treasury bond (which has the unlimited backing of the U.S. government). Treasuries that mature in the same length of time as a CD may pay the same or a better interest rate. Remember that bank CD interest is fully taxable, whereas a Treasury's interest is state-tax-free. Unless you really shop for a bank CD, you'll likely earn a lower return on a CD than on a Treasury. I explain how to purchase Treasury bonds in the section "Purchasing Treasuries," later in this chapter.

Municipal bonds

Municipal bonds are state and local government bonds that pay interest that's federal-tax-free and state-tax-free to residents in the state of issue. For example, if you live in California and buy a bond issued by a California government agency, you probably won't owe California state or federal income tax on the interest.

The government organizations that issue municipal bonds know that the investors who buy these bonds don't have to pay most or any of the income tax that's normally required on other bonds — which means that the issuing governments can pay a lower rate of interest.

TIP

If you're in a high tax bracket and want to invest in bonds outside of your tax-sheltered retirement accounts, you may end up with a higher after-tax yield from a municipal bond (often called *muni*) than from a comparable bond that pays taxable interest. Compare the yield on a given municipal bond (or muni bond fund) to the after-tax yield on a comparable taxable bond (or bond fund).

Corporate bonds

Companies such as Boeing and Johnson & Johnson issue corporate bonds. *Corporate bonds* pay interest that's fully taxable. Thus, they're appropriate for investing inside retirement accounts. Lower-tax-bracket investors should consider buying such bonds outside a tax-sheltered retirement account. (Higher-bracket investors should instead consider municipal bonds, which I discuss in the preceding section.) In the section "Understanding bond prices," later in this chapter, I show you how to read price listings for such bonds. If you buy corporate bonds through a mutual or exchange-traded fund, an approach I advocate, you don't need to price such bonds.

Mortgage bonds

Remember that mortgage you took out when you purchased your home? Well, you can actually purchase a bond, naturally called a *mortgage bond*, to invest in a portfolio of mortgages just like yours! Many banks actually sell their mortgages as bonds in the financial markets, which allows other investors to invest in them. The repayment of principal on such bonds is usually guaranteed at the bond's maturity by a government agency, such as the Government National Mortgage Association (GNMA, also known as *Ginnie Mae*) or the Federal National Mortgage Association (FNMA, also known as *Fannie Mae*).

REMEMBER

The vast majority of mortgage bonds are quite safe to invest in. The risky ones that were in the news in the late 2000s for defaulting were so-called subprime mortgages, which lacked government agency backing.

INTERNATIONAL BONDS

You can buy bonds outside of the country that you call home. If you live in the United States, for example, you can buy most of the bonds that I describe in this chapter from foreign issuers as well. These bonds, called *international bonds,* are often riskier to you because their interest payments can be offset by currency price changes.

The prices of international bonds tend not to move in tandem with U.S. bonds. International bond values benefit from and thus protect against a declining U.S. dollar and, therefore, offer some diversification value. Although the declining dollar during most of the 2000s boosted the return of international bonds, the U.S. dollar appreciated versus most currencies during the 1980s and 1990s, which lowered a U.S. investor's return on international bonds.

International bonds aren't a vital holding for a diversified portfolio. International bonds are generally more expensive to purchase and hold than comparable domestic bonds.

Convertible bonds

Convertible bonds are hybrid securities — they're bonds you can convert under a specified circumstance into a preset number of shares of stock in the company that issued the bond. Although these bonds do pay taxable interest, their yield is lower than nonconvertible bonds because convertibles offer you the potential to make more money if the underlying stock rises.

Inflation-protected Treasury bonds

The U.S. government offers bonds called *Treasury inflation-protected securities* (TIPS). Compared with traditional Treasury bonds (which I discuss earlier in this chapter), the inflation-indexed bonds carry a lower interest rate.

The reason for this lower rate is that the other portion of your return with these inflation-indexed bonds comes from the inflation adjustment to the principal you invest. The inflation portion of the return gets added back into principal. For example, if you invest $10,000 in an inflation-indexed bond and inflation increases 3 percent the first year you hold the bond, your principal would increase to $10,300 at the end of the first year.

What's appealing about these bonds is that no matter what happens with the rate of inflation, investors who buy inflation-indexed bonds always earn some return (the yield or interest rate paid) above and beyond the rate of inflation. Thus, holders of inflation-indexed Treasuries can't have the purchasing power of their principal or interest eroded by high inflation.

Because inflation-indexed Treasuries protect the investor from the ravages of inflation, they represent a less risky security. However, consider this little known fact: If the economy experiences *deflation* (falling prices), your principal isn't adjusted down, so these bonds offer deflation protection as well. As I discuss in Chapter 2, lower risk usually translates into lower returns.

WARNING

ZERO COUPON BONDS

Some bonds that you may have heard of or are interested in have unusual features. For instance, not all bonds make regular interest payments. An example is a *zero coupon bond,* which is sold at a substantial discount to its future maturity value. Thus, an investor in a zero coupon bond implicitly earns interest if the value of the bond should rise over time to reach full value by maturity. Zero coupon bonds are highly sensitive to interest rate changes, which is why I don't generally recommend them.

Buying Bonds

You can invest in bonds in one of two major ways: You can purchase individual bonds, or you can invest in a professionally selected and managed portfolio of bonds via a bond mutual fund or exchange-traded fund (see Chapter 8).

In this section, I help you decide how to invest in bonds. If you want to take the individual-bond route, I cover that path here, where I explain how to decipher bond listings you find in financial newspapers or online. I also explain the purchasing process for Treasuries (a different animal in that you can buy them directly from the government) and all other bonds. If you fall on the side of funds, head to Chapter 8 for more information.

Deciding between individual bonds and bond funds

Unless the bonds you're considering purchasing are easy to analyze and homogeneous (such as Treasury bonds), you're generally better off investing in bonds through a mutual fund or exchange-traded fund. Here's why:

>> **Diversification is more difficult with individual bonds.** You shouldn't put your money into a small number of bonds of companies in the same industry or that mature at the same time. It's difficult to cost-effectively build a diversified bond portfolio with individual issues, unless you have a substantial amount of money ($1 million) that you want to invest in bonds.

>> **Individual bonds cost you more money.** If you purchase individual bonds through a broker, you're going to pay a commission. In most cases, the commission cost is hidden — the broker quotes you a price for the bond that includes the commission. Even if you use a discount broker, these fees take a healthy bite out of your investment. The smaller the amount that you invest, the bigger the bite — on a $1,000 bond, the commission fee can equal several percent. Commissions take a smaller bite out of larger bonds — perhaps less than 0.5 percent if you use discount brokers.

On the other hand, investing in bonds through a fund is cost-effective. Great bond funds are yours for less than 0.5 percent per year in operating expenses. Selecting good bond funds isn't hard, as I explain in Chapter 8.

>> **You've got better things to do with your time.** Do you really want to research bonds and go bond shopping? Bonds are boring to most people! And bonds and the companies that stand behind them aren't that simple to

understand. For example, did you know that some bonds can be called before their maturity dates? Companies often *call* bonds (which means they repay the principal before maturity) to save money if interest rates drop significantly. After you purchase a bond, you need to do the same things that a good bond mutual fund portfolio manager needs to do, such as track the issuer's creditworthiness and monitor other important financial developments.

Understanding bond prices

Business-focused publications and websites provide daily bond pricing. You may also call a broker or browse websites to obtain bond prices. The following steps walk you through the bond listing for PhilEl (Philadelphia Electric) in Figure 7-1:

>> **Bond name:** This column tells you who issued the bond. In this case, the issuer is a large utility company, Philadelphia Electric.

>> **Funny numbers after the company name:** The first part of the numerical sequence here — $7^1/8$ — refers to the original interest rate (7.125 percent) that this bond paid when it was issued. This interest rate is known as the *coupon rate,* which is a percent of the maturity value of the bond. The second part of the numbers — 23 — refers to the year that the bond matures (2023, in this case).

>> **Current yield:** Divide the interest paid, 7.125, by the current price per bond, $93, to arrive at the current yield. In this case, it equals (rounded off) 7.7 percent.

>> **Volume:** Volume indicates the number of bonds that traded on this day. In the case of PhilEl, 15 bonds were traded.

>> **Close:** This shows the last price at which the bond traded. The last PhilEl bond price is $93.

>> **Change:** The change indicates how this day's close compares with the previous day's close. In the example figure, the bond rose $2^1/8$ points. Some bonds don't trade all that often. Notice that some bonds were up and others were down on this particular day. The demand of new buyers and the supply of interested sellers influence the price movement of a given bond.

REMEMBER

In addition to the direction of overall interest rates, changes in the financial health of the issuing entity that stands behind the bond strongly affect the price of an individual bond.

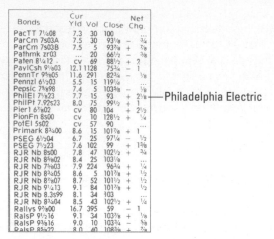

Bonds	Cur Yld	Vol	Close	Net Chg.	
PacTT 7¼08	7.3	30	100	...	
ParCm 7s03A	7.5	30	93⅛	− ¾	
ParCm 7s03B	7.5	5	93⅞	+ ⅞	
Pathmk zr03	...	20	66½	− ⅜	
Paten 8¼12	cv	69	88½	+ 2	
PaylCsh 9⅛03	12.1	1128	75¾	− 1	
PennTr 9⅝05	11.6	291	82¾	− ⅛	
Pennzl 6½03	5.5	15	119¼	...	
Pepsic 7⅝98	7.4	5	103⅝	− ⅛	
PhilEl 7⅛23	7.7	15	93	+ 2⅛	Philadelphia Electric
PhilPt 7.92s23	8.0	75	99½	+ 1	
Pier1 6⅞02	cv	80	104	+ 2½	
PionFn 8s00	cv	10	128½	+ ¼	
PotEl 5s02	cv	57	90	...	
Primark 8¾00	8.6	15	101⅞	+ 1	
PSEG 6½04	6.7	25	97¼	− ½	
PSEG 7½23	7.6	102	99	+ 1⅜	
RJR Nb 8s00	7.8	47	102½	+ ¾	
RJR Nb 8⅝02	8.4	25	103⅛	...	
RJR Nb 7⅝03	7.9	224	96¾	+ ¼	
RJR Nb 8¾05	8.6	5	101⅞	+ ½	
RJR Nb 8⅞07	8.7	52	101½	+ ½	
RJR Nb 9¼13	9.1	84	101⅞	+ ½	
RJR Nb 8.3s99	8.1	34	103	...	
RJR Nb 8¾04	8.5	43	102½	+ ¼	
Rallys 9⅞00	16.7	395	59	− 1	
RalsP 9½16	9.1	34	103⅞	+ ⅛	
RalsP 9⅜16	9.0	10	103¾	− ⅝	
RalsP 8⅝22	8.0	40	108⅜	+ ⅞	

FIGURE 7-1: Sample bond listings.

Purchasing Treasuries

If you want to purchase Treasury bonds, buying them through the Treasury Direct program is the lowest-cost option. Call 800-722-2678 or visit the U.S. Department of Treasury's website (`www.treasurydirect.gov`).

You may also purchase and hold Treasury bonds through brokerage firms and mutual funds. Brokers typically charge a flat fee for buying a Treasury bond. Buying Treasuries through a brokerage account makes sense if you hold other securities through the brokerage account and you like the ability to quickly sell a Treasury bond that you hold. Selling Treasury bonds held through Treasury Direct requires you to transfer the bonds to a broker.

REMEMBER

The advantage of a fund that invests in Treasuries is that it typically holds Treasuries of differing maturities, thus offering diversification. You can generally buy and sell *no-load* (commission-free) Treasury bond mutual funds easily and without fees. Funds, however, do charge an ongoing management fee. (See Chapter 8 for my recommendations of Treasury funds with good track records and low management fees.)

Shopping for other individual bonds

Purchasing other types of individual bonds, such as corporate and mortgage bonds, is a much more treacherous and time-consuming undertaking than buying Treasuries. Here's my advice for doing it right and minimizing the chance of mistakes:

TIP

ASSESSING INDIVIDUAL BONDS THAT YOU ALREADY OWN

If you already own individual bonds and they fit your financial objectives and tax situation, you can hold them until maturity because you already incurred a commission when they were purchased; selling them now would just create an additional fee. When the bonds mature, the broker who sold them to you will probably be more than happy to sell you some more. That's the time to check out good bond mutual funds (see Chapter 8).

Don't mistakenly think that your current individual bonds pay the yield that they had when they were originally issued. (That yield is the number listed in the name of the bond on your brokerage account statement.) As the market level of interest rates changes, the effective *yield* (the interest payment divided by the bond's price) on your bonds fluctuates to rise and fall with the market level of rates for similar bonds. So if rates have fallen since you bought your bonds, the value of those bonds has increased — which in turn reduces the effective yield that you're earning on your invested dollars.

>> **Don't buy through salespeople.** Brokerage firms that employ representatives on commission are in the sales business. Many of the worst bond-investing disasters have befallen customers of such brokerage firms. Your best bet is to purchase individual bonds through discount brokers (see Chapter 9).

>> **Don't be suckered into high yields — buy quality.** Yes, junk bonds pay higher yields, but they also have a much higher chance of default. Nothing personal, but you're not going to do as good a job as a professional money manager at spotting problems and red flags. Stick with highly rated bonds so you don't have to worry about and suffer through these consequences.

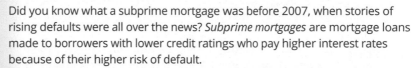

TECHNICAL STUFF

Did you know what a subprime mortgage was before 2007, when stories of rising defaults were all over the news? *Subprime mortgages* are mortgage loans made to borrowers with lower credit ratings who pay higher interest rates because of their higher risk of default.

>> **Understand that bonds may be called early.** Many bonds, especially corporate bonds, can legally be called before maturity. In this case, the bond issuer pays you back early because it doesn't need to borrow as much money or because interest rates have fallen and the borrower wants to reissue new bonds at a lower interest rate. Be especially careful about purchasing bonds that were issued at higher interest rates than those that currently prevail. Borrowers pay off such bonds first.

>> **Diversify.** To buffer changes in the economy that adversely affect one industry or a few industries more than others, invest in and hold bonds from a variety of companies in different industries.

Of the money that you want to invest in bonds, don't put more than 5 percent into any one bond; that means you need to hold at least 20 bonds. Diversification requires a good amount to invest, given the size of most bonds and because trading fees erode your investment balance if you invest too little. If you can't achieve this level of diversification, use a bond mutual fund or exchange-traded fund.

>> **Shop around.** Just like when you buy a car, shop around for good prices on the bonds that you have in mind. The hard part is doing an apples-to-apples comparison, because different brokers may not offer the same exact bonds. Remember that the two biggest determinants of what a bond should yield are its maturity date and its credit rating, both of which I discuss earlier in this chapter.

TIP

Unless you invest in boring, simple-to-understand bonds such as Treasuries, you're better off investing in bonds via the best bond mutual funds. One exception is if you absolutely, positively must receive your principal back on a certain date. Because bond funds don't mature, individual bonds with the correct maturity for you may best suit your needs. Consider Treasuries because they carry such a low default risk. Otherwise, you need a lot of time, money, and patience to invest well in individual bonds.

Considering Other Lending Investments

Bonds, money market funds, and bank savings vehicles are hardly the only lending investments. A variety of companies are more than willing to have you lend them your money and pay you a relatively fixed rate of interest. In most cases, though, you're better off staying away from the investments in the following sections.

WARNING

Too many investors get sucked into lending investments that offer higher yields. Always remember: Risk and return go hand in hand. Higher yields mean greater risk, and vice versa.

Guaranteed-investment contracts

Insurance companies sell and back *guaranteed-investment contracts* (GICs). The allure of GICs is that your account value doesn't appear to fluctuate. Like a one-year bank certificate of deposit, GICs generally quote you an interest rate for the next year. Some GICs lock in the rate for longer periods of time, whereas others may change the interest rate several times per year.

But remember that the insurance company that issues the GIC does invest your money, mostly in bonds and maybe a bit in stocks. Like other bonds and stocks, these investments fluctuate in value — you just don't see it.

Typically once a year, you receive a new statement showing that your GIC is worth more, thanks to the newly added interest. This statement makes otherwise-nervous investors who can't stand volatile investments feel all warm and fuzzy.

The yield on a GIC is usually comparable to those available on shorter-term, high-quality bonds. Yet the insurer invests in longer-term bonds and some stocks. The difference between what these investments generate for the insurer and what the GIC pays you in interest goes to the insurer.

WARNING

The insurer's take can be significant and is generally hidden. Unlike a mutual fund, which is required to report the management fee that it collects and subtracts before paying your return, GIC insurers have no such obligations. By having a return guaranteed in advance, you pay heavily — an effective fee of 2-plus percent per year — for the peace of mind in the form of lower long-term returns.

The high effective fees that you pay to have an insurer manage your money in a GIC aren't the only drawbacks. When you invest in a GIC, your assets are part of the insurer's general assets. Insurance companies sometimes fail, and although they often merge with a healthy insurer, you can still lose money. The rate of return on GICs from a failed insurance company is often slashed to help restore financial soundness to the company. So the only "guarantee" that comes with a GIC is that the insurer agrees to pay you the promised rate of interest (as long as it is able)!

Private mortgages

In the section "Mortgage bonds," earlier in this chapter, I discuss investing in mortgages that resemble the ones you take out to purchase a home. To directly invest in mortgages, you can loan your money to people who need money to buy or refinance real estate. Such loans are known as *private mortgages* or *second mortgages,* in the case where your loan is second in line behind someone's primary mortgage.

Private mortgage investments appeal to investors who don't like the volatility of the stock and bond markets and aren't satisfied with the seemingly low returns on bonds or other common lending investments. Private mortgages seem to offer the best of both worlds — stock-market-like, 10-plus percent returns without volatility.

WARNING

Mortgage and real estate brokers often arrange mortgage investments, so you must tread carefully because these people have a vested interest in seeing the deal done. Otherwise, the mortgage broker doesn't get paid for closing the loan, and the real estate broker doesn't get a commission for selling a property.

One broker who also happens to write about real estate wrote a newspaper column describing mortgages as the "perfect real estate investment" and added that mortgages are a "high-yield, low-risk investment." If that wasn't enough to get you to whip out your checkbook, the writer/broker further gushed that mortgages are great investments because you have "little or no management, no physical labor."

You know by now that a low-risk, high-yield investment doesn't exist. Earning a relatively high interest rate goes hand in hand with accepting relatively high risk. The risk is that the borrower can default — which leaves you holding the bag. (In the mid- to late 2000s, mortgage defaults escalated significantly.) More specifically, you can get stuck with a property that you need to foreclose on, and if you don't hold the first mortgage, you're not first in line with a claim on the property.

The fact that private mortgages are high risk should be obvious when you consider why the borrower elects to obtain needed funds privately rather than through a bank. Put yourself in the borrower's shoes. As a property buyer or owner, if you can obtain a mortgage through a conventional lender, such as a bank, wouldn't you do so? After all, banks generally give better interest rates. If a mortgage broker offers you a deal where you can, for example, borrow money at 10 percent when the going bank rate is, say, 6 percent, the deal must carry a fair amount of risk.

INVESTIGATE

I would avoid private mortgages. If you really want to invest in such mortgages, you must do some time-consuming homework on the borrower's financial situation. A banker doesn't lend someone money without examining a borrower's assets, liabilities, and monthly expenses, and you shouldn't either. Be careful to check the borrower's credit, and get a large down payment (at least 20 percent). The best circumstance in which to be a lender is if you sell some of your own real estate and you're willing to act as the bank and provide the financing to the buyer in the form of a first mortgage.

Also recognize that your mortgage investment carries interest rate risk: If you need to "sell" it early, you'll have to discount it, perhaps substantially if interest rates have increased since you purchased it. Try not to lend so much money on one mortgage that it represents more than 5 percent of your total investments.

OUT OF SIGHT: PRICE FLUCTUATIONS OF PRIVATE MORTGAGES, GICS, AND CDS

One of the allures of non-bond lending investments, such as private mortgages, GICs, and CDs, is that they don't fluctuate in value — at least not that you can see. Such investments appear safer and less volatile. You can't watch your principal fluctuate in value because you can't look up the value daily the way you can with bonds and stocks.

But the principal values of your mortgage, GIC, and CD investments really do fluctuate; you just don't see the fluctuations! Just as the market value of a bond drops when interest rates rise, so does the market value of these investments (and for the same reasons): At higher interest rates, investors expect a discounted price on your fixed-interest rate investment because they always have the alternative of purchasing a new mortgage, GIC, or CD at the higher prevailing rates. Some of these investments are actually bought and sold (and behave just like bonds) among investors on what's known as a *secondary market.*

If the normal volatility of a bond's principal value makes you queasy, try not to follow your investments so closely!

TIP

If you're willing to lend your money to borrowers who carry a relatively high risk of defaulting, consider investing in high–yield (junk) bond mutual funds instead. With these funds, you can at least diversify your money across many borrowers, and you benefit from the professional review and due diligence of the fund management team. You can also consider lending money to family members.

Chapter 8

Mastering Mutual Funds and Exchange-Traded Funds

Good mutual funds, which are big pools of money from investors that a fund manager uses to buy a bunch of stocks, bonds, and other assets that meet the fund's investment criteria, enable you to have some of the best money managers in the country direct the investment of your money. Because efficient funds take most of the hassle and cost out of deciding which companies to invest in, they're among the finest investment vehicles available today.

Different types of mutual funds can help you meet various financial goals, which is why investors have more than $15 trillion invested in these funds! You can use money market funds for something most everybody needs: an emergency savings stash of three to six months' living expenses. Or perhaps you're thinking about saving for a home purchase, retirement, or future educational costs. If so, you can consider some stock and bond funds.

TIP

If you haven't taken a comprehensive look at your personal finances, read Chapter 3 to begin this important process. Too many people plunge into mutual funds without looking at their overall financial situation and, in their haste, often end up paying more taxes and overlooking other valuable financial strategies.

Discovering the Benefits of the Best Funds

The best mutual funds are superior investment vehicles for people of all economic means, and they can help you accomplish many financial objectives. The following sections go over the main reasons for investing in mutual funds rather than individual securities. (If you wish to invest in individual stocks, I provide information on how best to do so in Chapter 6.)

Professional management

The mutual fund investment company hires a portfolio manager and researchers whose full-time jobs are to analyze and purchase suitable investments for the fund. These people screen the universe of investments for those that meet the fund's stated objectives.

Typically, fund managers are graduates of the top business and finance schools, where they learned portfolio management and securities valuation and selection. Many have additional investing credentials, such as being a Chartered Financial Analyst (CFA). In addition to their educational training, the best fund managers typically possess ten or more years of experience in analyzing and selecting investments.

For most fund managers and researchers, finding the best investments is more than a full-time job. Fund managers do tons of analysis that you probably lack the time or expertise to perform. For example, fund managers do the following: assess company financial statements; interview a company's managers to get a sense of the company's business strategies and vision; examine competitor strategies; speak with company customers, suppliers, and industry consultants; and attend trade shows and read industry periodicals.

REMEMBER

In short, a mutual fund management team does more research, number crunching, and due diligence than most people could ever have the energy or expertise to do in what little free time they have. Investing in mutual funds frees up time for friendships, family relationships, and maybe even your sex life — don't miss the terrific time-saving benefits of fund investing!

Cost efficiency

Mutual funds are a cheaper, more communal way of getting your investment work done. When you invest your money in an efficiently managed mutual fund, it likely costs you less than trading individual securities on your own. Fund managers can buy and sell securities for a fraction of the cost that you pay.

Funds also spread the cost of research over thousands of investors. The most efficiently managed mutual funds cost less than 1 percent per year in fees. (Bonds and money market funds cost much less — in the neighborhood of 0.5 percent per year or less.) Some of the larger and more established funds can charge annual fees of less than 0.2 percent per year — that's less than a $2 annual charge per $1,000 you invest.

Newer *exchange-traded funds* (ETFs) are like index mutual funds, except that ETFs trade on a stock exchange and, in the best cases, may have a slightly lower management fee than their sibling index mutual funds. See the later section "Keep exchange-traded funds on your radar" for more information.

Diversification

Diversification is a big attraction for many investors who choose mutual funds. Most funds own stocks or bonds from dozens of companies, thus diversifying against the risk of bad news from any single company or sector. Achieving such diversification on your own is difficult and expensive unless you have a few hundred thousand dollars and a great deal of time to invest.

Mutual funds typically invest in 25 to 100 securities or more. Proper diversification increases the fund's chances of earning higher returns with less risk.

WARNING

Although most mutual funds are diversified, some aren't. For example, some stock funds invest exclusively in stocks of a single industry (for example, healthcare) or country (such as Mexico). I'm not a fan of these funds because of the narrowness of their investments and their typically higher operating fees.

Reasonable investment minimums

Most funds have low minimum investment requirements. Many funds have minimums of $1,000 or less. Retirement account investors can often invest with even less. Some funds even offer monthly investment plans so you can start with as little as $50 per month.

REMEMBER

Even if you have lots of money to invest, you should consider mutual funds. Increasing numbers of fund companies offer their higher-balance customers special funds with lower annual operating expenses and thus even better returns. (I provide more information on these funds later in this chapter.)

Different funds for different folks

Some people think that mutual funds = stock market investing = risky. This line of thinking is wrong. The majority of money in funds isn't in the stock market. You can select the funds that take on the kinds of risks that you're comfortable with and that meet your financial goals. Following is a list of the three major types of funds:

>> **Stock funds:** If you want your money to grow over a long period of time (and you can handle down as well as up years), choose funds that invest more heavily in stocks.

>> **Bond funds:** If you need current income and don't want investments that fluctuate as widely in value as stocks do, consider some bond funds.

>> **Money market funds:** If you want to be sure that your invested principal doesn't decline in value because you may need to use your money in the short term, select a money market fund.

Most investors (myself included) choose a combination of these three types of funds to diversify and help accomplish different financial goals. (I cover each type of fund in depth later in this chapter.)

High financial safety

Thousands of banks and insurance companies have failed in recent decades. Banks and insurers can fail because their *liabilities* (the money that customers gave them to invest, which may need to be returned on short notice) can exceed their *assets* (the money that they've invested or lent).

For example, when big chunks of a bank's loans go sour at the same time that its depositors want their money, the bank fails, because banks typically have less than 15 cents on deposit for every dollar that you and I place with them. Likewise, if an insurance company makes several poor investments or underestimates the number of insurance policyholder claims, it, too, can fail.

Such failures can't happen with a mutual fund because the value of the fund's shares fluctuates as the securities in the fund rise and fall in value. For every dollar of securities they hold for their customers, mutual funds have a dollar's worth of securities. The worst that can happen with a fund is that if you want your money, you may get less money than you originally put into the fund due to a market value decline of the fund's holdings — but you won't lose all your original investment.

For added security, the specific stocks, bonds, and other securities that a mutual fund buys are held at a *custodian*, a separate organization independent of the mutual fund company. A custodian ensures that the fund management company can't embezzle your funds or use assets from a better-performing fund to subsidize a poor performer.

Accessibility

What's really terrific about dealing with mutual funds is that they're set up for people who value their time and don't like going to a local branch office and standing in long lines. With fund investing, you can fill out a simple form (often online, if you want) and write a check in the comfort of your home (or authorize electronic transfers from your bank or other accounts) to make your initial investment. You can then typically make subsequent investments by mailing in a check or zapping in money electronically.

Additionally, most money market funds offer check-writing privileges. Many mutual fund companies also allow you to electronically transfer money back and forth from your local bank account; you can access your money almost as quickly through a money market fund as you can through your local bank.

Selling shares of your mutual fund is usually simple. Generally, all you need to do is call the fund company's toll-free number or visit its website. Some companies have representatives available around the clock, year-round. Most fund companies also offer online account access and trading capabilities as well (although some people are prone to overtrading online, so beware).

Reviewing the Keys to Successful Fund Investing

This chapter helps explain why mutual and exchange-traded funds are good investment vehicles to use. However, keep in mind that not all funds are worthy of your investment dollars. Would you, for example, invest in a fund run by an inexperienced and unproven 18-year-old? How about a fund that charges high fees and produces inferior returns in comparison to similar funds? You don't have to be an investing wizard to know the correct answers to these questions.

When you select a fund, you can use a number of simple, common-sense criteria to greatly increase your chances of investment success. The criteria presented in the following sections have been proven to dramatically increase your fund investing returns. (Visit my website at www.erictyson.com to see the studies and discussion of various investing strategies.)

Minimize costs

The charges that you pay to buy or sell a fund, as well as the ongoing fund operating expenses, can have a big impact on the rate of return that you earn on your investments. So because hundreds of choices are available for a particular type of mutual fund (larger-company U.S. stock funds, for example), you have no reason to put up with inflated costs.

REMEMBER

Fund costs are an important factor in the return that you earn from a mutual fund because fees are deducted from your investment returns and can attack a fund from many angles. All other things being equal, high fees and other charges depress your returns.

TIP

Stick with funds that maintain low total operating expenses and that don't charge *sales loads* (commissions). Both types of fees come out of your pocket and reduce your rate of return. Plenty of excellent funds are available at reasonable annual operating expense ratios (less than 1 percent for stock funds; less than 0.5 percent for bond funds). See my recommendations in the sections on the best stock mutual funds, bond funds, and money market funds, later in this chapter.

Avoid load funds

The first fee you need to minimize is the *sales load*, which is a commission paid to brokers and "financial planners" who work on commission and sell mutual funds. Commissions, or *loads*, generally range from 4.0 to 8.5 percent of the amount that you invest. Sales loads are an additional and unnecessary cost that's deducted from your investment money. You can find plenty of outstanding *no-load* (commission-free) funds.

WARNING

Brokers, being brokers, sing the praises of buying a load fund, warn against no-loads, and sometimes even try to obscure the load. For example, brokers may tell you that the commission doesn't cost you because the mutual fund company pays it. Remember that the commission always comes out of your investment dollars, regardless of how cleverly some load funds and brokers disguise the commission.

Brokers also may say that load funds perform better than no-load funds. One reason, brokers claim, is that load funds supposedly hire better fund managers. Absolutely no relationship exists between paying a sales charge to buy a fund and gaining access to better investment managers. Remember that the sales commission goes to the selling broker, not to the fund managers. Objective studies demonstrate time and again that load funds not only don't outperform but in fact underperform no-loads. Common sense suggests why: When you factor in the higher commission and the higher average ongoing operating expenses charged on load funds, you pay more to own a load fund, so your returns are less.

WATCHING FOR HIDDEN LOADS

Unfortunately, some fund companies have crafty ways of hiding sales loads. Brokers and financial planners sell funds that they call no-loads, but these funds aren't no-loads.

In *back-end* or *deferred sales* load funds, the commission is hidden, thanks to the different classes of shares, known as A, B, C, and D classes. Salespeople tell you that as long as you stay in a fund for five to seven years, you need not pay the back-end sales charge that applies when you sell the investment. This claim may be true, but it's also true that these funds pay investment salespeople a hefty commission.

The salespeople can receive their commissions because the fund company charges you exorbitant continuing operating expenses (which are usually at least 1 percent more per year than the best funds). So one way or another, they get their commissions from your investment dollars.

Another problem with commission-driven load-fund sellers is the power of self-interest. This issue is rarely talked about, but it's even more important than the extra costs that you pay with load funds. When you buy a load fund through a salesperson, you miss out on the chance to get holistic advice on other personal finance strategies. For example, you may be better off paying down your debts or investing in something entirely different from a mutual fund. But in my experience, salespeople almost never advise you to pay off your credit cards or your mortgage — or to invest through your company's retirement plan or in real estate — instead of buying an investment through them.

Some mutual fund companies, such as Fidelity, try to play it both ways. They sell load funds (through brokers) as well as no-load funds (direct to investors). Be aware of this when a "financial advisor" says he can get you into funds from the leading companies, such as Fidelity, because what he really may be telling you is that he's pitching load funds.

Beware of high operating expenses

In addition to loads, the other costs of owning funds are the ongoing *operating expenses.* All funds charge fees as long as you keep your money in the fund. The fees pay for the costs of running a fund, such as employees' salaries, marketing, toll-free phone lines, printing and mailing *prospectuses* (legal disclosure of the fund's operations and fees), and so on.

A fund's operating expenses are essentially invisible to you because they're deducted from the fund's share price. Companies charge operating expenses on a daily basis, so you don't need to worry about trying to get out of a fund at a particular time of the year before the company deducts these fees.

Although operating expenses are invisible to you, their impact on your returns is quite real. Studying the expenses of various money market mutual funds and bond funds is critical; these funds buy securities that are so similar and so efficiently priced in the financial markets that most fund managers in a given type of money market or bond fund earn quite similar returns before expenses.

With stock funds, expenses may play less of an important role in your fund decision. However, don't forget that, over time, stocks have averaged returns of about 9 to 10 percent per year. So if one stock fund charges 1.5 percent more in operating expenses than another and your expected long-term return is about 10 percent per year, you give up an extra 15 percent of your expected (pre-tax) annual returns (and an even greater portion of your after-tax returns).

All types of funds with higher operating expenses tend to produce lower rates of return on average. Conversely, funds with lower operating costs can more easily produce higher returns for you than a comparable type of fund with high costs. This effect makes sense because companies deduct operating expenses from the returns that your fund generates. Higher expenses mean a lower return to you.

Fund companies quote a fund's operating expenses as a percentage of your investment. The percentage represents an annual fee or charge. You can find this number in a fund's prospectus, in the fund expenses section, usually in a line that says something like "Total Fund Operating Expenses." You also can call the fund's toll-free phone number and ask a representative, or you can find the information at the fund company's website. Make sure that a fund doesn't appear to have low expenses simply because it's temporarily waiving them. (You can ask the fund representative or look at the fees in the fund's prospectus to find this information.)

Reflect on performance and risk

A fund's historic rate of return or performance is another important factor to weigh when you select a mutual fund. However, keep in mind that, as all fund materials must tell you, past performance is no guarantee of future results. In fact, many former high-return funds achieved their results only by taking on high risk or simply by relying on short-term luck. Funds that assume higher risk should produce higher rates of return. But high-risk funds usually decline in price faster during major market declines. Thus, a good fund should consistently deliver a favorable rate of return given the level of risk that it takes.

A big mistake that many investors make when they choose a fund is overemphasizing the importance of past performance numbers. The shorter the time period you analyze, the greater the danger that you'll misuse high performance as an indicator for a good future fund.

Although past performance *can* be a good sign, high returns for a fund, relative to its peers, are largely possible only if a fund takes more risk (or if a fund manager's particular investment style happens to come into favor for a few years). The danger of taking more risk is that it doesn't always work the way you'd like. The odds are high that you won't be able to pick the next star before it vaults to prominence in the investing sky. You have a far greater chance of getting on board when a recently high-performing fund is ready to plummet back to Earth.

WARNING

One clever way that fund managers make their funds look better is to compare them to funds that aren't really comparable. The most common ploy is for a manager to invest a fund in riskier types of securities and then compare its performance to funds that invest in less risky securities. Examine the types of securities that a fund invests in, and then make sure that the comparison funds or indexes invest in similar securities.

Stick with experience

A great deal of emphasis is placed on who manages a specific mutual fund. Although the individual fund manager is important, a manager isn't an island unto himself. The resources and capabilities of the parent company are equally if not more important. Managers come and go, but fund companies usually don't.

Different companies maintain different capabilities and levels of expertise with different types of funds. Vanguard, for example, is terrific at money market, bond, and conservative stock funds, thanks to its low operating expenses. Fidelity has significant experience with investing in U.S. stocks.

A fund company gains more or less experience than others not only from the direct management of certain fund types but also through hiring out. For example, some fund families contract with private money management firms that possess significant experience. In other cases, private money management firms with long histories in private money management, such as PIMCO and Dodge & Cox, offer mutual funds.

Consider index funds

Index funds are funds that are mostly managed by a computer. Unlike other mutual funds, in which the portfolio manager and a team of analysts scour the market for the best securities, an index fund manager simply invests to match the makeup, and thus also the performance, of an index (such as the Standard & Poor's 500 index of 500 large U.S. company stocks). Most exchange-traded funds (ETFs), which I discuss in the next section, are simply index funds that trade on a stock exchange.

Index funds deliver relatively good returns by keeping expenses low, staying invested, and not trying to jump around. Over ten years or more, index funds typically outperform about three-quarters of their peers! Most so-called actively managed funds can't overcome the handicap of high operating expenses that pull down their rates of return. Index funds can run with far lower operating expenses because significant ongoing research isn't needed to identify companies to invest in.

The average U.S. stock mutual fund, for example, has an operating expense ratio of 1.4 percent per year. (Some funds charge expenses as high as 2 percent or more per year.) That being the case, a U.S. stock index fund with an expense ratio of just 0.2 percent per year has an advantage of 1.2 percent per year over the average fund. A 1.2 percent difference may not seem like much, but in fact it's a significant difference. Because stocks tend to return about 10 percent per year, you end up throwing away about 12 percent of your expected (pre-tax) stock fund returns with an "average fund" in terms of expenses (and an even greater portion of your post-tax returns).

With actively managed stock funds, a fund manager can make costly mistakes, such as not being invested when the market goes up, being too aggressive when the market plummets, or just being in the wrong stocks. An actively managed fund can easily underperform the overall market index that it's competing against.

WARNING

Don't try to pick *in advance* one of the few elite money managers who manage to beat the market averages by a few percentage points per year. Also, don't overestimate the pros' ability to consistently pick the right stocks. Index funds make sense for a portion of your investments, especially when you invest in bonds and larger, more conservative stocks, where beating the market is difficult for portfolio managers.

In addition to having lower operating expenses, which help boost your returns, index mutual funds and ETFs based upon an index are usually tax-friendlier when you invest outside retirement accounts. Mutual fund managers of actively managed portfolios, in their attempts to increase returns, buy and sell securities more frequently. However, this trading increases a fund's taxable capital gains distributions and reduces a fund's after-tax return.

ERIC'S
PICKS

Vanguard is the largest and best mutual fund provider of index funds and ETFs because it maintains the lowest annual operating fees in the business. Vanguard has all types of bond and stock (both U.S. and international) index mutual funds. See my recommended-fund sections later in this chapter.

Keep exchange-traded funds on your radar

Exchange-traded funds (ETFs) are relatively new. The first one was created in 1993. They've gained some traction in recent years and now hold about 10 percent of the total assets of the fund industry.

ETFs are similar to mutual funds. The most significant difference is that in order to invest, you must buy an ETF through a stock exchange where ETFs trade, just as individual stocks trade. Thus, you need a brokerage account to invest in ETFs. (See Chapter 9 for general information on selecting a brokerage firm.)

Most ETFs are also like index mutual funds in that each ETF generally tracks a major market index. (Beware that more and more companies are issuing ETFs that are actively traded or that track narrowly focused indexes such as an industry group or small country.) The best ETFs may also have slightly lower operating expenses than the lowest-cost index funds. However, you must pay a brokerage fee to buy and sell an ETF, and the current market price of the ETF may deviate slightly from the underlying market value of the securities in its portfolio.

Steer clear of leveraged and inverse exchange-traded funds

Since their introduction in 2006, leveraged and inverse exchange-traded funds have taken in tens of billions in assets. Here's the lowdown on these funds:

>> **Leveraged ETFs:** These funds claim to magnify the move of a particular index, such as the Standard & Poor's (S&P) 500 stock index, by double or even triple in some cases. So a double-leveraged S&P 500 ETF is supposed to increase by 2 percent for a 1 percent increase in the S&P 500 index.

>> **Inverse ETFs:** These funds are supposed to move in the opposite direction of a given index. For example, an inverse S&P 500 ETF is supposed to increase by 1 percent for a 1 percent decrease in the S&P 500 index.

The steep 2008 decline in stock market indexes around the globe and the increasing volatility in that year created the perfect environment for leveraged and inverse ETFs. With these new vehicles, you could easily make money from major stock market indexes when they were falling. Or if you were convinced a particular index or industry group was about to zoom higher, you could buy a leveraged ETF that would magnify market moves by double or even triple.

Suppose that back in early 2008, when the Dow Jones Industrial Average had declined about 10 percent from its then-recent peak above 14,000, you were starting to get nervous and wanted to protect your portfolio from a major market decline. So you bought some of the ProShares UltraShort Dow 30 ETF (trading symbol DXD), which is an inverse ETF designed to move twice as much in the opposite direction of the Dow. So if the Dow goes down, DXD goes up twice as much, and you make money.

Now consider what happened when you held on to the ETF through early 2010 — two years after you bought the fund in early 2008. Over this entire two-year period, the Dow was down about 20 percent. So your original thinking that the market was going to fall proved to be correct. If the ETF did what it was supposed to do and moved twice as much in the other direction, it should've increased 40 percent in value over this period, thus giving you a tidy return. But it didn't. It wasn't even close. The ETF actually plummeted nearly 50 percent in value over this two-year period!

My overall investigations of whether the leveraged (and inverse) ETFs actually deliver on their objectives show that they don't. In recent years, ETF issuers have come out with increasingly risky and costly ETFs. Leveraged and inverse ETFs are especially problematic in that regard. And now the issuers of these leveraged and inverse ETFs are in trouble for their poor disclosure and misleading marketing. Buried in the fine print of the prospectuses of these ETFs, you usually see notes that these ETFs are designed to accomplish their stated objectives for only one trading day. As a result, they're really suitable only for day traders! Of course, few investors read (and understand) the dozens of pages of legal boilerplate in a prospectus.

Brokerage firms and industry regulators are taking notice of these problems. The Financial Industry Regulatory Authority (FINRA), the largest independent regulator for U.S. securities firms, issued a lengthy warning to brokers and financial advisors that "inverse and leveraged ETFs that are reset daily typically are unsuitable for retail investors who plan to hold them for longer than one trading session, particularly in volatile markets."

Retail investors pumped billions of dollars into leveraged and inverse ETFs without FINRA's clear explanation and disclosure. If they had, and if they had known how poorly these ETFs actually do over extended periods of time, they wouldn't have invested.

A number of brokerage firms have suspended trading in these ETFs. They're worried about their legal exposure as well about what will happen if their customers invest in leveraged and inverse ETFs and get burned.

REMEMBER

Leveraged and inverse ETFs aren't investments. They're gambling instruments for day traders. As an individual investor, if you happen to guess correctly before a short-term major market move, you may do well over a short period of time (longer than one day but no more than a few months). However, the odds are heavily stacked against you. You can reduce risk and hedge yourself through sensible diversification. If, for example, you don't want 80 percent of your portfolio exposed to stock market risk, invest a percentage you're comfortable with and don't waste your time and money with leveraged and inverse ETFs.

Creating Your Fund Portfolio with Asset Allocation

Asset allocation simply means that you decide what percentage of your investments you place — or allocate — into bonds versus stocks and into international stocks versus U.S. stocks. (Asset allocation can also include other assets, such as real estate and small business, which are discussed throughout this book.)

When you invest money for the longer term, such as for retirement, you can choose among the various types of funds that I discuss in this chapter. Most people get a big headache when they try to decide how to spread their money among the choices. This section helps you begin cutting through the clutter. (I discuss recommended funds for shorter-term goals later in this chapter as well.)

Allocating for the long term

Many working folks have time on their side, and they need to use that time to make their money grow. You may have two or more decades before you need to draw on some portion of your retirement account assets. If some of your investments drop a bit over a year or two — or even over five years — the value of your investments has plenty of time to recover before you spend the money in retirement.

REMEMBER

Your current age and the number of years until you retire are the biggest factors in your allocation decision. The younger you are and the more years you have before retirement, the more comfortable you should be with volatile, growth-oriented investments, such as stock funds. (See Chapter 2 for the risks and historic returns of different investments.)

Table 8-1 lists guidelines for allocating fund money that you've earmarked for long-term purposes, such as retirement. You don't need an MBA or PhD to decide your asset allocation — all you need to know is how old you are and the level of risk that you desire!

TABLE 8-1   Asset Allocation for the Long Haul

Your Investment Attitude	Bond Fund Allocation (%)	Stock Fund Allocation (%)
Play it safe	= Age	= 100 – Age
Middle of the road	= Age – 10	= 110 – Age
Aggressive	= Age – 20	= 120 – Age

What's it all mean, you ask? Consider this example: If you're a conservative sort who doesn't like a lot of risk, but you recognize the value of striving for some growth to make your money work harder, you're a middle-of-the-road type. Using Table 8-1, if you're 35 years old, you may consider putting 25 percent (35 – 10) into bond funds and 75 percent (110 – 35) into stock funds.

TIP

Now divvy up your stock investment money between U.S. and international funds. Here's what portion of your stock allocation I recommend investing in overseas stocks:

>> 20 percent (for a play-it-safe attitude)

>> 35 percent (for a middle-of-the-road attitude)

>> 50 percent (for an aggressive attitude)

Using Table 8-1, if a 35-year-old, middle-of-the-road investor puts 75 percent in stocks, she can then invest about 35 percent of the stock fund investments (which works out to be around 25 percent of the total) in international stock funds. So here's what the 35-year-old, middle-of-the-road investor's portfolio asset allocation looks like:

Bonds	25%
U.S. stocks	50%
International stocks	25%

Diversifying your stock fund investments

Suppose that your investment allocation decisions suggest that you invest 50 percent in U.S. stock funds. Which ones do you choose? As I explain in the later section "Exploring different types of stock funds," stock funds differ on a number of levels. You can choose from growth-oriented stocks and funds and those that focus on value stocks as well as from funds that focus on small-, medium-, or large-company stocks. I explain these types of stocks and funds later in this chapter. You also need to decide what portion you want to invest in index funds (which I discuss earlier in "Consider index funds") versus actively managed funds that try to beat the market.

Generally, it's a good idea to diversify using different types of funds. You can diversify in one of two ways:

>> **Purchase several individual funds, each of which focuses on a different style.** For example, you can invest in a large-company value stock fund and in a small-company growth fund. I find this approach somewhat tedious. Granted, it does allow a fund manager to specialize and gain greater knowledge about a particular type of stock. But many of the best managers invest in more than one narrow range of security.

>> **Invest in a handful of funds (five to ten), each of which covers several bases and that together cover them all.** Remember, the investment delineations are somewhat arbitrary, and most funds focus on more than just one type of investment. For example, a fund may focus on small-company value stocks but may also invest in medium-company stocks. It may also invest in some that are more growth oriented.

Deciding how much you should use index versus actively managed funds is really a matter of personal taste. If you're satisfied knowing that you'll get the market rate of return and that you can't underperform the market (after accounting for your costs), index your entire portfolio. On the other hand, if you enjoy the challenge of trying to pick the better managers and want the potential to earn better than the market level of returns, don't use index funds at all. Investing in a happy medium of both, like I do, is always a safe bet.

If you haven't experienced the sometimes significant plummets in stock prices that occur, you may feel queasy the next time it happens and you've got a chunk of your nest egg in stocks. Be sure to read Chapters 2 and 5 to understand the risk in stocks and what you can and can't do to reduce the volatility of your stock holdings.

The Best Stock Funds

Stock mutual and exchange-traded funds are excellent investment vehicles that reduce your risk, compared to purchasing individual stocks, because they

>> **Invest in dozens of stocks:** Unless you possess a lot of money to invest, you're likely to buy only a handful of stocks. If you end up with a lemon in your

portfolio, it can devastate your other good choices. If such a stock represents 20 percent of your holdings, the rest of your stock selections need to increase about 25 percent in value just to get you back to even. Stock funds mitigate this risk.

For example, if a fund holds equal amounts of 50 stocks and one goes to zero, you lose only 2 percent of the fund value if the stock was an average holding. Similarly, if the fund holds 100 stocks, you lose just 1 percent. Remember that a good fund manager is more likely than you to sidestep disasters (see the earlier section "Professional management" for details).

>> **Invest in different types of stocks:** Some funds invest in stocks of different sizes of companies in a variety of industries. Others may hold U.S. and international stocks. Different types of stocks (which I explain in the upcoming section titled "Exploring different types of stock funds") generally don't move in tandem. So if smaller-company stocks get beat up, larger-company stocks may fare better. If U.S. stocks are in the tank, international stocks may be on an upswing.

In Chapters 2 and 5, I make the case for investing in stocks (also known as *equities*) to make your money grow. However, stocks sometimes plummet or otherwise remain depressed for a few years. Thus, stock funds (also known as *equity funds*), which, as their name suggests, invest in stocks, aren't a place for money that you know you may need to protect in the next few years.

Making money with stock funds

When you invest in stock funds, you can make money in three ways:

>> **Dividends:** As a mutual fund investor, you can choose to receive your share of the dividends paid out to the fund as cash or to reinvest them in purchasing more shares in the fund. Higher-growth companies tend to pay lower dividends.

Unless you need the income to live on (if, for example, you're already retired), reinvest your dividends into buying more shares in the fund. If you reinvest outside of a retirement account, keep a record of those reinvestments because you need to factor those additional purchases into the tax calculations that you make when you sell your shares. (Most brokers will allow you to reinvest dividends paid on ETFs without a fee.)

>> **Capital gains distributions:** When a fund manager sells stocks for more than he paid, the resulting profits, known as *capital gains,* must be netted against losses and paid out to the fund's shareholders. Just as with dividends, you can reinvest your capital gains distributions in the fund.

>> **Appreciation:** The fund manager isn't going to sell all the stocks that have gone up in value. Thus, the price per share of the fund increases to reflect the gains in its stock holdings. For you, these profits are on paper until you sell the fund and lock them in. Of course, if a fund's stocks decline in value, the share price depreciates.

If you add together dividends, capital gains distributions, and appreciation, you arrive at the *total return* of a fund.

Exploring different types of stock funds

Stock funds and the stocks that they invest in are usually pigeonholed into particular categories based on the types of stocks that they focus on. Categorizing stock funds is often tidier in theory than in practice, though, because some funds invest in an eclectic mix of stocks. So don't get bogged down with the names of funds — they sometimes have misleading names and don't necessarily do what those names imply. The investment strategies of the fund and the fund's typical investments are what matter. The following characteristics are what you need to pay attention to:

>> **Company size:** The first dimension on which a stock fund's stock selection differs is based on the size of the companies in which the fund invests — small, medium, or large. The total market value *(capitalization)* of a company's outstanding stock defines the categories that define the stocks that the fund invests in. (The term *capitalization* is often shortened to "cap," so you may hear financial folks tossing around terms like *large cap* and *small cap*.) The dollar amounts are arbitrary, and as stock prices increase over time, investment market analysts have moved up their cutoffs. Here's the latest:

- **Small-capitalization stocks** are usually defined as stocks of companies that possess total market capitalization of less than $2 billion.

- **Medium-capitalization stocks** have market values between $2 billion and $10 billion.

- **Large-capitalization stocks** are those of companies with market values greater than $10 billion.

>> **Growth versus value:** Stock fund managers and their funds are further categorized by whether they invest in growth or value stocks:

- *Growth stocks* have high prices in relation to the company's assets, profits, and potential profits. Growth companies typically experience rapidly expanding revenues and profits. These companies tend to reinvest most of their earnings in the company to fuel future expansion; thus, these stocks pay low dividends. For example, eBay pays no dividends and reinvests most of its profits in its business.

- *Value stocks* are priced cheaply in relation to the company's assets, profits, and potential profits. Value stocks tend to pay higher dividends and historically have produced higher total returns than growth stocks.

Fund companies sometimes use other terms to describe other types of stock funds. *Aggressive growth funds* tend to invest in the most growth-oriented companies and may undertake riskier investment practices, such as frequent trading. *Growth and income funds* tend to invest in stocks that pay higher-than-average dividends, thus offering the investor the potential for growth and income. *Income funds* tend to invest more in higher-yielding stocks. Bonds usually make up the other portion of income funds.

>> **Company location:** Stocks and the companies that issue them are also divvied up based on the location of their main operations and headquarters. Funds that specialize in U.S. stocks are, not surprisingly, called *U.S. stock funds;* those focusing in overseas stocks are typically called *international* or *overseas funds.*

Putting together two or three of these major classifications, you can start to comprehend all those silly, lengthy names that fund companies give their stock funds. You can have funds that focus on large-company value stocks or small-company growth stocks. You can add in U.S., international, and worldwide funds to further subdivide these categories into more fund types. So you can have international stock funds that focus on small-company stocks or growth stocks.

You can purchase several stock funds, each focusing on a different type of stock, to diversify into various types of stocks. Two potential advantages result from doing so:

>> Not all your money rides in one stock fund and with one fund manager.

>> Each of the different fund managers can look at and track particular stock investment possibilities.

Using the selection criteria I outline in the earlier section "Reviewing the Keys to Successful Fund Investing," the following sections describe the best stock funds that are worthy of your consideration. The funds differ primarily in terms of the types of stocks that they invest in. Keep in mind as you read through these funds that they also differ in their tax-friendliness (see Chapter 3). However, if you invest inside a retirement account, you don't need to worry about tax-friendliness.

U.S. stock funds

Of all the different types of funds offered, U.S. stock funds are the largest category. Stock funds differ mainly in terms of the size of the companies that they invest in and in whether the funds focus on growth or value companies. Some funds hold all these characteristics, and some funds may even invest a bit overseas.

INVESTIGATE

The only way to know for sure where a fund currently invests (or where the fund may invest in the future) is to ask. You can call the fund company that you're interested in to start your information search, or you can visit the company's website. You can also read the fund's annual report (just a little light reading before heading off to the land of Nod). Don't waste your time looking for this information in the fund's prospectus, because it doesn't give you anything beyond general parameters that guide the range of investments. The prospectus generally doesn't tell you what the fund currently invests in or has invested in.

For funds that you hold outside of retirement accounts, you owe current income tax on distributed dividends and capital gains. As I discuss in Chapter 3, long-term capital gains and stock dividends are taxed at lower rates than ordinary income and other investment income.

ERIC'S PICKS

Here's my short list of U.S. stock funds:

>> Dodge & Cox Stock

>> Fairholme Fund

>> Fidelity Low-Priced Stock

>> Sequoia

>> T. Rowe Price Spectrum Growth (holds some foreign stocks)

>> Vanguard Total Stock Market Index, PRIMECAP, Selected Value, Tax-Managed Capital Appreciation, Tax-Managed Small Cap, and Total Stock Market (ETF)

International stock funds

For diversification and growth potential, you should include in your portfolio stock funds that invest overseas. Normally, you can tell that you're looking at a fund that focuses its investments overseas if its name contains words such as *international* (foreign only), *global* (foreign and U.S.), or *worldwide* (foreign and U.S.).

WARNING

As a general rule, avoid foreign funds that invest in just one country, regardless of whether that country is Australia, Zimbabwe, or anywhere in between. As with investing in a sector fund that specializes in a particular industry (see the following section), this lack of diversification defeats the whole purpose of investing in funds. Funds that focus on specific regions, such as Southeast Asia, are better but still generally problematic because of poor diversification and higher expenses than other, more–diversified international funds.

EQUAL-WEIGHT STOCK INDEX FUNDS WORTH CONSIDERING

I've never cared for the S&P 500 index when investing in index funds. I dislike it as a core index investment because it's *capitalization weighted* (which simply means that stocks in the index must be held in proportion to their market value in the index) and because it includes only larger-cap stocks. Back in the late 1990s, during the technology stock bubble, the S&P 500 index was overloaded with bloated technology stocks selling at grossly inflated valuations, so S&P 500 index funds were forced to overweight pricey technology holdings. (And just prior to the bear market in the late 2000s, the same phenomenon happened with large financial companies in the index.)

Enter a new breed of index funds. Instead of using the stocks' capitalization to weight the holdings of stocks, these new index funds equally weight their holdings of all stocks in a given index (such as the S&P 500) or weight the holdings by some measure of company fundamentals.

Here are two equally or fundamentally weighted index funds that appear solid, have reasonable fees, and are worth considering:

- **Guggenheim S&P 500 Equal Weight (ticker RSP):** This ETF holds all 500 S&P 500 stocks in equal amounts (0.2 percent per holding). Thus, compared to a traditional S&P 500 index fund, this fund has more mid-cap and small-cap weighting. Expense ratio is 0.40 percent, which is a bit more than a Vanguard index fund or ETF but quite reasonable.

- **PowerShares FTSE RAFI US 1000 (ticker PRF):** This ETF has similarities to the Russell 1000 index but weights its holdings based upon fundamentals such as book value, dividends, sales, and cash flow rather than market capitalization. This weighting gives the fund a slightly more smaller-cap value flavor. Expense ratio is 0.39 percent.

Over their tenure, these two funds have posted excellent returns compared to their comparable indexes. Of course, there's no guarantee that the outperformance of these alternative weight index funds will continue. (WisdomTree is another large provider of ETFs that weight their index holdings using fundamental criteria.)

Be mindful of fees and the fact that high fees can sabotage an index fund. I wouldn't pay more than 0.5 percent for an index or index-like stock fund.

If you want to invest in more geographically limiting international funds, take a look at T. Rowe Price's and Vanguard's offerings, which invest in broader regions, such as just Europe, Asia, and the volatile but higher-growth-potential emerging markets in Southeast Asia and Latin America.

In addition to the risks normally inherent with stock fund investing, changes in the value of foreign currencies relative to the U.S. dollar cause price changes in the international securities. A decline in the value of the U.S. dollar helps the value of foreign stock funds (and conversely, a rising dollar versus other currencies can reduce the value of foreign stocks). Some foreign stock funds hedge against currency changes. Although this hedging helps reduce volatility a bit, it does cost money.

Here are my picks for diversified international funds:

>> Dodge & Cox International

>> Harbor International

>> Litman Gregory Masters' International

>> Oakmark International and Oakmark Global (holds some U.S. stocks)

>> Tweedy, Browne Global Value (invests in the U.S. as well)

>> Vanguard Global Equity (invests in the U.S., too), International Growth, Tax-Managed International, Total International Stock Index, FTSE All-World ex-US (ETF), and Total International Stock (ETF)

Sector funds

Sector funds invest in securities in specific industries. In most cases, you should avoid sector funds for a number of reasons, including the following:

>> **Lack of diversification:** Investing in stocks of a single industry defeats a major purpose of investing in mutual funds — you give up the benefits of diversification. Also, even if you're lucky enough to jump into a sector fund just before it becomes "hot," you can't assume that the fund will pick the right securities within that sector.

>> **High fees:** They tend to carry much higher fees than other mutual funds.

>> **Taxable distributions:** Many sector funds have high rates of trading or turnover of their investment holdings. Investors who use these funds outside of retirement accounts have to pay the tax man for the likely greater taxable distributions that this trading produces.

The only types of specialty funds that may make sense for a small portion (10 percent or less) of your entire investment portfolio are funds that invest in real estate or precious metals. These funds can help diversify your portfolio because they can perform better during times of higher inflation — which often depresses bond and stock prices. (However, you can comfortably skip these funds because diversified stock funds tend to hold some of the same stocks as these specialty funds.) Here are some details about these two specialty fund types:

>> **Real estate funds:** *Real estate investment trusts* (REITs) are stocks of companies that invest in real estate. REITs typically invest in properties such as apartment buildings, shopping centers, and other rental properties. REITs allow you to invest in real estate without the hassle of being a landlord. Evaluating REIT stocks is a hassle, but you can always invest in a fund of REITs.

REITs usually pay healthy levels of dividends, which, unlike stock dividends, are taxed at ordinary income tax rates. As such, they're less appropriate for people in a higher tax bracket who invest money outside of retirement accounts. Some good no-load REIT funds include Fidelity Real Estate, T. Rowe Price Real Estate, and Vanguard REIT Index.

>> **Precious metals:** If you expect higher inflation, consider a gold fund. But know that these funds swing wildly in value and aren't for the faint of heart. A good precious-metals fund is the Vanguard Precious Metals and Mining Fund.

WARNING

Don't buy bullion itself; storage costs and the concerns over whether you're dealing with a reputable company make buying gold bars a pain. Also avoid futures and options, which are gambles on short-term price movements (see Chapter 1 for information).

The Best Bond Funds

Bond funds can make you money in the same three ways that a stock fund can: dividends, capital gains distributions, and appreciation. (See the earlier section "Making money with stock funds" for more on these ways of making money.) However, most of the time, the bulk of your return in a bond fund comes from dividends.

REMEMBER

Although an overwhelming number of bond fund choices exists (thousands, in fact), not that many remain after you eliminate high-cost funds (those with loads and high ongoing fees), low-performance funds (which are often the high-cost funds), and funds managed by fund companies and fund managers with minimal experience investing in bonds. Here are the aspects to consider when choosing bond funds:

- » **Length to maturity:** Bond fund objectives and names usually fit one of three maturity categories — short-, intermediate-, and long-term. You can earn a higher yield from investing in a bond fund that holds longer-term bonds, but as I explain in Chapter 7, such bond prices are more sensitive to changes in interest rates.

- » **Quality:** Generally speaking, the lower their issuer's credit rating, the riskier the bond. As with the risk associated with longer maturities, a fund that holds lower-quality bonds should provide higher returns for the increased risk you take. A higher yield is the bond market's way of compensating you for taking greater risk. Funds holding higher-quality bonds provide lower returns but more security.

- » **Loads and fees:** After you settle on the type of bonds that you want, you must consider a bond fund's costs, including its sales commissions and annual operating fees. Stick with no-load funds that maintain lower annual operating expenses.

- » **Tax implications:** Pay attention to the taxability of the dividends that bonds pay. If you're investing in bonds inside of retirement accounts, you want taxable bonds. If you invest in bonds outside of retirement accounts, the choice between taxable versus tax-free depends on your tax bracket (see Chapter 3).

WARNING

Bond funds fluctuate in value, so invest in them only if you have sufficient money in an emergency reserve.

If you invest money for longer-term purposes, particularly retirement, you need to come up with an overall plan for allocating your money among a variety of different funds, including bond funds. (See the section "Allocating for the long term" earlier in this chapter.)

Avoiding yield-related missteps

When selecting bond funds to invest in, investors are often led astray as to how much they can expect to make. The first mistake is to look at recent performance and assume that you'll get that return in the future. Investing in bond funds based on recent performance is particularly tempting immediately after a period where interest rates have declined (as in the 1990s and the early and late 2000s), because declines in interest rates pump up bond prices and therefore bond fund total returns. Remember that an equal but opposite force waits to counteract pumped-up bond returns: Bond prices fall when interest rates rise.

Don't get me wrong: Past performance is an important issue to consider. In order for performance numbers to be meaningful and useful, you must compare bond funds that are comparable (such as intermediate-term funds that invest exclusively in high-grade corporate bonds).

Bond funds calculate their yield after subtracting their operating expenses. When you contact a fund company seeking a fund's current yield, make sure you understand what time period the yield covers. Fund companies are supposed to give you the SEC yield, which is a standard yield calculation that allows for fairer comparisons among bond funds. The SEC yield, which reflects the bond fund's yield to maturity, is the best yield to use when you compare funds because it captures the effective rate of interest that an investor can receive in the future.

WARNING

Unfortunately, if you select bond funds based on advertised yield, you're quite likely to purchase the wrong bond funds. Bond funds and the fund companies that sell them can play more than a few games to fatten a fund's yield. Such sleights of hand make a fund's marketing and advertising departments happy because higher yields make it easier for salespeople and funds to hawk their bond funds. But remember that yield-enhancing shenanigans can leave you poorer. Here's what you need to watch out for:

>> **Lower quality:** When comparing one short-term bond fund to another, you may discover that one pays 0.5 percentage points more and decide that it looks better. However, you may find out later that the higher-yielding fund invests 20 percent of its money in junk (non-investment grade) bonds, whereas the other fund fully invests in high-quality bonds.

>> **Longer maturities:** Bond funds can usually increase their yield just by increasing their maturity a bit. So if one long-term bond fund invests in bonds that mature in an average of 17 years and another fund has an average maturity of 12 years, comparing the two is a classic case of comparing apples and oranges.

>> **Giving your money back without your knowing it:** Some funds return a portion of your principal in the form of dividends. This move artificially pumps up a fund's yield but depresses its total return. When you compare bond funds, make sure you compare their total return over time (in addition to making sure that the funds have comparable portfolios of bonds).

>> **Waiving of expenses:** Some bond funds, particularly newer ones, waive a portion or even all of their operating expenses to temporarily inflate the fund's yield. Yes, you can invest in a fund that has a sale on its operating fees, but you'd also buy yourself the bother of monitoring things to determine when the sale is over. Bond funds that engage in this practice often end sales quietly when the bond market is performing well. Don't forget that if you sell a bond fund (held outside of a retirement account) that has appreciated in value, you owe taxes on your profits.

Treading carefully with actively managed bond funds

Some bond funds are aggressively managed. Managers of these funds possess a fair degree of latitude to purchase and trade bonds that they think will perform best in the future. For example, if a fund manager thinks interest rates will rise, she usually buys shorter-term bonds and keeps more of a fund's assets in cash. The fund manager may invest more in lower-credit-quality bonds if she thinks that the economy is improving and that more companies will prosper and improve their credit standing.

WARNING

Aggressively managed funds are a gamble. If interest rates fall instead of rise, the fund manager who moved into shorter-term bonds and cash experiences worse performance. If interest rates fall because the economy sinks into recession, the lower-credit-quality bonds will likely suffer from a higher default rate and depress the fund's performance even further.

Some people think the "experts" have no trouble predicting which way interest rates or the economy is heading. The truth is that economic predictions are always difficult, and the experts are often wrong. Few bond fund managers have been able to beat a buy-and-hold approach. However, William Gross, who manages the PIMCO and Harbor bond funds, is one fund manager who has pretty consistently beaten the market averages.

But remember that trying to beat the market can lead to getting beaten! Recent years have shown an increasing number of examples of bond funds falling on their faces after risky investing strategies backfire. Interestingly, bond funds that charge sales commissions (loads) and higher ongoing operating fees are the ones that are more likely to blow up, perhaps because these fund managers are under more pressure to pump up returns to make up for higher operating fees.

TIP

It's fine to invest some of your bond fund money in funds that try to hold the best position for changes in the economy and interest rates, but remember that if these fund managers are wrong, you can lose more money. Over the long term, you'll probably do best with efficiently managed funds that stick with an investment objective and that don't try to time and predict the bond market. Index funds (and their companion exchange-traded funds) that invest in a relatively fixed basket of bonds so as to track a market index of bond prices are a good example of this passive approach.

Stabilizing your portfolio by investing in short-term bond funds

Of all bond funds, short-term bond funds are the least sensitive to interest rate fluctuations. The stability of short-term bond funds makes them appropriate investments for money that you seek a better rate of return on than a money market fund can produce for you. But with short-term bond funds, you also have to tolerate the risk of losing a percent or two in principal value if interest rates rise.

TIP

Short-term bonds work well for money that you earmark for use in a few years, such as the purchase of a home or a car, or for money that you plan to withdraw from your retirement account in the near future.

Taxable short-term bond funds

ERIC'S
PICKS

Consider bond funds that pay taxable dividends when you're not in a high tax bracket and for investing inside of retirement accounts. With yields generally low for shorter-term bonds, expenses are ultra-important with this type of fund. My picks in this category are the Vanguard Short-Term Investment-Grade fund and Vanguard Short-Term Corporate Bond ETF.

Important note: Many of the Vanguard funds recommended in this chapter offer "Admiral" versions that have even lower operating fees for customers investing at least $10,000 for an index fund that offers Admiral shares, $50,000 for an actively managed fund, and $100,000 for certain sector-specific index funds and tax-managed funds.

U.S. Treasury short-term bond funds

ERIC'S
PICKS

U.S. Treasury bond funds may be appropriate if you prefer a bond fund that invests in U.S. Treasuries (which possess the safety of government backing; see Chapter 7 for details). They're also a fine choice if you're not in a high federal tax bracket but you're in a high state tax bracket (5 percent or higher). Vanguard Short-Term Treasury is a good choice, but with short-term yields as low as they've been in recent years, consider buying short-term bonds directly from the Treasury Department.

I don't recommend Treasuries for retirement accounts because they pay less interest than fully taxable bond funds.

Federally tax-free short-term bond funds

State and federally tax-free short-term bond funds are scarce. If you want shorter-term bonds, and if you're in a high federal bracket but in a low state bracket (less than 5 percent), consider investing in these *federally* tax-free bond funds (whose dividends are state taxable):

>> Vanguard Short-Term Tax-Exempt

>> Vanguard Limited-Term Tax-Exempt

If you live in a state with high taxes, consider checking out the state and federally tax-free intermediate-term bond funds (which I discuss in the next section) — if you can withstand their somewhat higher volatility. Another option is to use a state money market fund, which is covered later in this chapter in "The Best Money Market Funds."

Earning higher returns with intermediate-term bond funds

Intermediate-term bond funds hold bonds that typically mature in a decade or so. They're more volatile than shorter-term bonds but can also prove more rewarding. The longer you own an intermediate-term bond fund, the more likely you are to earn a higher return on it than on a short-term fund, unless interest rates continue to rise over many years.

TIP

As an absolute minimum, don't purchase an intermediate-term fund unless you expect to hold it for three to five years — or even longer, if you can. You need to make sure that the money you put into an intermediate-term fund is money that you don't expect to use in the near future.

Taxable intermediate-term bond funds

Taxable intermediate-term bond funds to consider include the following:

>> Dodge & Cox Income

>> Harbor Bond

>> PIMCO Total Return (ETF)

>> Vanguard GNMA, High-Yield Corporate, Total Bond Market Index, and Intermediate-Term Corporate Bond (ETF)

U.S. Treasury intermediate-term bond funds

Consider U.S. Treasury bond funds if you prefer a bond fund that invests in U.S. Treasuries (which maintain the safety of government backing). You can also invest in them if you're not in a high federal tax bracket but you're in a high state tax bracket (5 percent or higher). I don't recommend Treasuries for retirement accounts because they pay less interest than fully taxable bond funds.

ERIC'S
PICKS

A couple of my favorites are Vanguard Inflation-Protected Securities and Vanguard Intermediate-Term Treasury.

Federally tax-free intermediate-term bond funds

You should consider *federally* tax-free bond funds if you're in a high federal bracket but in a relatively low state bracket (less than 5 percent).

ERIC'S
PICKS

Good federally tax-free bond funds include the following:

>> T. Rowe Price Summit Municipal Intermediate

>> Vanguard Intermediate-Term Tax-Exempt

If you're in high federal and state tax brackets, refer to the state and federally tax-free bonds that I mention later in this chapter.

Using long-term bond funds to invest aggressively

Long-term bond funds are the most aggressive and volatile bond funds around. If interest rates on long-term bonds increase substantially, you can easily see the principal value of your investment decline 10 percent or more. (See Chapter 7 for a discussion of how interest rate changes impact bond prices.)

TIP

Long-term bond funds are generally used for retirement investing in one of two situations:

>> Investors don't expect to tap their investment money for a decade or more.

>> Investors want to maximize current dividend income and are willing to tolerate volatility.

Remember: Don't use these funds to invest money that you plan to use within the next five years, because a bond market drop can leave your portfolio short of your monetary goal.

Taxable long-term bond funds

Be careful with longer-term bond funds, as they're generally much more volatile than most bond funds. My recommendations in this category are the Vanguard Long-Term Investment-Grade fund and the Vanguard Long-Term Corporate Bond ETF.

U.S. Treasury long-term bond funds

U.S. Treasury bond funds may be advantageous if you want a bond fund that invests in U.S. Treasuries. They're also great if you're not in a high federal tax bracket but you're in a high state tax bracket (5 percent or higher). I recommend Treasuries for non-retirement accounts only, because Treasuries pay less interest than fully taxable bond funds.

I recommend the Vanguard Long-Term Treasury fund.

Federally tax-free long-term bond funds

Municipal (federally tax-free) long-term bond funds that I recommend are Fidelity Municipal Income and Vanguard Long-Term Tax-Exempt.

State and federally tax-free long-term bond funds

State and federally tax-free bond funds may be appropriate when you're in high federal *and* high state (5 percent or higher) tax brackets. Fidelity, T. Rowe Price, and Vanguard offer good funds for a number of states. If you can't find a good, state-specific fund for where you live or if you're only in a high federal tax bracket, you can use the nationwide Vanguard Municipal bond funds.

Balanced and Asset Allocation Funds: The Best Hybrid Funds

Hybrid funds invest in a mixture of different types of securities. Most commonly, they invest in both bonds and stocks. These funds are usually less risky and less volatile than funds that invest exclusively in stocks; in an economic downturn, bonds usually hold value better than stocks.

Hybrid funds make it easier for investors who are skittish about investing in stocks to hold stocks, because the hybrids reduce the volatility that normally comes with pure stock funds. Because of their extensive diversification, hybrid funds are excellent choices for an investor who doesn't have much money to start with.

Hybrid funds come in two forms:

>> **Balanced funds** generally try to maintain a fairly constant percentage of investment in stocks and bonds.

>> **Asset allocation funds,** by contrast, normally adjust the mix of different investments according to the portfolio manager's expectations.

Some asset allocation funds, however, tend to keep more of a fixed mix of stocks and bonds, whereas some balanced funds shift the mix around quite frequently. (Although the concept of a manager being in the right place at the right time and beating the market averages sounds good in theory, most funds that shift assets fail to outperform a buy-and-hold approach.)

WARNING

Because hybrid funds pay decent dividends from the bonds that they hold, they're not appropriate for some investors who purchase funds outside tax-sheltered retirement accounts. With the exception of the Vanguard Tax-Managed Balanced Fund, which holds federally tax-free bonds, avoid hybrid funds if you're in a higher tax bracket. (Chapter 7 has details on tax-free bonds.) You should consider buying separate tax-friendly stock funds and tax-free bond funds (both discussed earlier in this chapter) to create your own hybrid portfolio.

ERIC'S PICKS

Here's my recommended short list of great balanced-type mutual funds:

>> Dodge & Cox Balanced

>> Fidelity Freedom funds and Fidelity Puritan

>> FPA Crescent

>> T. Rowe Price Balanced and T. Rowe Price Retirement funds

>> Vanguard LifeStrategy funds, Wellesley Income, and Wellington

The Best Money Market Funds

As I explain in Chapter 7, money market funds are a safe, higher-yielding alternative to bank accounts. (If you're in a higher tax bracket, money market funds have even more appeal because you can get tax-free versions of money market funds.) Under Securities and Exchange Commission regulations, money market funds can invest only in the highest-credit-rated securities, and their investments must have an average maturity of less than 60 days. The short-term nature of these securities effectively eliminates the risk of money market funds being sensitive to changes in interest rates.

The securities that money market funds use are extremely safe. General-purpose money market funds invest in government-backed securities, bank certificates of deposit, and short-term corporate debt that the largest and most creditworthy companies and the U.S. government issue.

When shopping for a money market fund, consider these factors:

>> **Expenses:** Within a given category of money market funds (general, Treasury, municipal, and so on), fund managers invest in the same basic securities. The market for these securities is pretty darn efficient, so "superstar" money market fund managers may eke out an extra 0.1 percent per year in yield but not much more.

TIP

Select a money market fund that does a good job controlling its expenses. The operating expenses that the fund deducts before payment of dividends are the biggest determinant of yield. All other things being equal (which they usually are with different money market funds), lower operating expenses translate into higher yields for you.

You have no need or reason to tolerate annual operating expenses of greater than 0.5 percent. Some top-quality funds charge 0.3 percent or less annually. Remember, lower expenses don't mean that a fund company cuts corners or provides poor service. Lower expenses are possible in most cases because a fund company is successful in attracting a lot of money to invest. (Note that many money market funds have been waiving a portion of their management fee in recent years due to ultra-low interest rates. Otherwise, the yield on their funds would be negative.)

>> **Tax consequences:** With money market funds, all your return comes from dividends. What you actually get to keep of these returns (on non-retirement account investments) is what's left over after the federal and state governments take their cut of your investment income. If you invest money that's held outside of a retirement account and you're in a high tax bracket, you may come out ahead if you invest in tax-free money market funds. If you're in a high-tax state, then a state money market fund, if good ones exist for your state, may be a sound move.

REMEMBER

Tax-free refers to the taxability of the dividends that the fund pays. You don't get a tax deduction for money that you put into the fund, as you do with 401(k) or other retirement-type accounts.

>> **Location of other funds:** Consider what other investing you plan to do at the fund company where you establish a money market fund. Suppose that you decide to make fund investments in stocks and bonds at T. Rowe Price. In that case, keeping a money market fund at a different firm that offers a slightly higher yield may not be worth the time and administrative hassle, especially if you don't plan on holding much cash in your money market fund.

>> **Associated services:** Good money market funds offer other useful services, such as free check writing, telephone exchange and redemptions, and automated electronic exchange services with your bank account.

Most fund companies don't have many local branch offices. Generally, this fact helps these companies keep their expenses low so they can pay you greater money market fund yields. You may open and maintain your mutual fund account via the fund's toll-free phone lines, the mail, or the company's website. You don't really get much benefit, except psychological, if you select a fund company with an office in your area. However, having said that, I don't want to diminish the importance of your emotional comfort level.

In the following sections, using the criteria that I just discussed, I recommend the best money market funds — those that offer competitive yields, check-writing, access to other excellent mutual funds, and other commonly needed money market services.

Taxable money market funds

Money market funds that pay taxable dividends may be appropriate for retirement account funds that await investment as well as for non-retirement account money when you're not in a high federal tax bracket *and* aren't in a high state tax bracket (less than 5 percent).

ERIC'S PICKS

Here are the best taxable money market funds to consider:

>> Fidelity Cash Reserves

>> T. Rowe Price Summit Cash Reserves (higher yields if you invest $25,000)

>> Vanguard's Prime Money Market

U.S. Treasury money market funds

Consider U.S. Treasury money market funds if you prefer a money market fund that invests in U.S. Treasuries, which maintain the safety of government backing, or if you're not in a high federal tax bracket but *are* in a high state tax bracket (5 percent or higher).

The following lists U.S. Treasury funds that I recommend:

>> Fidelity's Government Money Market ($25,000 minimum)

>> USAA's Treasury Money Market

>> Vanguard Admiral Treasury Money Market

Municipal money market funds

Municipal (also known as *muni*) money market funds invest in short-term debt that state and local governments issue. A municipal money market fund, which pays you federally tax-free dividends, invests in munis issued by state and local governments throughout the country. A state-specific municipal fund invests in state and local government-issued munis for one state, such as New York. So if you live in New York and buy a New York municipal fund, the dividends on that fund are federal and New York state-tax-free.

HOW TO CONTACT FUND PROVIDERS

The following list provides the phone numbers and websites you can use to contact mutual fund companies and discount brokers that sell the mutual funds I discuss in this chapter. To find out more about selecting and investing in mutual funds, pick up a copy of the latest edition of my book *Mutual Funds For Dummies,* published by Wiley.

- Dodge & Cox Funds: 800-621-3979; www.dodgeandcox.com

- Fairholme Funds: 866-202-2263; www.fairholmefunds.com

- Fidelity Funds: 800-544-8888; www.fidelity.com

- FPA Funds: 800-982-4372; www.fpafunds.com

- Harbor Funds: 800-422-1050; www.harborfunds.com

- Litman Gregory Masters Funds: 800-960-0188; www.mastersselect.com

- Oakmark: 800-625-6275; www.oakmark.com

- Sequoia: 800-686-6884; www.sequoiafund.com

- T. Rowe Price Funds: 800-638-5660; www.troweprice.com

- Tweedy, Browne Funds: 800-432-4789; www.tweedybrowne.com

- USAA Funds: 800-382-8722; www.usaa.com

- The Vanguard Group: 800-662-7447; www.vanguard.com

So how do you decide whether to buy a nationwide or state-specific municipal money market fund? Money market funds that are only federally tax-free may be appropriate when you're in a high federal tax bracket but not in a high state bracket (less than 5 percent). State-tax-free municipal money market funds are worth considering when you're in a high federal *and* a high state tax bracket (5 percent or higher).

If you're in a higher state tax bracket, your state may not have good (or any) state-tax-free municipal money market funds available. If you live in any of those states, you're likely best off with one of the following national municipal money market funds:

>> T. Rowe Price Summit Municipal Money Market ($25,000 minimum)

>> USAA Tax-Exempt Money Market

>> Vanguard Tax-Exempt Money Market

Fidelity, USAA, and Vanguard have good funds for a number of states. If you can't find a good, state-specific fund for your state or you're only in a high federal tax bracket, use one of the nationwide muni money markets that I describe in the preceding list.

Chapter 9

Choosing a Brokerage Firm

When you invest in certain securities — such as stocks and bonds and exchange-traded funds — and when you wish to hold mutual funds from different companies in a single account, you need brokerage services. Brokers execute your trades to buy or sell stocks, bonds, and other securities and enable you to centralize your holdings of mutual funds and other investments. Your broker can also assist you with other services that may interest you.

In this chapter, I explain the ins and outs of discount brokers and online brokers to help you find the right one for your investment needs.

Getting Your Money's Worth: Discount Brokers

Prior to 1975, all securities brokerage firms charged the same fee, known as a *commission*, to trade stocks and bonds. The Securities and Exchange Commission (SEC), the federal government agency responsible for overseeing investment firms and their services, regulated these commissions.

Beginning May 1, 1975 — which is known in the brokerage business as "May Day" — brokerage firms were free to compete with one another on price, like companies in almost all other industries. Most of the firms in existence at that time, such as Prudential, Merrill Lynch, E. F. Hutton, and Smith Barney, largely continued with business as usual, charging relatively high commissions.

However, a new type of brokerage firm, the *discount broker*, was born. The earlier generations of discount brokerage firms charged substantially lower commissions — typically 50 to 75 percent lower — than the other firms. Today, discount brokers, which include many online brokers, abound and continue to capture the lion's share of new business. Many do stock trades, regardless of size, for a flat rate of less than $40, and some do them for less than $20 or even $10 per transaction.

REMEMBER

When you hear the word *discount*, you probably think of adjectives like *cheap*, *inferior-quality*, and such. However, in the securities brokerage field, the discount brokers who place your trades at substantial discounts can offer you even better value and service than high-cost brokers. The following list offers some of the reasons discount brokers give you more bang for your buck:

>> They can place your trades at a substantially lower price because they have much lower overhead.

>> They tend not to rent the posh downtown office space, complete with mahogany-paneled conference rooms, in order to impress customers.

>> They don't waste tons of money employing economists and research analysts to produce forecasts and predictive reports.

In addition to lower commissions, another major benefit of using discount brokers is that they generally work on salary. Working on salary removes a significant conflict of interest that continues to get commission-paid brokers and their firms into trouble. People who sell on commission to make a living aren't bad people, but given the financial incentives they have, don't expect to receive holistic, in-your-best-interest investing counsel from them.

Assessing the high-commission salespeople's arguments

WARNING

One of the many sales tactics of high-commission brokerage firms is to try to disparage discounters by telling you, "You'll receive poor service from discounters." My own experience, as well as that of others, suggests that in many cases, discounters actually offer *better* service.

Many of the larger discounters with convenient branch offices offer assistance with filling out paperwork and access to independent research reports. From discounters, you also can buy *no-load* (commission-free) mutual funds that are run by management teams that make investment decisions for you. Such funds can be bought from mutual fund companies as well. (See Chapter 8 for more on these mutual funds.)

High-commission firms used to argue that discount brokerage customers received worse trade prices when they bought and sold. This assertion is a bogus argument because all brokerage firms use a computer-based trading system for smaller retail trades. Trades are processed in seconds. High-commission brokers also say that discounters are only "for people who know exactly what they're doing and don't need any help." This statement is also false, especially given the abundance of financial information and advice available today.

Selecting a discount broker

Which discount broker is best for you depends on what your needs and wants are. In addition to fees, consider how important having a local branch office is to you. If you seek to invest in mutual funds, the discount brokerage firms that I list later in this section offer access to good funds (you can access all exchange-traded funds through a broker because ETFs trade like stocks on exchanges). In addition, these firms offer money market funds into which you can deposit money awaiting investment or proceeds from a sale.

Within the discount brokerage business, *deep discounters* are firms that offer the lowest rates but fewer frills and other services. Generally, deep discounters don't have local branch offices like big discounters do, and they also don't offer money market funds with the highest yields.

WARNING

Be careful of some deep discounters that offer bargain commissions but stick it to you in other ways, such as by charging high fees for particular services or offering below-market interest rates on money awaiting investment.

ERIC'S PICKS

Here are my top picks for discount brokers:

>> **T. Rowe Price (800-225-5132; www.troweprice.com):** T. Rowe Price offers a solid family of no-load mutual funds. The company's brokerage fees are competitive and among those on the lower end for discounters. Its six branch offices are primarily in the Baltimore-Washington metro areas, Florida, and Colorado.

>> **Vanguard (800-992-8327; www.vanguard.com):** Vanguard is best known for its excellent family of no-load mutual funds, but its discount brokerage services have improved over the years. Vanguard has also reduced its brokerage fees in recent years, and its prices are now near the low end of discount brokers.

>> **TD Ameritrade (800-454-9272; www.tdameritrade.com):** This firm was created by the merger of TD Waterhouse with Ameritrade. (Waterhouse Securities merged in the late 1990s with Jack White and company to form TD Waterhouse.) TD Ameritrade offers competitive commission rates and more than 100 branch offices. The company offers round-the-clock customer assistance.

CAN FINANCIAL ADVISORS ACCESS BETTER FUNDS THAT AREN'T AVAILABLE TO YOU?

Some financial advisors promote their services in part by saying that they can get you into funds that are sold only through advisors. Please allow me to separate the hype from reality in assessing advisor/institutional funds.

Some investment management companies offer different share classes of some of their funds. Some of these are much-higher-minimum funds (for example, $100,000 or $1,000,000 minimum) that are targeted to wealthy individuals or institutions. Such funds tend to have slightly lower expense ratios, which of course should translate into slightly higher returns for the fund's investors.

Some institutional funds can be accessed only by financial advisors. That said, that doesn't mean that the funds an advisor can get you into are worthy of your investing dollars. Just because a fund restricts access, that doesn't make the fund among the best to invest in (consider the many mediocre and lousy hedge funds).

The bottom line is that access to advisor/institutional funds is a consideration — a minor one — if and only if the advisor is actually doing a good job seeking out funds that are in your best interests and that have the best characteristics. You should evaluate a financial advisor on many factors, especially and including how the advisor is compensated and what conflicts of interest he or she may have.

Some of the larger fund companies, such as Vanguard and T. Rowe Price, offer lower-expense, higher-minimum-investment fund share classes that are available to anyone who can pay the minimum. For example, Vanguard has "Admiral" funds, which have $10,000 minimums (for index funds) or $50,000 minimums (for actively managed funds). T. Rowe Price has higher-minimum "Summit" funds with a $25,000 minimum initial investment.

There are also exchange-traded funds (ETFs), such as Vanguard's, that generally have expense ratios that are even lower than or as low as their high-balance Admiral funds — without having any minimum investment requirement. That said, you generally have to pay brokerage fees to buy and sell ETFs through a broker.

REMEMBER

All the preceding firms offer mutual funds from many fund companies in addition to their family of funds (if they have a family of funds). In other words, you may purchase mutual funds that aren't in the T. Rowe Price family of funds through the T. Rowe Price brokerage department. Other discounters certainly have good service and competitive rates, so shop around if you desire. Note, however, that you generally pay a transaction fee to buy funds from firms that don't offer their own family of funds.

Absent from my list are the large discounters Fidelity and Schwab. The simple reason they're missing is that they charge significantly higher transaction fees than the competition does. These firms can get away with premium pricing, despite comparable services, because enough investors prefer to do business with name-brand companies. Although I think that both companies can offer investors a fine base from which to do their investing, I don't feel that their fees are justified unless you want to do business with a broker that maintains a branch office in your area. If you're going to invest in individual stocks (as discussed in Chapter 6), Schwab and Fidelity deserve more consideration because they offer a comprehensive array of useful and independent research resources.

Considering Online Brokers

To get the lowest trading commissions, you generally must place your trades online. Even if you've never visited an online brokerage site, ads for them online, in print publications, and even on national television have surely bombarded you. Visit any website that's remotely related to investing in stocks, and you're sure to find ads for various Internet brokers. Anyone familiar with the economics of running a brokerage firm can tell you that technology, when properly applied, reduces a broker's labor costs. Some brokerages — thanks to technology — can now perform *market orders* (which means they'll execute your trade at the best current available price) for a few bucks. Hence the attraction of online trading.

Before you jump at the chance to save a few dollars by trading online, read the following sections for other considerations that should factor in to your choice of an online broker — or your decision to trade online at all.

Examining your online trading motives

If trading online attracts you, first examine why. If you're motivated by how easily you can check account balances, beware. Tracking prices daily (or, worse, minute by minute) and frequently checking your account balances leads to addictive trading. A low fee of $5 or $10 per trade doesn't really save you any money if you trade a lot and rack up significant total commissions, and you pay more in capital gains taxes when you sell at a profit. Don't forget that as with trading through a regular brokerage firm, you also lose the *spread* (difference between the bid and ask prices when you trade stocks and bonds) and incur the explicit commission rates that online brokers charge.

Frankly, trading online is also an unfortunately easy way for people to act impulsively and emotionally when making important investment decisions. If you're prone to such actions or if you find yourself tracking and trading investments too closely, stay away from this form of trading and use the Internet only to check account information and gather factual information.

Most of the best investment firms also allow you to trade via touch-tone phone. In most cases, touch-tone phone trading is discounted when you compare it to trading through a live broker, although it's admittedly less glamorous than trading through a website.

Some brokers also offer account information and trading capabilities via apps and smartphones, which, of course, add to your costs. Trading through such handheld technology can also promote addictive investment behaviors.

Investment websites also push the surging interest in online trading with the pitch that you can beat the market averages and professionals at their own game if you do your own research and trade online. Beating the market and professionals is highly unlikely. You can save some money trading online but perhaps not as much as the hype has you believe. Online trading is good for the convenience and low costs if you're not obsessive about it.

Taking other costs into account

Online brokerage customers often shop for low costs. However, by simply talking with many folks who have traded online and by reviewing online message boards where customers speak their minds, I've discovered that shopping merely for low-cost trading prices often causes investors to overlook other important issues. The biggest problem is firms that nickel-and-dime you with fees. For instance, some charge fees for real-time stock quotes (as opposed to quotes that may be 15 to 20 minutes old and are free). Other brokers whack you $20 here and $50 there for services such as wiring money or simply closing your account. Also beware of "inactivity fees" that some brokers levy on accounts that have infrequent trading. So before you sign up with any broker, make sure you examine its entire fee schedule.

Also beware below-market rates on money market accounts and many cut-rate brokers. When you buy or sell an investment, you may have cash sitting around in your brokerage account. Not surprisingly, the online brokers pitching their cheap online trading rates in 3-inch-high numbers don't reveal their money market rates in such large type (if at all). Some don't pay interest on the first $1,000 or so of your cash balance, and even then, some companies pay half a percent to a full percent less than their best competitors. In the worst cases, some online brokers have paid up to 3 percent less during periods of normal interest rates. Under those terms, you'd earn up to $150 less in interest per year if you averaged a $5,000 cash balance during the year.

Looking at service quality

Common complaints among customers of online brokers include slow responses to email queries, long wait times to speak with a live person to answer questions or resolve problems, delays in opening accounts and receiving literature, unclear statements, incorrect processing of trading requests, and slow web response during periods of heavy traffic. With a number of firms that I called, I experienced phone waits of up to ten minutes and was transferred several times to retrieve answers to simple questions, such as whether the firm carried a specific family of mutual funds.

INVESTIGATE

When you shop for an online broker, check your prospects thoroughly. Here are some things to do:

>> **Call for literature and to see how long it takes you to reach a live human being.** Ask some questions and see how knowledgeable and helpful the representatives are. For non-retirement accounts, if you want to gauge the quality of the firm's year-end account statements, ask prospective brokerages to send you a sample. If you're a mutual fund investor, check out the quality of the funds that the company offers. In other words, don't allow the sheer number of funds that the company offers impress you. Also, inquire about the interest rates that the company pays on cash balances as well as the rates that the company charges on margin loans, if you want such borrowing services. Try sending some questions to the broker's website and see how accurate and timely the response is.

>> **Consider checking online message boards to see what current and past customers say about the firms that you're considering.** Most online brokers that have been around for more than six months lay claim to a number-one rating with some survey or ranking of online brokers. Place little value on such claims.

>> **Examine what the firm did before it got into the online brokerage business.** Would you rather put your money and trust in the hands of an established and respected financial service company that has been around for a number of years or an upstart firm run by a couple of people hoping to

strike it rich on the Internet? Transact business only with firms that offer sufficient account insurance (enough to protect your assets) through the Securities Investor Protection Corporation (SIPC). The severe stock market downturns in the early and late 2000s led to major shakeouts, and you need to protect yourself.

Listing the best online brokers

ERIC'S PICKS

Among the e-brokers I've reviewed, my top picks are the following:

Broker	Phone Number	Website
E*Trade	800-387-2331	etrade.com
Scottrade	800-619-7283	scottrade.com
T. Rowe Price	800-638-5660	troweprice.com
Vanguard	800-992-8327	vanguard.com
TD Ameritrade	800-934-4448	tdameritrade.com

WHY YOU SHOULD KEEP YOUR SECURITIES IN A BROKERAGE ACCOUNT

When most investors purchase stocks or bonds today, they don't receive the actual paper certificate demonstrating ownership. Brokerage accounts often hold the certificate for your stocks and bonds on your behalf. Holding your securities through a brokerage account is beneficial because most brokers charge an extra fee to issue certificates.

Sometimes people hold stock and bond certificates themselves, though this practice was more common among previous generations. The reason: During the Great Depression, many brokerage firms failed and took people's assets down with their sinking ships. Since then, various reforms have greatly strengthened the safety of money and the securities that you hold in a brokerage account.

Just as the FDIC insurance system backs up money in bank accounts, the Securities Investor Protection Corporation (SIPC) provides insurance to investment brokerage firm customers. The base level of insurance is $500,000 per account. However, many firms purchase additional protection — some as high as $100 million total!

Brokerage firms don't often fail these days, but unlike during the Depression, the SIPC protects you if they do. However, the SIPC coverage doesn't protect you against a falling stock market. If you invest your money in stocks or bonds that drop in value, that's your own problem!

Besides not having to worry about losing your securities if a brokerage firm fails, another good reason to hold securities with a broker is so you don't lose them — literally! Surprising numbers of people — the exact number is unknown — have lost their stock and bond certificates. Those who realize their loss can contact the issuing firms to replace them, but doing so takes a good deal of time. However, just like future goals and plans, some certificates are simply lost, and owners never realize their loss. This financial fiasco sometimes happens when people die and their heirs don't know where to look for the certificates or the securities that their loved ones held.

Another reason to hold your securities in a brokerage account is that doing so cuts down on processing all those dividend checks. For example, if you own a dozen stocks and each pays you a quarterly dividend, you must receive, endorse, and otherwise deal with 48 separate checks. Some people enjoy this practice — they say that doing so is part of the "fun" of owning securities. My advice: Stick all your securities in one brokerage account that holds your paid dividends. Brokerage accounts offer you the ability to move these payments into a reasonably good-yielding money market fund. Most of the better discount brokers even allow you to reinvest stock dividends in the purchase of more shares of that stock at no charge.

3

Growing Wealth with Real Estate

Chapter 10
Investing in a Home

For most people, buying a home in which to live is their first, best, and only real estate investment. Homes may require a lot of financial feeding, but over the course of your life, owning a home (instead of renting) can make and save you money. Although the pile of mortgage debt seems daunting in the years just after your purchase, someday your home's *equity* (the market value of the home minus the outstanding mortgage debt) may be among your biggest assets.

And, yes, real estate is still a good investment despite its declines in the late 2000s in many areas. Like stocks, real estate does well over the long term but doesn't go continuously higher (see my website at www.erictyson.com for up-to-date, long-term graphs of housing prices in different parts of the U.S.). Smart investors take advantage of down periods; they consider these periods to be times to buy at lower prices just like they do when their favorite retail stores are having a sale.

Considering How Home Ownership Can Help You Achieve Your Financial Goals

Even though your home consumes a lot of dough (mortgage payments, property taxes, insurance, maintenance, and so on) while you own it, it can help you accomplish important financial goals:

>> **Retiring:** By the time you hit your 50s and 60s, the size of your monthly mortgage payment, relative to your income and assets, should start to look

small or nonexistent. Lowered housing costs can help you afford to retire or cut back from full-time work. Some people choose to sell their homes and buy less-costly ones or to rent the homes out and use some or all of the cash to live on in retirement. Other homeowners enhance their retirement income by taking out a reverse mortgage to tap the equity that they've built up in their properties.

>> **Pursuing your small-business dreams:** Running your own business can be a source of great satisfaction. Financial barriers, however, prevent many people from pulling the plug on a regular job and taking the entrepreneurial plunge. You may be able to borrow against the equity that you've built up in your home to get the cash you need to start your own business. Depending on what type of business you have in mind, you may even be able to run your enterprise from your home. (I discuss small-business issues in Part 4.)

>> **Financing college:** It may seem like only yesterday that your kids were born, but soon enough they'll be ready for an expensive four-year undertaking: college. Borrowing against the equity in your home is a viable way to help pay for your kids' educational costs.

Perhaps you won't use your home's equity for retirement, a small business, educational expenses, or other important financial goals. But even if you decide to pass your home on to your children, a charity, or a long-lost relative, it's still a valuable asset and a worthwhile investment. This chapter explains how to make the most of it.

The Buying Decision

I believe that most people should buy and own a home. But homeownership isn't for everybody and certainly not at all times in your adult life.

The decision of if and when to buy a home can be complex. Money matters, but so do personal and emotional issues. Buying a home is a big deal — you're settling down. Can you really see yourself coming home to this same place day after day, year after year? Of course, you can always move, but doing so, especially within just a few years of purchasing the home, can be costly and cumbersome, and now you've got a financial obligation to deal with.

Weighing the pros and cons of ownership

Some people — particularly enthusiastic salespeople in the real estate business — believe everybody should own a home. You may hear them say things like "Buy a home for the tax breaks" or "Renting is like throwing your money away."

REMEMBER

As I discuss later in this chapter, the bulk of homeownership costs — namely, mortgage interest and property taxes — are tax-deductible. However, these tax breaks are already largely factored into the higher cost of owning a home. So don't buy a home just because of the tax breaks. (If such tax breaks didn't exist, housing prices would be lower because the effective cost of owning would be so much higher. I wouldn't be put off by tax reform discussions that mention eliminating home-buying tax breaks — though the odds of these reforms passing are slim to none.)

Renting isn't necessarily equal to "throwing your money away." In fact, renting can have a number of benefits, such as the following:

» **In some communities, with a given type of property, renting is less costly than buying.** Happy and successful renters I've seen include people who pay low rent, perhaps because they've made housing sacrifices. If you can sock away 10 percent or more of your earnings while renting, you're probably well on your way to accomplishing your future financial goals.

» **You can save money and hopefully invest in other financial assets.** Stocks, bonds, and mutual and exchange-traded funds (see Part 2) are quite accessible and useful in retirement. Some long-term homeowners, by contrast, have a substantial portion of their wealth tied up in their homes. (*Remember:* Accessibility is a double-edged sword because it may tempt you as a cash-rich renter to blow the money in the short term.)

» **Renting has potential emotional and psychological rewards.** The main reward is the not-so-inconsequential fact that you have more flexibility to pack up and move on. You may have a lease to fulfill, but you may be able to renegotiate it if you need to move on. As a homeowner, you have a major monthly payment to take care of. To some people, this responsibility feels like a financial ball and chain. After all, you have no guarantee that you can sell your home in a timely fashion or at the price you desire if you want to move.

WARNING

Although renting has its benefits, renting has at least one big drawback: exposure to inflation. As the cost of living increases, your landlord can keep increasing your rent (unless you live in a rent-controlled unit). If you're a homeowner, however, the big monthly expense of the mortgage payment doesn't increase, assuming that you buy your home with a fixed-rate mortgage. (Your property taxes, home-owners insurance, and maintenance expenses are exposed to inflation, but these expenses are usually much smaller in comparison to your monthly mortgage payment or rent.)

Here's a quick example to show you how inflation can work against you as a long-term renter. Suppose that you're comparing the costs of owning a home that costs $160,000 to renting a similar property for $800 a month. (If you're in a high-cost urban area and these numbers seem low, please bear with me and focus on the general insights, which you can apply to higher-cost areas.) Buying at $160,000 sounds a lot more expensive than renting for $800, doesn't it? But this isn't an apples-to-apples comparison. You must compare the monthly cost of owning to the monthly cost of renting. You must also factor the tax benefits of homeownership in to your comparison so that you compare the after-tax monthly cost of owning versus renting (mortgage interest and property taxes are tax-deductible). Figure 10-1 does just that over 30 years.

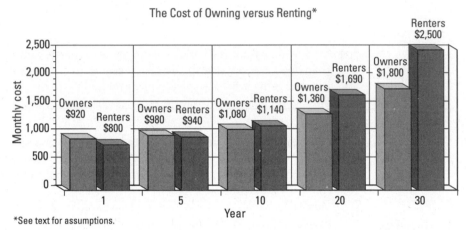

The Cost of Owning versus Renting*

*See text for assumptions.

© John Wiley & Sons, Inc.

FIGURE 10-1: Because of inflation, renting is generally more costly in the long run.

As you can see in Figure 10-1, although owning costs more in the early years, it should be less expensive in the long run. Renting is costlier in the long term because all your rental expenses increase with inflation. *Note:* I haven't factored in the potential change in the value of your home over time. Over long periods of time, home prices tend to appreciate, which makes owning even more attractive.

TECHNICAL STUFF

The example in Figure 10-1 assumes that you make a 20 percent down payment and take out a 7 percent fixed-rate mortgage to purchase the property. It also assumes that the rate of inflation of your homeowners insurance, property taxes, maintenance, and rent is 4 percent per year. If inflation is lower, renting doesn't necessarily become cheaper in the long term. In the absence of inflation, your rent should escalate less, but your homeownership expenses, which are subject to inflation (property taxes, maintenance, and insurance), should increase less, too. And with low inflation, you can probably refinance your mortgage at a lower interest rate, which reduces your monthly mortgage payments. With low or no inflation, owning can still cost less, but the savings versus renting usually aren't as dramatic as when inflation is greater.

KNOWING WHEN TO BUY

If you're considering buying a home, you may be concerned about whether home prices are poised to rise or fall. No one wants to purchase a home that then plummets in value. And who wouldn't like to buy just before prices go on an upward trajectory?

It's not easy to predict what's going to happen with real estate prices in a particular city, state, or country over the next one, two, three, or more years. Ultimately, the economic health and vitality of an area drive the demand and prices for homes in that area. An increase in jobs, particularly ones that pay well, increases the demand for housing. And when demand goes up, so do prices.

If you first buy a home when you're in your 20s, 30s, or even your 40s, you may end up as a homeowner for several decades. Over such a long time, you may experience numerous ups and downs. But you'll probably see more ups than downs, so don't be too concerned about trying to predict what's going to happen to the real estate market in the near term. I know some long-term renters who avoided buying homes decades ago because they thought that prices were high. Consequently, they missed out on tremendous appreciation in real estate values. (The one silver lining to the late 2000s decline in home prices is that homes became more affordable than they had been in a long time.)

That said, you may be, at particular times in your life, ambivalent about buying a home. Perhaps you're not sure whether you'll stay put for more than three to five years. Therefore, part of your home-buying decision may hinge on whether current home prices in your local area offer you a good value. The state of the job market, the number of home listings for sale, and the level of real estate prices as compared to rent are useful indicators of the housing market's health. Trying to time your purchase has more importance if you think you may move in less than five years. In that case, avoid buying in a market where home prices are relatively high compared to their rental costs. If you expect to move so soon, renting generally makes more sense because of the high transaction costs of buying and selling real estate.

Recouping transaction costs

Financially speaking, I recommend that you wait to buy a home until you can see yourself staying put for a minimum of three years. Ideally, I'd like you to think that you have a good shot of staying with the home for five or more years. Why? Buying and selling a home cost big bucks, and you generally need at least five years of low appreciation to recoup your transaction costs. Some of the expenses you face when buying and selling a home include the following:

>> **Inspection fees:** You shouldn't buy a property without thoroughly checking it out, so you'll incur inspection expenses. Good inspectors can help you identify problems with the plumbing, heating, and electrical systems. They also check out the foundation, roof, and so on. They can even tell you whether termites are living in the house. Property inspections typically cost a few hundred dollars up to $1,000 for larger homes.

>> **Loan costs:** The costs of getting a mortgage include items such as the *points* (upfront interest that can run 1 to 2 percent of the loan amount), application and credit report fees, and appraisal fees.

>> **Title insurance:** When you buy a home, you and your lender need to protect yourselves against the chance — albeit small — that the property seller doesn't actually legally own the home that you're buying. That's where title insurance comes in — it protects you financially from unscrupulous sellers. Title insurance costs vary by area; 0.5 percent of the purchase price of the property is about average.

>> **Moving costs:** You can transport all your furniture, clothing, and other personal belongings yourself, but your time is worth something, and your moving skills may be limited. Besides, do you want to end up in a hospital emergency room after being pinned at the bottom of a staircase by a runaway couch? Moving costs vary wildly, but you can count on spending hundreds to thousands of dollars.

>> **Real estate agents' commissions:** A commission of 5 to 7 percent of the purchase price of most homes is paid to the real estate salespeople and the companies they work for.

REMEMBER

On top of all these transaction costs of buying and then selling a home, you'll also face maintenance expenses — for example, fixing leaky pipes and painting. To cover all the transaction and maintenance costs of homeownership, the value of your home needs to appreciate about 15 percent over the years that you own it for you to be as well off financially as if you had continued renting. Fifteen percent! If you need or want to move elsewhere in a few years, counting on that kind of appreciation in those few years is risky. If you happen to buy just before a sharp rise in housing prices, you may get this much appreciation in a short time. But you can't count on this upswing — you're more likely to lose money on such a short-term deal.

Some people invest in real estate even when they don't expect to live in the home for long, and they may consider turning their home into a rental if they move within a few years. Doing so can work well financially in the long haul, but don't underestimate the responsibilities that come with rental property, which I discuss in Chapter 11.

Deciding How Much to Spend

Buying a home is a long-term financial commitment. You'll probably take out a 15- to 30-year mortgage to finance your purchase, and the home that you buy will need maintenance over the years. So before you decide to buy, take stock of your overall financial health.

WARNING

If you have good credit and a reliable source of employment, lenders will eagerly offer to loan you money. They'll tell you how much you may borrow from them — the maximum that you're qualified to borrow. Just because they offer you that maximum amount, however, doesn't mean that you should borrow the maximum.

HOMEOWNERSHIP TAX SAVINGS

Your mortgage interest and property taxes are tax-deductible on Form 1040, Schedule A of your personal tax return. When you calculate the costs of owning a home, subtract the tax savings to get a more complete and accurate sense of what homeownership will cost you.

When you finally buy a home, be sure to refigure how much you need to pay in income tax, because your mortgage interest and property tax deductions can help lower your tax bill. If you work for an employer, ask your payroll/benefits department for Form W-4. If you're self-employed, you can complete a worksheet that comes with Form 1040-ES. Call 800-TAX-FORM (800-829-3676) for a copy. Many new homebuyers don't bother with this step, and they receive a big tax refund on their next filed income tax return. Although getting money back from the IRS may feel good, it means that at a minimum, you gave the IRS an interest-free loan. In the worst-case scenario, the reduced cash flow during the year may cause you to accumulate debt or miss out on contributing to tax-deductible retirement accounts.

If you want a more precise estimate as to how homeownership may affect your tax situation, get out your tax return and plug in some reasonable numbers to guesstimate how your taxes may change. You can also speak with a tax advisor.

Last but not least, eligible homeowners can exclude from taxable income a significant portion of their gain on the sale of a principal residence: up to $250,000 for single tax-payers and up to $500,000 for married couples filing jointly.

Buying a home without considering your other monthly expenditures and long-term goals may cause you to end up with a home that dictates much of your future spending. Have you considered, for example, how much you need to save monthly to reach your retirement goals? How about the amount you want to spend on recreation and entertainment?

If you want to continue your current lifestyle, you have to be honest with yourself about how much you can really afford to spend as a homeowner. First-time home-buyers in particular run into financial trouble when they don't understand their current spending. Buying a home can be a wise decision, but it can also be a huge burden. And you can buy all sorts of nifty things for a home. Some people prop up their spending habits with credit cards — a dangerous practice.

REMEMBER

Don't let your home control your financial future. Before you buy a property or agree to a particular mortgage, be sure that you can afford to do so — be especially careful not to ignore your retirement planning (if you hope to someday retire). Start by reading Chapter 3. After reading the following sections, you can also check out Chapter 12, where I cover mortgages and financing options in greater detail.

Looking through lenders' eyes

Mortgage lenders calculate the maximum amount that you can borrow to buy a piece of real estate. All lenders want to gauge your ability to repay the money that you borrow, so you have to pass a few tests.

For a home in which you will reside, lenders total your monthly housing expenses. They define your housing costs as

> Mortgage payment + property taxes + insurance

REMEMBER

A lender doesn't consider maintenance and upkeep expenses (including utilities) in owning a home. Although lenders may not care where you spend money outside your home, they do care about your other debt. A lot of other debt, such as credit cards or auto loans, diminishes the funds that are available to pay your housing expenses. Lenders know that having other debt increases the possibility that you'll fall behind or actually default on your mortgage payments.

If you have consumer debt (for example, credit cards, auto loans, and so on) that requires monthly payments, lenders calculate another ratio to determine the maximum that you can borrow. Lenders add the amount that you need to pay down your other consumer debt to your monthly housing expense.

Consumer debt is bad news even without considering that it hurts your qualification for a mortgage. This type of debt is costly and encourages you to live beyond your means. Unlike the interest on mortgage debt, consumer debt interest isn't tax-deductible. Get rid of it — curtail your spending and adjust to living within your means. If you can't live within your means as a renter, doing so is going to be even harder as a homeowner.

Determining your down payment

When deciding how much to borrow for a home, keep in mind that most lenders require you to purchase *private mortgage insurance* (PMI) if your down payment is less than 20 percent of your home's purchase price. PMI protects the lender from getting stuck with a property that may be worth less than the mortgage you owe, in the event that you default on your loan. On a moderate-size loan, PMI can add hundreds of dollars per year to your payments.

If you have to take PMI to buy a home with less than 20 percent down, keep an eye on your home's value and your loan balance. Over time, your property should appreciate, and your loan balance should decrease as you make monthly payments. After your mortgage represents 80 percent or less of the market value of the home, you can get rid of the PMI. Doing so usually entails contacting your lender and paying for an appraisal.

As I've said in the earlier editions of this book, I have never been a fan of *interest-only* loans, which entice cash-strapped buyers with lower monthly payments, because all the initial payments go toward interest. These loans typically have worse *terms* (interest rate and fees) than conventional mortgages and cause some buyers to take on more debt than they can handle. After a number of years, the payment amount jumps higher when the principal and interest begin to be repaid together.

What if you have so much money that you can afford to make more than a 20 percent down payment? How much should you put down then? (This problem doesn't usually arise — most buyers, especially first-time buyers, struggle to get a 20 percent down payment together.) The answer depends on what else you can or want to do with the money. If you're considering other investment opportunities, determine whether you can expect to earn a higher rate of return on those other investments versus the interest rate that you'd pay on the mortgage. Forget about the tax deduction for your mortgage interest. The interest is deductible, but remember that the earnings from your investments are ultimately taxable.

During the past century, stock market and real estate investors have enjoyed average annual returns of around 9 percent per year. So if you borrow mortgage money at around 5 to 6 percent, in the long term you should come out a few percent ahead if you use the money you would have put toward a larger down payment to invest in such growth investments. You aren't guaranteed, of course, that your investments will earn 9 percent yearly. (Remember that past returns don't guarantee the future.) And don't forget that all investments come with risk. The advantage of putting more money down and borrowing less is that it's essentially a risk-free investment (as long as you have adequate insurance on your property).

TIP

If you prefer to put down just 20 percent and invest more money elsewhere, that's fine. Just don't keep the extra money (beyond an emergency reserve) under the mattress, in a savings account, or in bonds that pay less interest than your mortgage costs you in interest. Invest in stocks, real estate, or a small business. Otherwise, you don't have a chance at earning a higher return than the cost of your mortgage, and you'd therefore be better off paying down your mortgage.

Selecting Your Property Type

If you're ready to buy a home, you must make some decisions about what and where to buy. If you grew up in the suburbs, your image of a home may include the traditional single-family home with a lawn, kids, and family pets. But single-family homes, of course, aren't the only or even the main type of residential housing in many areas, especially in some higher-cost, urban neighborhoods. Other common types of higher-density ("shared") housing include the following:

>> **Condominiums:** *Condominiums* are generally apartment-style units that are stacked on top of and adjacent to one another. Many condo buildings were originally apartments that were converted — through the sale of ownership of separate units — into condos. When you purchase a condominium, you purchase a specific unit as well as a share of the common areas (for example, the pool, landscaping, entry and hallways, laundry room, and so on).

>> **Townhomes:** *Townhome* is just a fancy way of saying attached or row home. Think of a townhome as a cross between a condominium and a single-family house. Townhomes are condolike because they're attached (generally sharing walls and a roof) and are homelike because they're often two-story buildings that come with a small yard.

>> **Cooperatives:** *Cooperatives* (usually called co-ops) resemble apartment and condominium buildings. When you buy a share in a cooperative, you own a share of the entire building, including some living space. Unlike in a condo, you generally need to get approval from the cooperative association if you want to remodel or rent your unit to a tenant. In some co-ops, you must even gain approval from the association for the sale of your unit to a proposed buyer. Co-ops are generally much harder to obtain loans for and to sell, so I don't recommend that you buy one unless you get a good deal and can easily obtain a loan.

All types of shared housing in the preceding list offer two potential advantages:

>> **This type of housing generally gives you more living space for your dollars.** This value makes sense because with a single-family home, a good chunk of the property's cost is for the land that the home sits on. Land is good for decks, recreation, and playing children, but you don't live "in" it the way you do with your home. Shared housing maximizes living space for the housing dollars that you spend.

>> **In many situations, you're not personally responsible for general maintenance.** Instead, the homeowners association (which you pay into) takes care of it. If you don't have the time, energy, or desire to keep up a property, shared housing can make sense. Shared housing units may also give you access to recreation facilities, such as a pool, tennis courts, and exercise equipment.

So why doesn't everyone purchase shared housing? Well, as investments, single-family homes generally outperform other housing types. Shared housing is easier to build (and to overbuild) — and the greater supply tends to keep its prices from rising as much. Single-family homes tend to attract more potential buyers — most people, when they can afford it, prefer a standalone home, especially for the increased privacy.

If you can afford a smaller single-family home instead of a larger shared-housing unit and don't shudder at the thought of maintaining a home, buy the single-family home. Shared housing makes more sense for people who don't want to deal with building maintenance and who value the security of living in a larger building with other people. Keep in mind that shared-housing prices tend to hold up better in developed urban environments. If possible, avoid shared housing units in suburban areas where the availability of developable land makes building many more units possible, thus increasing the supply of housing and slowing growth in values.

If shared housing interests you, make sure that you have the property thoroughly inspected. Also, examine the trend in maintenance fees over time to ensure that these costs are under control. (See Chapter 11 for specifics on how to check out property.)

Finding the Right Property and Location

Some people know where they want to live, so they look at just a handful of properties and then buy. Most people take much more time; finding the right house in a desired area at a fair price can take a lot of time. Buying a home can also entail much compromise when you buy with other family members, particularly spouses.

Be realistic about how long it may take you to get up to speed about different areas and to find a home that meets your various desires. If you're like most people and have a full-time job that allows only occasional weekends and evenings to look for a house, three to six months is a short time period to settle on an area and actually find and successfully negotiate on a property. Six months to a year isn't unusual or slow. Remember that you're talking about an enormous purchase that you'll come home to daily.

WARNING

Real estate agents can be a big barrier to taking your time with this monumental decision. Some agents are pushy and want to make a sale and get their commission. Don't work with such agents as a buyer — they can make you miserable, unhappy, and broke. If necessary, begin your search without an agent to avoid this outside pressure. See Chapter 12 for additional information on working with an agent.

Keeping an open mind

Before you start your search for a new home, you may have an idea about the type of property and location that interests you or that you think you can afford. You may think, for example, that you can only afford a condominium in the neighborhood that you want. But if you take the time to check out other communities, you may find another area that meets most of your needs and has affordable single-family homes. You'd never know that, though, if you narrowed down your search too quickly.

REMEMBER

Even if you've lived in an area for a while and think that you know it well, look at different types of properties in a variety of locations before you start to narrow down your search. Be open-minded and make sure that you know which of your many criteria for a home you *really* care about. You'll likely have to be flexible with some of your preferences.

TIP

After you focus on a particular area or neighborhood, make sure you see the full range of properties available. If you want to spend $200,000 on a home, look at properties that are more expensive. Most real estate sells for less than its listing price, and you may feel comfortable spending a little bit more after you see what you can purchase if you stretch your budget a little bit. Also, if you work with an agent, make sure that you don't overlook homes that are for sale by their owners (that is, properties not listed with real estate agents). Otherwise, you may miss out on some good prospects.

Research, research, research

Thinking that you can know what an area is like from anecdotes or from a small number of personal experiences is a mistake. You may have read or heard that someone was mugged in a particular area. That incident doesn't make that area dangerous — or more dangerous than others. *Get the facts.* Anecdotes and people's perceptions often aren't accurate reflections of the facts. Check out the following key items in an area:

>> **Amenities:** Hopefully, you don't spend all your time at work, slaving away to make your monthly mortgage payment. I hope that you have time to use parks, sports and recreation facilities, and so on. You can drive around the neighborhood you're interested in to get a sense of these attractions. Most real estate agents just love to show off their favorite neighborhoods. Websites for cities and towns detail what they have to offer and where you can find it.

>> **Schools:** If you have kids, you care about this issue a lot. Unfortunately, many people make snap judgments about school quality without doing their homework. Visit the schools and don't blindly rely on test scores. Talk to parents and teachers and discover what goes on at the schools.

TIP

If you don't have (or want!) school-age children, you may be tempted to say, "What the heck does it matter about the quality of the schools?" You need to care about the schools because even if you don't have kids, the quality of the local schools and whether they're improving or faltering affects property values. Consider schooling issues even if they're not important to you, because they can affect the resale value of your property.

>> **Property taxes:** What will your property taxes be? Property tax rates vary from community to community. Check with the town's assessment office or with a good real estate agent.

>> **Crime:** Call the local police department or visit your public library to get the facts on crime. Cities and towns keep all sorts of crime statistics for neighborhoods — use them!

>> **Future development:** Check with the planning department in towns that you're considering living in to find out what types of new development and major renovations are in the works. Planning people may also be aware of problems in particular areas.

>> **Catastrophic risks:** Are the neighborhoods that you're considering buying a home in susceptible to major risks, such as floods, tornadoes, mudslides, fires, or earthquakes? Although homeowners insurance can protect you financially, consider how you may deal with such catastrophes emotionally. Insurance eases only the financial pain of a home loss. All areas have some risk, and a home in the safest of areas can burn to the ground. Although you can't eliminate all risks, you can at least educate yourself about the potential catastrophic risks in various areas.

If you're new to an area or don't have a handle on an area's risks, try a number of different sources. Knowledgeable and honest real estate agents may help, but you can also dig for primary information. For example, the U.S. Geologic Survey (USGS) puts together maps that help you see potential earthquake risks by area. The USGS maintains offices all around the country — check your local phone directory in the government White Pages section (or visit the agency online at www.usgs.gov). The Federal Emergency Management Agency (FEMA) provides maps that show flood risk areas. (Call FEMA at 800-358-9616 or check its website at www.fema.gov.) Insurance companies and agencies can also tell you what they know about risks in particular areas.

Understanding market value

Over many months, you'll look at perhaps dozens of properties for sale. Use these viewings as an opportunity to find out what specific homes are worth. The listing price isn't what a house is worth — it may be, but odds are it's not. Property that's priced to sell usually does just that: It sells. Properties left on the market are often overpriced. The listing price on such properties may reflect what an otherwise greedy or uninformed seller and his agent hope that some fool will pay.

Of the properties that you see, keep track of the prices that they end up selling for. (Good agents can provide this information.) Properties usually sell for less than the listed price. Keeping track of selling prices gives you a good handle on what properties are really worth and a better sense of what you can afford.

Pounding the pavement

After you set your sights on that special home, thoroughly check out the surroundings — you should know what you're getting yourself into.

At different times of the day and on different days of the week, go back to the neighborhood in which the property is located. Knock on a few doors and meet your potential neighbors. Ask questions. Talk to property owners as well as renters. Because renters don't have a financial stake in the area, they're often more forthcoming with negative information about an area.

After you decide where and what to buy, you're ready to try to put a deal together. I cover issues common to both home and investment property purchases — such as mortgages, negotiations, inspections, and so on — in Chapter 12.

Chapter 11

Investing in Real Estate

I f you've already bought your own home (and even if you haven't), using real estate as an investment may interest you. Over the decades and generations, real estate investing, like the stock market and small-business investments, has generated tremendous wealth for participants. (See Chapter 2 for more on the rate of return from various investments.)

REMEMBER

Real estate is like other types of ownership investments, such as stocks, where you have an ownership stake in an asset. Although you have the potential for significant profits, don't forget that you also accept greater risk. Real estate isn't a gravy train or a simple way to get wealthy. Like stocks, real estate goes through good and bad performance periods. Most people who make money investing in real estate do so because they invest and hold property over many years. The vast majority of people who don't make money in real estate don't because they make easily avoidable mistakes. In this chapter, I discuss how to make the best real estate investments and avoid the rest.

Discussing Real Estate Investment Attractions

Many people build their wealth by investing in real estate. Some people focus exclusively on property investments, but many others build their wealth through the companies that they started or through other avenues and then diversify into real estate investments. What do these wealthy folks know, and why do they choose to invest in real estate? In the following sections, I cover real estate's attractions.

REMEMBER

Real estate, like all investments, has its pros and cons. Investing in real estate is time-intensive, and it carries risks. Invest in real estate because you enjoy the challenge and because you want to diversify your portfolio. Real estate's value doesn't move in lockstep with other investments, such as stocks or small-business investments that you hold, so it's a useful diversification tool.

Limited land

The supply of buildable, desirable land on this planet is limited. And because people are prone to reproduce, demand for land and housing continues to grow. Land and what you can do with it are what make real estate valuable. Cities and islands such as Hawaii, Hong Kong, San Francisco, Los Angeles, and New York City have the highest housing costs around because land is limited in these places.

Leverage

Real estate is different from most other investments because you can borrow 75 to 80 percent (or more) of the value of the property to buy it. Thus, you can use your down payment of 20 to 25 percent of the purchase price to buy, own, and control a much larger investment; this concept is called *leverage.* Of course, you hope that the value of your real estate goes up — if it does, you make money on your original dollars invested as well as on the money that you borrowed.

Here's a quick example to illustrate. Suppose you purchase a rental property for $150,000 and make a $30,000 down payment (and borrow the other $120,000). Over the next three years, imagine that the property appreciates to $180,000. Thus, you have a profit (on paper at least) of $30,000 on an investment of just $30,000. In other words, you've made a 100 percent return on your investment. (Note that in this scenario, I ignore whether your expenses from the property exceed the rental income that you collect.)

WARNING

Leverage is good for you if property prices appreciate, but leverage can also work against you. Say, for example, that your $150,000 property decreases in value to $120,000. Even though it has dropped only 20 percent in value, you actually lose (on paper) 100 percent of your original $30,000 investment. If you have an out-standing mortgage of $120,000 on this property and you need to sell, you actually have to pay money into the sale to cover selling costs — in addition to losing your entire original investment. Ouch!

Appreciation and income

Another reason that real estate is a popular investment is that you can make money from it in two major ways: through appreciation and from income. I explain both in the following list:

>> **Appreciation:** You hope and expect that over the years, your real estate investments will appreciate in value. The appreciation of your properties compounds without tax (tax-deferred, actually) during your years of owner-ship. You don't pay tax on this profit until you sell your property — and even then you can roll over your gain into another investment property to avoid paying tax. (See the sidebar "Roll over those rental property profits" for details on tax-deferred exchanges of investment properties.)

If you choose to simply take your profits and not roll them over, the federal tax rate on gains from property held more than one year — known as *long-term capital gains* — are taxed at no more than 20 percent. (Obamacare adds an additional 3.8 percent to that for high-income earners.) That's beneficial when you consider that ordinary income can be taxed at rates approaching 40 percent. (Chapter 10 details the capital gains tax rules on the sale of a primary residence, which enable a single taxpayer to make up to $250,000 tax-free and a married couple up to $500,000 tax-free.)

>> **Income:** You also hope and expect to make money from the ongoing business that you run: renting the property. You rent out investment property to make a profit based on the property's rental income in excess of its expenses (mortgage, property taxes, insurance, maintenance, and so on). Unless you make a large down payment, your monthly operating profit is usually small (or nonexistent) in the early years of rental property ownership. Over time, your operating profit, which is subject to ordinary income tax, should rise as you increase your rental prices faster than your expenses. During soft periods in the local economy, however, rents may rise more slowly than your expenses (or rents may even fall).

ROLL OVER THOSE RENTAL PROPERTY PROFITS

TIP

When you sell a stock or fund investment that you hold outside a retirement account, you must pay tax on your profits. By contrast, if you roll over your real estate gain into another like-kind investment real estate property, you can avoid paying tax on your rental property profit when you sell.

The rules for properly making one of these (IRS code section) *1031 exchanges* (also called *Starker exchanges*) are complex and usually involve third parties. With like-kind transactions, you don't receive the proceeds of the sale. Instead, they must go into an escrow account (explained in Chapter 12). You must complete the rollover within a six-month time limit, and you must also identify a replacement property within 45 days of the sale of the first property. Make sure you find an attorney or tax advisor who's an expert at these transactions to ensure that everything goes smoothly (and legally).

If you don't roll over your gain, you may owe significant taxes because of how the IRS defines your gain. For example, if you buy a property for $200,000 and sell it for $250,000, not only do you owe tax on that difference, but you also owe tax on an additional amount that depends on the property's depreciation. The amount of depreciation that you deducted on your tax returns reduces the original $200,000 purchase price, making the taxable difference that much larger. For example, if you deducted $25,000 for depreciation over the years that you owned the property, you owe tax on the difference between the sale price of $250,000 and $175,000 ($200,000 purchase price minus $25,000 depreciation).

Ability to add value

You, as a small investor, can't add value to stocks by "fixing them up," but you may have some good ideas about how to improve a property and make it more valuable. Perhaps you can fix up a property or develop it further and raise the rental income and resale value accordingly. Through legwork, persistence, and good negotiating skills, you may also be able to make money by purchasing a property below its fair market value.

REMEMBER

Relative to investing in the stock market, tenacious and savvy real estate investors can more easily buy property below its fair market value. You can do the same in the stock market, but the legions of professional, full-time money managers who analyze stocks make finding bargains more difficult.

Ego gratification

Face it. Investing in real estate appeals to some investors because land and buildings are tangible. Although few admit it, some real estate investors get an ego rush from a tangible display of their wealth. You can drive past investment real estate and show it off to others.

In a *New York Times* article titled "What My Ego Wants, My Ego Gets," Donald Trump publicly admitted what most everyone knew long ago: He holds his real estate investments partly for his ego. Trump confessed of his purchase of the famed Plaza Hotel in the Big Apple, "I realized it was 100 percent true — ego did play a large role in the Plaza purchase and is, in fact, a significant factor in all of my deals."

Longer-term focus

One problem with investing in the securities markets, such as the stock market, is that prices are constantly changing. Television news programs, websites, smartphones, and other communication devices dutifully report the latest price quotes.

WARNING

REAL ESTATE INVESTING ISN'T AS WONDERFUL AS THEY SAY

If you've read some of the many real estate investment books or have attended seminars, you may need deprogramming! Too often, pundits attempt to make real estate investments sound like the one and only sure way to become a multimillionaire with little effort. Consider the following statements made by real estate book authors. My rebuttals to their claims follow.

"Rather than yielding only a small interest payment or dividend, real estate in prime locations can appreciate 20 percent a year or more."

Bank accounts, bonds, and stocks pay interest or dividends that typically amount to a few percent per year or less (the total return on stocks has historically been about 9 percent per year). However, bank accounts and bonds aren't comparable investments to real estate — they're far more conservative and liquid and therefore don't offer the potential for double-digit returns. Stock market investing is comparable to investing in real estate, but you shouldn't go into real estate investments expecting annual returns of 20 percent or more. Those who purchased good Los Angeles real estate in the 1950s and held onto it for the next three decades earned handsome returns as the population of this area boomed. However, keep in mind that finding areas like Los Angeles and knowing how long to hold on to investments in these areas is easier said than done.

(continued)

(continued)

> *"A good piece of property can't do anything but go up!"*
>
> Every city, town, or community has good pieces of real estate. But that doesn't mean communities can't and won't have slow or depressed years. The real estate decline of the late 2000s, which hit most communities, was a reminder that real estate prices can do something other than go up!
>
> *"Real estate is the best way of preserving and enhancing wealth . . . . [It] stands head and shoulders above any other form of investment."*
>
> Investing in stocks or in a small business is every bit as profitable as investing in real estate. In fact, more great fortunes have been built in small business than in any other form of investment. Over the long term, stock market investors have enjoyed (with less hassle) average annual rates of return comparable to real estate investors' returns.

From my observations and work with individual investors, I've seen that the constant reports on price changes cause some investors to lose sight of the long term and the big picture. In the worst cases, large short-term drops, such as what happened during the 2008 financial crisis, led investors to panic and sell at what end up being bargain prices. Or headlines about big increases pull investors in lemminglike fashion into an overheated and peaking market. Because all you need to do is click your computer mouse or dial a toll-free phone number to place your sell or buy order, some stock market investors fall prey to snap judgments.

REMEMBER

While the real estate market is constantly changing, short-term, day-to-day, and week-to-week changes are invisible. Publications don't report the value of your real estate holdings daily, weekly, or even monthly. These less-frequent publications are good because they encourage a longer-term focus. If prices do decline over months and years, you're much less likely to sell in a panic with real estate. Preparing a property for sale and eventually getting it sold take a good deal of time, and this barrier to quickly selling helps keep your vision in focus.

Figuring Out Who Should Avoid Real Estate Investing

WARNING

Real estate investing isn't for everyone. Most people do better financially when they invest their ownership holdings in a diversified portfolio of stocks, such as through stock funds. Definitely shy away from real estate investments that involve managing property if you fall into either of the following categories:

>> **You're time starved and anxious.** Buying and owning investment property and being a landlord take a lot of time. If you fail to do your homework before purchasing real estate, you can end up overpaying — or buying a heap of trouble. You can hire a property manager to help with screening and finding good tenants and troubleshooting problems with the building you purchase, but this step costs money and still requires some time involvement. Also, remember that most tenants don't care for a property the same way property owners do. If every little scratch or carpet stain sends your blood pressure skyward, avoid distressing yourself as a landlord.

>> **You're not interested in real estate.** Some people simply don't feel comfortable and informed when it comes to investing in real estate. If you've had experience and success with other investments, such as stocks, stick with them and avoid real estate. Over long periods of time, both stocks and real estate provide comparable returns.

Examining Simple, Profitable Real Estate Investments

Investing in rental real estate that you're responsible for can be a lot of work. Think about it this way: With rental properties, you have all the headaches of maintaining a property, including finding and dealing with tenants, without the benefits of living in and enjoying the property.

TIP

Unless you're extraordinarily interested in and motivated to own investment real estate, start with and perhaps limit yourself to a couple of the much simpler yet still profitable methods I discuss in the following sections.

Finding a place to call home

During your adult life, you need to put a roof over your head. You may be able to sponge off your folks or some other relative or friend for a number of years to cut costs and save money. If you're content with this arrangement, you can minimize your housing costs and save more for a down payment and possibly toward other goals. Go for it, if your friend or relative will!

But what if neither you nor your loved ones are up for the challenge of cohabitating? For the long term, because you need a place to live, why not own real estate instead of renting it? Real estate is the only investment that you can live in or rent to produce income. You can't live in a stock, bond, or mutual fund! Unless you expect to move within the next few years or live in an area where owning costs much more than renting, buying a place probably makes good long-term financial sense. In the long term, owning usually costs less than renting, and it allows you to build equity in an asset. Read Chapter 10 to find out more about profiting from homeownership.

Trying out real estate investment trusts

Real estate investment trusts (REITs) are entities that generally invest in different types of property, such as shopping centers, apartments, and other rental buildings. For a fee, REIT managers identify and negotiate the purchase of properties that they believe are good investments, and then they manage these properties, including all tenant relations. Thus, REITs are a good way to invest in real estate if you don't want the hassles and headaches that come with directly owning and managing rental property.

THINK CAREFULLY BEFORE CONVERTING YOUR HOME INTO A RENTAL

If you move into another home, turning your current home into a rental property may make sense. After all, it saves you the time and cost of finding a separate rental property.

Unfortunately, many people hold on to their current home for the wrong reasons when they buy another. Homeowners often make this mistake when they must sell their homes in a depressed market (such as the one that existed in many areas in the late 2000s). Nobody likes to sell their home for less than they paid for it, so some owners hold on to their homes until prices recover.

If you plan to move and want to keep your current home as a long-term investment property, you can. But turning your home into a short-term rental is usually a bad move for the following reasons:

- You may not want the responsibilities of a landlord, yet you force yourself into the landlord business when you convert your home into a rental.

- If the home eventually does rebound in value, you owe tax on the profit if your property is a rental when you sell it and you don't buy another rental property. You can purchase another rental property through a 1031 exchange to defer paying taxes on your profit. (See the "Roll over those rental property profits" sidebar in this chapter.)

WARNING

Surprisingly, most books that focus on real estate investing neglect REITs. Why? I've come to the conclusion that they overlook these entities for the following reasons:

>> **If you invest in real estate through REITs, you don't need to read a long, complicated book on real estate investment.** Therefore, books often focus on more complicated direct real estate investments (where you buy and own property yourself).

>> **Real estate brokers write many of these books.** Not surprisingly, the real estate investment strategies touted in these books include and advocate the use of such brokers. You can buy REITs without real estate brokers.

>> **A certain snobbishness prevails among people who consider themselves to be "serious" real estate investors.** These folks thumb their noses at the benefit of REITs in an investment portfolio. One real estate writer/investor went so far as to say that REITs aren't "real" real estate investments.

Please. No, you can't drive your friends by a REIT to show it off. But those who put their egos aside when making real estate investments are happy that they considered REITs and have enjoyed double-digit annualized gains over the decades.

You can research and purchase shares in individual REITs, which trade as securities on the major stock exchanges. An even better approach is to buy a mutual fund that invests in a diversified mixture of REITs (see Chapter 8).

In addition to providing you with a diversified, low-hassle real estate investment, REITs offer an additional advantage that traditional rental real estate doesn't: You can easily invest in REITs through a retirement account (for example, an IRA). As with traditional real estate investments, you can even buy REITs and mutual fund REITs with borrowed money. You can buy with 50 percent down, called *buying on margin,* when you purchase such investments through a non-retirement brokerage account.

Evaluating Direct Property Investments

Every year, *Forbes* magazine profiles the 400 wealthiest Americans, known as the *Forbes 400.* To get on the list, you must make the money through legitimate and legal channels (*Forbes* leaves out mobsters and drug kingpins). Numerous people made the most recent list primarily because of their real estate investments. For others on the list, real estate was an important secondary factor that contributed to their wealth.

Consider the case of Thomas Flatley, an Irish immigrant. He was practically broke when he came to the United States in 1950 at age 18. After dabbling in his own small business, he got into real estate development and accumulated thousands of apartments, more than a dozen hotels, and millions of square feet of office and retail space, growing his net worth to more than $1 billion.

If you think you're cut out to be a landlord and are ready for the responsibility of buying, owning, and managing rental real estate, you have lots of direct real estate investment options from which to choose.

TIP

Before you begin this potentially treacherous journey through the process of real estate investing, read Chapter 10. Many concepts that you need to know to be a successful real estate investor are similar to those that you need when you buy a home. The rest of this chapter focuses on issues that are more unique to real estate investing.

Some investors prefer to buy properties, improve them, and then move on. Ideally, however, you should plan to make real estate investments that you hold until (and perhaps through) your retirement years. But what should you buy? The following is my take on various real estate investments.

Residential housing

TIP

Your best bet for real estate investing is to purchase residential property. People always need places to live. Residential housing is easier to understand, purchase, and manage than most other types of property, such as office and retail property. If you're a homeowner, you already have experience locating, purchasing, and maintaining residential property.

The most common residential housing options are single-family homes, condominiums, and townhouses. You can also purchase multi-unit buildings. In addition to the considerations that I address in Chapter 10, from an investment and rental perspective, consider the following issues when you decide what type of property to buy:

>> **Tenants:** Single-family homes with just one tenant (which could be a family, a couple, or a single person) are simpler to deal with than a multiunit apartment building that requires the management and maintenance of multiple renters and units.

>> **Maintenance:** From the property owner's perspective, condominiums are generally the lowest-maintenance properties because most condominium associations deal with issues such as roofing, gardening, and so on for the entire building. Note that as the owner, you're still responsible for

maintenance that's needed inside your unit, such as servicing appliances, interior painting, and so on. Beware, though, that some condo complexes don't allow rentals.

With a single-family home or apartment building, you're responsible for all the maintenance. Of course, you can hire someone to do the work, but you still have to find the contractors and coordinate, oversee, and pay for the work they do.

>> **Appreciation potential:** Look for property where simple cosmetic and other fixes may allow you to increase rents and increase the market value of the property. Although condos may be easier on the unit owner to maintain, they tend to appreciate less than homes or apartment buildings, unless the condos are located in a desirable urban area.

One way to add value to some larger properties is to "condo-ize" them. In some areas, if zoning allows, you can convert a single-family home or multi-unit apartment building into condominiums. Keep in mind, however, that this metamorphosis requires significant research, both on the zoning front as well as with estimating remodeling and construction costs.

>> **Cash flow:** As I discuss in the "Estimating cash flow" section later in the chapter, your rental property brings in rental income that you hope covers and exceeds your expenses. The difference between the rental income that you collect and the expenses that you pay out is known as your *cash flow*. With all properties, as time goes on, generating a positive cash flow gets easier as you pay down your mortgage debt and (hopefully) increase your rents.

WARNING

Unless you can afford a large down payment of 25 percent or more (to help pay down your debt), the early years of rental property ownership may financially challenge you. Making a profit in the early years from the monthly cash flow of a single-family home may be hard because some properties sell at a premium price relative to the rent that they can command. Remember, you pay extra for the land, which you can't rent. Also, the downside to having just one tenant is that when you have a vacancy, you have no rental income.

Apartment buildings, particularly those with more units, can generally produce a small positive cash flow, even in the early years of rental ownership.

REMEMBER

Unless you really want to minimize maintenance responsibilities, avoid condominium investments. Similarly, apartment building investments are best left to sophisticated investors who like a challenge and can manage more-complex properties. Single-family home investments are generally more straightforward for most people. Just make sure you run the numbers on your rental income and expenses to see whether you can afford the negative cash flow that often occurs in the early years of ownership (I show you how in the "Estimating cash flow" section later in this chapter). As I discuss in Chapter 12, do thorough inspections before you buy any rental property.

Land

If tenants are a hassle and maintaining a building is a never-ending pain, you can consider investing in land. To do so, you buy land in an area that will soon experience a building boom, hold on to it until prices soar, and then cash in.

WARNING

Such an investment idea sounds good in theory. In practice, however, making the big bucks through land investments isn't easy. Although land doesn't require upkeep and tenants, it does require financial feeding. Here are some reasons investing in land can be problematic:

>> **Investing in land is a cash drain, and because it costs money to purchase land, you also have a mortgage payment to make.** Mortgage lenders charge higher interest rates on loans to purchase land because they see it as a more speculative investment.

>> **You don't get depreciation tax write-offs because land isn't depreciable.** You also have property tax payments to meet as well as other expenses. However, with land investments, you don't receive income from the property to offset these expenses.

>> **If you decide that you someday want to develop the property, you'll have to fork over a hefty chunk of money.** Obtaining a loan for development is challenging and more expensive (because it's riskier for the lender) than obtaining a loan for a developed property.

>> **Identifying many years in advance which communities will experience rapid population and job growth isn't easy.** Land in those areas that people believe will be the next hot spot already sells at a premium price. If property growth doesn't meet expectations, appreciation will be low or nonexistent.

TIP

If you decide to invest in land, be sure that you

>> **Can afford it:** Tally up the annual carrying costs so you can see what your cash drain may be. What are the financial consequences of this cash outflow? For example, will you be able to fund your tax-advantaged retirement accounts? If you can't, count the lost tax benefits as another cost of owning land.

>> **Understand what further improvements the land needs:** Running utility lines, building roads, landscaping, and so on all cost money. If you plan to develop and build on the land that you purchase, research what these things may cost. Remember that improvements almost always cost more than you expect.

>> **Know its zoning status:** The value of land depends heavily on what you can develop on it. Never purchase land without thoroughly understanding its zoning status and what you can and can't build on it. Also research the disposition of the planning department and nearby communities. Areas that

are antigrowth and antidevelopment are less likely to be good places for you to invest in land, especially if you need permission to do the type of project that you have in mind. Beware that zoning can change for the worse — sometimes a zoning alteration can reduce what you can develop on a property and, consequently, the property's value.

>> **Become familiar with the local economic and housing situations:** In the best of all worlds, buy land in an area that's home to rapidly expanding companies and that has a shortage of housing and developable land. I discuss how to research these issues in the upcoming section "Deciding Where and What to Buy."

Commercial real estate

Ever thought about owning and renting out a small office building or strip mall? If you're really motivated and willing to roll up your sleeves, you may want to consider commercial real estate investments. However, you're generally better off not investing in such real estate because it's much more complicated than investing in residential real estate. It's also riskier from an investment and tenant-turnover perspective. When tenants move out, new tenants sometimes require extensive and costly improvements.

If you're a knowledgeable real estate investor and you like a challenge, here are two good times to invest in commercial real estate:

>> When your analysis of the local market suggests that it's a good time to buy

>> When you can use some of the space to run your own small business

Just as owning your home is generally more cost-effective than renting over the years, so it is with commercial real estate if — and this is a big *if* — you buy at a reasonably good time and hold the property for many years.

INVESTIGATE

So how do you evaluate the state of your local commercial real estate market? Examine the supply-and-demand statistics over recent years. Determine how much space is available for rent and how that number has changed over time. Also discover the vacancy rate, and find out how it has changed in recent years. Finally, investigate the rental rates, usually quoted as a price per square foot. See the next section to find out how to gather this kind of information.

TIP

Here's one sign that purchasing a commercial property in a particular area is not wise: The supply of available space in the market has increased faster than demand, leading to falling rental rates and higher vacancies. A slowing local economy and an increasing unemployment rate also spell trouble for commercial real estate prices. Each market is different, so make sure you check out the details of your area.

Deciding Where and What to Buy

If you're going to invest in real estate, you can do tons of research to decide where and what to buy. Keep in mind, though, that as in other aspects of life, you can spend the rest of your days looking for the perfect real estate investment, never find it, never invest, and miss out on lots of opportunities, profit, and even fun. In the following sections, I explain what to look for in a community and area that you seek to invest in.

REMEMBER

I'm not suggesting that you need to conduct a nationwide search for the best areas. In fact, investing in real estate closer to home is best because you're probably more familiar with the area, allowing you to have an easier time researching and managing the properties.

Considering economic issues

INVESTIGATE

People need places to live, but an area doesn't generally attract homebuyers if jobs don't exist there. Ideally, look to invest in real estate in communities that maintain diverse job bases. If the local economy relies heavily on jobs in a small number of industries, that dependence increases the risk of your real estate investments. The U.S. Bureau of Labor Statistics compiles this type of data for metropolitan areas and counties. Visit www.bls.gov for more information.

Also, consider an area's likelihood of appreciation or depreciation. Determine which industries are more heavily represented in the local economy. If most of the jobs come from slow-growing or shrinking employment sectors, real estate prices are unlikely to rise quickly in the years ahead. On the other hand, areas with a greater preponderance of high-growth industries stand a greater chance of faster price appreciation.

Finally, check out the unemployment situation and examine how the jobless rate has changed in recent years. Good signs to look for are declining unemployment and increasing job growth. The Bureau of Labor Statistics also tracks this data.

Taking a look at the real estate market

The price of real estate, like the price of anything else, is driven by supply and demand. The smaller the supply and the greater the demand, the higher prices climb. An abundance of land and available credit, however, inevitably lead to overbuilding. When the supply of anything expands at a much faster rate than demand, prices usually fall.

Upward pressure on real estate prices tends to be greatest in areas with little buildable land. This characteristic was one of the things that attracted me to invest in real estate in the San Francisco Bay Area decades ago. If you look at a map of this area, you can see that the city of San Francisco and the communities to the south are on a peninsula. Ocean, bay inlets, and mountains bound the rest of the Bay Area. More than 80 percent of the land in the greater Bay Area isn't available for development because state and federal government parks, preserves, and other areas protect the land from development or because the land is impossible to develop. Of the land available for development, nearly all of it in San Francisco and the vast majority of it in nearby counties had been developed.

In the long term, the lack of buildable land in an area can be a problem. Real estate prices that are too high may cause employers and employees to relocate to less expensive areas. If you want to invest in real estate in an area with little buildable land and sky-high prices, run the numbers to see whether the deal makes economic sense. (I explain how to do this later in this chapter.)

INVESTIGATE

In addition to buildable land, consider these other important real estate market indicators to get a sense of the health, or lack thereof, of a particular market:

» **Building permits:** The trend in the number of building permits tells you how the supply of real estate properties may soon change. A long and sustained rise in permits over several years can indicate that the supply of new property may dampen future price appreciation.

» **Vacancy rates:** If few rentals are vacant, you can assume that the area has more competition and demand for existing units, which bodes well for future real estate price appreciation. Conversely, high vacancy rates indicate an excess supply of real estate, which may put downward pressure on rental rates as many landlords compete to attract tenants.

» **Listings of property for sale and number of sales:** Just as the construction of many new buildings is bad for future real estate price appreciation, increasing numbers of property listings are also an indication of potential future trouble. As property prices reach high levels, some investors decide that they can make more money cashing in and investing elsewhere. When the market is flooded with listings, prospective buyers can be choosier, exerting downward pressure on prices. At high prices (relative to the cost of renting), more prospective buyers elect to rent, and the number of sales relative to listings drops.

A sign of a healthy real estate market is a decreasing and relatively low level of property listings, indicating that the demand from buyers meets or exceeds the supply of property for sale from sellers. When the cost of buying is relatively low compared with the cost of renting, more renters can afford and choose to purchase, thus increasing the number of sales.

» **Rents:** The trend in rental rates that renters are willing and able to pay over the years gives a good indication of the demand for housing. When the demand for housing keeps up with the supply of housing and the local economy continues to grow, rents generally increase. This increase is a positive sign for continued real estate price appreciation. Beware of buying rental property subject to rent control; the property's expenses may rise faster than you can raise the rents.

Examining property valuation and financial projections

How do you know what a property is really worth? Some say it's worth what a ready, willing, and financially able buyer is willing to pay. But some buyers pay more than what a property is truly worth. And sometimes buyers who are patient, do their homework, and bargain hard are able to buy property for less than its fair market value.

TIP

REFUTING THE WISDOM OF BUYING IN THE "BEST" AREAS

Some people, particularly those in the real estate business, say, "Buy real estate in the best school districts" or "Buy the least expensive home in the best neighborhood." Such conventional wisdom is sometimes wrong.

Remember that as a real estate investor, you hope to profit from someday selling your properties, many years in the future, for a much higher price than you purchased them. If you buy into the "best," you may not have as much room for price appreciation.

Take school districts, for example. Conventional wisdom says that you should look at the test scores of different districts and buy real estate in the best (that is, highest-scoring) districts. But odds are that real estate in those areas is probably already priced at a premium level. If the situation deteriorates, such an area may experience more decline than an area where property buyers haven't bid prices up into the stratosphere.

The biggest price increases often come from those areas and properties that benefit the most from improvement. Identifying these in advance isn't easy. Look for communities where the trend in recent years has been positive. Even some "average" areas perform better in terms of property value appreciation than today's "best" areas.

TIP

Crunching some numbers to figure what revenue and expenses a rental property may have is one of the most important exercises that you can go through when determining a property's worth and making an offer. In the sections that follow, I walk you through these important calculations.

Estimating cash flow

Cash flow is the money that a property brings in minus what goes out for its expenses. If you pay so much for a property that its expenses (including the mortgage payment and property taxes) consistently exceed its income, you have a money drain on your hands. Maybe you have the financial reserves to withstand the temporary drain for the first few years, but you need to know upfront what you're getting yourself into.

WARNING

Here are two big mistakes that novice rental property investors make:

>> **They fail to realize all the costs associated with investment property.** In the worst cases, some investors end up in personal bankruptcy from the drain of *negative cash flow* (expenses exceeding income). In other cases, negative cash flow hampers investors' ability to accomplish important financial goals.

>> **They believe the financial statements that sellers and their real estate agents prepare.** Just as an employer views a résumé with some skepticism, you should always view such financial statements as advertisements rather than sources of objective information. In some cases, sellers and agents fib or spin things in the most favorable way. In most cases, these statements contain lots of projections and best-case scenarios.

TIP

For property that you're considering purchasing, ask for a copy of Schedule E (Supplemental Income and Losses) from the property seller's federal income tax return. When most people complete their tax returns, in order to minimize their income taxes, they try to minimize their revenue and maximize their expenses — the opposite of what they and their agents normally do on the statements they sometimes compile to hype the property sale. Confidentiality and privacy aren't an issue when you ask for Schedule E because you're asking only for this one schedule and not the person's entire income tax return. (If the seller owns more than one rental property for which financial data is compiled on Schedule E, he can simply black out this other information if he doesn't want you to see it.)

You should prepare financial statements based on facts and a realistic assessment of a property (see Figures 11-1, 11-2, and 11-3). There's a time and a place for unbridled optimism and positive thinking, such as when you're lost in a major snowstorm. But deciding whether to buy a rental property isn't a life-or-death situation. Take your time, and make the decision with your eyes and ears open and with a healthy degree of skepticism.

REMEMBER

The monthly rental-property financial statement that you prepare in Figures 11-1 through 11-3 is for the present. Over time, you hope and expect that your rental income will increase faster than the property's expenses, thus increasing the cash flow. If you want, you can use this financial statement for future years' projections as well.

Valuing property

Estimating a property's cash flow is an important first step to figuring a property's value. But on its own, a building's cash flow doesn't provide enough information to intelligently decide whether to buy a particular real estate investment. Just because a property has a positive cash flow doesn't mean you should buy it. In areas where investors expect to earn lower rates of appreciation, real estate generally sells for less and may have better cash flow.

	Per Month
Rents: Ask for copies of current lease agreements and also check comparable unit rental rates in the local market. Ask if the owner made any *concessions* (such as a month or two of free rent), which may make rental rates appear inflated. Make your offer contingent on the accuracy of the rental rates.	$_____
Garage rentals: Some properties come with parking spaces that the tenants rent. As with unit rental income, make sure that you know what the spaces really rent for.	+$_____
Laundry income: Dirty laundry isn't just on the evening news — it can make you wealthier! Don't underestimate or neglect to include the cost of laundry machine maintenance when you figure the expenses of your rental building.	+$_____
Other income: Other potential income streams for residential properties can include late charges, vending, Internet services, storage, concierge services, and so on. For commercial properties, common area maintenance charges (CAM) and telecommunications income, among other sources, are possible.	+$_____
Vacancy allowance: Keeping any rental occupied all the time is difficult, and finding a good tenant who is looking for the type of unit(s) that you have to offer may take some time. You can do occasional maintenance and refurbishing work in between tenants. Allow for a vacancy rate of 5 to 10 percent (multiply 5 to 10 percent by the rent figured in the first line).	–$_____
TOTAL INCOME	=$_____

FIGURE 11-1:
Monthly rental-property financial statement (Page 1 of 3).

	Per Month
Mortgage: Enter your expected mortgage payment.	$_____
Property taxes: Ask a real estate person, mortgage lender, or your local assessor's office what your annual property tax bill would be for a rental property of comparable value to the one that you're considering buying. Divide this annual amount by 12 to arrive at your monthly property tax bill.	+$_____
Utilities: Get copies of utility bills from the current owner. Get bills over the previous 12-month period — a few months won't cut it because utility usage may vary greatly during different times of the year. (In a multi-unit building, it's a plus for each unit to have a separate utility meter so that you can bill each tenant for what he/she uses.)	+$_____
Insurance: Ask for a copy of the current insurance coverage and billing statement from the current owner. If you're considering buying a building in an area that has floods, earthquakes, and so on, make sure that the cost of the policy includes these coverages. Although you can insure against most catastrophes, I would avoid buying property in a flood-prone area. Flood insurance does not cover lost rental income.	+$_____
Water: Again, ask the current owner for statements that document water costs over the past 12 months.	+$_____
Garbage: Get the bills for the last 12 months from the owner.	+$_____
Repairs/maintenance/cleaning: You can ask the current owner what to expect and check the tax return, but even doing this may provide an inaccurate answer. Some building owners defer maintenance. (A good property inspector can help to ferret out problem areas before you commit to buying a property.) Estimate that you'll spend at least 1 to 2 percent of the purchase price per year on maintenance, repairs, and cleaning. Remember to divide your annual estimate by 12!	+$_____
Rental advertising/management expenses: Finding good tenants takes time and promotion. If you list your rental through rental brokers, they normally take one month's rent as their cut. Owners of larger buildings sometimes have an on-site manager to show vacant units and deal with maintenance and repairs. Put the monthly pay for that person on this line or the preceding line. If you provide a below-market rental rate for an on-site manager, make sure that you factor this into the rental income section.	+$_____
Extermination/pest control: Once a year or every few years, you likely need to take care of pest control. Spraying and/or inspections generally start at $200 for small buildings.	+$_____
Legal, accounting, and other professional services: Especially with larger rental properties, you'll likely need to consult with lawyers and tax advisors from time to time.	+$_____
TOTAL EXPENSES	=$_____

FIGURE 11-2: Monthly rental-property financial statement (Page 2 of 3).

(continued)

© *John Wiley & Sons, Inc.*

(continued)

	Per Month
Total Income (from Page 1)	$_____
Total Expenses (from Page 2)	–$_____
CASH FLOW (Pre-tax Profit or Loss)	=$_____
Depreciation: The tax law allows you to claim a yearly tax deduction for depreciation, but remember that you can't depreciate land. Break down the purchase of your rental property between the building and land. You can make this allocation based on the assessed value for the land and the building or on a real estate appraisal. Residential property is depreciated over **27½** years (3.64 percent of the building value per year), and nonresidential property is depreciated over 39 years (2.56 percent of the building value per year). For example, if you buy a residential rental property for $300,000 and $200,000 of that is allocated to the building, that means that you can take $7,273 per year as a depreciation tax deduction ($200,000 x 0.0364).	–$_____
NET INCOME	=$_____

FIGURE 11-3: Monthly rental-property financial statement (Page 3 of 3).

Important note: *Although depreciation is a deduction that helps you reduce your profit for tax purposes, it doesn't actually cost you money. Your cash flow from a rental property is the revenue minus your out-of-pocket expenses.*

© John Wiley & Sons, Inc.

In the stock market, you have more clues about a specific security's worth. Most companies' stocks trade on a daily basis, so you at least have a recent sales price to start with. Of course, just because a stock recently traded at $20 per share doesn't mean that it's worth $20 per share. Investors may be overly optimistic or pessimistic.

Just as you should evaluate a stock versus other comparable stocks, so, too, should you compare the asking price of a property with the prices of comparable real estate. But what if all real estate is overvalued? Such a comparison doesn't reveal the state of inflated prices. So in addition to comparing a real estate investment property to comparable properties, you need to perform some local area evaluations of whether prices from a historic perspective appear too high, too low, or just right. To answer this last question, see Chapter 10.

Here are the pros and cons of the different approaches you can use to value property:

>> **Appraisers:** The biggest advantage of hiring an appraiser is that she values property for a living. An appraisal also gives you some hard numbers to use for negotiating with a seller. Hire a full-time appraiser who has experience valuing the type of property that you're considering. Ask her for examples of a dozen similar properties in the area that she has appraised in the past three months.

The drawback of appraisers is that they cost money. A small home may cost several hundred dollars to appraise, and a larger multi-unit building may cost

$1,000 or more. The danger is that you can spend money on an appraisal for a building that you don't end up buying.

>> **Real estate agents:** If you work with a good real estate agent (I discuss how to find one in Chapter 12), ask him to draw up a list of comparable properties and help you estimate the value of the property that you're considering buying. The advantage of having your agent help with this analysis is that you don't pay extra for this service.

WARNING

The drawback of asking an agent what to pay for a property is that his commission depends on your buying a property and on the amount that you pay for that property. The more you're willing to pay for a property, the more likely the deal is completed, and the more the agent makes on commission.

>> **Do-it-yourself:** If you're comfortable with numbers and analysis, you can try to estimate the value of a property yourself. The hard part is identifying comparable properties. Finding identical properties is usually impossible, so you need to find similar properties and then make adjustments to their selling prices so you can do an apples-to-apples comparison.

Among the factors that should influence your analysis of comparable properties are the date each property sold; the quality of the location; the lot size; the building age and condition; the number of units; the number of rooms, bedrooms, and bathrooms; the number of garages and fireplaces; and the size of the yard. A real estate agent can provide this information, or you can track it down for properties that you've seen or that you know have recently sold.

Through a series of price adjustments, you can then compare the value of your target property to others that have recently sold. For example, if a similar property sold six months ago for $250,000 but prices overall have decreased 3 percent in the last six months, subtract 3 percent from the sales price. Ultimately, you have to attach a value or price to each difference between comparable properties and the one that you're considering buying.

TIP

These approaches for valuing property aren't mutually exclusive. Obtain the numbers and analysis that an appraiser or real estate agent puts together.

Discovering the information you need

When you evaluate properties, you need to put on your detective hat. If you're creative and inquisitive, you soon realize that this isn't a hard game to play. You can collect useful information about a property and the area in which it's located in many ways.

TIP

Begin your inquiries with the real estate agent who listed the property for sale. One thing that most agents love to do is talk and schmooze. Try to understand why the seller is selling. This knowledge helps you negotiate an offer that's appealing to the seller.

As for specifics on the property's financial situation, ask the sellers for specific independent documents, including Schedule E from their tax return. (See the earlier section "Estimating cash flow" for more information.) Hire inspectors to investigate the property's physical condition (I advise you on hiring inspectors in Chapter 12).

Local government organizations can be treasure-troves of information about their communities. Check out the other recommended sources in Chapter 10 as well as those that I suggest earlier in this chapter.

Digging for a Good Deal

Everyone likes to get a deal or feel like they bought something at a relatively low price. How else can you explain the American retail practice of sales? Merchandise is first overpriced, and what doesn't sell quickly enough is then marked down to create the illusion that you're getting a bargain! Some real estate sellers and agents do the same thing. They list property for sale at an inflated price and then mark it down after they realize that no one will pay their asking price. "A $30,000 price reduction!" the new listing screams. Of course, such reductions aren't a deal.

REMEMBER

It's possible to get a good buy on a problem property that provides a discount larger than the cost of fixing the property. However, these opportunities are hard to find, and sellers of such properties are often unwilling to sell at a discount that's big enough to leave you much room for profit. If you don't know how to thoroughly and correctly evaluate the property's problems, you can end up overpaying.

Scores of books claim to have the real estate investment strategy that can beat the system. Often these promoters claim that you can become a multimillionaire through investing in distressed properties. A common suggested strategy is to purchase property that a seller has defaulted on or is about to default on. Or how about buying a property in someone's estate through probate court? Maybe you'd like to try your hand at investing in a property that has been condemned or has toxic-waste contamination!

In some cases, the strategies that these real estate gurus advocate involve taking advantage of people's lack of knowledge. For example, some people don't know that they can protect the equity in their home through filing for personal bankruptcy. If you can find a seller in such dire financial straits and desperate for cash, you may get a bargain buy on the home. (You may struggle with the moral issues of buying property cheaply this way, however.)

Other methods of finding discounted property take lots of time and digging. Some involve cold-calling property owners to see whether they're interested in selling.

This method is a little bit like trying to fill a job opening by interviewing people you run into on a street corner. Although you may eventually find a good candidate this way, if you factor in the value of your time, the deal seems like less of a bargain.

Without making things complicated or too risky, you can use some of the following time-tested and proven ways to buy real estate at a discount to its fair market value:

>> **Find a motivated seller.** Be patient and look at lots of properties, and sooner or later you'll come across one that someone needs to sell (and these aren't necessarily the ones advertised as having motivated sellers). Perhaps the seller has bought another property and needs the money to close on the recent purchase. Having access to sufficient financing can help secure such deals.

>> **Buy unwanted properties with fixable flaws.** The easiest problems to correct are cosmetic. Some sellers and their agents are lazy and don't even bother to clean a property. One single-family home that I bought had probably three years' worth of cobwebs and dust accumulated. It seemed like a dungeon at night because half the light bulbs were burned out.

Painting; tearing up old, ugly carpeting; refinishing hardwood floors; and putting new plantings in a yard are relatively easy jobs. They make the property worth more and make renters willing to pay higher rent. Of course, these tasks take money and time, and many buyers aren't interested in dealing with problems. If you have an eye for improving property and are willing to invest the time that coordinating the fix-up work requires, go for it! Just make sure you hire someone to conduct a thorough property inspection before you buy. (See Chapter 12 for details.)

WARNING

Be sure to factor in the loss of rental income if you can't fully rent the property during the fix-up period. Some investors have gone belly up from the double cash drain of fix-up expenses and lost rents.

>> **Buy when the real estate market is depressed.** When the economy takes a few knocks and investors rush for the exits (as in the late 2000s downturn), it's time to go shopping! Buy real estate when prices and investor interest are down. Interest rates are usually lower then too. During times of depressed markets, obtaining properties that produce a positive cash flow (even in the early years) is easier. In Chapter 10, I explain how to spot a depressed market.

>> **Check for zoning opportunities.** Sometimes you can make more productive use of a property. For example, you can legally convert some multi-unit apartment buildings into condominiums. Some single-family residences may include a rental unit if local zoning allows for it. A good real estate agent, contractor, and the local planning office in the town or city where you're looking at the property can help you identify properties that you can convert. However, if you're not a proponent of development, you probably won't like this strategy.

REMEMBER

If you buy good real estate and hold it for the long term, you can earn a healthy return from your investment. Over the long haul, having bought a property at a discount becomes an insignificant issue. You make money from your real estate investments as the market appreciates and as a result of your ability to manage your property well. So don't obsess over buying property at a discount and don't wait for the perfect deal, because it won't always come along.

Recognizing Inferior Real Estate "Investments"

Some supposedly "simple" ways to invest in real estate rarely make sense because they're near-certain money losers. In this section, I discuss real estate investments that you should generally (but not always) avoid.

Avoiding ticking time shares

WARNING

Time shares are near-certain money losers. With a time share, you buy a week or two of ownership or usage of a particular unit, usually a condominium, in a resort location. If you pay $8,000 for a week of "ownership," you would pay the equivalent of more than $400,000 a year for the whole unit ($8,000/week × 52 weeks). However, a comparable unit nearby may sell for only $150,000. The extra markup pays the salespeople's commissions, administrative expenses, and profits for the time-share development company. (This little analysis also ignores the not-so-inconsequential ongoing time-share maintenance fees.)

People usually get hoodwinked into buying a time share when they're enjoying a vacation someplace. Vacationers are easy prey for salespeople who, often using high-pressure sales tactics, want to sell them a souvenir of the trip. The cheese in the mousetrap is an offer of something free (for example, a free night's stay in a unit) for sitting through a sales presentation.

TIP

If you can't live without a time share, consider buying a used one. Many previous buyers, who almost always have lost much of their original investment, try to dump their time shares. (This fact tells you that time shares are a crummy investment.) You may be able to buy a time share from an existing owner at a fair price, but why commit yourself to taking a vacation in the same location and building at the same time each year? Many time shares let you trade your weeks; however, doing so is a hassle, and you're limited by what time slots you can trade for, which are typically dates that other people don't want.

KEEPING A SECOND HOME

Some folks dream of having a weekend cottage or condo — a place they can retreat to when crowded urban or suburban living conditions get on their nerves. When their vacation home isn't in use, they may decide to rent it out to earn some income to help defray part of the maintenance expenses.

If you can realistically afford the additional costs of a second, or vacation, home, I'm not going to tell you how to spend your money. *Investment real estate* is property that you rent out 90 percent or more of the time. Most second-home owners I know rent out their property very little — 10 percent or less of the time. As a result, second homes are usually money drains. Even if you do rent your second home most of the time, high tenant turnover decreases your net rental income.

I've seen some people make a decent return with second homes that were infrequently rented. Usually these homes are held over many years and are located in areas that have become increasingly popular.

Part of the allure of a second home is the supposed tax benefits. Even when you qualify for some or all of them, tax benefits only partially reduce the cost of owning a property. I've seen more than a few cases in which the second home is such a cash drain that it prevents its owners from contributing to and taking advantage of tax-deductible retirement savings plans.

If you don't rent out a second home most of the time, ask yourself whether you can afford such a luxury. Can you accomplish your other financial goals — saving for retirement, paying for the home in which you live, and so on — with this added expense? Keeping a second home is more of a consumption than an investment decision.

Staying away from limited partnerships

In Chapter 2, I give you good reasons to avoid limited partnerships. High sales commissions and ongoing management fees burden limited partnerships sold through stockbrokers and financial planners who work on commission. Quality real estate investment trusts (REITs), which I discuss earlier in this chapter, are infinitely better alternatives. REITs, unlike limited partnerships, are also completely liquid.

Ignoring hucksters and scams

WARNING

Real estate investors with lofty expectations for high returns become bait for various hucksters who promise these investors great riches. It's bad enough when the deck is stacked against you. Even worse is putting your money into scams.

In the following sections, I provide some examples of hucksters and scams that could severely hamper your financial success. Take heed, my friend.

REMEMBER

If an investment "opportunity" sounds too good to be true, it is. If you want to invest in real estate, avoid the hucksters and scams and instead invest directly in properties that you can control or invest through reputable REITs (or REIT mutual funds), which I discuss earlier in this chapter.

Don't believe the hucksters

Cable television infomercials (and now websites) bring investors a never-ending stream of real estate hucksters. The faces and names change over the years, but the pitch is the same. If you're a cable television viewer, you've likely seen the chirpy Dean Graziosi and his lengthy real estate infomercials on various cable television channels, including CNBC. Graziosi claims that he can teach you to make great riches investing in real estate without putting up any of your own money.

Graziosi has been selling advice since 1999. He started with advice about inspecting a car with his CarPro VHS tapes. However, Graziosi didn't have the expertise — he interviewed an experienced auto mechanic. He then pitched a program on television called *Motor Millions,* which he claimed could help folks break into the billion-dollar used car market and make an easy profit to "make your dreams a reality." Graziosi has been selling his book *Profit from Real Estate Right Now! The Proven No Money Down System for Today's Market.* Over the years, Graziosi has written and promoted other real estate books with similar content.

If the descriptions of these programs and books aren't enough to make you run in the other direction, Graziosi also appears to have no training or educational background to qualify him for his self-anointed real-estate guru status. In his books and through interviews, Graziosi says that he "chose" not to go to college and got started in the working world by joining his father in his small car business. That business, according to Graziosi, subsequently failed.

In the mid-2000s, Graziosi began flogging various real estate programs to the public. The books, audio tapes, and DVDs I've reviewed are filled with excessive motivational nonsense wherein Graziosi preaches about the importance of having the right mindset and attitude to succeed as a real estate investor. He provides little in the way of details and how-to information. It turns out that there's a good reason for this lack of information (besides his lack of training and experience). After customers buy a book or DVD set directly from his company, his salespeople use high-pressure tactics to sell personal real estate coaching services for thousands of dollars.

Graziosi's lack of experience and lack of common sense are exposed many times in his publications. Consider the following:

>> In *Profit from Real Estate Right Now!* he claims that when he saw a real estate agent putting up a for sale sign on a $525,000 house across the street from a home he already owned, he did a quick walk-through of the property and immediately wrote a near full-price purchase offer. In that offer, he claimed to buy the home as-is without having it professionally inspected. This tactic is dangerous for anyone who isn't a contractor and an expert on all the operating systems of a home. Graziosi clearly lacks this expertise; his not telling the reader the importance of doing such an inspection is a horrible oversight.

>> Recent years have shown that Graziosi changes his stripes and story. In the mid-2000s, he encouraged taking out risky mortgages and layering on heavy debts. The real estate market slide in the late 2000s exposed the dangers in that short-sighted approach.

Now that real estate prices have corrected significantly in most parts of the country, Graziosi is claiming that his system enables novice investors to take advantage of low prices and depressed market conditions. Graziosi suggests that people buy foreclosures (for no money down, of course) and then rent out the property. He also claims that by getting such good deals when you buy foreclosed property, you can refinance and pull lots of cash out of your property and buy more. If you believe this idea is simplistic and naïve, go to the head of the class! Most foreclosures happen in highly depressed areas where decent renters are hard to come by. And it's wishful thinking to expect that you'll get such a steal on a property that you can turn around and find a lender willing to do a refinancing that enables you to pull out cash.

Stand strong against the scams

In addition to hucksters, the real estate field has outright scams you should be on guard against. Here are just a few examples:

>> First Pension was an outfit run by loan broker William Cooper, who bilked investors out of more than $100 million. First Pension was sold as a limited partnership that invested in mortgages. Using a Ponzi-type scheme, Cooper used the money from new investors to pay dividends to earlier investors.

>> New York attorney Alan Harris defrauded real estate investors (including actress Shirley Jones) out of millions of dollars when he pocketed money that was set aside for property investments. The lure: Harris promised investors far higher yields than they could get elsewhere.

>> Stephen Murphy, a real estate investor who claimed to make a fortune by buying foreclosed commercial real estate, wrote and self-published a book to share his techniques with the public. Murphy's organization called the people who bought his book and pitched them into collaborating with him on property purchases that supposedly would return upwards of 100 percent or more per year. However, Murphy had other ideas, and he siphoned off nearly two-thirds of the money for himself and for promotion of his books! He even hoodwinked Donald Trump into writing praise for his book and work.

>> Time shares, a truly terrible investment that I discuss earlier in this chapter, have also been subject to bankruptcy and fraud problems.

Chapter 12

Real Estate Financing and Deal Making

I n this chapter, I discuss issues such as understanding and selecting mortgages, working with real estate agents, negotiating, and other important details that help you put a real estate deal together. I also provide some words of wisdom about taxes and selling your property that may come in handy down the road. (In Chapter 10, I cover what you need to know to purchase a home, and in Chapter 11, I review the fundamentals of investing in real estate.)

Financing Your Real Estate Investments

Unless you're affluent or buying a low-cost property, you likely need to borrow some money via a mortgage to make the purchase happen. Without financing, your dream to invest in real estate remains just that: a dream. So first you have to maximize your chances of getting approved for a loan, which has become harder since the real estate market downturn in the late 2000s. Shopping wisely for a good mortgage can save you thousands, perhaps even tens of thousands, of dollars in extra interest and fees. Don't get saddled with a loan that you may not be able to afford someday and that could push you into foreclosure or bankruptcy.

Getting your loan approved

Even if you have perfect or near-perfect credit, you may encounter financing problems with some properties. And, of course, not all real estate buyers have a perfect credit history, tons of available cash, and no debt. Because of the soft real estate market in the late 2000s and the jump in foreclosures since that time, lenders tightened credit standards to avoid making loans to people likely to default. If you're one of those borrowers who ends up jumping through more hoops than others to get a loan, don't give up hope. Few borrowers are perfect from a lender's perspective, and many problems are fixable.

TIP

To head off some potential rejections before you apply for a loan, disclose to your lender anything that may cause a problem. For example, if you already know that your credit report indicates some late payments from when you were out of the country for several weeks five years ago, write a letter that explains this situation.

Solving down payment problems

Most people, especially when they make their first real estate purchase, are strapped for cash. In order to qualify for the most attractive financing, lenders typically require that your down payment be at least 20 percent of the property's purchase price. Investment property loans sometimes require 25 to 30 percent down for the best terms. In addition, you need reserve money to pay for other closing costs, such as title insurance and loan fees.

TIP

If you don't have 20-plus percent of a property's purchase price available, don't despair. You can still own real estate with the following strategies:

>> **Take out private mortgage insurance.** Some lenders may offer you a mortgage even though you can put down only, say, 10 percent of the purchase price. These lenders will likely require you to purchase *private mortgage insurance* (PMI) for your loan, however. This insurance generally costs a few hundred dollars per year and protects the lender if you default on your loan. When you have at least 20 percent equity in the property, you can generally eliminate the PMI.

>> **Dip into your retirement savings.** You may be able to borrow against your retirement account balance through your employer's retirement savings plan under the condition that you repay the loan within a set number of years. Subject to eligibility requirements, first-time homebuyers can make penalty-free withdrawals of up to $10,000 from IRA accounts. (**Note:** You still must pay regular income tax on the withdrawal.)

>> **Postpone your purchase.** If you don't want the cost and strain of extra fees and bad mortgage terms, you can also postpone your purchase. Go on a financial austerity program and boost your savings rate.

>> **Consider lower-priced properties.** Lower-priced properties can help keep down the purchase price and the required down payment.

>> **Find a partner.** Sharing the financial load with a partner often makes buying real estate easier. Just make sure you write up a legal contract to specify what happens if a partner wants out. Family members sometimes make good partners. Your parents, grandparents, and even your siblings may have some extra cash they'd like to loan, invest, or give to you as a gift!

>> **Look into seller financing.** Some property owners or developers may finance your purchase with as little as 5 to 10 percent down. However, you can't be as picky about such seller-financed properties because a limited supply is available. Many that are available need work or haven't yet sold for other reasons.

Improving your credit score

Late payments, missed payments, or debts that you never bothered to pay can tarnish your credit report and squelch a lender's desire to offer you a mortgage. If you're turned down for a loan because of your less-than-stellar credit history, find out the details of why by requesting (at no charge to you) a copy of your credit report from the lender that turned down your loan.

TIP

If you think that your credit history may be a problem as you're looking for a loan, the first thing to do is get the facts. By law, you're entitled to one free credit report per year from each of the three consumer credit reporting companies — Equifax, Experian, and TransUnion. You can get all three reports at once or space them out throughout the year (checking in on one each at four-month intervals). The companies have set up one central website where you can access these reports (www.annualcreditreport.com), or you can call toll-free at 877-322-8228. Just be careful not to buy the ongoing credit services these companies will pitch you.

If you do find credit report problems, explain them to your lender. If the lender is unsympathetic, try calling other lenders. Tell them your credit problems upfront and see whether you can find one willing to offer you a loan. Mortgage brokers may also be able to help you shop for lenders in these cases. (I discuss working with mortgage brokers later in this chapter.)

Sometimes you may feel that you're not in control when you apply for a loan. In reality, however, you can fix a number of credit problems yourself, and you reap great rewards (access to better loan terms, including lower interest rates) for doing so. And you can often explain those that you can't fix. Remember that some lenders are more lenient and flexible than others. Just because one mortgage lender rejects your loan application doesn't mean that all the others will as well.

If you discover erroneous information on your credit report, get on the phone to the credit bureaus and start squawking. If specific creditors are the culprits, call them, too. Keep notes from your conversations and make sure that you put your case in writing and add your comments to your credit report. If the customer service representatives you talk with are no help, send a letter to the president of each company. Let the head honcho know that his or her organization caused you problems in obtaining credit. For more information on examining and disputing items on your credit report and managing credit in general, check out the Federal Trade Commission's website at www.ftc.gov/credit.

Besides late or missed payments, another common credit problem is having too much consumer debt at the time you apply for a mortgage. The more consumer debt you rack up (including credit card and auto loan debt), the less mortgage credit you qualify for. If you're turned down for a mortgage, consider it a wake-up call to get rid of your high-cost debt. Hang on to the dream of buying real estate and plug away at paying off your debts before you attempt another foray into real estate.

To find out more about how credit scores work and techniques to improve yours, see the latest edition of my book *Personal Finance For Dummies* (Wiley).

Dealing with low appraisals

Even if you have sufficient income, a clean credit report, and an adequate down payment, a lender may deny your loan if the appraisal of the property that you want to buy comes in lower than you agreed to pay for the property.

If you still like the property, renegotiate a lower price with the seller by using the low appraisal to strengthen your case. You need to follow a different path should you encounter a low appraisal on a property that you already own and are refinancing. If you have the cash available, you can simply put more money down to get the loan balance to a level for which you qualify. If you don't have the cash, you may need to try another lender or forgo the refinance until you save more money or until the property value rises. (I discuss refinancing in more detail later in this chapter.)

Handling insufficient income

If you're self-employed or have changed jobs, your current income may not resemble your past income or, more importantly, your income may be below what a mortgage lender likes to see given the amount that you want to borrow. A way around this problem, although challenging, is to make a larger down payment.

If you can't make a large down payment, another option is to get a cosigner for the loan. For example, your relatives may be willing to sign with you. As long as they aren't overextended themselves, they may be able to help you qualify for a larger loan than you can get on your own. As with partnerships, put your agreement in writing so that no misunderstandings occur.

Comparing fixed-rate with adjustable-rate mortgages

Two major types of mortgages exist: those with a fixed interest rate and those with an adjustable rate. Your choice depends on your financial situation, how much risk you're willing to accept, and the type of property you want to purchase. For example, obtaining a fixed-rate loan on a property that lenders perceive as a riskier investment is more difficult than getting an adjustable-rate mortgage for the same property.

Locking into fixed-rate mortgages

Fixed-rate mortgages, which are typically for a 15- or 30-year term, have interest rates that stay fixed or level — you lock in an interest rate that doesn't change over the life of your loan. Because the interest rate stays the same, your monthly mortgage payment stays the same. You have nothing complicated to track and no uncertainty. Fixed-rate loans give people peace of mind and payment stability.

WARNING

Fixed-rate mortgages do, however, carry risks. If interest rates fall significantly after you obtain your mortgage and you're unable to refinance, you face the danger of being stuck with a higher-cost mortgage, which could be problematic if you lose your job or the value of your property decreases. (This scenario — declining interest rates and falling real estate values — happened to plenty of people in the late 2000s.) Even if you're able to refinance, you'll probably have to spend significant time and money to complete the paperwork.

Understanding adjustable-rate mortgages (ARMs)

In contrast to a fixed-rate mortgage, an *adjustable-rate mortgage* (ARM) carries an interest rate that varies over time (based on a formula the lender establishes). Such a mortgage begins with one interest rate, and you may pay different rates for every year, possibly even every month, that you hold the loan. Thus, the size of your monthly payment fluctuates. Because a mortgage payment makes a large dent in most property owners' checkbooks, signing up for an ARM without fully understanding it is fiscally foolish.

The advantage of an ARM is that if you purchase your property during a period of higher interest rates, you can start paying your mortgage with a relatively low initial interest rate, compared with fixed-rate loans. (With a fixed-rate mortgage, a mortgage lender takes extra risk in committing to a fixed interest rate for 15 to 30 years. To be compensated for accepting this additional risk, lenders charge a premium with fixed-rate mortgages in case interest rates, which they have to pay on their source of funds in the form of deposits, move much higher in future years.) If interest rates decline, an ARM allows you to capture many of the benefits of lower rates without the cost and hassle of refinancing.

⚠ BEWARE OF BALLOON LOANS

WARNING

Balloon loans generally start the way traditional fixed-rate mortgages start. You make level payments based on a long-term payment schedule — over 15 or 30 years, for example. But at a predetermined time, usually within 10 years of the loan's inception, the remaining loan balance becomes fully due.

Balloon loans may save you money because they have a lower interest rate than a longer-term fixed-rate mortgage and you pay that interest over a shorter period of time. However, balloon loans are dangerous — your financial situation can change, and you may not be able to refinance when your balloon loan is due. What if you lose your job or your income drops? What if the value of your property drops and the appraisal comes in too low to qualify you for a new loan? What if interest rates rise and you can't qualify at the higher rate on a new loan? You're still going to have to pay off your balloon loan when it comes due.

Sometimes, balloon loans may be the only option for the buyer (or so the buyer thinks). Buyers are more commonly backed into these loans during periods of high interest rates. When a buyer can't afford the payments on a conventional mortgage and really wants a particular property, a seller may offer a balloon loan.

Shun balloon loans. Consider a balloon loan if, and only if, such a loan is your only financing option, you've really done your homework to exhaust other financing alternatives, and you're certain that you can refinance when the balloon comes due. If you take a balloon loan, get one with as much time as possible, preferably ten years, before it becomes due.

Choosing between fixed and adjustable mortgages

You can't predict the future course of interest rates. Even the professional financial market soothsayers and investors can't predict where rates are heading. If you could foretell interest rate movements, you could make a fortune investing in bonds and interest-rate futures and options. So cast aside your crystal ball and ask yourself the following two vital questions to decide whether a fixed or adjustable mortgage will work best for you.

How comfortable are you with taking risk?

How much of a gamble can you take with the size of your monthly mortgage payment? For example, if your job and income are unstable and you need to borrow an amount that stretches your monthly budget, you can't afford much risk. If you're in this situation, stick with fixed-rate mortgages because you likely won't be able to handle a large increase in interest rates and the payment on an ARM.

If, on the other hand, you're in a position to take the financial risks that come with an adjustable-rate mortgage, you have a better chance of saving money with an adjustable loan rather than a fixed-rate loan. Your interest rate starts lower and stays lower if the market level of interest rates remains unchanged. Even if rates go up, they'll likely come back down over the life of your loan. If you can stick with your adjustable-rate loan for better and for worse, you may come out ahead in the long run.

Adjustables also make more sense if you borrow less than you're qualified for. Or perhaps you regularly save a sizable chunk — more than 10 percent — of your monthly income. If your income significantly exceeds your spending, you may feel less anxiety about fluctuating interest rates. If you do choose an adjustable loan, you may be more financially secure if you have a hefty financial cushion (at least six months' to as much as a year's worth of expenses reserved) that you can access if rates go up.

TIP

Almost all adjustables limit, or *cap,* the rise in the interest rate that your loan allows. Typical caps are 2 percent per year and 6 percent over the life of the loan. Ask your lender to calculate the highest possible monthly payment that your loan allows. The number that the lender comes up with is the *lifetime cap,* the payment that you face if the interest rate on your loan goes to the highest level allowed. If you can't afford the highest-allowed payment on an adjustable-rate mortgage, don't take one. You shouldn't take the chance that the rate won't rise that high — it can, and you could lose the property.

REMEMBER

Don't take an adjustable mortgage just because the lower initial interest rates allow you to afford the property that you want to buy (unless you're absolutely certain that your income will rise to meet future payment increases). Instead, try setting your sights on a property that you can afford to buy with a fixed-rate mortgage.

How many years do you expect to stay put?

Saving interest on most adjustables is usually a certainty in the first two or three years. By nature, an adjustable-rate mortgage starts at a lower interest rate than a fixed-rate mortgage. However, if rates rise while you hold an ARM, you can end up giving back the savings that you achieve in the early years of the mortgage.

TIP

If you aren't going to keep your mortgage for more than five to seven years, you'll probably end up paying more interest to carry a fixed-rate mortgage. Also consider a hybrid loan, which combines features of fixed- and adjustable-rate mortgages. For example, the initial rate may hold constant for several years and then adjust once a year or every six months thereafter. Such loans may make sense for you if you foresee a high probability of keeping your loan seven years or less but want some stability in your monthly payments. The longer the initial rate stays locked in, the higher the interest rate.

Landing a great fixed-rate mortgage

You may think that comparing one fixed-rate loan to another is simple because the interest rate on a fixed-rate loan is the rate that you pay every month over the entire life of the loan. And as with your golf score and the number of times that your boss catches you showing up late for work, a lower number (or interest rate) is better, right?

Unfortunately, banks generally charge an upfront interest fee, known as *points*, in addition to the ongoing interest over the life of the loan. Points are actually percentages: One point is equal to 1 percent of the loan amount. So when a lender tells you a quoted loan has 1.5 points, you pay 1.5 percent of the amount you borrow as points. On a $100,000 loan, for example, 1.5 points cost you $1,500. The interest rate on a fixed-rate loan must always be quoted with the points on the loan, if the loan has points.

TIP

You may want to take a higher interest rate on your mortgage if you don't have enough cash to pay for a lot of points, which you pay upfront when you close the loan. On the other hand, if you're willing and able to pay more points, you can lower your interest rate. You may want to pay more points because the interest rate on your loan determines your payments over a long period of time — 15 to 30 years.

Suppose that one lender quotes you a rate of 5.75 percent on a 30-year fixed-rate loan and charges one point (1 percent). Another lender, which quotes 6 percent for 30 years, doesn't charge any points. Which is better? The answer depends on how long you plan to keep the loan.

The 5.75 percent loan is 0.25 percent less than the 6 percent loan. However, it takes you about four years to earn back the savings to cover the cost of that point because you have to pay 1 percent (one point) upfront on the 5.75 percent loan. So if you expect to keep the loan more than four years, go with the 5.75 percent option. If you plan to keep the loan less than four years, go with the 6 percent option.

TIP

To make it easier to perform an apples-to-apples comparison of mortgages from different lenders, get interest rate quotes at the same point level. For example, ask each lender for the interest rate on a loan for which you pay one point. And remember that if a loan has no points, it's sure to have a higher interest rate. I'm not saying that no-point loans are better or worse than comparable loans from other lenders. Just don't get sucked into a loan because of a no-points sales pitch. Lenders who spend big bucks on advertising these types of loans rarely have the best mortgage terms.

All things being equal, no-point loans make more sense for refinances because points aren't immediately tax-deductible as they are on purchases. (You can deduct the points that you pay on a refinance *only* over the life of the mortgage.)

On a mortgage for a property that you're purchasing, a no-point loan may help if you're cash poor at closing.

Consider a no-point loan if you can't afford more out-of-pocket expenditures now or if you think that you'll keep the loan only a few years. Shop around and compare different lenders' no-point loans.

Finding a suitable adjustable-rate mortgage

Selecting an ARM has a lot in common with selecting a home to buy. You need to make trade-offs and compromises. In the following sections, I explain the numerous features and options — caps, indexes, margins, and adjustment periods — that you find with ARMs (these aren't issues with fixed-rate loans).

Getting off to a good start rate

WARNING

Just as the name implies, your *start rate* is the rate that your adjustable mortgage begins with. Think of the start rate as a teaser rate — the initial rate on ARMs is often set artificially low to entice you. Don't judge an ARM by this rate alone. You won't pay this attractively low rate for long. With ARMs, interest rates generally rise as soon as the terms of the mortgage allow. Even if the market level of interest rates doesn't change, your adjustable rate is destined to increase. An increase of 1 or 2 percentage points is common.

The formula for determining the rate caps and the future interest rates on an adjustable-rate mortgage (see the next section) are far more important in determining what a mortgage will cost you in the long run. For more on rate caps, see the section "Analyzing adjustments," later in this chapter.

Determining your future interest rate

The first thing you need to ask a mortgage lender or broker about an adjustable rate is the exact formula they use for determining the future interest rate on your particular loan. You need to know how a lender figures your interest rate changes over the life of your loan. All adjustables are based on the following general formula, which specifies how the interest rate is set on your loan in the future:

Index + Margin = Interest rate

The *index* determines the base level of interest rates that the mortgage contract specifies in order to calculate the specific interest rate for your loan. Indexes are generally (but not always) widely quoted in the financial press.

For example, suppose that the current index value for a given loan is equal to the 6-month Treasury bill index, which is, say, 2 percent. The *margin* is the amount added to the index to determine the interest rate that you pay on your mortgage. Most loans have margins of around 2.5 percent. Thus, the rate of a mortgage driven by the following formula

6-month Treasury bill rate + 2.5 percent

is set at 2 + 2.5 = 4.5 percent. This figure is known as the *fully indexed rate.* If the advertised start rate for this loan is just 3 percent, you know that if the index (6-month Treasuries) stays at the same level, your loan will increase to 4.5 percent.

TIP

Compare the fully indexed rate to the current rate for fixed-rate loans. During particular time periods, you may be surprised to discover that the fixed-rate loan is at about the same interest rate or even a tad lower. This insight may cause you to reconsider your choice of an adjustable-rate loan, which can, of course, rise to an even higher rate in the future.

Looking at common indexes for adjustable-rate mortgages

The different indexes vary mainly in how rapidly they respond to changes in interest rates. Some common indexes include the following:

>> **Treasury bills:** *Treasury bills,* which are often referred to as T-bills, are IOUs (bonds) that the U.S. government issues. Most adjustables are tied to the interest rate on 6-month or 12-month T-bills. T-bill interest rates move relatively quickly.

>> **Certificates of deposit:** *Certificates of deposit,* or CDs, are interest-bearing bank investments that lock you in for a specific period of time. ARMs are usually tied to the average interest rate that banks are currently paying on 6-month CDs. Like T-bills, CDs tend to respond quickly to changes in the market's level of interest rates.

>> **The 11th District cost of funds:** The *cost of funds index* (COFI) is among the slower-moving indexes. Adjustable-rate mortgages tied to the 11th District cost of funds index tend to start out at a higher interest rate. (The *11th District* is a Western region of several states.) A slower-moving index has the advantage of moving up less quickly when rates are on the rise. On the other hand, you have to be patient to benefit from falling interest rates.

If you select an adjustable-rate mortgage that's tied to one of the faster-moving indexes, you take on more of a risk that the next adjustment will reflect interest rate increases. Because you take on this risk, lenders cut you breaks in other ways, such as through lower caps or points. If you want the security of an ARM tied to a slower-moving index, you pay for that security in one form or another, such as through a higher start rate, caps, margin, or points.

Trying to predict interest rates is risky business. When selecting a mortgage, keeping sight of your financial situation is far more important than trying to guess future interest rates.

Analyzing adjustments

After the initial interest rate expires, the interest rate on an ARM fluctuates based on the loan formula that I discuss earlier in the chapter. Most ARMs adjust every 6 or 12 months, but some adjust as frequently as monthly. In advance of each adjustment, the lender sends you a notice telling you your new rate.

All things being equal, the less frequently your loan adjusts, the less financial uncertainty you have in your life. However, less-frequent adjustments usually have a higher starting interest rate.

Almost all adjustables come with an *adjustment cap,* which limits the maximum rate change (up or down) at each adjustment. On most loans that adjust every 6 months, the adjustment cap is 1 percent. In other words, the interest rate that the loan charges can move up or down no more than one percentage point in a given adjustment period.

Loans that adjust more than once per year usually limit the maximum rate change that's allowed over the entire year as well. On the vast majority of such loans, 2 percent is the annual rate cap. Likewise, almost all adjustables come with *lifetime caps.* These caps limit the highest rate allowed over the entire life of the loan. It's common for adjustable loans to have lifetime caps 5 to 6 percent higher than the initial start rate.

Never take an ARM without rate caps! Doing so is worse than giving a credit card with an unlimited line of credit to your teenager for the weekend (at least you get the credit card back on Monday!). When you want to take an ARM, you must identify the maximum payment that you can handle. If you can't handle the highest allowed payment, don't look at ARMs.

Avoiding negative amortization ARMs

As you make mortgage payments over time, the loan balance you still owe is gradually reduced, or *amortized. Negative amortization* — increasing your loan balance — is the reverse of this process. Some ARMs allow negative amortization. How can your outstanding loan balance grow when you continue to make mortgage payments? This phenomenon occurs when your mortgage payment is less than it really should be.

Some loans cap the increase of your monthly payment but don't cap the interest rate. Thus, the size of your mortgage payment may not reflect all the interest that you owe on your loan. So rather than paying the interest that you owe and paying off some of your loan balance (or principal) every month, you end up paying off some, but not all, of the interest that you owe. Thus, lenders add the extra, unpaid interest that you still owe to your outstanding debt.

Negative amortization resembles paying only the minimum payment that your credit card bill requires. You continue to rack up finance charges (in this case, greater interest) on the balance as long as you make only the artificially low payment. Taking a loan with negative amortization defeats the whole purpose of borrowing an amount that fits your overall financial goals.

REMEMBER

Avoid adjustables with negative amortization. Most lenders and mortgage brokers aren't forthcoming about telling you, so the only way to know whether a loan includes negative amortization is to explicitly ask. You find negative amortization more frequently on loans that lenders consider risky. If you have trouble finding lenders that will deal with your financial situation, make sure you're especially careful.

Examining other mortgage fees

INVESTIGATE

In addition to points and the ongoing interest rate, lenders tack on all sorts of other upfront charges when processing your loan. Get an itemization of these other fees and charges in writing from all lenders that you're seriously considering. (I explain how to find the best lenders for your needs in the next section.) You need to know the total of all lender fees so you can accurately compare different lenders' loans and determine how much closing on your loan will cost you. These other mortgage fees can pile up in a hurry. Here are the common ones you may see:

>> **Application and processing fees:** Most lenders charge a few hundred dollars to work with you to complete your paperwork and funnel it through their loan evaluation process. If your loan is rejected, or if it's approved and you decide not to take it, the lender needs to cover its costs. Some lenders return this fee to you upon closing with their loan.

>> **Credit report charge:** Most lenders charge you for the cost of obtaining your credit report, which tells the lender whether you've repaid other loans on time. Credit report fees typically run about $20.

>> **Appraisal fee:** The property for which you borrow money needs to be valued. If you default on your mortgage, a lender doesn't want to get stuck with a property that's worth less than you owe. The cost for an appraisal typically ranges from several hundred dollars for most residential properties to as much as $1,000 or more for larger investment properties.

Some lenders offer loans without points or other lender charges. However, remember that if they don't charge points or other fees, they charge a higher interest rate on your loan to make up the difference. Such loans may make sense for you when you lack the cash to close a loan or when you plan to keep the loan for just a few years.

TIP

To minimize your chances of throwing money away applying for a loan that you may not qualify for, ask the lender whether he sees any reason your loan request may be denied. (Also consider getting pre-approved.) Be sure to disclose any problems on your credit report or any problems with the property that you're aware of. Lenders may not take the time to ask about these sorts of things in their haste to get you to complete their loan applications.

Finding the best lenders

You can easily save thousands of dollars in interest charges and other fees if you shop around for a mortgage deal. It doesn't matter whether you do so on your own or hire someone to help you, but you definitely should shop because a lot of money is at stake!

Shopping through a mortgage broker

A competent mortgage broker can be a big help in getting you a good loan and closing the deal, especially if you're too busy or uninterested to dig for a good deal on a mortgage. A good mortgage broker also stays abreast of the many different mortgages in the marketplace. She can shop among lots of lenders to get you the best deal available. The following list presents some additional advantages to working with a mortgage broker:

>> An organized and detail-oriented mortgage broker can help you through the process of completing all those tedious documents that lenders require.

>> Mortgage brokers can help polish your loan package so the information you present is favorable yet truthful.

>> The best brokers can help educate you about various loan options and the pros and cons of available features.

WARNING

Be careful when you choose a mortgage broker, because some brokers are lazy and don't shop the market for the best current rates. Even worse, some brokers direct their business to specific lenders so they can take a bigger cut or commission.

INVESTIGATE

A mortgage broker typically gets paid a percentage, usually 0.5 to 1 percent, of the loan amount. This commission is completely negotiable, especially on larger loans that are more lucrative. So be sure to ask what the commission is on loans that a broker pitches. Some brokers may be indignant that you ask, but that's their problem. You have every right to ask. After all, it's your money.

Even if you plan to shop on your own, talking to a mortgage broker may be worthwhile. At the very least, you can compare what you find with what brokers say they can get for you. But again, be careful. Some brokers tell you what you want to hear — that they can beat your best find — and then can't deliver when the time comes.

If your loan broker quotes you a really good deal, ask who the lender is. (However, do be aware that most brokers refuse to reveal this information until you pay the necessary fee to cover the appraisal and credit report.) You can then check with the actual lender to verify the interest rate and points that the broker quotes you and make sure that you're eligible for the loan.

Shopping by yourself

Many mortgage lenders compete for your business. Although having a large number of lenders to choose from is good for keeping interest rates lower, it also makes shopping a chore, especially if you're going it alone (instead of using a broker). But there's no substitute for taking the time to speak with numerous lenders and exploring the range of options.

Real estate agents may refer you to lenders with whom they've done business. Just keep in mind that those lenders won't necessarily offer the most competitive rates — the agent simply may have done business with them in the past or received client referrals from them.

TIP

You can start searching for a good deal by looking in the real estate section of a large, local Sunday newspaper for charts of selected area lender interest rates. You also can visit Internet sites that advertise rates. However, newspaper tables and Internet sites are by no means comprehensive or reflective of the best rates available. In fact, many of these rates are sent to newspapers for free by firms that distribute mortgage information to mortgage brokers. Use them as a starting point and then call the lenders that list the best rates.

Refinancing for a better deal

When you buy a property, you take out a mortgage based on your circumstances and available loan options at that time. But things change. Maybe interest rates have dropped, or you have access to better loan options now than when you first purchased. Or perhaps you want to tap into some of your real estate equity for other investments.

WHEN TO CONSIDER A HOME EQUITY LOAN

Home equity loans, also known as *second mortgages,* allow you to borrow against the equity in your home in addition to the mortgage that you already have (a first mortgage).

A home equity loan may benefit you if you need more money for just a few years or if your first mortgage is at such a low interest rate that refinancing it to get more cash would be too costly. Otherwise, I advise you to avoid home equity loans.

If you need a larger mortgage, why not refinance the first one and wrap it all together? Home equity loans have higher interest rates than comparable first mortgages because they're riskier from a lender's perspective. They're riskier because the first mortgage lender gets first claim against your property if you file bankruptcy or you default on the mortgage.

Interest on home mortgage loans of up to $1 million (first or second residences) is tax-deductible for loans taken out after October 13, 1987. (Loans taken before that date have no monetary limit.) Interest deduction on home equity loans is limited to the first $100,000 of such debt.

If interest rates drop and you're able to refinance, you can lock in interest rate savings. But getting a lower interest rate than the one you got when you took out your original mortgage isn't reason enough to refinance your mortgage. When you refinance a mortgage, you have to spend money and time to save money. So you need to crunch a few numbers to determine whether refinancing makes financial sense for you.

TIP

Calculate how many months it will take you to recoup the costs of refinancing, such as appraisal costs, loan fees and points, title insurance, and so on. You also have to consider tax issues. For example, if the refinance costs you $2,000 to complete and reduces your monthly payment by $100, it may appear that you can recoup the cost of the refinance in 20 months. However, because you lose some tax write-offs if you reduce your mortgage interest rate and payment, you can't simply look at the reduced amount of your monthly payment.

For a better estimate without spending hours crunching numbers, take your tax rate as specified in Chapter 3 (for example, 28 percent) and reduce your monthly payment savings on the refinance by this amount. That means, continuing with the preceding example, that if your monthly payment drops by $100, you're actually saving only around $72 a month after you factor in the lost tax benefits. So it takes about 28 months ($2,000 divided by $72), not 20 months, to recoup the refinance costs.

REMEMBER

Consider refinancing when you can recover the costs of the refinance within a few years or less and you don't plan to move in that time frame. If it takes longer to recoup the refinance costs, refinancing may still make sense if you anticipate keeping the property and mortgage that long. If you estimate that breaking even will take more than five to seven years, refinancing is probably too risky to justify the costs and hassles.

Refinancing a piece of real estate that you own to pull out cash for some other purpose can make good financial sense because under most circumstances, mortgage interest is tax-deductible. Perhaps you want to purchase another piece of real estate, start or purchase a business, or get rid of an auto loan or some high-cost credit card debt. The interest on consumer debt isn't tax-deductible and is usually at a much higher interest rate than what mortgage loans charge you.

WARNING

Be careful that you don't borrow more than you need to accomplish your financial goals. For example, just because you can borrow more against the equity in your real estate doesn't mean you should do so to buy an expensive new car or take your dream vacation.

Working with Real Estate Agents

If you're like most people, when you purchase real estate, you enlist the services of a real estate agent. A good agent can help screen property so you don't spend all your free time looking at potential properties, negotiating a deal, helping coordinate inspections, and managing other pre-closing items.

Recognizing agent conflicts of interest

All real estate agents (good, mediocre, and awful) are subject to a conflict of interest because of the way they're compensated: on commission. I respect real estate agents for calling themselves what they are. They don't hide behind an obscure job title, such as "shelter consultant." (Many financial "planners," "advisors," or "consultants," for example, actually work on commission and sell investments and life insurance and therefore are really stockbrokers and insurance brokers, not planners or advisors.)

Real estate agents aren't in the business of providing objective financial counsel. Just as car dealers make their living selling cars, real estate agents make their living selling real estate. Never forget this fact as a buyer.

The pursuit of a larger commission may encourage an agent to get you to do things that aren't in your best interest, such as the following:

>> **Buy, and buy sooner rather than later:** If you don't buy, your agent doesn't get paid for all the hours she spends working with you. The worst agents fib and use tricks to motivate you to buy. They may say, for example, that other offers are coming in on a property that interests you, or they may show you a bunch of dumps and then one good listing that has much of what you're looking for to motivate you to buy the nicer property.

>> **Spend more than you should:** Because real estate agents get a percentage of the sales price of a property, they have a built-in incentive to encourage you to spend more on a property than what fits comfortably with your other financial objectives and goals. An agent doesn't have to consider or care about your other financial needs.

>> **Purchase their company's listings:** Agents also have a built-in incentive (higher commission) to sell their own listings. So don't be surprised when an agent pushes you in the direction of one of her own company's properties.

>> **Buy in their territory:** Real estate agents typically work a specific territory. As a result, they usually can't objectively tell you the pros and cons of the surrounding region.

>> **Use people who scratch their backs:** Some agents refer you to mortgage brokers, lenders, inspectors, and title insurance companies that have referred customers to them. Some agents also solicit and receive referral fees (or bribes) from mortgage lenders, inspectors, and contractors to whom they refer business.

Selecting a good agent

A mediocre, incompetent, or greedy agent can be a real danger to your finances. Whether you're hiring an agent to work with you as a buyer or as a seller, you want someone who's competent and with whom you can get along. Working with an agent costs a good deal of money, so make sure you get your money's worth out of him.

Interview several agents and check references. Ask agents for the names and phone numbers of at least three clients with whom they've worked in the past six months in the geographical area in which you're looking. By narrowing the period during which they worked with these references, you maximize the chances of speaking with clients other than the agent's all-time-favorite clients.

As you speak with an agent's references, ask about these traits in any agent that you're considering working with, whether as a buyer or as a seller:

>> **Full-time employment:** Some agents work in real estate as a second or even third job. Information in this field changes constantly, so keeping track of it is challenging on a full-time basis. It's hard to imagine a good agent being able to stay on top of the market on a part-time basis while moonlighting elsewhere.

>> **Experience:** Hiring someone with experience doesn't necessarily mean looking for an agent who's sold real estate for decades. Many of the best agents come into the field from other occupations, such as business and teaching. Agents can acquire some sales, marketing, negotiation, and communication skills in other fields. However, keep in mind that some experience in real estate does count.

>> **Honesty and integrity:** You need to trust your agent with a lot of information. If the agent doesn't level with you about what a neighborhood or particular property is really like, you suffer the consequences.

>> **Interpersonal skills:** An agent must get along not only with you but also with a whole host of other people who are involved in a typical real estate deal: other agents, property sellers, inspectors, mortgage lenders, and so on. An agent needs to know how to put your interests first without upsetting others.

>> **Negotiation skills:** Putting a real estate deal together involves negotiation. Is your agent going to exhaust all avenues to get you the best deal possible? Most people don't like the sometimes aggravating process of negotiation, so they hire someone else to do it for them. Be sure to ask the agent's former client references how the agent negotiated for them.

>> **High quality standards:** Sloppy work can lead to big legal or logistical problems down the road. If an agent neglects to recommend an inspection, for example, you may get stuck with undiscovered problems after the deal is done and paid for.

Agents who pitch themselves as buyers' brokers claim that they work for your interests. However, agents who represent you as a buyer's broker still get paid only when you buy. And agents still get paid a commission that's a percentage of the purchase price. So they still have an incentive to sell you a piece of real estate that's more expensive because their commission increases.

WARNING

Some agents market themselves as *top producers*, meaning that they sell a relatively larger volume of real estate. This title doesn't matter much to you, the buyer. In fact, you may use this information as a potential red flag for an agent who focuses on completing as many deals as possible. Such an agent may not be able to give you the time and help that you need to get the house you want.

BUYING WITHOUT A REAL ESTATE AGENT

You can purchase property without an agent if you're willing to do some additional leg-work. You need to do the things that a high-quality real estate agent does, such as searching for properties, scheduling appointments to see those properties, determining fair market value, negotiating the deal, and coordinating inspections.

If you don't work with an agent, have a real estate attorney review the various contracts. Having someone else not vested in the transaction look out for your interests helps your situation. Real estate agents generally aren't legal experts, so getting legal advice from an attorney is generally better. (In fact, in some states, you need to hire an attorney in addition to the real estate agent.)

One possible drawback to working without an agent is performing the negotiations yourself. Negotiating can be problematic if you lack these skills or get too caught up emotionally in the situation.

When you buy a home, you need an agent who is patient and allows you the necessary time to educate yourself and who helps you make the decision that's best for you. The last thing you need is an agent who tries to push you into making a deal.

You also need an agent who's knowledgeable about the local market and community. If you want to buy a home in an area where you don't currently live, an informed agent can have a big impact on your decision.

TIP

Finding an agent with financing knowledge is a plus for buyers, especially first-time buyers or those with credit problems. Such an agent may be able to refer you to lenders that can handle your type of situation, which can save you a lot of legwork.

Closing the Deal

After you locate a property that you want to buy and you understand your financing options, the real fun begins. At this point, you have to put the deal together. The following sections discuss key things to keep in mind.

Negotiating 101

When you work with an agent, she usually carries the burden of the negotiation process. But even if you delegate that responsibility to your agent, you still should have a strategy in mind. Otherwise, you may overpay for real estate. Here's what you should do:

>> **Find out about the property and the owner before you make your offer.** How long has the property been on the market? What are its flaws? Why is the owner selling? The more you understand about the property you want to buy and the seller's motivations, the better your ability to draft an offer that meets everyone's needs. Some listing agents love to talk and will tell you the life history of the seller. Either you or your agent may be able to get a listing agent to reveal helpful information about the seller.

>> **Bring facts to the bargaining table. Get comparable sales data to support your price.** Too often, homebuyers and their agents pick a number out of the air when they make an offer. If you were the seller, would you be persuaded to lower your asking price? Pointing to recent and comparable home sales to justify your offer price strengthens your case.

REMEMBER

Price is only one of several negotiable items. Sometimes sellers fixate on selling their homes for a certain amount. Perhaps they want to get at least what they paid for it several years ago. You may get a seller to pay for certain repairs or improvements or to offer you an attractive loan without all the extra fees that a bank charges. Also, be aware that the time for closing on the purchase is a bargaining point. Some sellers may need cash fast and may concede other terms if you can close quickly. Likewise, the real estate agent's commission is negotiable.

>> **Try to leave your emotions out of any property purchase.** Being objective rather than emotional regarding a purchase is easier said than done, and it's hardest to do when buying a home in which you'll live. So do your best not to fall in love with a property. Keep searching for other properties even when you make an offer because you may be negotiating with an unmotivated seller.

Inspecting the property

Unless you've built homes and other properties and performed contracting work yourself, you probably have no idea what you're getting yourself into when it comes to furnaces and termites.

TIP

Spend the money and take the time to hire inspectors and other experts to evaluate the major systems and potential problem areas of the home. Because you can't be certain of the seller's commitment, I recommend that you do the inspections *after* you've successfully negotiated and signed a sales contract. Even though you won't have the feedback from the inspections to help with this round of negotiating, you can always go back to the seller with the new information. Make your purchase offer contingent on a satisfactory inspection.

Hire people to help you inspect the following features of the property:

» Overall condition of the property (for example, look for peeling paint, level floors, appliances that work properly, and so on)

» Electrical, heating and air conditioning, and plumbing systems

» Foundation

» Roof

» Pest control and dry rot

» Seismic/slide/flood risk

With multi-unit rental property, be sure to read Chapter 11 for other specifics that you need to check out.

Inspection fees often pay for themselves. If you uncover problems that you weren't aware of when you negotiated the original purchase price, the inspection reports give you the information you need so you can go back and ask the property seller to fix the problems or reduce the property's purchase price.

WARNING

Never accept a seller's inspection report as your only source of information. When a seller hires an inspector, he may hire someone who isn't as diligent and critical of the property. Review the seller's inspection reports if available, but also get your own evaluation. Also, beware of inspectors who are popular with real estate agents. They may be popular because they don't bother to document all the property's problems.

As with other professionals whose services you retain, interview a few different inspection companies. Ask which systems they inspect and how detailed of a report they can prepare for you. Consider asking the company that you're thinking of hiring for customer references. Ask for names and phone numbers of three people who used the company's services within the past six months. Also request from each inspection company a sample of one of its reports.

TIP

The day before you close on the purchase, take a brief walk-through of the property to make sure that everything is still in the condition it was before and that all the fixtures, appliances, curtains, and other items the contract lists are still there. Sometimes, sellers ignore or don't recall these things, and consequently, they don't leave what they agreed to leave in the sales contract.

Shopping for title insurance and escrow services

Mortgage lenders require *title insurance* to protect against someone else claiming legal title to your property. For example, when a husband and wife split up, the one who remains in the home may decide to sell and take off with the money. If the title lists both spouses as owners, the spouse who sells the property (possibly by forging the other's signature) has no legal right to do so. The other spouse can come back and reclaim rights to the home even after it has been sold. In this event, both you and the lender can get stuck holding the bag. (If you're in the enviable position of paying cash for a property, buying title insurance is still wise to protect your investment, even though a mortgage lender won't prod you to do so.)

TIP

Title insurance and escrow charges vary from company to company. (*Escrow charges* pay for neutral third-party services to ensure that the instructions of the purchase contract or refinance are fulfilled and that everyone gets paid.) Don't simply use the company that your real estate agent or mortgage lender suggests — shop around. When you call around for title insurance and escrow fee quotes, make sure that you understand all the fees. Many companies tack on all sorts of charges for things such as courier fees and express mail. If you find a company with lower prices and want to use it, consider asking for an itemization in writing so you don't receive any unpleasant surprises.

An insurance company's ability to pay claims is always important. Most state insurance departments monitor and regulate title insurance companies. Title insurers rarely fail, and most state departments of insurance do a good job of shutting down financially unstable ones. Check with your state's department if you're concerned. You can also ask the title insurer for copies of its ratings from insurance-rating agencies.

Selling Real Estate

Buying and holding real estate for the long term really pays off. If you do your homework, buy in a good area, and work hard to find a fairly priced or underpriced property, why sell it quickly and incur all the selling costs, time, and hassle to locate and negotiate another property to purchase?

WARNING

Some real estate investors like to buy properties in need of improvement, fix them up, and then sell them and move on to another. Unless you're a contractor or experienced real estate investor and have a real eye for this type of work, don't expect to make a windfall or even to earn back more than the cost of the improvements. The process of buying, fixing, and flipping can be profitable, but it's not as easy as the home-improvement television shows and some books would have you believe. In fact, it's more likely that you'll erode your profit through the myriad costs of frequent buying and selling. The vast majority of your profits should come from the long-term appreciation of the overall real estate market in the communities in which you own property.

Use the reasons that you bought in an area as a guide for considering selling. Review the criteria that I discuss in Chapter 11 as a guideline. For example, if the schools in the community are deteriorating and the planning department is allowing development that will hurt the value of your property and the rents that you can charge, you may have cause to sell. Unless you see significant problems like these in the future, holding good properties over many years is a great way to build your wealth and minimize transaction costs.

Negotiating real estate agents' contracts

Most people use an agent to sell real estate. As I discuss in "Selecting a good agent," earlier in this chapter, selling and buying a home demand agents with different strengths. When you sell a property, you want an agent who can get the job done efficiently and for the highest possible sales price.

TIP

As a seller, seek agents who have marketing and sales expertise and who are willing to put in the time and money necessary to sell your house. Don't be impressed by an agent just because she works for a large company. What matters more is what the agent can do to market your property.

When you list a property for sale, the contract that you sign with the listing agent includes specification of the commission that you pay the agent if she succeeds in selling your property. In most areas of the country, agents usually ask for a 6 percent commission for single-family homes. In an area that maintains lower-cost housing, agents may ask for 7 percent. For small multifamily properties and commercial properties, commissions often hover around the 3 to 5 percent range.

REMEMBER

Regardless of the commission an agent says is "typical," "standard," or "what my manager requires," always remember that you can negotiate commissions. Because the commission is a percentage, you have a much greater ability to get a lower commission on a higher-priced property. If an agent makes 6 percent selling both a $200,000 and a $100,000 property, the agent makes twice as much on the $200,000 property. Yet selling the higher-priced property doesn't usually take twice as much work.

If you live in an area with generally higher-priced properties, you may be able to negotiate a 5 percent commission. For really expensive properties, a 4 percent commission is reasonable. You may find, however, that your ability to negotiate a lower commission is greatest when an offer is on the table. Because of the cooperation of agents who work together through the multiple listing service (MLS), if you list your real estate for sale at a lower commission than most other properties, some agents won't show it to prospective buyers. For this reason, you're better off having your listing agent cut his take instead of cutting the commission that you pay to a real estate agent who brings a buyer for your property.

TIP

In terms of the length of the listing agreement, 3 months is reasonable. If you give an agent too long to list your property (6 to 12 months), the agent may simply toss your listing into the multiple listing database and not expend much effort to get your property sold. Practically speaking, you can fire your agent whenever you want, regardless of the length of the listing agreement, but a shorter listing may motivate your agent more. A shorter listing period also allows you to part company with your agent if he doesn't do a good job and to move on to someone who will.

Forgoing a real estate agent

The temptation to sell real estate without an agent is usually to save the commission that an agent deducts from your property's sale price. If you have the time, energy, and marketing experience, you can sell sans agent and possibly save some money.

WARNING

The major problem with attempting to sell real estate on your own is that you can't list it in the MLS, which, in most areas, only real estate agents can access. If you're not listed in the MLS, many potential buyers never know that your home is for sale. Agents who work with buyers don't generally look for or show properties that are for sale by owner or listed with discount brokers.

Besides saving you time, a good agent can help ensure that you're not sued for failing to disclose known defects of your property. If you decide to sell on your own, contact a local real estate legal advisor who can review the contracts. Take the time to educate yourself about the many facets of selling property for top dollar. Read the latest edition of *House Selling For Dummies,* which I coauthored with Ray Brown (published by Wiley).

4
Savoring Small Business

Explore the investment opportunities of your own small business by developing a business plan, identifying marketable products or services, finding customers, and understanding and beating the competition.

Consider your options and do due diligence if you prefer to buy an existing small business instead of establishing your own.

Chapter 13

Assessing Your Appetite for Small Business

Many people dream about running their own companies — and for good reason. If you start your own business, you can pursue something that you're passionate about, *and* you have more control over how you do things. Plus, successful business owners can reap major economic bounties.

WARNING

But tales of entrepreneurs becoming multimillionaires focus attention on the financial rewards without revealing the business and personal challenges and costs associated with being in charge. Consider what your company has to do well to survive and succeed in the competitive business world:

>> Develop products and services that customers will purchase

>> Price your offerings properly and promote them

>> Deal with the competition

>> Manage the accounting

>> Interpret lease contracts and evaluate office space

>> Stay current with changes in your field

>> Hire, train, and retain good employees

Business owners also face personal and emotional challenges, which rarely get airtime among all the glory of the rags-to-riches tales of multimillionaire entrepreneurs. Major health problems, divorces, fights and lawsuits among family members who are in business together, the loss of friends, and even suicides have been attributed to the passions of business owners who are consumed with winning or become overwhelmed by their failures. I'm not trying to scare you, but I do want you to be realistic about starting your own business.

In this chapter, I help you to assess whether starting a company fits with your goals and aptitude. I also present numerous alternatives that may better fit you and your situation.

Testing Your Entrepreneurial IQ

The keys to success and enjoyment as an entrepreneur vary as much as the businesses do. But if you can answer *yes* to most of the following questions, you probably have the qualities and perspective needed to succeed as a small-business owner:

>> **Are you a self-starter? Do you like challenges? Are you persistent? Are you willing to do research to solve problems?** Most of the time, running your own business isn't glamorous, especially in the early years. You have many details to remember and many things to do. Success in business is the result of doing lots of little things well. If you're accustomed to working for large organizations where much of the day is spent attending meetings and keeping up on office politics and gossip, with little accountability, running your own business may come as a bit of a shock at first.

>> **Do you value independence and self-control?** Particularly in the early days of your business, you need to enjoy working on your own. When you leave a company environment and work on your own, you give up a lot of socializing. Of course, if you work in an unpleasant environment or with people you don't really enjoy socializing with, venturing out on your own may be a plus.

REMEMBER

If you're a people person, many businesses offer lots of contact. But you must recognize the difference between socializing for fun with co-workers versus the often more demanding and goal-oriented networking with business contacts and customers.

>> **Can you develop a commitment to an idea, a product, or a principle?** If you work about 50 hours per week over 50 or so weeks per year, you'll work

around 2,500 hours per year. If the product, service, or cause you're pursuing doesn't excite you and you can't motivate others to work hard for you, you're going to have a long year!

WARNING

One of the worst reasons to start your own business is solely for the pursuit of great financial riches. Don't get me wrong — if you're good at what you do and you know how to market your services or products, you may make more money working for yourself. But for most people, money isn't enough of a motivation, and many people make the same or less money on their own than they did working for a company.

» **Are you willing to make financial sacrifices and live a reduced lifestyle before and during your early entrepreneurial years?** "Live like a student before and during the startup of your small business" was the advice that my best business school professor, James Collins, gave me before I started my business. With most businesses, you expend money during the startup years and likely have a reduced income compared to the income you receive while working for a company. You also have to buy your own benefits.

TIP

To make your entrepreneurial dream a reality, you need to live within your means both before and after you start your business. But if running your own business really makes you happy, sacrificing expensive vacations, overpriced luxury cars, the latest designer clothing, and $4 lattes at the corner cafe shouldn't be too painful.

» **Do you recognize that when you run your own business, you must still report to bosses?** Besides the allure of huge profits, the other reason some people mistakenly go into business for themselves is that they're tired of working for other people. Obnoxious, evil bosses can make anyone want to become an entrepreneur.

When you run your own business, you may have customers and other people to please who are miserable to deal with. Fortunately, even the worst customers usually can't make your life anywhere near as miserable as the worst bosses. (And if you have enough customers, you can simply decide not to do business with such misfits.)

» **Can you withstand rejection, naysayers, and negative feedback?** "I thought every *no* that I got when trying to raise my funding brought me one step closer to a *yes*," says an entrepreneur I know. Unless you come from an entrepreneurial family, don't expect your parents to endorse your "risky, crazy" behavior. Even other entrepreneurs can ridicule your good ideas. Two of my entrepreneurial friends were critical of each other's ideas, yet both have succeeded!

Some people (especially parents) simply think that working for a giant company makes you safer and more secure (which, of course, is a myth, because corporations can lay you off in a snap). It's also easier for them to say to their friends and neighbors that you're a big manager at a well-known corporation (such as IBM, GE, Enron, Lehman Brothers, or WorldCom) than to explain that you're working on some kooky business idea out of a spare bedroom. How secure do you think those former employees of Enron, Lehman Brothers, and WorldCom feel now about having lost their jobs at their former large company?

>> **Are you able to identify your shortcomings and hire or align yourself with people and organizations that complement your skills and expertise?** To be a successful entrepreneur, you need to be a bit of a jack-of-all-trades: marketer, accountant, customer service representative, administrative assistant, and so on. Unless you get lots of investor capital, which is rare for a true startup, you can't afford to hire help in the early months, or perhaps even years, of your business.

REMEMBER

Partnering with or buying certain services or products rather than trying to do everything yourself may make sense for you. And over time, if your business grows and succeeds, you should be able to afford to hire more help. If you can be honest with yourself and surround and partner yourself with people whose skills and expertise complement yours, you can build a winning team!

>> **Do you deal well with ambiguity? Do you believe in yourself?** When you're on your own, determining whether you're on the right track is difficult. Some days, things don't go well — and such days are much harder to take flying solo. Therefore, being confident, optimistic, and able to work around obstacles are necessary skills.

>> **Do you understand why you started the business or organization and how you personally define success?** Many business entrepreneurs define success by such measures as sales revenue, profits, number of branch offices and employees, and so on. These are fine measures, but other organizations, particularly nonprofits, have other measures. For example, the Jacksonville, Florida–based nonpartisan Wounded Warrior Project was founded by a "group of veterans and friends who took action to help the injured service men and women of this generation." Money is necessary for the Wounded Warrior Project to accomplish its purpose, but such a cause-focused organization has a "bottom line" that's very different from that of a for-profit organization.

>> **Can you accept lack of success in the early years of building your business?** A few rare businesses are instant hits, but most businesses take time to build momentum — it may take years, perhaps even decades. Some successful corporate people suffer from anxiety when they go out on their own and encounter the inevitable struggles and lack of tangible success as they build their companies.

REMEMBER

Don't be deterred by the questions that you can't answer in the affirmative. A perfect entrepreneur doesn't exist. Part of succeeding in business is knowing what you can and can't do and then finding creative ways (or people) to help you achieve your goals.

Considering Alternative Routes to Owning a Small Business

Sometimes entrepreneurial advocates imply that running your own business or starting your own nonprofit is the greatest thing in the world and that all people would be happy owning their own businesses if they just set their minds to it.

REMEMBER

The reality is that some people won't be blissful as entrepreneurs. If you didn't score highly on my ten-question entrepreneur assessment in the preceding section, don't despair. You can probably be happier and more successful doing something other than starting your own business. Some people are better off working for someone else. If you're one of these people, consider the options in the following sections.

Being an entrepreneur inside a company

A happy medium is available for people who want the challenge of running their own show without giving up the comforts and security that come with a company environment. For example, you can manage an entrepreneurial venture at a company. That's what John Kilcullen, president and chief executive officer of IDG Books Worldwide (former publisher of this book), did when he helped launch the book publishing division of IDG in 1990. (IDG Books was subsequently bought by John Wiley & Sons, Inc.)

Kilcullen had publishing industry experience and wanted to take on the responsibility of growing a successful publishing company. But he also knew that being a player in the book publishing industry takes a lot of money and resources. Because he was a member of the founding team of the new IDG Books division, Kilcullen had the best of both worlds.

Kilcullen always had a passion to start his own business but found that most traditional publishers weren't interested in giving autonomy and money to a division and letting it run with the ball. "I wanted the ability to build a business on my own instincts . . . . The appeal of IDG was that it was decentralized. IDG was willing to invest and provide the freedom to spend as we saw fit."

If you're able to secure an entrepreneurial position inside a larger company, in addition to significant managerial and operational responsibility, you can also negotiate your share of the financial success that you help create. The parent company's senior management wants you to have the incentive that comes from sharing in the financial success of your endeavors. Bonuses, stock options, and the like are often tied to a division's performance.

Investing in your career

Some people are happy or content as employees. Companies need and want lots of good employees, so you should be able to find a job if you have skills, a solid work ethic, and the ability to get along with others.

TIP

You can improve your income–earning ability and invest in your career in a variety of ways:

>> **Work:** Be willing to work extra hours and take on more responsibility. Those who take extra initiative and then deliver really stand out in a company where many people working on a salary have a time-clock, 9-to-5 mentality. But be careful that the extra effort doesn't contribute to *workaholism,* a dangerous addiction that causes too many people to neglect important personal relationships and their own health. Don't bite off more than you can chew; otherwise, your supervisors won't have faith that they can count on you to deliver. Find ways to work smarter, not just longer, hours.

>> **Read:** One of the reasons you don't need a PhD, master's degree, or even an undergraduate college degree from a top college to succeed in business is that you can find out a lot on your own. You can gain insight by doing, but you can also gain expertise by reading a lot. A good bookstore has no entrance requirements, such as an elevated high school grade point average or high SAT scores. A good book isn't free, but it costs a heck of lot less than taking college or graduate courses!

>> **Study:** If you haven't completed your college or graduate degree and the industry you're in values those who have, consider investing the time and money to finish your education. Speak with others who have taken that path and see what they have to say.

Exploring Small-Business Investment Options

Only your imagination limits the ways you can make money with small businesses. Choosing the option that best meets your needs isn't unlike choosing other investments, such as in real estate (see Part 3) or in the securities markets (see Part 2). In the following sections, I discuss the major ways you can invest in small business, including what's attractive and what isn't for each option.

Starting your own business

Of all your small-business options, starting your own business involves the greatest amount of work. Although you can perform this work on a part-time basis in the beginning, most people end up working in their business full time.

For most of my working years, I've run my own business, and overall, I really like it. In my experience counseling small-business owners, I've seen many people of varied backgrounds, interests, and skills achieve success and happiness running their own businesses.

REMEMBER

Most people perceive starting their own business as the riskiest of all small-business investment options. But if you get into a business that uses your skills and expertise, the risk isn't nearly as great as you may think. Suppose, for example, that as a teacher you make $35,000 per year, and now you decide you want to set up your own tutoring service, making a comparable amount of money. If you find through your research that others who perform these services charge $40 per hour, you need to tutor about 20 or so hours per week, assuming that you work 50 weeks per year. Because you can run this business from your home (which can possibly generate small tax breaks) without purchasing new equipment, your expenses should be minimal.

Instead of leaving your job cold turkey and trying to build your business from scratch, you can start moonlighting as a tutor. Over a couple of years, if you can build the tutoring up to ten hours per week, you're halfway to your goal. If you leave your job and focus all your energies on your tutoring business, getting to 20 hours per week of billable work shouldn't be a problem. Still think starting a business is risky?

REMEMBER

You can start many businesses with little money by leveraging your existing skills and expertise. If you have the time to devote to building "sweat equity," you can build a valuable company and job. As long as you check out the competition and offer a valued product or service at a reasonable cost, the principal risk with your business is that you won't do a good job marketing what you have to offer. If you can market your skills, you should succeed. See Chapter 14 for more details on starting and running your own business.

Buying an existing business

If you don't have a specific idea for a business that you want to start but you have business management skills and an ability to improve existing businesses, consider buying an established business. Although you don't have to go through the riskier startup period if you take this route, you'll likely need more capital to buy a going enterprise.

DON'T START A BUSINESS FOR TAX WRITE-OFFS

"Start a small business for fun, profit, and huge tax deductions," declares a financial advice book, adding that "the tax benefits alone are worth starting a small business." A seminar company offers a course titled "How to Have Zero Taxes Deducted from Your Paycheck." This tax seminar tells you how to solve your tax problems: "If you have a sideline business, or would like to start one, you're eligible to have little or no taxes taken from your pay."

All this sounds too good to be true — and of course it is. Not only are the strategies sure to lead to IRS-audit purgatory, but such books and seminars may also seduce you to pony up $100 or more for audiotapes or notebooks of "inside information."

Unfortunately, many self-proclaimed self-help gurus state that you can slash your taxes simply by finding a product or service that you can sell on the side of your regular employment. The problem, they argue, is that as a regular wage earner who receives a paycheck from an employer, you can't write off many of your other (personal) expenses. Open a sideline business, they say, and you can deduct your personal expenses as business expenses.

The pitch is enticing, but the reality is something quite different. You have to spend money to get tax deductions, and the spending must be for legitimate purposes of your business in its efforts to generate income. If you think that taking tax deductions as a hobby is worth the risk because you won't get caught unless you're audited, the odds are stacked against you. The IRS audits an extraordinarily large portion of small businesses that show regular losses.

The bottom line is that you need to operate a real business for the purpose of generating income and profits, not tax deductions. The IRS considers an activity a hobby (and not a business) if it shows a loss for three or more of the preceding five tax years. (Exception: The IRS considers horse racing and breeding a hobby if it shows a loss for at least six of the preceding seven tax years.) Some years, a certain number of businesses lose money, but a real business can't afford to do so year after year and remain in operation. Even if your sideline business passes this hobby test as well as other IRS requirements, deducting any expenses that aren't directly applicable to your business is illegal.

If these loss rules indicate that you're engaging in a hobby but you still want to claim your losses, you must convince the IRS that you're seriously trying to make a profit and run a legitimate business. The IRS wants to see that you're actively marketing your services, building your skills, and accounting for income and expenses. The IRS also wants to see that you don't derive too much pleasure from an activity. If you do, the IRS says that what you're doing is a hobby and not a business. Business isn't supposed to give you too much enjoyment!

You also need to be able to deal with potentially sticky personnel and management issues. The history of the organization and the way things work predates your ownership of the business. If you don't like making hard decisions, firing people who don't fit with your plans, and coercing people into changing the way they did things before you arrived on the scene, buying an existing business likely isn't for you. Also realize that some of the good employees may be loyal to the old owner and his style of running the business, so they may split when you arrive.

WARNING

Some people perceive that buying an existing business is safer than starting a new one, but buying someone else's business can actually be riskier. You have to put out far more money upfront, in the form of a down payment, to buy a business. And if you don't have the ability to run the business and it does poorly, you may lose much more financially. Another risk is that the business may be for sale for a reason — perhaps it's not very profitable, it's in decline, or it's generally a pain in the posterior to operate.

Good businesses that are for sale don't come cheaply. If the business is a success, the current owner has removed the startup risk from the business, so the price of the business should include a premium to reflect this lack of risk. If you have the capital to buy an established business and the skills to run it, consider going this route. Chapter 15 discusses how to buy a good business.

Investing in someone else's business

If you like the idea of profiting from successful small businesses but don't want the day-to-day headaches of being responsible for managing the enterprise, you may want to invest in someone else's small business. Although this route may seem easier, fewer people are actually cut out to be investors in other people's businesses.

Choosing to invest for the right reasons

Consider investing in someone else's business if you meet the following criteria:

>> **You have sufficient assets.** You need enough assets so that what you invest in small privately held companies is a small portion (20 percent or less) of your total financial assets.

>> **You can afford to lose what you invest.** Unlike investing in a diversified stock fund (see Chapter 8), you may lose all of your investment when you invest in a small, privately held company.

>> **You're astute at evaluating financial statements and business strategies.** Investing in a small, privately held company has much in common with investing in a publicly traded firm. A main difference is that private firms aren't

required to produce comprehensive, audited financial statements that adhere to certain accounting principles the way that public companies are. Thus, you have a greater risk of not receiving sufficient or accurate information when you evaluate a small private firm. (There are also liquidity differences; with a small, private company, you may not be able to sell out when you want and at a fair current price.)

Putting money into your own business (or someone else's) can be a high-risk — but potentially high-return — investment. The best options are those that you understand well. If you hear about a great business idea or company from someone you know and trust, do your research and make your best judgment. That company or idea may be a terrific investment.

TIP

Before you invest, ask to see a copy of the business plan and compare it with the business plan model that I suggest later in this chapter. Thoroughly check out the people running the business. Talk to others who don't have a stake in the investment; you can benefit from their comments and concerns. But don't forget that many a wise person has rained on the parade of what turned out to be a terrific business idea. See the sidebar in this chapter "Wet blankets throughout history" for some amusing rejections that turned out to be huge mistakes.

Avoiding investing mistakes

WARNING

Although some people are extra careful when they invest other people's money, others aren't. For example, many small-business owners seek investors' money for the wrong reasons, including the following:

>> They are impatient and perhaps don't understand the feasibility of making do with a small amount of capital (a process called *bootstrapping,* which I discuss in Chapter 14).

>> They need money because they're in financial trouble. A small furniture retailer in my area conducted a stock offering to raise money. On the surface, everything seemed fine, and the company made it onto the *Inc. 500* list of fast-growing small companies. But it turns out that the company wanted to issue stock because it expanded too quickly and didn't sell enough merchandise to cover its high overhead. The company ended up in bankruptcy.

Here's another problem with small businesses that seek investors: Many small-business owners take more risk and do less upfront planning and homework with other people's money. In fact, many well-intentioned people fail at their businesses.

An MBA I know from a top business school — I'll call him Jacob — convinced an investor to put up about $300,000 to purchase a small manufacturing company.

Jacob put a small amount of his own money into the business and immediately blew about $100,000 on a fancy computer-scheduling and order-entry system. Jacob wasn't interested much in sales (a job that the previous owner managed), so he also hired a sales manager. The sales manager he hired was a disaster — many of the front-line salespeople fled to competitors, taking key customers with them. He tried to cut costs, but doing so hurt the quality and timeliness of the company's products. By the time Jacob came to his senses, it was too late. The business dissolved, and the investor lost everything.

Drawing Up Your Business Plan

If you're motivated to start your own business, the next step is to figure out what you want to do and how you're going to do it. In other words, you need a *business plan.* You need a general plan that helps you define what you think you want to do and the tasks that you need to perform to accomplish your goal. The business plan — which you use to plan your goals, obtain loans, and show potential investors — should be a working document or blueprint for the early days, months, and years of your business.

You don't need a perfectly detailed plan that spells out all the minutiae. Making such an involved plan is a waste of your time because things change and evolve. The amount of detail that your plan needs depends on your goals and the specifics of your business. A simple, more short-term focused plan (10 pages or so) is fine if you don't aspire to build an empire. However, if your goal is to grow, hire employees, and open multiple locations, your plan needs to be longer (20 to 50 pages) to cover longer-term issues. If you want to pick up outside investor money, a longer business plan is a necessity.

TIP

As you put together your plan and evaluate your opportunities, open your ears and eyes. Expect to do research and speak with other entrepreneurs and people in the industry. Most folks will spend time talking with you as long as they realize that you don't want to compete with them. For more details on crafting a business plan, check out the latest edition of my book *Small Business For Dummies,* written with Jim Schell and published by Wiley.

Identifying your business concept

What do you want your business to do? What product or service do you want to offer? Maybe, for example, your business goal is to perform tax-preparation services for small-business owners. Or perhaps you want to start a consulting firm, open a restaurant that sells healthy fast-food, run a gardening service, or design and manufacture toys.

REMEMBER

Your concept doesn't need to be unique to survive in the business world. Consider the legions of self-employed consultants, plumbers, tax preparers, and restaurant owners. The existence of many other people who already do what you want to do validates the potential for your small-business ideas. I know many wage slaves who say they would love to run their own business if they could only come up with "the idea." Most of these people still dream about their small-business plans as they draw their Social Security checks. Being committed to the idea of running your own business is more important than developing the next great product or service. In the beginning, the business opportunities that you pursue can be quite general to your field of expertise or interest. What you eventually do over time will evolve.

I'm not saying that innovative ideas lack merit. Indeed, a creative idea gives you the chance to hit a big home run, and being the first person to successfully develop a new idea can help you achieve big success.

Even if you aspire to build the next billion-dollar company, you can put a twist on older concepts. Suppose that you're a veterinarian, but you don't want a traditional office where people must bring their cats and dogs for treatment. You believe that because many people are starved for free time or have pets that despise a trip to the vet's office, they want a vet who makes house calls. Thus, you open your Vet on Wheels business. You may also want to franchise the business and open locations around the country. However, you can also succeed by doing what thousands of other vets are now doing and have done over the years with a traditional office.

WET BLANKETS THROUGHOUT HISTORY

"This 'telephone' has too many shortcomings to be seriously considered as a means of communication. The device is inherently of no value to us." —Western Union internal memo in response to Alexander Graham Bell's telephone, 1876

"The concept is interesting and well formed, but in order to earn better than a C, the idea must be feasible." —A Yale University management professor in response to Fred Smith's paper proposing reliable overnight delivery service (Smith went on to found Federal Express Corporation.)

"We don't tell you how to coach, so don't tell us how to make shoes." —A large sporting shoe manufacturer to Bill Bowerman, inventor of the waffle shoe and cofounder of NIKE, Inc.

"So we went to Atari and said, 'Hey, we've got this amazing thing, even built with some of your parts, and what do you think about funding us? Or we'll give it to you. We just want to do it. Pay our salary, we'll come work for you.' And they said, 'No.' So then we went to Hewlett-Packard, and they said, 'Hey, we don't need you. You haven't got through college yet.'" —Steve Jobs, speaking about attempts to get Atari and Hewlett-Packard interested in his and Steve Wozniak's personal computer (Jobs and Wozniak founded Apple Computer.)

"'You should franchise them,' I told them. 'I'll be your guinea pig.' Well, they just went straight up in the air! They couldn't see the philosophy. . . . When they turned us down, that left Bud and me to swim on our own." —Sam Walton, describing his efforts to get the Ben Franklin chain interested in his discount retailing concept in 1962 (Walton went on to found Wal-Mart.)

"We don't like their sound, and guitar music is on the way out." —Decca Recording Company when rejecting The Beatles, 1962

In 1884, John Henry Patterson was ridiculed by his business friends for paying $6,500 for the rights to the cash register — a product with "limited" or no potential. Patterson went on to found National Cash Register (NCR) Corporation.

"What's all this computer nonsense you're trying to bring into medicine? I've got no confidence at all in computers, and I want nothing whatsoever to do with them." —A medical professor in England to Dr. John Alfred Powell, about the CT scanner

"That is good sport. But for the military, the airplane is useless." —Ferdinand Foch, Commander in Chief, Allied Forces on the Western Front, World War I

"The television will never achieve popularity; it takes place in a semi-darkened room and demands continuous attention." —Harvard Professor Chester L. Dawes, 1940

These quotes were reprinted with permission from *Beyond Entrepreneurship: Turning Your Business into an Enduring Great Company,* by James C. Collins and William C. Lazier (Prentice Hall).

Outlining your objectives

The reasons for starting and running your own small business are as varied as the entrepreneurs behind their companies. Before you start your firm, it's useful to think about your *objectives*, or what you're seeking to achieve. Your objectives need not be cast in concrete and will surely change over time. If you like, you can write a short and motivating mission statement.

Introductory economics courses teach students that the objective of every for-profit firm is to maximize profits. As with many things taught in economics courses, this theory has one problem: It doesn't hold up in reality. Most small-business owners I know don't manage their businesses maniacally in the pursuit of maximum profits. The following list gives you some other possible objectives to consider:

>> **Working with people you like and respect:** Some customers may buy your products and services, and some employees and suppliers may offer you their services for a good price, but what if you can't stand working with them? If you have sufficient business or just have your own standards, you can choose whom you do business with.

>> **Educating others:** Maybe part of your business goal is to educate the public about something that you're an expert in. I know that when I started my financial counseling and writing business, I saw education as a core part of my company's purpose.

>> **Improving an industry or setting a higher standard:** Perhaps part of your goal in starting your business is to show how your industry can better serve its customers. John Bogle, who founded the Vanguard Group of mutual funds, is a good example of someone who wanted to improve an industry. When he started Vanguard, Bogle structured the company so the shareholders (customers) of the company's individual mutual funds would own the company.

Because he relinquished ownership of his company, Bogle gave up the opportunity to build a personal net worth that would easily be worth several billion dollars today. But Bogle wanted to build a mutual fund company that kept operating costs to a minimum and returned profits to the customers in the form of lower operating fees, which are deducted from a mutual fund's returns. He's also been outspoken about how owners of many mutual fund companies operate their funds too much out of self-interest instead of keeping their customers in mind.

Of course, you can't accomplish these objectives without profits, and doing these things isn't inconsistent with generating greater profits. But if your objectives are more than financial or your financial objectives aren't your number-one concern, don't worry — that's usually a good sign. Remember the expression "Do what you love; the money will follow."

Analyzing the marketplace

REMEMBER

The single most important area to understand is the marketplace in which your business competes. To be successful, not only must your business produce a good product or service, but it must also reach customers and convince them to buy your product at a price at which you can make a profit. You should discern what the competition has to offer as well as its strengths and vulnerabilities. In most industries, you also need to understand government regulations that affect the type of business that you're considering.

Meeting customer needs

If the market analysis is the most important part of the business plan, understanding your potential customers is the most important part of your market analysis. Understanding your desired customers and their needs is one key to having a successful business.

If you're in a business that sells to consumers, consider your customers' characteristics, including gender, age, income, geographic location, marital status, number of children, education, living situation (rent or own), and the reasons they want your product or service. In other words, find out who your prospective customers are. Find out where they live and what they care about. If you sell to businesses, you need to understand similar issues. For instance, what types of businesses may buy your product or services? Why?

TIP

The best way to get to know your potential customers is to get out and talk to them. Even though live interviews are more time consuming, they allow you to go with the flow of the conversation, improvise questions, and probe more interesting areas. Although you can mail, email, or fax paper-based surveys to many people with a minimal investment of your time, the response rate is usually quite low, and the answers aren't usually as illuminating. To encourage better response, offer a product or service sample or some other promotional item to those who help you with your research. Doing so attracts people who are interested in your product or service, which helps you define your target customers.

Also try to get a sense of what customers do pay and will pay for the products or services that you offer. Analyzing the competition's offerings helps, too. Some products or services require follow-up or additional servicing. Understand what customers need and what they'll pay for your services.

If you want to raise money from investors, include some estimates as to the size of the market for your product or services. Of course, such numbers are ballpark estimates, but sizing the market for your product helps you estimate profitability, the share of the market needed to be profitable, and so on.

Besting the competition

Always examine the products, services, benefits, and prices that competitors offer. Otherwise, you go on blind faith that what you offer stacks up well to the alternatives in the industry.

TIP

Examine your competitors' weaknesses so you can exploit them. Instead of trying to beat them on their terms, maybe you've identified a need for a neighborhood pet supply store that offers a more specialized range of pet supplies than the big-selling brands of dog and cat food that warehouse stores sell. Providing knowledgeable customer sales representatives to answer customer questions and make product suggestions can also give you a competitive edge. Thus, you may be able to surpass the warehouse stores on three counts: convenience of location for people in your neighborhood, breadth of product offerings, and customer assistance.

WARNING

Even if you have a completely innovative product or service that no other business currently offers, don't make the mistake of thinking that you don't have competitors. All businesses have competitors. In the event that you've developed something truly unique that has little competition, your success will surely breed competition as imitators follow or attempt to leapfrog your lead.

Complying with regulations

Most businesses are subject to some sort of regulation. If you want to start a retail business, for example, few communities permit you to run it out of your home. If you lease or purchase a private location, the zoning laws in that location may restrict you. Therefore, you need to check what you can and can't sell at that location. Check with your city's or town's zoning department — don't simply believe a real estate broker or property owner who says, "No problem!" That person's goal, after all, is to sell the property.

If, for instance, you were going to start a veterinary practice, you would quickly discover that special zoning is required to use a piece of real estate for a vet's office. Convincing a local zoning board to allow a new location to get such special zoning is quite difficult, if not impossible.

Many businesses face other local, state, and even federal regulatory issues, including ordinances, laws, and the need for specific licenses and filings. For example, if you were opening a restaurant, you'd have to heed ordinances and laws that regulate everything from signage to operating hours to your ability to serve alcohol. And you'd be subject to an amazing array of health codes, building codes, and fire codes, to name a few.

TIP

If you enter an industry that you're relatively new to, ask questions and open your ears to find out more about where you should locate and how you should design and run your business. Speak to people who are currently in the field and to your local chamber of commerce to see what, if any, licenses or filings you must complete. Read books and trade magazines that may deal with your questions. Libraries have books and online services that can help you locate specific articles on topics that interest you.

Delivering your service or product

Every business has a product or service to sell. How are you going to provide this product or service to your customers? Suppose, for example, that you want to start a business that delivers groceries and runs errands for busy people or older and disabled people who can't easily perform daily tasks for themselves. Delineate the steps that you'll take to provide the service.

When potential customers call to inquire about your business, what kinds of information do you want to record about their situation? Contact software can assist with this task. Also, you can create a pricing sheet and other marketing literature (discussed in the next section) that you can send to curious potential customers.

If you want to manufacture a product, you definitely need to scope out the process that you're going to use. Otherwise, you have no idea how much time the manufacturing process may take or what the process may cost.

As your business grows and you hire employees to provide services or create your products, the more you codify what you do and the better your employees can replicate your good work.

Marketing your service or product

After you determine more in-depth information about delivering your company's services or products, you need to decide on specific marketing information. Answer the following questions:

>> **How much will you charge for your services and products?** Look at what competing products and services cost. Estimating your costs helps you figure out what you need to charge to cover your costs and make a reasonable profit.

>> **How will you position your products and services compared to the competition?** Consider, for example, how books position themselves in the

book marketplace. I hope, in your mind, that my financial books are down-to-earth, practical, answer-oriented, and educational.

>> **Where will you sell your product or service?** Business consultants call this decision the *distribution channel* question. For example, if you have a toy to sell, you may consider selling via mail order and the Internet, through toy stores, or through discount warehouse stores. Selling through each of these different distribution channels requires unique marketing and advertising programs. If you market a product or service to companies, you need to find out who the key decision makers are at the company and what will persuade them to buy your product or service.

Having a great product or service isn't enough if you keep it a secret; you gotta get the word out. You likely won't have the budget or the desire to reach the same region as television and radio, so start marketing your product to people you know. Develop a punchy, informative one-page letter that announces your company's inception and the products or services it offers, and then mail it to your contacts. Include an envelope with a reply form that allows recipients to provide the addresses of others who may be interested in what you have to offer. Send these folks a mailing as well, referencing who passed their names along to you.

Finding and retaining customers is vital to any business owner who wants his company to grow and be profitable. One simple, inexpensive way to stay in touch with customers you've dealt with or others who have made inquiries and expressed interest in your company's offerings is via a mailing list. Once a quarter, once a year, or whatever makes sense for your business, send out a simple, professional-looking postcard or newsletter announcing new information about your business and the customer needs you can fulfill. Such mailings allow you to remind people that you're still in business and that you provide a wonderful product or service. Computer software and websites (for example, Constant Contact) give you fast, efficient ways to keep customer mailing lists up-to-date and to print mailing labels.

WARNING

Emailing your marketing information has the attraction of no out-of-pocket expenses. However, due to the deluge of junk email most people get, your email is likely to be deleted without being opened. At least a snail-mailed postcard gets a prospective customer's attention, even if only for a brief period.

Organizing and staffing your business

Many small businesses are one-person operations. So much the better for you — you have none of the headaches of hiring, payroll, and so on. You only have to worry about you — and that may be a handful in itself!

But if you hope to grow your business and would rather manage the work being done instead of doing all of it yourself, you eventually want to hire people. (I explain the best way to fill your personnel needs in Chapter 14.) Give some thought now to the skills and functional areas of expertise that future hires need. If you want to raise money, the employment section of your business plan is essential to show your investors that you're planning long-term.

Maybe you want an administrative assistant, researcher, marketing director, or sales representative. What about a training specialist, finance guru, or real estate manager if your company expands? Consider the background that you want in those you hire, and look at the types of people that similar companies select.

REMEMBER

You should also consider what legal form of organization — for example, a sole proprietorship, partnership, S corporation, or limited liability company — your business will adopt. The legal form of your organization impacts, among other important issues, how the business is taxed and what its liabilities are in the event of a lawsuit. See Chapter 14 for details.

Projecting finances

WARNING

An idea may become a business failure if you neglect to consider or are unrealistic about the financial side of the business that you want to start. If you're a creative or people-person type who hates numbers, the financial side may be the part of the business plan that you most want to avoid. Don't — doing so can cost you tens of thousands of dollars in avoidable mistakes. Ignoring the financial side can even lead to the bankruptcy of a business founded with a good idea.

Before you launch your business, do enough research so you can come up with some decent financial estimates. Financial projections are mandatory, and knowledgeable investors will scrutinize them if you seek outside money. You also need to think through how and when investors can cash out.

Startup and development costs

Spending money to get your business from the idea stage to an operating enterprise is inevitable. Before the revenue begins to flow in, you incur expenditures as you develop and market your products and services. Therefore, you need to understand what you must spend money on and the approximate timing of the needed purchases.

If you were going to build a house, you'd develop a list of all the required costs. How much are the land, construction, carpeting, landscaping, and so on going to cost? You can try to develop all these cost estimates yourself, or you can speak with local builders and have them help you. Likewise, with your business, you can hire a business consultant who knows something about your type of business. However, I think you're best served by doing the homework yourself — you discover a lot more, and it's cheaper.

If you're going to work in an office setting, whether at home or in outside space, you need furniture (such as a desk, chair, filing cabinets, and so on), a computer, printer, and other office supplies. Don't forget to factor in the costs of any licenses or government registrations that you may need.

If you run a retailing operation, you also need to estimate your cost for establishing and maintaining an inventory of goods. Remember, selling your inventory takes time, especially when you first start up, and you need to have adequate stock on hand to fulfill reasonable customer orders in a timely fashion. And as a new business, suppliers won't give you months on end to pay. Be realistic — otherwise, the money that you tie up in inventory can send you to financial ruin.

Income statement

Preparing an estimated *income statement* that summarizes your expected revenue and expenses is a challenging and important part of your business plan. (I explain the elements of an income statement in Chapter 6.) Many estimates and assumptions go into it. As you prepare your estimated income statement, you may discover that making a decent profit is tougher than you thought. This section of your business plan helps you make pricing decisions.

Consider the Vet on Wheels business idea that I discuss in the "Identifying your business concept" section earlier in this chapter. What range of veterinary services can you provide if you make house calls? You can't perform all the services that you can in a larger office setting, so decide which ones are feasible. What equipment do you need to perform the services? How much should you charge for the services? You need to estimate all these things to develop a worthwhile income statement. You should be able to answer these questions from the insights and information you pulled together regarding what customers want and what your competitors are offering.

WARNING

With service businesses in which you or your employees sell your time, be realistic about how many hours you can bill. You may end up being able to bill only a third to half of your time, given the other management activities that you need to perform.

Because building a customer base takes several years, try to prepare estimated income statements for the first three years. In the earlier years, you have more startup costs, so creating income statements more often ensures you have a good handle on this typically lean period. In later years, you reap more profits as your customer rolls expand. Doing income statements over several years is also essential if you're seeking investor money.

Balance sheet

An income statement measures the profitability of a business over a span of time, such as a year, but it tells you nothing of a business's resources and obligations. That's what a *balance sheet* does. Just as your personal balance sheet itemizes your personal assets (for example, investments) and liabilities (debts you owe), a business balance sheet details a company's assets and liabilities.

If you operate a cash business — you provide a service and are paid for that service, and you don't hold any inventory, for example — a balance sheet has limited use. An exception is if you're trying to get a bank loan for your service business.

TIP

A detailed balance sheet isn't as important as tracking your available cash, which will likely be under pressure in the early years of a business because expenses can continue to exceed revenue for quite some time.

A complete balance sheet is useful for a business that owns significant equipment, furniture, inventory, and so on. The asset side of the balance sheet provides insight into the financial staying power of the company. For example, how much cash does your business have on hand to meet expected short-term bills? Conversely, the liability side of the ledger indicates the obligations, bills, and debts the company has coming due in the short and long term. See Chapter 6 for more information on all the elements of a balance sheet.

Writing an executive summary

An *executive summary* is a 2- to 3-page summary of your entire business plan that you can share with interested investors who may not want to first wade through a 40- to 50-page plan. The executive summary whets the prospective investor's appetite by touching on the highlights of your entire plan. Although this summary should go in the front of your plan document, I list this element last because you can't write an intelligent summary of your plan until you flesh out the body of your business plan.

Chapter 14

Starting and Running a Small Business

After you research and evaluate the needs of your prospective business (see Chapter 13 for more information), at some point you need to decide whether to actually *start* your business. If you really want to, you can conduct and analyze market research and crunch numbers until the cows come home. Even if you're a linear, logical, analytic, quantitative kind of person, you ultimately need to make a gut-level decision: Do you jump in the water and start swimming, or do you stay on the sidelines and remain a spectator? In my opinion, watching isn't nearly as fun as doing. If you feel ready but have some trepidation, you're normal — just go for it!

Starting Up: Your Preflight Checklist

When you take off into the world of small-business ownership, you need to make decisions about a number of important issues. Just like a pilot before he takes flight, you should make sure that all systems are in order and ready to do the job. If your fuel tanks aren't adequately filled, your engines aren't clean and in working order, and your wing flaps aren't in the proper position, you may never get your business off the ground or be able to stay in business long enough to succeed.

Preparing to leave your job

REMEMBER

You may never discover that you have the talent to run your own business, and perhaps have a good idea to boot, unless you prepare yourself financially and psychologically to leave your job. Financial and emotional issues cause many aspiring entrepreneurs to remain chained to their employers and cause those who do break free to soon return to bondage.

The money side of this self-exploration is easier to deal with than the emotional side, so I'll focus on finances. Dealing with a net reduction in the income that you bring home from work — at least in the early years of your business — is a foregone conclusion for the vast majority of small-business opportunities that you may pursue. Accept this fact and plan accordingly.

TIP

Do all you can to reduce your expenses to a level that fits the entrepreneurial life that you want to lead. Examine your monthly spending patterns to make your budget lean, mean, and entrepreneurially friendly. Determine what you spend each month on your rent (or mortgage), groceries, eating out, phone calls, insurance, and so on. Unless you're someone who keeps all this data detailed, you need to compile your checking and ATM transactions, credit card statements, and anything else that documents your spending habits. Don't forget to estimate your cash purchases that don't leave a trail, like when you eat lunch out.

Beyond the bare essentials of food, shelter, healthcare, and clothing, most of what you spend money on is discretionary — that is, you spend money on luxuries. Even the amount that you spend on the necessities, such as food and shelter, is probably only part necessity and may include a fair amount of luxury and waste. So make sure you question all expenditures! If you don't, you'll have to continue working as an employee, and you'll never be able to pursue your entrepreneurial dream. If you need a helping hand and an analyst's eye in preparing and developing strategies for reducing your spending, pick up a copy of the latest edition of my book *Personal Finance For Dummies* (Wiley).

In addition to reducing your spending before and during the period that you start your business, also figure out how to manage the income side of your personal finances. The following list gives you some proven strategies to ensure that you have sufficient income:

>> **Transition gradually.** One way to pursue your entrepreneurial dreams (and not starve while doing so) is to continue working part time in a regular job while you work part time at your own business. If you have a job that allows you to work part time, seize the opportunity. Some employers may even allow you to maintain your benefits. In addition to ensuring a steady source of income, splitting your time allows you to adjust to a new way of making a living. Some people have a hard time adjusting to their new lifestyle if they quit their jobs cold turkey and plunge headfirst into full-time entrepreneurship.

Another option is to completely leave your job but line up a chunk of work that provides a decent income for a portion of your weekly work hours. Consulting for your most recent employer is a time-tested first "entrepreneurial" option with low risk.

>> **Get (or stay) married.** Actually, as long as you're attached (married or not) to someone who maintains a regular job and you manage your spending so you can live on that person's income alone, you're golden! Just make sure you talk things through with the love of your life to minimize misunderstandings and resentment. Maybe someday you can return the favor — that's what my wife and I did. She was working in education (no big bucks there!) when I started an entrepreneurial venture after business school. We lived a Spartan lifestyle and made do just fine on her income. Several years later, when things were going well for me, she left her job to work on her own business.

Valuing and replacing your benefits

For many people, walking away from their employer's benefits, including insurance, retirement funds, and paid days off, is both financially and emotionally challenging. Benefits are valuable, but you may be surprised by how efficiently you can replicate them in your own business.

Health insurance

Some prospective entrepreneurs fret over finding new health insurance. However, unless you have a significant existing medical problem (known as a *preexisting condition*), getting health insurance as an individual isn't difficult. If you have such a condition, many states have high-risk pools that offer coverage options. You also have new protections under the 2010 federal healthcare bill (also known as Obamacare). This bill includes numerous provisions affecting small businesses. However, as of this writing, it's unclear exactly when some of the small business provisions will take effect. For updated information on this topic, visit my website at www.erictyson.com.

When you're seeking health insurance, first explore whether you can convert your existing coverage through your employer's group plan into individual coverage. Just don't act on this potentially attractive option until you've explored other health plans on your own, which may offer similar benefits at lower cost. Also, get proposals for individual coverage from major health plans in your area.

TIP

Take a high deductible, if available, to keep costs down. Having a *high-deductible health plan,* which is defined as an individual plan with a deductible of at least $1,250 or a family plan with a minimum $2,500 deductible for tax year 2011 (this amount increases over time with inflation), qualifies you to contribute money into a Health Savings Account (HSA). The contribution limits are up to $3,300 for individuals and $6,550 for families for tax year 2014, and these amounts increase over time with inflation. (Folks age 55 or older can put away an extra $1,000 per year.) Contributions to an HSA reduce your current year's taxable income, and the money compounds without taxation over time. Withdrawals aren't taxed so long as you use the money for qualified healthcare expenses, which are fairly broadly defined and include traditional out-of-pocket medical expenses (doctors and hospital care) as well as dental care, prescription drugs, psychologist expenses, vision care, and so on.

WARNING

Government regulations called *COBRA* require an employer with 20 or more employees to continue health insurance coverage (at your own expense) for up to 18 months after terminating employment. Moreover, if you have or develop a health problem while covered under COBRA, the law enables you to purchase an individual policy at the same price that a healthy individual can. These laws create a nice buffer zone for the budding entrepreneur, but don't get lazy and wait until the last minute of the 18th month to start shopping for your individual plan — COBRA plans can be costly. Shopping around and locking in an individual plan as soon as possible can save money and prevent headaches.

Long-term disability insurance

For most working people, their greatest asset is their ability to earn money. If you suffer a disability and can't work, how would you manage financially? Long-term disability insurance protects your income in the event of a disability.

REMEMBER

Before you leave your job, secure an individual long-term disability policy. After you leave your job and are no longer earning steady income, you won't qualify for a policy. Most insurers want to see at least six months of self-employment income before they'll write you a policy. If you become disabled during this time, you're uninsured and out of luck — that's a big risk to take!

TIP

Check with any professional associations that you belong to or could join to see whether they offer long-term disability plans. Association plans are sometimes less expensive because of the group's purchasing power.

Life insurance

If you have dependents who count on your income, you need life insurance. And unlike with disability insurance, you can generally purchase a life insurance policy at a lower cost than you can purchase additional coverage through your employer.

Retirement plans

If your employer offers retirement savings programs, such as a 401(k) plan or a pension plan, don't despair about not having these in the future. (Of course, what you've already earned and accumulated while employed is yours.) One of the best benefits of self-employment is the availability of retirement savings plans — SEP-IRAs (Simplified Employee Pension Individual Retirement Accounts) and Keoghs — that allow you to sock away a hefty chunk of your earnings on a tax-deductible basis.

Retirement plans are a terrific way for you and your employees to shield a sizeable portion of earnings from taxation. If you don't have employees, regularly contributing to one of these plans is usually a no-brainer. With employees, the decision is a bit more complicated but often still a great idea. Small businesses with a number of employees can also consider 401(k) plans. I explain retirement plans in more detail in Chapter 3.

Other benefits

Besides insurance and retirement plans, employers offer other benefits that you may value. But don't get too bummed yet. These benefits aren't true benefits, so you won't miss much if you branch out on your own. For example, you *seem* to get paid holidays and vacations. In reality, though, your employer simply spreads your salary over 52 weeks, thus paying you for actually working the other 47 weeks or so out of the year. You can do the same by building the cost of this paid time off into your product and service pricing.

Another "benefit" of working for an employer is that the employer pays for half of your Social Security and Medicare taxes. Although you must pay the entire tax when you're self-employed, the IRS allows you to take half of this amount as a tax deduction on your annual tax Form 1040. So, really, this tax isn't as painful as you think. As with vacations and holidays, you can simply build the cost of this tax into your product and service pricing. Just think: Your employer could pay you a higher salary if it weren't paying half of these taxes as a benefit.

TIP

Some employers offer other insurance plans, such as dental or vision care plans. Ultimately, these plans only cover small out-of-pocket expenditures that aren't worth insuring. Don't waste your money purchasing such policies when you're self-employed. (*Note:* One of the reasons that Obamacare-compliant health insurance plans are costly is the mandated pediatric dental and vision coverage.)

Financing Your Business

When you create your business plan (which I explain how to do in Chapter 13), you should estimate your startup and development costs. Luckily, you can start many worthwhile small businesses with little capital. The following sections explain methods for financing your business.

Going it alone by bootstrapping

Making do with a small amount of capital and spending only what you can afford is known as *bootstrapping.* Bootstrapping is just a fancy way of saying that a business lives within its own means and without external support. This strategy forces a business to be more resourceful and less wasteful. Bootstrapping is also a great training mechanism for producing cost-effective products and services. It offers you the advantage of getting into business with little capital.

Millions of successful small companies were bootstrapped at one time or another. Like small redwood saplings that grow into towering trees, small companies that had to bootstrap in the past can eventually grow into hundred million–dollar (and even multi-billion-dollar) companies. For example, Hewlett-Packard's founders started their company out of a garage in Palo Alto, California. Microsoft, Motorola, Sony, and Disney were all bootstrapped, too.

Whether you want to maintain a small shop that employs just yourself, hire a few employees, or dream about building a large company, you need capital. However, misconceptions abound about how much money a company needs to achieve its goals and sources of funding.

"There's an illusion that most companies need tons of money to get established and grow," says James Collins, former lecturer at the Stanford Graduate School of Business and coauthor of the bestsellers *Built to Last* and *Good to Great: Why Some Companies Make the Leap . . . and Others Don't.* "The Silicon Valley success stories of companies that raise gobs of venture capital and grow 4,000 percent are very rare. They are statistically insignificant but catch all sorts of attention," he adds.

Studies show that the vast majority of small businesses obtain their initial capital from personal savings and family and friends rather than outside sources, such as banks and venture capital firms. A Harvard Business School study of the *Inc. 500* (500 large, fast-growing private companies) found that more than 80 percent of the successful companies started with funds from the founder's personal savings. The median startup capital was a modest $10,000, and these are successful, fast-growing companies! Slower-growing companies tend to require even less capital.

With the initial infusion of capital, many small businesses can propel themselves for years after they develop a service or product that brings in more cash flow. Jim

Gentes, the founder of Giro, the bike helmet manufacturer, raised $35,000 from personal savings and loans from family and friends to make and distribute his first product. He then used the cash flow from the first product for future products.

REMEMBER

Eventually, a successful, growing company may want outside financing to expand faster. Raising money from investors or lenders is much easier after you demonstrate that you know what you're doing and that a market exists for your product or service. (Check out the following section for info on getting a bank loan.)

As I explain in the earlier section "Preparing to leave your job," aspiring entrepreneurs must examine their personal finances for opportunities to reduce their own spending. If you want to start a company, the best time for you to examine your finances is years before you want to hit the entrepreneurial path. As with other financial goals, advance preparation can go a long way toward helping start a business. The best funding source and easiest investor to please is you.

Alan Tripp, founder and CEO of Score Learning, a chain of storefront interactive learning centers, planned for seven years before he took the entrepreneurial plunge. He funded his first retail center fully from personal savings. He and his wife lived frugally to save the necessary money. Tripp's first center proved the success of his business concept: retail learning centers where kids can use computers to improve their reading, math, and science skills. With a business plan crafted over time and hard numbers to demonstrate the financial viability of his operation, Tripp then successfully raised funds from investors to open many more centers. (Kaplan Inc. ultimately bought his company.)

Some small-business founders put the cart before the horse and don't plan and save for starting their business the way Tripp did. And in many cases, small-business owners want capital but don't have a clear plan or need for it.

Taking loans from banks and other outside sources

If you're starting a new business or have been in business for just a few years, borrowing, particularly from banks, may be difficult. Borrowing money is easier when you don't really need to do so. No one knows this fact better than small-business owners.

REMEMBER

Small-business owners who successfully obtain bank loans do their homework. To borrow money from a bank, you generally need a business plan, three years of financial statements and tax returns for the business and its owner, and projections for the business. Seek out banks that are committed to and understand the small-business marketplace.

The Small Business Administration (SBA) guarantees some small-business loans that banks originate. Because many small businesses lack collateral and pose a higher loan risk, banks wouldn't otherwise make many of these loans. The SBA, in addition to guaranteeing loans for existing businesses, grants about 20 percent of its loans to startup businesses, which must have founders who put up at least a third of the funds needed and demonstrate a thorough understanding of the business, ideally through prior related industry experience.

ERIC'S
PICKS

The SBA offers a number of workshops and counseling services for small-business owners. Its SCORE (Service Corps of Retired Executives) consulting services provide free advice and critiques of business plans as well as advice on raising money for your business (www.score.org; 800-634-0245). The SBA charges a nominal fee for seminars. To get more information on SBA's services and how to contact a local office, call 800-827-5722 or visit its website at www.sba.gov.

If you don't have luck with banks or the SBA, consider the following:

>> **Credit unions can be a source of financial help.** They're often more willing to make personal loans to individuals.

>> **Borrowing against the equity in your home or other real estate is advantageous.** This strategy is helpful because real estate loans generally entail lower and tax-deductible interest.

>> **Retirement savings plans can bridge the gap.** You may be able to borrow against your investment balance, and such loans are usually available at competitive rates through employer-based plans. Just make sure you don't take on too much debt and jeopardize your retirement savings.

>> **Credit cards may be useful as a last resort.** If you've got the itch to get your business going but can't wait to save the necessary money and lack other ways to borrow, the plastic in your wallet may be your ticket to operation. You can acquire some credit cards at interest rates of 10 percent or less. *Remember:* Because credit cards are unsecured loans, if your business fails and you can't pay back your debt, your home equity and assets in retirement accounts aren't at risk.

REMEMBER

No matter what type of business you have in mind and how much money you think you need to make it succeed, be patient. Start small enough that you don't need outside capital (unless you're in an unusual situation where your window of opportunity is now and will close if you don't get funding quickly). Starting your business without outside capital instills the discipline required for building a business piece by piece over time. The longer you can wait to get a loan or an equity investment, the better the terms generally are for you and your business because the risk is lower for the lender or investor.

Borrowing from family and friends

Because they know you and hopefully like and trust you, your family and friends may seem like good sources of investment money for your small business. They also likely have the added advantage of offering you better terms than a banker, wealthy investor, or a venture capitalist.

However, before you solicit and accept money from those you love, consider the following pitfalls:

>> **Defaulting on a loan can cause hard feelings.** If your business hits the skids, defaulting on a loan made by a large, anonymous lender is one thing, but defaulting on a loan from your dear relatives can make future Thanksgiving meals mighty uncomfortable!

>> **Most entrepreneurs receive surprisingly little encouragement from the people they're close to.** Your parents, for example, may think that you've severed some of your cerebral synapses if you announce your intention to quit your job, which provides a lofty job title, decent pay, and benefits. The lack of emotional support may discourage you more than the lack of financial support.

>> **You lose out on the experience of a seasoned investor.** Family and friends may lack important practical experience with similar ventures and may be unable to provide the type of guidance that a seasoned investor could.

Family investments in a small business work best under the following conditions:

>> **You prepare and sign a letter of agreement that spells out the terms of the investment or loan.** In other words, you act as if you're doing business with a banker or some other investor you know for business purposes only. I also recommend clearly disclosing in writing the risk of losing one's entire investment. As time goes on, people have selective recall. Putting things in writing reminds everyone what was agreed to and what's at risk.

>> **You're quite certain that you can repay the loan.** Otherwise, you run into the issue I discuss earlier: You default on the loan and burn bridges with your closest loved ones. No business is worth losing your family or friends.

>> **You can start your business with an equity investment.** With an equity investment, a person is willing and able to lose all the money invested but hopes to hit a home run while helping you with your dream. (Check out the next section for more on equity investments.)

Courting investors and selling equity

Beyond family members and friends, private individuals with sufficient funds — also known as wealthy individuals — are your next best source of capital if you want an equity investor (and not a loan from a lender). However, before you approach wealthy people, you must have a solid business plan, which I explain how to prepare in Chapter 13.

A worthwhile *angel investor* (a wealthy individual who invests in small companies) has a track record of success with somewhat similar businesses that she's funded and brings other things to the table besides money, such as strategic advice, helpful business contacts, and so on.

Although you want an investor to care about your business, it's best if his investment in your business is no more than 5 to 10 percent of his total investment portfolio. No one wants to lose money, but doing so is less painful when you diversify well. A $50,000 investment from an investor with a $5 million portfolio is risking just 1 percent of his portfolio.

TIP

Finding people who may be interested in investing requires persistence and creativity. Consider these approaches:

>> Consult tax advisors and attorneys you know who may have contacts.

>> Network with successful entrepreneurs in similar fields.

>> Think about customers or suppliers who like your business and believe in its potential.

One friend of mine sent hundreds of letters to people who lived in upscale neighborhoods in the city where he lived. The letter, a one-page summary of his investment opportunity, got an astounding 5 percent response for interest in receiving a business plan. Ultimately through this search method, he found one wealthy investor who funded his entire deal.

Here's how to determine how much of the business you're selling for the amount invested. Basically, the equity percentage should hinge on what the whole business is worth (see Chapter 15 for details on valuing a business). If your whole business is worth $500,000 and you're seeking $100,000 from investors, that $100,000 should buy 20 percent of the business.

REMEMBER

New businesses are the hardest to value — yet another reason you're best off trying to raise money *after* you demonstrate some success. The further along you are, the lower the risk to an investor and the lower the cost to you (in terms of how much equity you must give up) to raise money.

THE *SHARK TANK* PHENOMENON

The television show *Shark Tank* is popularizing small business and angel investors investing in those small businesses. I enjoy the show, which first aired in 2009, and watch it regularly.

Small-business owners pitch their business to a panel of five wealthy and highly successful businesspeople turned angel investors. After a brief explanation of their business and product or service, the small-business owners ask for a specific investment amount in exchange for a particular portion of equity in the business. For example, a business owner might be seeking $100,000 in exchange for a 10 percent equity stake in their business. This would imply that their business has an overall value of $1,000,000.

In a typical one-hour episode, four different businesses make their pitches. (Thousands of businesses seek to be on the show, but few are selected.) So the small-business owners seeking an investment have to get to the point and be able to answer questions concisely. Of course, the real world of business doesn't work so quickly. It takes time to court an investor, meet with them, and so on. (Investors on the panel on the show are provided background about the business beyond what they hear on the show.)

What I think is most helpful about the show is that it enables you to hear how very successful businesspeople evaluate a business for investment purposes and what they're looking for and looking out for. You also get to see what business opportunities small-business owners are pursuing and what's working and not working for them.

Deciding Whether to Incorporate

Most businesses operate as *sole proprietorships*, a status limited to one owner or a married couple. If you run a sole proprietorship, you report your business income and costs on your tax return on Schedule C (Profit or Loss From Business), which you attach to your personal income tax return, Form 1040.

Incorporating, which establishes a distinct legal entity under which you do business, takes time and costs money. Therefore, incorporation must offer some benefits. Here are two main benefits of going through the process:

>> **Because corporations are legal entities distinct from their owners, they offer features that a proprietorship or partnership doesn't.** For example, corporations can have shareholders who own a piece or percentage of the company. These shares can be sold or transferred to other owners, subject to any restrictions in the shareholder's agreement.

>> **Corporations offer continuity of life.** In other words, corporations can continue to exist despite an owner's death or the owner's transfer of her stock in the company.

In the following sections, I detail the other benefits, along with possible drawbacks, of incorporating so you can decide whether it's the right choice for you.

TIP

Don't waste your money incorporating if you simply want to maintain a corporate-sounding name. If you operate as a sole proprietor, you can choose to operate under a different business name ("doing business as," or d.b.a.) without the cost and hassles of incorporating.

Looking for liability protection

A major reason to consider incorporation is liability protection. Incorporation effectively separates your business from your personal finances, thereby better protecting your personal assets from lawsuits that may arise from your business.

INVESTIGATE

Before you incorporate, ask yourself (and perhaps others in your line of business or advisors — legal, tax, and so on — who work with businesses like yours) what can cause someone to sue you. Then see whether you can purchase insurance to protect against these potential liabilities. Insurance is superior to incorporation because it pays claims, and people can still sue you if you're incorporated. If you incorporate and someone successfully sues you, your company must cough up the money for the claim, and doing so may sink your business. Only insurance can cover such financially destructive claims.

People can also sue you if, for example, they slip and suffer an injury while on your property. To cover these types of claims, you can purchase a property or premises liability policy from an insurer.

TIP

Accountants, doctors, and a number of other professionals can buy liability insurance. A good place to start searching for liability insurance is through the associations for your profession. Even if you're not a current member, check out the associations anyway — you may be able to access the insurance without membership, or you can join the association long enough to sign up. (Associations also sometimes offer competitive rates on disability insurance.)

Taking advantage of tax-deductible insurance and other benefits

A variety of insurance and related benefits are tax-deductible for all employees of an incorporated business. These benefits include the full cost of health and disability insurance as well as up to $50,000 in term life insurance per employee.

A new health insurance premium tax credit is available to qualifying small employers. Among other requirements, employers must have fewer than 25 full-time employees, and the annual employee wages must average less than $50,000. For tax year 2014 and beyond, the credit is 50 percent of the employer's qualifying health insurance premium expenses. The credit is calculated and claimed on IRS Form 8941.

In addition to insurance, incorporated companies can also hold dependent-care plans in which up to $5,000 per employee may be put away on a tax-deductible basis for childcare and care for elderly parents. Corporations can also offer cafeteria or flexible spending plans that allow employees to pick and choose which benefits they spend their benefit dollars on.

If your business isn't incorporated, you and the other business owners can't deduct the cost of insurance plans for yourselves. However, you can deduct these costs for your employees as well as your health insurance costs for yourself and covered family members.

Cashing in on corporate taxes

Aside from the tax treatment of insurance and other benefits, another difference between operating as a sole proprietor and as a corporation is that the government taxes a corporation's profits differently from those realized in a sole proprietorship. Which is better for your business depends on your situation.

Suppose that your business performs well and makes lots of money. If your business isn't incorporated, the government taxes all profits from your business on your personal tax return in the year that your company earns those profits. If you intend to use these profits to reinvest in your business and expand, incorporating can potentially save you some tax dollars. (However, this tax-reducing tactic doesn't work for personal service corporations, such as accounting, legal, and medical firms, which pay a higher tax rate.)

Resist the short-term temptation to incorporate just so you can have money left in the corporation taxed at a lower rate. If you want to pay yourself the profits in the future, you can end up paying more taxes. Why? Because you first pay taxes at the corporate tax rate in the year that your company earns the money, and then you pay taxes again on your personal income tax return when the corporation pays you.

Another reason not to incorporate, especially in the early months of a business, is that you can't immediately claim the losses for an incorporated business on your personal tax return. Because most businesses produce little revenue in their early years and have all sorts of startup expenditures, losses are common.

S CORPORATIONS AND LIMITED LIABILITY COMPANIES: THE BEST OF BOTH WORLDS?

Wouldn't it be nice to get the liability protection and other benefits that come with incorporating without the tax complications and hassles? Well, S corporations or limited liability companies may be for you.

Subchapter S corporations provide the liability protection that comes with incorporation. Likewise, the business profit or loss passes through to the owner's personal tax return, so if the business shows a loss in some years, the owner may claim those losses in the current year of the loss on his personal tax return. If you plan to take all the profits out of the company (instead of reinvesting them), an S corporation may make sense for you.

The IRS allows most small businesses to operate as S corporations but not all. In order to be an S corporation, a company must be a U.S. company, have just one class of stock, and have no more than 35 shareholders (who are all U.S. residents or citizens and who are not partnerships, corporations, or, with certain exceptions, trusts).

Limited liability companies (LLCs) offer business owners benefits similar to those of S corporations but are even better in some cases. Like an S corporation, an LLC offers liability protection for the owners. LLCs also pass the business's profits and losses through to the owner's personal income tax returns.

But limited liability companies have fewer restrictions regarding shareholders. For example, LLCs have no limits on the number of shareholders, and the shareholders in an LLC can be foreigners, corporations, and partnerships.

Compared with S corporations, the only additional restriction LLCs carry is that sole proprietors and professionals can't always form an LLC (although they can in some states). Most state laws require you to have at least two partners and not be a professional service firm (for example, accounting, legal, or medical firms).

Making the decision to incorporate

If you're totally confused about whether to incorporate because your business is undergoing major financial changes, it's worth getting competent professional help. The hard part is knowing where to turn, because finding one advisor who can put together all the pieces of the puzzle (including the financial, legal, and tax-related aspects) is challenging. Also be aware that you may get wrong or biased advice.

TIP

Although most attorneys and tax advisors don't understand the business side of business, some do. So try to find one who does. You may need to hire a business advisor along with your attorney or tax advisor. Attorneys who specialize in advising small businesses can help explain the legal issues. Tax advisors who perform a lot of work with business owners can help explain the tax considerations.

If you've weighed the factors and you still can't decide, my advice is to keep your business simple — don't incorporate. Why? Because after you incorporate, unincorporating takes time and money. Start off your business as a sole proprietorship and then take it from there. Wait until the benefits of incorporating your business clearly outweigh the costs and drawbacks.

Finding and Keeping Customers

When you write your business plan (see Chapter 13), you need to think about your business's customers. Just as the sun is the center of the solar system, everything in your business revolves around your customers. If you take care of your customers, they'll take care of you and your business for many years.

Obtaining a following

When you're ready to attract customers, put together a mailing list of people you know who may be interested in what you're offering. Draft and mail an upbeat, one-page letter that provides an overview of what your business offers. As you have news to report — successes, new products and services, and so on — do another mailing.

REMEMBER

Short letters are read more than glossy advertising newsletters. Most people are busy and don't care about your business enough to read a lengthy piece of mail. Email lists may work as well and are attractive due to their lower costs. Use a service like Constant Contact, which enables you to track how many people actually open and click on links in your emails.

In addition to mailings, other successful ways to get the word out and attract customers are limited only to your imagination and resourcefulness. Consider the following ideas:

>> **If your business idea is innovative or somehow different, or if you have grand expansion plans, add some local media people to your mailing list.** Newspaper, radio, and even television business reporters are always looking for story ideas. So include them in your mailings, and send them the one-page updates as well. Just remember to make your press releases information pieces and not advertisements.

>> **If your business seeks customers in a specific geographic area, blanket that area by mailing your one-page letter or delivering it door to door.** You can include a coupon that offers your products or services at a reduced cost (perhaps at the cost you pay) to get people to try them. Make sure that people know this deal is a special opening-for-business bargain.

Providing solid customer service

REMEMBER

After you attract customers, treat them as you would like to be treated by a business. If customers like your products and services, not only do they come back to buy more when the need arises, but they also tell others. (However, keep in mind that they're even more likely to tell others when they have a bad experience!) Satisfied customers are every business's best cost-effective marketers.

I never cease to be amazed by how many businesses have mediocre or poor customer service. One reason for poor service is that as your business grows, your employees are on the customer service front lines. If you don't hire good people and give them the proper incentives to serve customers, many of them won't do it. For most employees on a salary, the day-to-day task of assisting customers may be just an annoyance for them.

TIP

One way to make your staff care about customer service is to base part of their pay on the satisfaction of the customers they work with. Tie bonuses and increases at review time to this issue. You can easily measure customer satisfaction with a simple survey form.

Treating the customer right starts the moment that the selling process begins. Honesty is an often-underused business tool. More than a few salespeople mislead and lie in order to close a sale. Many customers discover after their purchase that they've been deceived, and they get angry. These unethical businesses likely lose not only future business from customers but also surely — and justifiably — referrals.

If your business doesn't perform well for a customer, apologize and bend over backward to make the customer happy. Offer a discount on the problem purchase or, if possible, a refund on product purchases. Also, make sure you have a clear return-and-refund policy. Bend that policy if doing so helps you satisfy an unhappy customer or rids you of a difficult customer.

Setting Up Shop

No matter what type of business you have in mind, you need space to work from, whether it's a spare room in your home, shared office space, or a small factory. You also need to outfit that space with tools of your trade. This section explains how to tackle these tasks.

Finding business space and negotiating a lease

Unless you can run your business from your home, you may be in the market for office or retail space. Finding good space and buying or leasing it both take plenty of time if done right.

WARNING

In the early years of your business, buying an office or a retail building generally doesn't make sense. The down payment consumes important capital, and you may end up spending lots of time and money on a real estate transaction for a location that may not interest you in the long term. Buying this type of real estate rarely makes sense unless you plan to stay put for five or more years. Leasing a space for your business is far more practical.

Renting office space is simpler than renting retail space because a building owner worries less about your business and its financial health. Your business needs more credibility to rent a retail building because your retail business affects the nature of the strip mall or shopping center where you lease. Owners of such properties don't want to move in quick failures or someone who does a poor job of running his business.

If you and your business don't have a track record with renting space, getting references is useful. If you seek well-located retail space, you must compete with national chains like Walgreens, so you better have a top-notch credit rating and track record. Consider subletting — circulate flyers to businesses that may have some extra space in the area in which you want to locate your business. Also prepare financial statements that show your personal and business creditworthiness.

Brokers list most spaces for lease. Working with a broker can be useful, but the same conflicts exist as with residential brokers (see Chapter 12). So also examine spaces for lease without a broker, and deal with the landlord directly. Such landlords may give you a better deal, and they don't worry about recouping a brokerage commission.

INVESTIGATE

The biggest headaches with leasing space are understanding and negotiating the lease contract. Odds are that the lessor presents you with a standard, preprinted lease contract that she says is fair and is the same lease that everyone else signs. Don't sign it! This contract is the lessor's first offer. Have an expert review it and help you modify it. Find yourself an attorney who regularly deals with such contracts.

SHOULD YOU WORK FROM HOME?

You may be able to run a relatively simple small business from your home. If you have the choice of running your business out of your home versus securing outside office space, consider the following issues:

- **Cost control:** As I discuss earlier in this chapter, bootstrapping your business can make a lot of financial and business sense. If you have space in your home that you can use, you've found yourself a rent-free business space. (However, if you're considering buying a larger home to have more space, you can't really say that your home office is rent-free.)

- **Business issues:** What are the needs of your business and customers? If you don't require fancy office space to impress others or to meet with clients, work at home. If you operate a retail business that requires lots of customers coming to you, getting outside space is probably the best (and legally correct) choice. Check with the governing authorities of your town or city to find out what local regulations exist for home-based businesses.

- **Discipline:** At home, do you have the discipline to work the number of hours that you need and want, or will the kitchen goodies tempt you to make half a dozen snack trips? Can you refrain from turning on the television every hour for late-breaking news or constantly surfing the Internet for stock quotes, personal research, and entertainment? The sometimes amorphous challenge of figuring out how to grow the business may cause you to focus your energies elsewhere.

- **Family matters:** Last but not least, your home life should factor into where you decide to work. One advantage to working at home when you're a parent is that you can be a more involved parent. If nothing else, you can spend the one to two hours per day with your kids that you would have spent commuting! Just make sure you try to set aside work hours during which time your office is off limits.

Ask other family members how they feel about your working at home. Be specific about what you plan to do, where, when, and how. Will clients come over? What time of day and where in the home will you meet with them? You may not think that your home office is an imposition, but your spouse may. Home business problems come between many couples. If you're single and living alone, home life is less of an issue.

Office leases are usually simpler than retail leases. About the most complicated issue you face with office leases is that they can be *full service,* which includes janitorial benefits. Retail leases, however, are usually *triple-net,* which means that you as the tenant pay for maintenance (for example, resurfacing the parking lot, cleaning, and gardening), utilities, and property taxes. You're correct to worry about a triple-net retail lease because you can't control many of these expenses. For example, if the property is sold, property taxes can jump.

REMEMBER

Here are provisions to keep in mind when dealing with a triple-net lease:

>> Compare your site's costs to other sites to evaluate the deal that the lessor offers you.

>> Your lease contract needs to include a cap for the triple-net costs at a specified limit per square foot.

>> Try to make sure that the lease contract doesn't make you responsible for removal costs for any toxic waste you may discover during your occupation. Also exclude increased property taxes that the sale of the property may cause.

>> If feasible, get your landlord to pay for remodeling. It's cheaper for the landlord to do it and entails fewer hassles for you.

>> With retail leases, get an option for renewal. This renewal option is critical in retail, where location is important. The option should specify the cost — for example, something like 5 percent below market, as determined by arbitration.

>> Get an option that the lease can be transferred to a new owner if you sell the business.

If you really think you want to purchase (not lease) because you can see yourself staying in the same place for at least five years, head to Chapter 11.

Equipping your business space

You can easily go overboard spending money when leasing or buying office space and outfitting that space. The most common reason that small-business owners spend more than they should is to attempt to project a professional, upscale image. You can have an office or retail location that works for you and your customers without spending a fortune if you observe some simple rules:

>> **Buy — don't lease or finance — equipment.** Unless you're running a manufacturing outfit where the cost of buying equipment is prohibitive, try to avoid borrowing and leasing. If you can't buy office furniture, computers, cash registers, and so on with cash, you probably can't afford them! Buying such things on credit or leasing them — leasing is invariably the most expensive way to go — encourages you to spend beyond your means.

Consider buying used equipment, especially furniture, which takes longer to become obsolete. The more popular a piece of equipment, the more beneficial it is for you to purchase rather than lease: If many other businesses would be willing to buy the equipment, you'll have an easier time unloading it if you ever want to sell it. Leasing may make more sense with oddball-type equipment that is more of a hassle and costly for you to unload after a short usage period.

>> **Don't get carried away with technological and marketing gadgets.** Some small-business owners spend excessively on the latest tech gadgets that they don't really need because they feel the need to be "competitive" and "current." Don't forget the virtues of picking up the phone or meeting in person — these forms of communication are much more personal ways of doing business.

Bootstrap-equipping your office makes sense within certain limits (see "Going it alone by bootstrapping," earlier in this chapter). If customers come to you, of course, you don't want a shabby-looking store or office. However, you don't have to purchase the Rolls-Royce equivalent of everything that you need for your office.

Accounting for the Money

One of the less glamorous aspects of running your own business is dealing with accounting. Unlike when you work for an employer, you must track your business's income, expenses, and taxes (for you *and* your employees). Although you may be able to afford to hire others to help with these dreary tasks, you still must know the inner workings of your business to keep control of your company, to stay out of trouble with the tax authorities, and to minimize your taxes. The following sections explain how to handle the accounting aspect of your business.

Maintaining tax records and payments

With revenue hopefully flowing into your business and expenses surely heading out, you must keep records to help satisfy your tax obligations and keep a handle on the financial status and success of your business. You can't accurately complete the necessary tax forms for your business if you don't properly track your income and expenses. And should the IRS audit you (the probability of being audited as a small-business owner is about four times higher than when you're an employee at a company), you may need to prove some or even all of your expenses and income.

REMEMBER

In order to keep your sanity, and keep the IRS at bay, make sure you do the following:

>> **Pay your taxes each quarter and on time.** When you're self-employed, you're responsible for the accurate and timely filing of all taxes that you owe on your income on a quarterly basis. You must pay taxes by the 15th of January, April, June, and September. (If the 15th falls on the weekend, payment is due the Monday that follows the 15th.) Call the IRS at 800-TAX-FORM (800-829-3676) and ask for Form 1040-ES (Estimated Tax for Individuals), or download this form from www.irs.gov. This form comes with an easy-to-use estimated tax worksheet and four payment coupons that you send in with your quarterly tax payments. Mark the due dates for your quarterly taxes on your calendar so you don't forget!

If you have employees, you also need to withhold taxes from each paycheck they receive. You must then use the money that you deduct from their paychecks to make timely payments to the IRS and the appropriate state authorities. In addition to federal and state income tax, you need to withhold and send in Social Security and any other state or locally mandated payroll taxes. Pay these taxes immediately after withholding them from your employees' paychecks, and *never* use the money to fund your business needs.

I recommend using a payroll service to ensure that your payments are made correctly and on time to all the different places that these tax filings need to go.

>> **Keep your business accounts separate from your personal accounts.** The IRS knows that small-business owners have more opportunity to hide business income and inflate business expenses. Thus, the IRS looks skeptically at business owners who use and commingle funds in personal checking and credit card accounts for business transactions.

Although you may find opening and maintaining separate business accounts bothersome, do so. And remember to pay for only legitimate business expenses through your business account. You'll be thankful come tax preparation time to have separate records. Having separate records can also make the IRS easier to deal with if you're audited.

>> **Keep good records of your business income and expenses.** You can use file folders, software, or a shoebox to collect your business income and expenses. Whatever your method, just do it! When you're ready to file your annual return, you need the documentation that allows you to figure your business income and expenses.

Charging expenses on a credit card or writing a check can make the documentation for most businesses easier. These methods of payment leave a paper trail that simplifies the task of tallying up your expenses come tax time, and they also make the IRS auditor less grumpy in the event that he audits you. (Just make sure you don't overspend, as many people do with credit cards!)

In addition to keeping good records, you also need to decide on what basis, cash or accrual, you want your company to keep its books. Here's the lowdown on the options:

>> **Cash:** Most small-business owners use the *cash* method, which simply means that for tax purposes, you recognize or report income in the year it's received and expenses in the year they're paid.

>> **Accrual:** The *accrual* method, by contrast, records income when the sale is made, even if the customer hasn't yet paid; expenses are recognized when incurred even if your business hasn't paid the bill yet.

Sole proprietorships, partnerships, and S and personal service corporations generally can use the cash method. C corporations and partnerships that have C corporations as partners may not use the cash accounting method.

TIP

The advantage of operating on a cash basis is that you can have some control over the amount of your business income and expenses that your business reports for tax purposes year to year. Doing so can lower your tax bill. Suppose that, looking ahead to the next tax year, you have good reason to believe that your business will make more money, pushing you into a higher tax bracket. You can likely reduce your tax bill if you pay more of your expenses in the next year. For example, instead of buying a new computer late this year, you can wait until early next year. (*Note:* The IRS recognizes credit card expenses by the date when you make the charges, not when you pay the bill.) Likewise, you can somewhat control when your customers pay you. If you expect to make less money next year, simply don't invoice customers in December of this year. Wait until January so you receive the income from those sales next year.

Paying lower taxes(legally)

Every small business must spend money, and spending money in your business holds the allure of lowering your tax bill. But don't spend money on your business just for the sake of generating tax deductions. Spend your money to make the most of the tax breaks that you can legally take. The following are some examples of legal tax breaks:

>> **Take it all off now or spread it around for later.** As a small-business owner, if you have net income, you can deduct up to $500,000 (for tax year 2013) per year for equipment purchases (for example, espresso machines, computers, desks, and chairs) for use in your business. (Unless Congress amends the tax laws, this expense limitation is set to revert to its previous and much lower $25,000 limit in 2014.) By deducting via a Section 179 deduction, you can

immediately deduct the entire amount that you spend on equipment for your business. Normally, equipment for your business is depreciated over a number of years. With *depreciation,* you claim a tax deduction yearly for a portion of the total purchase price of the equipment. For example, if you drop two grand on a new computer, you can take a $400 deduction annually for this computer's depreciation (if you elect straight-line depreciation). If you elect the special 179 deduction, you can claim the entire $2,000 outlay at once (as long as you haven't exceeded the annual cap).

REMEMBER

Taking all the deduction in one year by using the Section 179 deduction method is enticing, but you may pay more taxes in the long run that way. Consider that in the early years of most businesses, profits are low. When your business is in a low tax bracket, the value of your deductions is low. If your business grows, you may come out ahead if you depreciate your early-year big-ticket expenses, thereby postponing to higher-tax-bracket years some of the deductions that you can take off.

>> **Make the most of your auto deductions.** If you use your car for business, you can claim a deduction, but don't waste a lot of money on a new car, thinking that the IRS pays for it — because it doesn't. The IRS limits how large an annual auto expense you can claim for depreciation. Another advantage of purchasing a more reasonably priced car: You won't be burdened with documenting your actual auto expenses and calculating depreciation. You can use the auto expense method of just claiming a flat 56 cents per mile (for tax year 2014).

>> **Deduct travel, meal, and entertainment expenses.** For the IRS to consider your expense deductible, your travel must be for a bona fide business purpose. For example, if you live in Chicago, fly to Honolulu for a week, and spend one day at a seminar for business purposes and then the other six days snorkeling and sunning, you can deduct only the expenses for the one day of your trip that you devoted to business. (An exception to this rule enables you to write off more of your trip: If you extend a business trip to stay over a Saturday night to qualify for a lower airfare and you save money in total travel costs, you can claim the extra costs that you incurred to stay over through Sunday!)

Don't waste your money on meal and entertainment expenses. You can deduct only 50 percent of your business expenses; by all means, take that 50 percent deduction when you can legally do so, but don't spend frivolously on business trips and think that you can deduct everything. The IRS doesn't allow business deductions for club dues (such as for health, business, airport, or social clubs) or entertainment (such as executive boxes at sports stadiums).

Keeping a Life and Perspective

David Packard, co-founder of Hewlett-Packard, said, "You are likely to die not of starvation for opportunities, but of indigestion of opportunities."

Most small businesses succeed in keeping their owners more than busy — in some cases, too busy. If you provide needed products or services at a fair price, customers will beat a path to your door. Your business will grow and be busier than you can personally handle. You may need to start hiring people. I know small-business owners who work themselves into a frenzy by putting in 70 or more hours a week.

If you enjoy your work so much that it's not really work and you end up putting in long hours because you enjoy it, terrific! But success in your company can cause you to put less energy into other important aspects of your life that perhaps don't come as easily.

REMEMBER

Although careers and business successes are important, don't place these successes higher than fourth on your overall priority list. You can't replace your health, family, and friends, but you can replace a job or a business.

Chapter 15

Purchasing a Small Business

Each year, hundreds of thousands of small businesses are sold to new owners. This chapter is for those of you who want to run or invest in an existing small business but don't want to start the business yourself. And of course, this chapter can show you how to make good money and have fun along the way!

Examining the Advantages of Buying

I don't want to scare you off if you want to start a business. However, buying someone else's business works better for some people. The following list reflects the main advantages of buying a business:

>> **You avoid startup hassles and headaches.** Starting a business from scratch requires dealing with many issues. For instance, in the early years, along with formulating a business plan, you must also develop a marketing plan, find

customers, locate space, hire employees, and incorporate. If you buy a good existing business, you buy into an ongoing enterprise with customers, assets, and hopefully profits (although you still need to fix any problems the business may have).

REMEMBER

Consider the learning curve for the type of business you're contemplating purchasing. Buying an existing business makes more sense if the business is complicated. For example, purchasing a business that manufactures musical instruments may make more sense than starting one on your own. Unless you've built musical instruments before and understand the intricacies of the production process, starting such a business from scratch is quite risky and perhaps foolhardy. (Purchasing an existing business also makes sense if, for example, you don't want to build a stable of customers from scratch.)

>> **You reduce risk.** Although investing in something with a solid track record is still far from a sure thing, your risk may be significantly lower than the risk involved in a startup. After a business has an operating history and offers a product or service with a demonstrated market, some of the risk in the company is removed. Looking at historic financial statements also helps you make more accurate financial forecasts than you could make with a startup venture.

>> **You enhance your ability to attract investor or lender money.** You should have less difficulty raising money from investors and lenders for your existing business than with a startup. Why? You'll likely find it easier to attract investors to something that's more than an idea. And for the amount that they invest, investors demand a smaller piece of an existing business than they would with an investment in an idea.

>> **You can enter industries where buying an existing business is your only ticket in.** You can enter some industries only through your purchase of a business that already exists. For instance, if you want to be involved in a bottling or car dealership business, you're mostly limited to purchasing existing businesses.

>> **You can find businesses where you can add value.** Some entrepreneurs who start businesses don't see the potential for growth or don't want to grow their businesses — they may be burned out, content with their current profit, or simply ready to retire. Finding businesses where the potential exists to improve operating efficiency and to expand into new markets isn't too hard. Finding small companies that are undervalued relative to the potential that they can offer is easier for a business-minded person.

WARNING

Just because you think you see potential to improve a business doesn't mean you should pay a high price based on your high expectations. You can be wrong — you may be looking at the business through rose-colored glasses. Even if you're correct about the potential, don't pay the current owner for the hard work and ingenuity that you'll bring to the business if you purchase it. Offer a fair price based on the conditions and value of the business *now* — I explain how to figure this value in the section "Evaluating a Small Business" later in this chapter.

Understanding the Drawbacks of Buying

Not everyone enjoys running or cooking, and similarly, some people don't enjoy the negatives that come with buying an existing business. If the following issues don't turn you off, purchasing an existing business may be right for you:

>> **You buy the baggage.** When you buy an existing business, the bad comes with the good, and all businesses include their share of the bad. The business may employ problem employees, for example, or it may have a less-than-stellar reputation in the marketplace. Even if the employees are good, they and the company culture may not mesh with where you want to take the company in the future.

Do you have the ability to motivate people to change — or to fire them if they aren't willing or able to adapt to your agenda? Do you have the patience to work at improving the company's products and reputation? You need these types of skills and traits to run and add value to a company. Some people enjoy and thrive on such challenges, and others find such pressures hard to swallow. Think back on your other work experiences for information about what challenges you've tackled and how you felt about them.

>> **You need to do a lot of inspection.** If you think that buying a company is easier than starting one, think again. You must know what you're buying *before* you buy it. So you need to do a thorough inspection. For example, you need to rip apart financial statements to ascertain whether the company is really as profitable as it appears and to determine its financial health.

REMEMBER

After you close the deal and the money is transferred, you can't change your mind. Unless a seller commits fraud or lies, which is difficult and costly for a buyer to legally prove, it's "buyer beware" about the quality of the business you're buying. (In "Evaluating a Small Business," later in this chapter, I cover the homework that you need to do before you buy.)

>> **You need more capital.** Existing businesses have value, which is why you generally need more money to buy a business than you do to start one. If you're short on cash, starting a company is generally a lower-cost path.

>> **Lower risk means lower returns.** If you purchase a good business and run it well, you can make decent money. In some cases, you can make a lot of money. But you generally have less potential for hitting it big with an existing business than you do with a business you start. Those who have built the greatest wealth from small businesses are generally those who have started them rather than those who have purchased existing ones.

>> **You don't get the satisfaction of creating a business.** Entrepreneurs who build their own businesses get a different experience from those who buy someone else's enterprise. You can make your mark on a business that you buy, but doing so takes a number of years. Even then, the business is never completely your own creation.

Prerequisites to Buying a Business

Not everyone is cut out to succeed when buying an existing business. Meeting a couple of prerequisites improves your chances of success, as the following sections explain.

Business experience

You definitely need business experience to succeed when buying an existing business. If you were an economics or business major in college and took accounting and other quantitatively oriented courses, you're off to a good start.

Even better than academic learning, however, is work experience in the type of business that you want to buy. If you want to run a restaurant, go to work in a good one. Consider the experience as paid on-the-job training for running your own restaurant.

If you've worked as a consultant on business-management issues with a variety of industries, you also have a good background. However, the danger in having done only consulting is that you're usually not on the front lines where operational issues arise.

Should none of the previous examples apply to you, I won't say that you're doomed to fail if you buy a business, but I will say that the odds are against you.

TIP

If you don't have business experience, you'll likely do far better in your first business venture after some remedial work. Get some hands-on experience, which is more valuable than any degree or credential that you can earn through course work. No substitute exists for the real-life experiences of marketing to and interacting with customers, grappling with financial statements, dealing with competitive threats, and doing the business of business. However, I don't endorse skipping academic course work. You may, in fact, be required to get a credential to be able to do the work that you want to do. If you don't need a specific credential, taking selected courses and reading good business books (I recommend some in Chapter 18) can boost your knowledge.

Financial resources

To purchase a business, as with real estate, you need to make a down payment on the purchase price. Bankers and business sellers who make loans to business buyers normally require down payments of 25 to 30 percent to protect their loans. Small-business buyers who make sizeable down payments are less likely to walk away from a loan obligation if the business gets into financial trouble.

TIP

If you lack sufficient capital for a down payment, try asking family or friends to invest. You can also set your sights on a less expensive business or seek business owners willing to accept a smaller down payment. If you can find a business for sale where the owner wants less than 20 percent down, you may be on to something good. Be careful, though, because an owner who accepts such a small down payment may be having a difficult time selling because of problems inherent in the business or because the business is overpriced.

You can purchase some existing small businesses with a loan from the selling owner. Also, check for loans with banks in your area that specialize in small-business loans. (See Chapter 14 for other financing ideas.)

Focusing Your Search for a Business to Buy

Unless you're extraordinarily lucky, finding a good business to buy takes a great deal of time. If you spend time outside of your work hours, finding a quality business that's right for you can easily take a year or two. Even if you can afford to look full time, finding and closing on a business can still take you many months.

REMEMBER

Above all else, it pays to be persistent, patient, and willing to spend time on things that don't lead to immediate results. You must be willing to sort through some rubbish. If you require immediate gratification in terms of completing a deal, you can make yourself miserable in your search or rush into a bad deal.

Unless you set some boundaries for your business search, you're going to end up spinning your wheels (and likely end up with the wrong type of business for yourself). You don't need to be rigid or to precisely define every detail of the business that you want to purchase, but you do need to set some parameters so you can start laying the groundwork to purchase.

Each person has unique shopping criteria. The following list exemplifies some useful ones to narrow your search:

>> **Size/purchase price:** The money you have available to invest in a business determines the size of business you can afford. As a rough rule, figure that you can afford to pay a purchase price of about three times the amount of cash you have earmarked for the business. For example, if you have $50,000 in the till, you should look at buying a business for about $150,000. Because many business sellers overprice their businesses, you can probably look at businesses listed at a price above $150,000, perhaps as high as $200,000.

>> **Location:** If you're already rooted and don't want to move or deal with a long commute, the business's location further narrows the field. Although you may be willing to look at a broader territory, maybe even nationally if you're willing to relocate, evaluating businesses long-distance is difficult and costly. Unless you want a highly specialized type of company, try to keep your business search local.

>> **Industry:** Industry-specific expertise that you want to use in the business you buy can help whittle the pool of businesses down further. If you don't have industry-specific expertise, I highly recommend that you focus on some specific niches in industries that interest you or in which you have some knowledge or expertise. Focusing on an industry helps you conduct a more thorough search and find higher-quality companies. The industry knowledge that you accumulate in your search process can pay big dividends during your years of ownership in the business.

TIP

If you have a hard time brainstorming about specific industries, use this trick to jump-start your creativity: Take a walk through the Yellow Pages! Many business types known to exist in your area are listed alphabetically. Remember that a separate Yellow Pages directory exists for businesses that sell mainly to consumers; a business-to-business Yellow Pages directory lists businesses whose customers are primarily other businesses. Look at either or both, depending on the types of businesses that interest you. You also may want to buy a business in a sector that's experiencing fast growth so you, too, can ride the wave. Check out *Inc.* magazine's annual *Inc. 5,000* list of the fastest-growing private companies in America.

>> **Opportunity to add value:** Some buyers want to purchase a business with untapped opportunities or problems that need to be fixed. As with real estate, however, many people are happier leaving the fixer-uppers to the contractors. Some businesses without major problems can offer significant untapped potential.

After you define your shopping criteria, you're ready to go to the marketplace of businesses for sale. I recommend that you type up your criteria on a single page so you can hand it to others who may put you in touch with businesses for sale. The following sections give you the best techniques for identifying solid businesses that meet your needs.

Perusing publications

If you're focused on specific industry sectors, you may be surprised to find out that all sorts of specialty newsletters and magazines are published. Just think of the fun you can have reading publications such as *Alternative Energy Retailer, Specialty Foods Merchandising, Coal Mining Newsletter, Advanced Battery Technology,* or *Gas Turbine World!* Specialty publications get you into the thick of an industry and also contain ads for businesses for sale or business brokers who work in the industry.

Conducting literature searches of general interest business publications can help you identify articles on your industry of interest. Online computer searches can help you find articles as well. Websites worth examining include www.bizbuysell.com and www.sba.gov.

ERIC'S
PICKS

A useful reference publication that you can find in public libraries with decent business sections is a two-volume set titled *Small Business Sourcebook* (Gale). Organized alphabetically by industry, this reference contains listings of publications, trade associations, and other information sources.

Networking with advisors

Speak with accountants, attorneys, bankers, and business consultants who specialize in working with small businesses. These advisors are sometimes the first to hear of a small-business owner's desire to sell. Advisors may also suggest good businesses that aren't for sale but whose owners may consider selling (see the next section).

Knocking on some doors

Some business owners who haven't listed their businesses for sale may be thinking about selling, so if you approach enough owners, you may find some of these not-yet-on-the-market businesses with owners interested in selling. You can increase the possibility of finding your desired business and may get a good deal on such a business because you can negotiate with such a seller from the beneficial position of not having to compete with other potential buyers.

Instead of calling on the phone or literally knocking on the business's door, start your communications by mail. Sending a concise letter of introduction explaining what kind of business you're looking for and what a wonderful person you are demonstrates that you're investing some time in this endeavor. Follow up with a call a week or so after you send the letter.

Working with business brokers

Numerous small businesses for sale list their enterprises through business brokers. Just as a real estate agent makes a living selling real estate, a business broker makes a living selling businesses.

Business brokers generally sell smaller small businesses — those with less than $1 million in annual sales. These businesses tend to be family-owned companies or sole proprietorships, such as restaurants, dry cleaners, other retailers, and service firms. About half of such small businesses are sold through brokers. Most business brokerage firms sell different types of businesses. Some firms, however, specialize in one industry or a few industries.

One advantage of working with brokers to buy a business is that a broker can expose you to other businesses you may not have considered (a doughnut shop, for example, instead of a restaurant). Brokers can also share their knowledge with you — like the fact that you need to get up at 4 a.m. to make doughnuts.

The pitfalls of working with brokers include the following:

>> **Commission conflicts:** Brokers aren't your business advisors; they're salespeople. That fact doesn't necessarily make them corrupt or dishonest, but it does mean that their interests aren't aligned with yours. Their goal is to do a deal and to do the deal as soon as possible. And the more you pay for your business, the more they make. Business brokers typically get paid 10 to 12 percent of the sales price of a business. Technically, the seller pays this fee, but as with real estate deals done through brokers, the buyer actually pays. Remember, if a broker isn't involved, the seller can sell for a lower price and still clear more money, and the buyer is better off, too.

>> **Undesirable businesses:** Problem businesses are everywhere, but a fair number end up with brokers when the owners encounter trouble selling on their own.

>> **Packaging:** This problem relates to the preceding two. Brokers (who are on commission) help not-so-hot businesses look better than they really are. Doing so may involve lying, but more typically, it involves stretching the truth, omitting negatives, and hyping potential. (Owners who sell their businesses themselves may do these things as well.)

You (and your advisors) need to perform due diligence on any business that you may buy. Never, ever trust or use the selling package that a broker prepares for a business as your sole source of information. *Remember:* Brokers as well as sellers may stretch the truth, lie, and commit fraud.

>> **Access to limited inventory:** Unlike real estate brokers (who can access all homes listed with brokers for sale in an area through a shared listing service), a business broker can generally tell you only about his office's listings. (Confidentiality is an issue because a shared listing service increases the number of people who can find out that a business is for sale and the particulars of the sale. This information may cause some customers to find another company to do business with and may lead some key employees to leave as well.)

If you want to work with a business broker, use more than one. Working with a larger business brokerage firm or one that specializes in listing the type of business that you're looking for can maximize the number of possible prospects that you see. Some state associations of business brokers share their listings. However, even in such states, some of the larger brokerages opt not to include themselves because they benefit less from sharing their information.

>> **Few licensing requirements:** The business brokerage field isn't tightly regulated. The majority of states have no requirements — anyone can hang out a shingle and work as a business broker. Some states allow those with securities brokerage licenses to operate as business brokers, whereas most states require real estate licenses.

Ask tax, legal, and business consultants for names of good brokers they may know. If you find a broker you'd like to work with, first check references from other buyers who have worked with that broker. Be sure the broker works full time and has solid experience. (Some business brokers dabble in the field part time and make a living in other ways.)

TIP

Ask the broker you're interested in for the names of several buyers of similar businesses whom she's worked with over the past six months. By narrowing down the field to the past six months and your particular business interest, the broker can't just refer you to the three best deals of her career. Also, check whether anyone has filed complaints against the brokerage with the local Better Business Bureau, or BBB (although the BBB favors member companies and is less likely to entertain and retain complaints against members), and the state regulatory departments (real estate, attorney general, department of corporations, and so on) that oversee business brokers.

Considering a Franchise or Multilevel Marketing Company

Among the types of businesses that you may buy are franchises and multilevel marketing companies. Both of these types of businesses offer more of a prepackaged and defined system for running a business. Although both types may be worth your exploration, significant pitfalls can trip you up, especially with multilevel marketing companies.

Finding a franchise

Some companies expand their locations through selling replicas, or *franchises,* of their business. Purchasing a good franchise can be your ticket into the world of small-business ownership. When you purchase a franchise, you buy the local rights to a specified geographic territory to sell the company's products or services under the company's name and to use the company's system of operation. In addition to an upfront franchisee fee, franchisers also typically charge an ongoing royalty.

Franchising makes up a huge part of the business world. Companies that franchise — such as McDonald's, Pizza Hut, H&R Block, Jiffy Lube, 7-Eleven stores, Gymboree, Century 21 Real Estate, Holiday Inn, Avis, Subway, and Foot Locker — account for more than $1 trillion in sales annually.

Franchise advantages

When you purchase a new franchise, you don't automatically have customers. As with starting a business, you must find your patrons. However, the parent company should have a track record and multiple locations with customers. (You can also purchase existing franchises from owners who want to sell, and these businesses come complete with customers.)

So why would you want to pay a good chunk of money to buy a business without customers?

>> **Proven business:** A company that has been in business for a number of years and has successful franchisees proves the demand for the company's products and services and shows that the company's system for providing those products and services works. The company has worked out the bugs and has hopefully solved common problems. As a franchise owner, you benefit from and share in the experience that the parent company has gained over the years.

>> **Name-brand recognition:** Some consumers recognize the company name of a larger and successful franchise company and may be more inclined to purchase its products and services. For example, some consumers feel more comfortable getting an oil change at franchiser Jiffy Lube rather than from a local Ollie's Oil Changers. The comfort that comes from dealing with Jiffy Lube may stem from the influence of advertisements, recommendations of friends, or your own familiarity with their services in another part of the country. Most freestanding small businesses for sale in a community lack this name-brand recognition.

>> **Centralized purchasing power:** You would hope and expect that Jiffy Lube, as a corporation made up of hundreds of locations, buys oil and other car supplies at a low price. (Volume purchasing generally leads to bigger discounts.) In addition to possibly saving franchisees money on supplies, the parent company can take the hassle out of figuring out where and how to purchase supplies. Again, most unattached small businesses that you could buy won't offer this advantage. However, quality business associations can provide some of these benefits.

Franchise pitfalls

WARNING

As with purchasing other small businesses, pitfalls abound in buying a franchise. Franchises aren't for everyone. Here are some common problems that may cause you to reconsider buying a franchise:

>> **You're not the franchise type.** When you buy a franchise, you buy into an established system. People who like structure and following established rules and systems adapt more easily to the franchise life. But if you're the creative sort who likes to experiment and change things, you may be an unhappy franchisee. Unlike starting your own business, where you can get into the game without investing lots of your time and money, buying a franchise that you end up not enjoying can make for an expensive learning experience.

>> **You may be locked in to buying overpriced supplies.** Centralized, bulk purchasing through the corporate headquarters supposedly saves franchisees time and money on supplies and other expenditures. Some franchisers, however, take advantage of franchisees through large markups on proprietary items that franchisees must buy from the franchisers.

>> **The franchise is unproven.** If the company's concept hasn't stood the test of time, don't make yourself a guinea pig. Some franchisers show more interest in simply selling franchises to collect the upfront franchise money. Reputable franchisers want to help their franchisees succeed so they can collect an ongoing royalty from the franchisees' sales.

> **» The franchise is a pyramid scheme.** Unscrupulous, short-term-focused business owners sometimes attempt to franchise their businesses and sell as many franchises as they can as quickly as possible. Some push their franchisees to sell franchises. The business soon focuses on selling franchises rather than operating a business that sells a product or service well. In rare cases, franchisers engage in fraud and sell next to nothing, except the hopes of getting rich quick.

Evaluating a franchise

Make sure you do plenty of homework before you agree to buy a franchise. You may be tempted to cut corners when reviewing a franchise from a long-established company. Don't. You may not be right for the specific franchise, or perhaps the "successful" company has mostly been good at keeping problems under wraps.

In "Evaluating a Small Business," later in this chapter, I explain the homework you should complete prior to buying an existing business. That section is especially important if you want to purchase an existing franchise from another franchisee.

Considering a multilevel marketing company

A twist, and in most cases a bad one, on the franchising idea is *multilevel marketing (MLM) companies.* Sometimes known as *network companies,* MLM companies can be thought of as a poor person's franchise. I know dozens of people, from clients I've worked with to students I've taught in my courses, who have been sorely disappointed with the money and time they've spent on MLM companies.

WARNING

In companies that use multilevel marketing, representatives who work as independent contractors recruit new representatives, known in the industry as your *downline,* as well as solicit customers. For those weary of traditional jobs, the appeal of multilevel marketing is obvious. You can work at home, part time if you want. You have no employees. You don't need any experience. Yet you're told you can still make big bucks ($10,000, $25,000, $50,000, or more per month). If your parents raised you right, however, you should be skeptical of deals like these.

A big problem to watch out for when dealing with MLM companies is the business equivalent of the pyramid scheme — businesses that exist to sign up other people. Beware of MLM companies that advocate the following: "Sell directly to those that you have direct influence over. The system works great because you don't need to resell month after month. It's an opportunity for anybody — it's up to that person how much work he wants to put into it."

WORK-FROM-HOME "OPPORTUNITIES"

WARNING

"We made $18,269.56 in just 2½ weeks! Remarkable home-based business! We do over 90 percent of the work for you! Free info: 800-555-8975."

"You can be earning $4,000 to $10,000 each month in less than 30 days! We'll even help you hire agents to do the work for you . . . FREE!"

You can find lots of ad copy like this, especially in magazines and emails and on websites that small-business owners and wannabe small-business owners read. In most cases, these ads come from grossly overhyped multilevel marketing companies. In other ads, no legitimate company exists; instead, a person (or two or three) simply tries to sell you some "information" that explains the business opportunity. This information may cost several hundred dollars or more. Sadly, such packages end up being worthless marketing propaganda and rarely provide useful information that you couldn't find at a far lower cost or no cost at all.

Remember: Never buy into anything like these ads that companies (or people) pitch to you through the mail or over the phone.

INVESTIGATE

Any MLM company examination should start with the company's product or service. How does its product or service stack up to the competition on price and quality? Contact the Better Business Bureau in the city where the MLM company is headquartered to see what kinds of complaints are on file.

REMEMBER

The bottom line on any network marketing "opportunity" is to remember that it's a job. No company is going to pay you a lot of money for little work. As with any other small-business venture, if you hope to earn a decent income, multilevel marketing opportunities require at least three to five years of low income to build up your business. Most people who pay to buy into networks make little money, and many quit and move on.

Also, think twice before you sign up relatives, friends, and co-workers — they're often the first people network marketers encourage you to sell to. A danger in doing business with those people whom you have influence over is that you put your reputation and integrity on the line. You could be putting your friendships and family relations on the line as well.

QUALITY MULTILEVEL MARKETING COMPANIES ARE THE EXCEPTION

A number of multilevel marketing (MLM) companies have achieved success over the years. Amway, Herbalife, and Mary Kay have stood the test of time and achieved significant size. Amway founders Richard DeVos and Jay Van Andel achieved multibillionaire status.

Not all MLM companies are created equal, and few are worth a look. However, Mary Kay, which sells primarily makeup and skincare products, is an example of a successful MLM company with a 30-plus year history. Mary Kay has hundreds of thousands of sales representatives and does business worldwide. Although not shy about the decent money that its more successful salespeople make, Mary Kay doesn't hype the income potential. Local sales directors typically earn $50,000 to $100,000 per year, but this income comes after many years of hard work. Mary Kay rewards top sellers with gifts, such as the famous pink Cadillac.

The ingredients for Mary Kay's success include competitive pricing, personal attention, and social interaction, which many stores don't or can't offer their customers. "We make shopping and life fun," says Mary Gentry, one of Mary Kay's sales directors. "We make people look and feel good."

Mary Kay encourages prospective representatives to try the products first and then host a group before they sign up and fork over the $100 to purchase a showcase of items to sell. To maximize sales, the company encourages Mary Kay reps to keep a ready inventory because customers tend to buy more when products are immediately available. If reps want out of the business, they can sell their inventory back to the company at 90 cents on the dollar originally paid, a good sign that the company stands behind its product and isn't simply signing up lots of new folks simply to sell inventory to.

Quality multilevel marketing companies make sense for people who really believe in and want to sell a particular product or service and don't want to or can't tie up a lot of money buying a franchise or other business. Just remember to check out the MLM company, and realize that you won't get rich in a hurry — or probably ever.

INVESTIGATE

Remember that due diligence requires digging for facts and talking to people who don't have a bias or reason to sell to you. Do the homework that I recommend in the later section "Evaluating a Small Business." Be skeptical of multilevel marketing systems, unless the company has a long track record and many people who are happy. In other words, assume that an MLM company isn't worth pursuing until your extensive due diligence proves otherwise.

Evaluating a Small Business

If you put in many hours, you may eventually come across a business that interests and intrigues you so much that you consider purchasing it. As with purchasing a piece of real estate, major hurdles stand between you and ownership of the business. You need to inspect what you want to buy, negotiate a deal, and finalize a contract. When done correctly, these processes take a lot of time.

Doing due diligence

The American legal system presumes a person is innocent until a jury proves that person is guilty beyond a reasonable doubt. When you purchase a business, however, you must assume that the selling business owner is guilty of making the business appear better than what it is (and possibly of lying) until you prove otherwise with due diligence.

I don't want to sound cynical, but a business owner can use more than a few tricks to make a business look more profitable, financially healthier, and more desirable than it really is. You can't decide how much inspection or due diligence to conduct on a business based on your gut feelings.

REMEMBER

Because you can't guess which surprises hide in a business, you must dig for them. Until you prove to yourself beyond a reasonable doubt that these surprises don't exist, don't go through with a business purchase.

When you find a business you may want to purchase, you absolutely, positively must do your homework before you buy. However, just as with purchasing a home, you don't want to expend buckets of money and time on detailed inspections until you can reach an agreement with the seller. What if the seller is unrealistic about what the business is worth? You need to perform the most serious, time-consuming, and costly due diligence *after* the seller has accepted your offer to purchase the business. Make such inspections a contingency in your purchase contract.

Ultimately, if you're going to buy a business, you need to follow a plan similar to but likely shorter than the business plan I present in Chapter 13. Addressing such issues in a plan goes a long way toward helping you perform your due diligence.

Following are some additional questions you should answer about a business you're contemplating purchasing (address as many of the questions as possible before you make your offer):

>> **Why is the owner selling?** Ask the owner or the owner's advisors why the owner wants to sell and why now. The answer may shed insight on the owner's motivations and need to sell. Some owners want to bail when they see things getting worse.

>> **What is the value of the assets that you want to buy?** This value includes not only equipment but also "soft" assets, such as the firm's name and reputation with customers and suppliers, customer lists, patents, and so on. Interview key employees, customers, suppliers, advisors, and competitors. Ask key customers and key employees whether they would still be loyal to the business if you took it over.

>> **What do the financial statements reveal?** Search for the same things that you would look for in a company whose stock you're considering purchasing. (See Chapter 6 for information on how to read financial statements and what to look for.) Don't take the financial statements at face value simply because they're audited. The accountant who did the audit may be incompetent or chummy with the seller.

TIP

One way to check for shenanigans is to ask the seller for a copy of the business's tax returns. Owners are more likely to try to minimize reported revenue and maximize expenses on their tax return to keep from paying more tax. After your purchase offer is accepted, ask a tax advisor experienced in such matters to do an audit (see the "Questioning profits" sidebar in this chapter for more information).

>> **If the company leases its space, what does the lease contract say?** A soon-to-expire lease at a low rate can ruin a business's profit margins. With a retail location, the ability to maintain a good location is also vital. Check *comparables* — that is, what other similar locations lease for — to see whether the current lease rate is fair, and talk to the building owner to determine his plans for the building. Ask for and review (with the help of a legal advisor) the current owner's lease contract.

>> **What liabilities, including those that may be hidden "off" the balance sheet, are you buying with a business?** Limit liabilities, such as environmental contaminations, through a contract. Conduct legal searches for liens, litigation, and tax problems.

>> **What does a background check turn up on the owners and key employees?** Do they have good business experience, or do they have criminal records and a trail of unpaid debts?

QUESTIONING PROFITS

Don't blindly take the profit from the bottom line of a business's financial statement as the gospel. As part of your due diligence, ask a tax advisor to perform an audit after you negotiate a deal.

Even if the financial statements of a business are accurate, you (and your tax advisor) must still look for subtle problems that can make the profits of the business appear better than they truly are. The issues that I tell you to look for in Chapter 6, when you analyze the financial statements of public companies that issue stock, also apply to evaluating the financial statements of small businesses.

If necessary, factor out one-time events from the profit analysis. For example, if last year the business received an unusually large order that is unlikely to be repeated and hasn't been the norm in the past, subtract this amount from the profitability analysis. Also, examine the owner's salary to see whether it's low for the field. Owners can reduce their draw to a minimum or pay family members less than fair market salaries to pump up the profitability of their company in the years before they sell. Also examine whether the rent or mortgage expense may change when you buy the business. Consider what will happen to profits when you factor in your expected rent or mortgage costs.

Determining a business's value

After you find what you think is a good business and do your homework, you're ready to make an offer. Negotiating done well takes time and patience. Unless you're legally savvy, find an attorney who focuses her practice on small-business dealings. Have that attorney review and work with your contract. Also consider obtaining input from a qualified tax advisor.

Good advisors can help you inspect what you're buying and look for red flags in the company's financial statements. Advisors can also help structure the purchase to protect what you're buying and to gain you maximum tax benefits. If you work with a business broker, use an attorney and accountant as well.

The price that a business is listed for is often in excess of — and sometimes grossly so — the business's true worth. A smart homebuyer or real estate investor looks at comparable properties when he's ready to make an offer. So you should do the same and look at what similar businesses have sold for as a starting point for valuing a business that you want to buy.

When you look at sales prices of comparable businesses, calculate how many times the companies' earnings that these businesses sold for. (In Chapter 5, I discuss how the price/earnings ratio works for evaluating the value of larger, publicly traded companies.) Because they're less well established and riskier from an investment standpoint, small, privately held businesses sell for a lower multiple of earnings than comparable but larger companies.

Some advisors and business brokers advocate calculating how many times revenue a company should sell for to determine the value of the business. Revenue is a poor proxy for profitability: Two businesses in the same field can have identical revenue yet quite different profitability because of how well they're run, the pricing of their products and services, and the types of customers they attract.

In addition to looking at the sales price of other businesses relative to earnings, you can consider the value of a company's assets. The so-called *book value* of a company's assets is what the assets are worth per the company's balance sheet. Check these figures to ensure that their asset values are correct. Another, more conservative way to value such assets is to consider the liquidation or replacement cost.

5

Investing Resources

Wade through the ocean of investing sound bites, trivia, advice, and opinions to evaluate the reliability of a given source.

Filter the best from the rest as you read investing magazine articles, blogs, or books; peruse Internet sites; use software; watch television; or listen to the radio.

Chapter 16

Selecting Investing Resources Wisely

I n the past, sifting through financial information was much simpler, mainly because the available resources were limited. Today's investor faces information overload. Radio, television, magazines, newspapers, books, the Internet, family, friends, neighbors, and cabdrivers — everywhere you turn, someone is offering investing opinions, tips, and advice. You can't pick up a newspaper or magazine or turn on the television or radio without bumping into articles, stories, segments, and entire programs devoted to investment issues. Blogs on the topic continue to sprout like weeds during the dog days of summer.

Because investment information and advice is so widespread and constantly growing, knowing how to sift through it is just as important as hearing what the best resources are today. When chosen wisely, the best investing resources can further your investment knowledge and enable you to make better decisions. Throughout this book, I name the best investment resources that I'm familiar with, but in this chapter, I explain how you can separate the good from the mediocre and awful.

Dealing with Information Overload

Early in the year 2000, one of my clients, Roseanne, called me in a near panic. She said, "Eric, I'm not satisfied with my investments. Why are so many of my friends doubling and tripling their money in technology stocks, and my mutual funds are going nowhere? Everywhere I turn, people are talking about these high-growth companies. I want my piece of the pie, too!" I explained to her that many of her diversified mutual funds held some technology stocks as well as stocks in many other industries. I also reminded her that because she was nearing 50 years of age, she had a healthy helping of bonds in her portfolio as well.

She urged me to put her money in some technology stocks and technology-focused funds, but I stood my ground. I further encouraged her to read this book (the second edition was out at the time), wherein I highlighted technology stocks as a bubble waiting to burst (see Chapter 5). I'm glad that Roseanne followed my advice, and now, years later, she is, too. During the severe stock market decline in the early 2000s, technology stocks got clobbered, but other market segments (such as bonds and value-oriented stocks) actually increased in value.

A major reason so many people were talking about making money with technology stocks was that so many media outlets (radio, television, websites, and so on) were talking about these investments and other personal money management issues around the clock. All this talk logically makes one wonder why everybody in the media and publishing world is putting out investing information. Has money become that much more complicated over the years? Are there simply more media and publishing executives who want to help us?

The following list explains some of the reasons investing has become such a hot topic:

>> **Communications options are expanding.** Over the years, the number of television channels has mushroomed as a result of cable and satellite television. Flip through the channels at any hour of the day, and you see infomercials that promise to make you a real estate tycoon or stock market day trader in your spare time. Similarly, the explosion of the Internet has introduced a whole new medium. Now, at a relatively low cost, anybody can "publish" online. The accessibility of these communications mediums allows nearly everyone with an animated personality or access to a computer to appear to be an expert. These newer communications options are primarily structured around selling advertising rather than offering quality content.

>> **A rough decade combined with a panic.** The 2000s were the worst for U.S. stocks since the Great Depression. The decade featured two severe bear markets, the second of which (in 2008) culminated in a panic. Because many

folks invest through retirement accounts such as IRAs and 401(k)s, heightened stock market volatility gets more attention.

>> **Economic change breeds uncertainty.** Global competition and technological advances are causing most industries to undergo dramatic changes in much shorter periods of time. Fear of job loss and financial instability run high in people's minds. Economic change and widespread cynicism about Social Security's ability to provide a reasonable retirement income to baby boomers has also caused many to seek investment guidance.

>> **Investment choices and responsibilities are increasing.** Most employees today are forced to take responsibility for saving money for their retirement and deciding how to invest that money. In the past, more employers offered pension plans. In these plans, the employer set aside money on behalf of employees and retained a pension manager who decided how to invest it. All the employees had to do was learn the level of benefits they had earned and when they could begin drawing a monthly check.

REMEMBER

With today's retirement plans, such as 401(k)s, employees have to educate themselves about how much money they need to save and how to invest it. In addition to mastering retirement planning and investment allocation, individuals face a dizzying number of financial products, such as the thousands of mutual funds that are on the market.

Read the next section to find out how you can filter out the best information and advice and skip the rest.

Separating Financial Fact from Fiction

Just because more sources than ever offer investing advice doesn't mean that you should read, listen to, or watch all of it. In fact, most of the advice out there can easily steer you in the wrong direction. So in this section, I offer prescriptions for how to intelligently choose among all the available financial content.

Understanding how advertising corrupts the quality of investment advice

WARNING

The first rule for maximizing your chances of finding the best investing information and advice is to recognize that there are no free lunches. Too many people get sucked into supposedly free resources when looking for information.

The Internet is packed with scores of "free" investing sites. And if you turn on your television or radio, you come across mountains of "free" stuff. Of course, someone is paying for all this "free" content, and it's all available for some reason. Most of the free Internet sites are run by investment companies or someone else with something to sell. What these sites give away is nothing but subtle and not-so-subtle advertising for whatever products and services they sell. Advertising also foots the bill in the vast majority of cases involving free investment advice on TV and radio.

As I discuss in Chapter 18, many investing and personal finance books also contain subtly veiled advertisements. Some "authors" choose to write books that are the equivalent of an infomercial for something else — such as high-priced seminars — that they really want to sell. Such writers aren't interested in educating and helping you as much as they're seeking to sell you something. So for example, an author may write about how complicated the investing markets are and some indicators he follows to time investments. However, at the end of such a book, the author says that investing is too complicated to do on your own and that you really need a personal investment manager — which, to no great surprise, the author happens to be.

REMEMBER

Whether in print or on the Internet, television, or radio, advertising often compromises the quality of the investment advice it accompanies.

I won't say that you *can't* find some useful investment resources in mediums with lots of advertising. In fact, you can find some good investing programs on radio and television and some helpful investing sites on the Internet. However, these resources are the exception to the rule that sources with lots of advertising contain little valuable information and advice. Likewise, just because some publications have advertising doesn't mean that some of their columnists and articles aren't worthwhile.

In the following sections, I outline the problems that advertising can cause within all the media outlets.

Influencing content

Many organizations, such as newspaper and magazine publishers and radio and television stations that accept ads, say that their ad departments are separate from their editorial departments. The truth, however, is that in most of these organizations, advertisers wield influence over the content. At a minimum, the editorial environments at these organizations must be perceived as conducive to the sale of the advertiser's product.

The stock market cable television channels, for example, carry many ads from brokers catering to investors who pick and trade their own stocks. Furthermore, such stations carry ads from firms that purport to teach folks how to make big bucks day trading (see Chapter 5). Not surprisingly, such stations offer many "news" segments on their shows that cater to stock traders and condone and endorse foolish strategies, such as day trading, instead of condemning them. Instead of asking themselves what's in the best interests of their viewers, listeners, and readers, executives at too many media and publishing firms ask what will attract attention and advertisers.

Corrupting content

In most organizations, advertisers can have a direct and adulterating influence on editorial content. Specifically, some media organizations and publishers simply won't publish negative comments about a major advertiser. And sometimes they highlight and praise investment companies that are big advertisers.

More than a few publications have attempted to edit out critical comments that I've made about companies with lousy products. These companies always turned out to be advertisers in the publications. Some editors simply say they don't want to bite the hand that feeds them. Others are less candid about why they remove such criticism. The bottom line is still the same: Advertisers' influence prevents readers, viewers, and listeners from getting the truth and best advice. (By the way, I don't write for organizations that edit my work in such a fashion.)

Recognizing quality resources

With the tremendous increase in the coverage of investing and other personal money issues, more and more journalists are writing about increasingly technical issues — often in areas in which they have no expertise. (This type of reporting is true in traditional print publications but especially so online.) Some writers provide good information and advice. Unfortunately, others dish out bad advice. You probably aren't so willing to take medical or legal advice from non-experts, so why would you care any less about your money?

REMEMBER

How can you know what information is good and whom you can trust? Although I can suggest resources that I hold in high regard (as I do throughout this book, especially in Chapters 17, 18, and 19), I recognize that you may encounter many different investment resources and need to understand *how* to tell the best from the rest. The answer to the question, dear reader, rests in educating thyself. The more knowledgeable you are about sound and flawed investment strategies, the better able you are to tell good from not-so-good investment resources.

The best thing to do when you encounter a financial magazine, newspaper, website, or other resource for the first time is to scrutinize it. The following sections suggest some investigative work you should do before you take anyone's investment advice.

Following the money

All things being equal, you have a greater chance of finding quality content when subscriber fees account for the bulk of a company's revenue and advertising accounts for little or none of the revenue. This generalization, of course, is just that: a generalization. Some publications that derive a reasonable portion of their revenues from advertising have some good columns and content. Conversely, some relatively ad-free sources aren't very good.

Figuring out their philosophy and agenda

Deciphering an author's philosophy and agenda is important to determining whether she provides quality information. Readers of my books, for example, can clearly understand my philosophies about investing. I advocate buying and holding, not trading and gambling. I explain how to build wealth through proven vehicles, including stocks, real estate, and small-business ownership. My guiding beliefs are clearly detailed on the Cheat Sheet in the front of this book.

Unfortunately, many publications and programs don't make it as easy for you to see or hear their operating beliefs. You may have to do some homework. For example, with a radio program, you probably have to listen to at least portions of several shows to get a sense of the host's investment philosophies.

WARNING

Red flags include publications and programs that make investing sound overly complicated and that imply or say you won't succeed or do as well if you don't hire a financial advisor or follow your investments like a hawk.

Considering whether the information is constructive

Just about everywhere you turn these days — radio, television, and the Internet — you can get up-to-the-minute updates on financial markets around the globe. Although most investors have a natural curiosity about how their investments are doing, from my experience, the constant barrage of updates causes a loss of focus on the bigger, more important issues. In many cases, publishing and media companies report what I call the "noise" rather than the news of the day. Some companies are far worse about doing so than others.

INVESTIGATE

Over the next week, take a close look at how you spend your time keeping up with financial news and other information. Do the programs and publications that you use most heavily really help you better understand and map out sound investment strategies, or do they end up confusing, overwhelming, and paralyzing you with bits and pieces of contradictory and often hyped noise? I'm not saying that you should tune these resources out completely, but you should devote less time to the noise of the day and more time to self-education. How can you do that? Read some good books (a topic that I discuss in detail in Chapter 18).

Investigating their qualifications

Examine the backgrounds, including professional work experience and education credentials, of a resource's writers, hosts, or anchors. If such information isn't given or easily found, consider this secrecy a red flag. People who have something to hide or lack something significantly redeeming about themselves usually don't promote their backgrounds.

WARNING

Of course, just because someone seems to have a relatively impressive background doesn't mean that she has your best interests in mind or has honestly presented her qualifications. For example, *Forbes* journalist William P. Barrett was skeptical of financial author Suze Orman's biographical and business claims. He investigated and presented a sobering review of Orman's stated credentials and qualifications in *Forbes* magazine, revealing that they were largely exaggerated. A writer for *The San Francisco Chronicle* later substantiated this fact.

Examining gurus' claims

The tremendous growth in media outlets, such as through cable television, radio and television programs, and lots of websites, means that more pundits are making claims about the value of their predictions. Such activity also tends to increase after a major event, such as the severe recession and stock market decline and associated financial crisis in 2008. In the aftermath, many gurus claim "I told you so" status. Unfortunately, many publications and media outlets that interview and give airtime to these pundits fail to independently investigate most of such claims.

In Chapters 17, 18, and 19, I detail how to evaluate various claims. I also provide a short list of worthwhile resources. (Also visit the "Guru Watch" section of my website, www.erictyson.com, for analysis of many of the popular gurus in the media today.)

Chapter 17

Perusing Periodicals, Radio, and Television

Newspapers, magazines, newsletters, and radio and television programs inundate you and other investors with a constant barrage of investing information and advice. In this chapter, I explain what to look for — and what to look out for — when you tune in to these traditional media sources in the hopes of investing better.

In Print: Magazines and Newspapers

Visit a newsstand, and you find many investing publications as well as general interest publications with investing columns. I've written investing articles for various magazines and newspapers. Some of the experiences have been enjoyable, others okay, and a few miserable. The best publications and editors I've written for take seriously their responsibility to provide quality information and advice to their readers.

Taking the scribes to task

Perusing high-quality publications is fun, but reading those that include tons of hype and inaccurate information is mind-numbing. In the following sections, I discuss the problems with magazine and newspaper investment articles so you can easily recognize and avoid them.

Highlighting hype and horror

Whenever the stock market suffers a sharp decline, many in the media bring out the gloom and doom. For example, when the stock and real estate markets slid sharply in the late 2000s, scores of "Great Depression II" pieces populated the pages. First came talk that the "real" unemployment rate was actually closer to 20 percent instead of the reported (and already high) 10 percent. Other similar negative stories weren't far behind.

Then came the news stories that the local, state, and federal governments were so laden with debts that bankruptcy loomed and the very existence of the United States was in jeopardy. (Global stock prices, meanwhile, more than doubled from their lows in early 2009, once again proving that the best values and opportunities come to those brave enough to buy when others are fearful of doing so and when bad news is easy to find.)

Another particularly popular subject for such hyped-up reporting is the cost of a college education. (See, you can write a sentence about the cost of education without including the word *skyrocketing*.) Scores of these articles horrify parents with estimates of the expected costs associated with sending Junior to campus. The typical advice they provide goes like this: Start saving and investing early so you don't have to tell Junior that you can't afford to send him to college.

INVESTIGATE

Cost-of-college stories typify another failing of the media's horror stories. The *horror* is that the story and the accompanying advice can be shortsighted. Completely overlooked and ignored are the tax and financial aid consequences of the recommended investment strategies. For example, if parents don't take advantage of tax-deductible retirement accounts and instead save outside of them to pay for expected college costs, they not only pay more in taxes but also generally qualify for less financial aid. Sound investing decisions require a holistic approach that acknowledges that people have limited money and must make trade-offs. And, unfortunately, blogs and print publications can't always supply that type of advice.

Quoting "experts" who don't know their stuff

Historically, one way that finance journalists have attempted to overcome technical gaps in their knowledge is to interview and quote financial experts. Although these quotes may add to the accuracy and quality of a story, journalists who aren't experts themselves often have difficulty telling qualified experts from hacks. (See Chapter 16 for a discussion on examining the qualifications of writers who offer up financial guidance.)

WARNING

One glaring example of this phenomenon that continues to amaze me is how many newspaper and magazine financial writers quote unproven advice from investment newsletter writers. As I discuss in the section "Fillers and Fluff: Being Wary of Investment Newsletters," later in this chapter, the predictive advice of many newsletter writers is often poor and causes investors to earn lower returns and miss more investment gains due to frequent trading than if they simply bought and held. Journalists who simply parrot this type of information and provide an endorsement that unqualified sources are "experts" do readers an immense disservice.

Focusing on noise and minutiae

Daily financial press writers contribute to today's shortsighted investment environment and encourage readers to adopt similarly misguided outlooks. A focus on the noise of the day causes nervous investors to make panicked, emotionally based decisions, such as deciding to sell *after* major stock market falls.

Of course, the daily print media aren't the only ones chronicling the minutiae. As I discuss elsewhere, other media, including television, radio, and the Internet, cause many investors to lose sight of the long term and the big picture. (I discuss television and radio resources later in this chapter; you can read about Internet resources in Chapter 19.)

REMEMBER

The short length of online, newspaper, and magazine articles can easily lead writers to oversimplify complex issues and offer flawed advice, so be judicious when reading them. For example, some pieces on mutual funds focus on a fund's returns and investment philosophies, devoting little if any space to the risks or tax consequences of investing in the recommended funds.

Making the most of periodicals

So what should you do if you want to find out more about investing but don't want to be overloaded with information? Educate yourself and be selective. If you're considering subscribing to financial publications, review some old issues and articles first. Try to determine whether the information and advice was useful and error free. The more you know, the easier it is to separate the wheat from the chaff.

Shy away from publications that claim to be able to predict the future — few people have a knack for forecasting financial numbers, and those who do are usually busy managing money. Unfortunately, as the financial markets got more volatile in the late 1990s, the early 2000s, and then again in the late 2000s, I witnessed more and more publications promoting columnists and headlines that attempted to prognosticate the future.

INVESTIGATE

Read bylines and biographies and get to know writers' strengths and weaknesses. Ditto for the entire publication. Any writer or publisher can make mistakes. Some make many more than others, however, so follow their advice at your own peril. Start by evaluating advice in the areas that you know the most about. For example, if you're interested in investing in Microsoft or Intel and are reasonably familiar with the computer industry, find out what the publications say about technology investments.

And remember that you're not going to outfox the financial markets, because they're reasonably efficient (see Chapter 4). Seek information and advice that help you flesh out your goals and develop a plan instead of hunting for the next hot stock tip or worrying about short-term trends.

Broadcasting Hype: Radio and Television Programs

As you move from the world of magazines and newspapers to radio and television, the entertainment component usually increases. In this section, I highlight some common problems with radio and television programs.

I've been a guest on hundreds of radio and television programs. Just as Dorothy discovered in *The Wizard of Oz*, seeing how things work behind the scenes tends to deglamorize these mediums. Here are the main problems I've discovered from my years observing radio and television.

You often get what you pay for

Not surprisingly, some of the worst financial advice is brought to you for "free." Nationally, thousands of radio stations have financial and money talk shows. Money and investing shows are proliferating on television cable channels. Because listeners don't pay for these shows, advertising often drives who and what gets on the air, as I discuss in Chapter 16.

I've found that some of the worst offenders are local and even national radio advice programs. Some of these shows are "hosted" by a person who is nothing more than a financial salesperson. That person's first and sometimes only motivation for hosting the show is to pick up clients. Many local radio investing programs are hosted by a local stockbroker (who usually calls himself a financial consultant or planner). A broker who reels in just one big fish a month — a person with, say, $300,000 to invest — can generate commissions totaling $15,000 by selling investments with a 5 percent commission.

WARNING

I know from personal experience what too many radio stations look for in the way of hosts for financial programs. The host's integrity, knowledge, and lack of conflict of interest don't matter. Willingness to work for next to nothing helps. In fact, one radio station program director told me that she liked the broker who was hosting a financial talk show because the broker was willing to work for so little compensation from the radio station. Never mind the fact that the broker rarely gave useful advice and was obviously trolling for new clients. Those things didn't matter to the program director, who told me, "We're in the entertainment business."

Information and hype overload

At 9:30 a.m. EST, the New York Stock Exchange opens, and transactions start streaming across the bottom of television screens that are tuned to financial cable stations. Changes in the major market indexes — the Dow Jones Industrial Average, the S&P 500, and the NASDAQ index — also flash on the screen. In fact, these indexes are updated almost every *second* on the screen. Far more exciting than a political race or sporting event, this event never ends and offers constant change and excitement. Before the U.S. markets open and after they close, reporting of still-open overseas markets continues. The performance of futures of U.S. stock market indexes then appears on the screen.

WARNING

This constant reporting doesn't make people better investors. Although the conventionally accepted notion is that this information overload levels the playing field for the individual investor, I know too many investors who make emotionally based decisions prodded by all this noise, prognostication, opinion, and hearsay.

Poor method of guest selection

Some journalists, often in an effort to overcome their own lack of knowledge, interview "experts." A classic example of this problem is the media exposure that author Charles Givens used to receive. Givens became a darling of the media and the public following an unprecedented, consecutive three-day appearance on NBC's *Today* show.

"When Charles Givens talks, everyone listens," said Jane Pauley, then co-host of the *Today* show. Bryant Gumbel, the other co-host, said of Givens, "Last time he was here, the studio came to a complete stop . . . . Everyone started taking notes, and I was asking for advice." Givens regularly held court on the talk show circuit with the likes of Larry King and Oprah Winfrey.

The Givens case highlights some of the media's inability to distinguish between good and bad experts. It's relatively easy for the financially sophisticated to see the dangerous, oversimplified, and biased advice that Givens offers in his books. In his first bestseller, *Wealth Without Risk*, Givens recommended investing in limited partnerships and provided a phone number and address of a Florida firm, Delta Capital Corp., where readers could buy the partnerships. Those who bought these products ended up paying hefty sales commissions and owning investments worth half or less of their original value. Besides the problematic partnerships he recommended, court proceedings against Givens in a number of states uncovered that he owned a major share of Delta Capital.

WARNING

Other investing advice from Givens that gives true experts pause: In his chapters on investing, he said that the average yearly return you earn investing in mutual funds will be 25 percent or 30 percent. The reality: An investor would be fortunate to earn half of these inflated returns.

So how did Givens get on all these national programs? He had a shrewd publicist, and the show producers either didn't read his books or were financially illiterate themselves. Talk shows and many reporters often don't take the time to check out people like Givens. Most of the time, they never read the books these so-called experts write. Producers, who themselves usually don't know much about investing, often decide to put someone on the air on the basis of a press kit or a call from a publicist.

Fillers and Fluff: Being Wary of Investment Newsletters

Particularly in the newsletter business, prognosticators fill your mailbox and email inbox with promotional material making outrageous claims about their returns. Private money managers, not subject to the same scrutiny and auditing requirements as mutual fund managers, can do the same.

WARNING

Be especially wary of any newsletters making claims of high returns. Stephen Leeb's *Personal Finance* newsletter ads, for example, claim that he has developed a brilliant proprietary model, which he calls the "Master Key Indicator." His model supposedly has predicted the last 28 consecutive upturns in the market without a single miss. The odds of doing this, according to Leeb, are more than 268 million to 1! The ad goes on to claim that Leeb's "Master Key" market-timing system could have turned a $10,000 investment over 12 years into $39.1 million, a return of 390,000 percent!

Turns out that this outrageous claim was based on *backtesting,* looking back over historic returns and creating "what if" scenarios. In other words, Leeb didn't turn anyone's $10,000 into $39 million. Much too late after that ad appeared, the SEC charged Leeb with false advertising. Leeb settled out of court.

According to the *Hulbert Financial Digest,* the worst investment newsletters have underperformed the market averages by dozens of percentage points; some would even have caused you to lose money during decades when the financial markets performed extraordinarily well, like the 1980s and 1990s. Newsletter purveyor Joe Granville, for example, has long been known for making outrageous and extreme stock market predictions and is often quoted in financial publications. He claims to have the number-one-rated newsletter, but he fails to mention that it was number one for one year only (in 1989). Over the subsequent decade — one of the best decades ever for the stock market (with U.S. stocks more than quadrupling in value) — followers of Granville's advice *lost* 99 percent of their investments!

REMEMBER

Be highly suspicious of past investment performance claims made by investment newsletters. Don't believe a track record unless a reputable accounting firm with experience doing such audits has audited it. You don't need predictions and sooth-sayers to make sound investing choices. If you choose to follow this "expert" advice and you're lucky, little harm will be done. But more often than not, you can lose lots of money by following a prognosticator's predictions. Stay far away from publications that purport to be able to tell what's going to happen next. No one has a crystal ball.

The best investment publications can assist you with research and ideas. For individual stock selection, please see my recommended resources in Chapter 6.

Chapter 18

Selecting the Best Investment Books

WARNING

Over the years, I've read hundreds of investing and financial books. You may have read a few yourself! I hope that if you have, you've begun to learn that you need to be choosy and not take everything at face value.

Although most books have something to offer, too many investing books are burdened with biased, wrongheaded advice and misinformation. As a non-expert, you may have a hard time sifting through the heap for the tidbits of treasure. And, sadly, the bad stuff can pollute your thinking and cause you to make investing mistakes that millions before you have made.

When reading investing books, remember not to believe everything you read. Publishing is no different from any other business — companies are in it to make money. As with other industries, the shortsighted desire to reap quick profits causes some companies to publish content that seems attractive in the short term but may be toxic to readers in the long term. In this chapter, I help you sift through the confusion to find books worth reading.

Being Wary of Infomercial Books

When you're watching television, it's generally easy to identify infomercials. You've got the overly energetic salesman pitching a product or service for up to 30 minutes. With books, however, it's much more difficult to decipher such a pitch woven throughout a lengthy book. In the following sections, I highlight what to look out for and give you a ringside seat for a notorious book infomercial that duped too many folks.

Understanding how authors may take advantage of you

WARNING

The worst books steer you toward purchasing a crummy investment product that the author has a vested interest in selling you. They also tend to confuse more than they convey. In fact, some authors have an incentive to make things complicated and mysterious. Their agenda may be to sell you a high-priced newsletter or persuade you to turn your money over to them to manage.

One book author said to me, "I write books to hook people into my monthly newsletter. I can make $185 per year off of a $195 newsletter sale. You can't do that with a book." You sure can't. However, this salesman isn't satisfied to just turn out books that are short on information and advice but long on pitches to keep up with the latest market developments through his newsletter. When you subscribe to his newsletter, you're told that the financial markets are so complicated and change so rapidly that the newsletter is really no substitute for using his money-management service!

WARNING

Unfortunately, most publishers don't do their homework to check out prospective authors. They don't care what the author is up to or whether the author is really an expert on the topic. As long as she's willing and able to write and promote a salable book, the publishers are happy. Authors who run around the country conducting seminars and making publicity appearances are actually a plus to the publisher.

Learning by example

In his books and seminar promotional materials, Wade Cook claimed to be able to teach people how to earn monthly returns of 20 percent or more (that's right — *monthly*, not yearly) by using his stock market investing strategies. (If you've read this book, you know that the promise of such returns is a major red flag.)

Cook's self-published books, which were short on specifics, were largely infomercials for his high-priced seminars. His get-rich-quick investment seminars — which cost a whopping $4,695 — had been so successful at attracting attendees that Cook's company, Profit Financial Corporation, went public and generated more than $100 million in revenues annually! Cook wasn't shy about promising people they could get rich quick without much effort. Here's a passage from his book *Stock Market Miracles:*

> I want millions of dollars and I don't want to have to work a 9 to 5 job to get them. Boy, that's a conundrum. It's almost impossible to work a typical American job, with average income and accumulate millions. Yes, in 40 to 50 years maybe, but who wants to wait that long? That's the rub — accomplishing the task of having millions without having to work for millions.
>
> You see my method is simple. I want to use a small amount of money — risk capital if you will — to generate cash flow which will exponentially generate more income.

Cook promised his followers several hundred percent annualized returns by teaching them how to successfully gamble (not invest) in the stock market. Cook's "techniques" included trading in and out of stocks and options on stocks after short holding periods of weeks, days, or even hours.

Cook's trading strategies were loosely based on *technical analysis* — that is, examining a stock's price movements and volume history through charting. (See Chapter 6 for details on the foolishness of technical analysis.) His investment seminar, which was offered in cities throughout the country, was marketed to folks like this: "If you aren't getting 20 percent per month, or 300 percent annualized returns on your investments, you need to be there."

Steven Thomas, a truck driver, went to a seminar with his wife so both of them could follow and implement Cook's strategies. In addition to spending $4,695 on the seminar, they spent another $2,000 on audiotapes and videotapes. Six months later, Thomas spent $1,500 on a paging system from Cook's company. The results? Thomas eventually lost $36,000, which he borrowed against his home's equity, on investments that were made following Cook's strategies. "I saw this as an opportunity to quit my job and just invest in the stock market," says Thomas. "This has had a terrible impact on my family, and I'm super-depressed."

Of course, if Cook had invested just $1 million of the income he supposedly earned in real estate and indeed earned the 300 percent annual returns his seminars claimed to be able to teach the masses how to achieve, he would have, in about a decade, become the world's wealthiest individual. Look out, Bill Gates and Warren Buffett! Any investor starting with just $10,000 would vault to the top of the list of the world's wealthiest people in about 15 years if Cook's teachings really worked!

So how did Cook get his start in the investing world? Here's what his website said:

> He was a taxicab driver in the '70s. Borrowing $500 from his father, Wade Cook started buying real estate. His innovative ideas and gutsy follow-through enabled him to turn that $500 into several million. But that's nothing compared with what he's doing on Wall Street. Starting with $1,300, using his "Rolling Rock" and "Range Rider" methods, he's showing students how to create millions.
>
> Why is Wade so smart? He says he's "street smart." What he discovered driving a cab changed his life forever. While his fellow cabbies were out looking for the big runs, Wade was taking every little run he could find — $4 here, $5 here. You see it costs $2 just to get into a cab (something called a meter drop) even if you only go two blocks. At the end of a month, Wade made three times what every other taxicab driver made. Now, Wade applies his "meter drop" technique to his stock market investment business — making a ton of money on a lot of little deals.

Imagine that — this investing genius honed his craft driving a cab! Although Cook's investment return expectations were completely unrealistic, he got away with claiming these hyped and undocumented returns for many years because he didn't manage money for others. Seminar promoters and newsletter writers face no SEC scrutiny of their inflated performance claims or what they do in their seminars as long as no securities laws are violated. The SEC refers to such organizations as *non-regulated entities*.

Of course, Cook wasn't the first person to profit in this fashion. Numerous other seminar promoters and authors (some are discussed later in this chapter) have made big bucks as well, including the Beardstown Ladies investment club, which couldn't document its supposedly market-beating returns of 23-plus percent per year (see the next section for details). In addition to puffed-up expected stock market returns, Cook has more to his past than simply driving a taxi. According to *Smart Money* magazine, Cook's dubious business practices had him in trouble before his stock market exploits. At the end of his real estate seminars, which touted that average people could become millionaires by buying property with little money down, Cook began peddling stock in his own business ventures.

State securities regulators in six states — Missouri, Utah, Minnesota, Illinois, Oregon, and Arizona — issued Cook cease-and-desist orders for selling securities without a license, selling unregistered securities, and omitting material facts (such as the fact that he had previously declared bankruptcy). In fact, Arizona charged that Cook had duped $390,841 out of 150 investors by selling unregistered securities and funneling $48,000 of that money into a Scottsdale home purchase and federal income tax payments. The state ordered him to pay back the money and slapped him with a $150,000 penalty.

Cook answered by filing bankruptcy (again). He then moved back to his home state of Washington, where he didn't lay low for long. His new company, Profit Financial Corporation, became wildly successful when he began selling his Wall Street Workshop seminars and publishing his two stock-picking books. The attorneys general of several states sought millions of dollars in consumer refunds and sued the company. These states alleged the company lied about its investment track record. (Now that's a big surprise — the company only claimed you would make 300 percent per year in stocks!) Cook's company settled the blizzard of state and Federal Trade Commission (FTC) lawsuits against his firm by agreeing to accurately disclose his company's trading record in future promotions and to give refunds to customers who were misled by past inflated return claims.

Although Profit Financial Corporation was a public company, SEC documents indicated that it wasn't exactly shareholder friendly. Cook had set up a rather clever business structure whereby the public company (of which he is the majority owner) was required to pay him for the right to print his words and teach his methods. This enabled Cook to funnel much of the revenue stream directly into his pockets before it ever got to the shareholders. According to SEC filings, Cook's total corporate compensation in one year exceeded $8 million! According to a report by Bloomberg News, Cook's firm lost a whopping 89 percent of its own money trading in 2000. As Deb Bortner, director of the Washington State Securities Division and president of the North American Securities Administrators Association, observed, "Either Wade is unable to follow his own system, which he claims is simple to follow, or the system doesn't work."

And as if Cook's financial dealings didn't have enough unsavory aspects, he also was sentenced in 2007 to more than seven years in federal prison for tax evasion, filing false tax returns, and obstructing a tax investigation. He was ordered to pay nearly $4 million in additional taxes as well.

REMEMBER

The moral of the story is this: Be highly skeptical and suspicious of investing books that direct you to high-priced seminars and other expensive products and services from the author. The best investing books, which I recommend later in this chapter, seek to instruct and educate, not sell and scam.

Ignoring Unaudited Performance Claims

REMEMBER

Book authors' claims of especially high returns generally aren't scrutinized. But if a performance claim hasn't been independently audited, don't believe it. Remember also that the stock market, over the long term, provides annualized returns of about 9 to 10 percent. View skeptically any prognosticator or author claiming substantially higher returns that sound too good to be true.

Some book publishers are happy to look the other way or even to solicit and encourage great boasts that they then use in the packaging to sell books. Consider these two examples:

>> *The Beardstown Ladies' Common-Sense Investment Guide: How We Beat the Stock Market — and How You Can, Too:* The Beardstown Ladies investment club claimed a whopping 23.4 percent annualized return since the club's inception. In the book, the authors advocated forming an investment club, pooling your money, and using a simple stock selection method to beat the pants off the market and the suspendered managers of mutual funds. The bulk of this book walked readers through how this investment club evaluated and selected individual stocks.

>> *The Whiz Kid of Wall Street's Investment Guide* by Matt Seto: This book boasted, "Matt Seto manages a portfolio that consistently outperforms 99 percent of all mutual fund managers . . . and returns an annual average of 34 percent." In his book, this then 17-year-old investing genius told readers to forget bonds, real estate, and mutual funds and grow rich by investing entirely in individual stocks.

WARNING

Each of these books made prominently displayed and marketed performance claims. The Beardstown club's returns and Seto's returns, versus the market averages, would've placed them shoulder to shoulder with the legendary Peter Lynch, former manager of the Fidelity Magellan fund, and Warren Buffett, an investor whom Peter Lynch described as "the Greatest Investor of them all." Problem is, neither book contained information as to how these investment gurus calculated their returns, nor were the authors able to substantiate their claimed returns when asked to.

When I first wrote about the Beardstown book for *The San Francisco Examiner,* I offered to work with an accounting firm to calculate the club's returns if the club supplied the necessary information. I asked the same of Seto when I read his book. Neither of these authors could supply the documentation to prove their claims, and they backpedaled when pressed.

Initially, the Beardstown club said it would send the information, but months passed, and it never arrived. The club's media spokesperson then told me that the club has "chosen not to make our return an issue . . . . We're not out to be bragging." This statement was surprising, given the claims prominently plastered all over their book.

A later piece in *Chicago* magazine proved that although the Beardstown investment club claimed 23 percent per year returns versus 14 percent for the market over the same time period, the club actually tremendously underperformed the market and earned only 9 percent per year. The publisher of the Beardstown book, Buena Vista Publishing (which was doing business as Hyperion and Seth Godin Productions), was ultimately sued. Under the terms of the settlement, buyers of the Beardstown investment club's books, audiotapes, or videotapes received certificates that could be redeemed for other books published by Hyperion.

Do you think the Beardstown ladies would have acquired their book deal (and landed on bestseller lists) if the facts had been known? Seto, likewise, couldn't ever prove his claim of an astounding 34 percent return.

Investing Books Worth Reading

Exceptional investing books — ones that are readable, educational, and insightful — are rare. Some of the better investment books are technical in nature and are written by career investment folks, so don't be surprised if they require more than one read. Make the investment of time; it'll pay big dividends (and capital gains!). Following are my picks for books that are worth tracking down and reading.

A Random Walk Down Wall Street

ERIC'S PICKS

Now in its tenth edition, *A Random Walk Down Wall Street* (Norton), by Burton Malkiel, is a classic that was first published in 1973. Malkiel is an entertaining and intelligent writer. Drawing from examples from this century and others, Malkiel teaches how *speculative bubbles* (frenzied buying) and fear and greed, as well as economic and corporate fundamentals, can move the financial markets.

One fundamental premise of his book is that the financial markets can't be predicted, especially in the short term. Common sense confirms this premise: If someone could figure out a system to forecast the markets and make a fortune, that person wouldn't waste time writing a book, publishing a newsletter, and so on. Malkiel, in fact, is one of the pioneers and proponents of *index funds,* which simply invest in a relatively fixed basket of securities in order to track the overall market performance rather than to attempt to beat it. (See Chapter 8 to find out about index funds and how to use them.)

Malkiel explains how to look at some common-sense indicators, such as whether the stock and bond markets are fairly valued and your own personal goals and desire to take risk, to develop a thoughtful and successful investment plan. Instead of trying to predict the future, Malkiel explains how the level of risk an investor accepts with investments will ultimately determine future returns.

Stocks for the Long Run

Finance professor Jeremy J. Siegel loves investing data, especially data he can examine over long time periods. In *Stocks for the Long Run: The Definitive Guide to Financial Market Returns and Long-Term Investment Strategies,* 5th Edition (McGraw-Hill), Siegel presents an analysis of U.S. stock and bond returns since 1802!

The book is packed with charts and graphs for the analytic, graphical folks. Even if you don't completely comprehend all these graphs, the book can still be beneficial. Siegel provides comprehensive discussion of the worldwide financial markets as well as how the economic environment affects stocks. The book focuses on stock market investing, but it also discusses bonds if for no other reason than to compare their returns and risk to stocks.

Built to Last and Good to Great

Some people may think that *Built to Last: Successful Habits of Visionary Companies* (HarperCollins) is just for the small number of people who want to build a large company. However, the book, written by management consultant James Collins and Stanford Business School Professor Jerry Porras, is an excellent book for all entrepreneurs and people who work in leadership positions. It's also great for people interested in investing in individual stocks.

The book presents the findings from an extensive six years' worth of research into what's behind the success of companies such as 3M, Boeing, Ford, Hewlett-Packard, Motorola, Sony, and Wal-Mart, all of which have achieved great success in their respective industries over many years. The average company in the Collins and Porras study was founded in 1897. In all, the authors tracked 18 extraordinary companies (referred to as the gold-medal winners in their respective industries) and compared the traits of these companies with those of similarly long-lived but less successful peer companies (in the same industries).

Not only do Collins and Porras's findings yield insight into how to build or identify a great business in which to invest, but they also destroy some commonly held myths. For example, some people feel that a great idea is behind every great company. This concept is wrong, and in fact, according to the authors' research, companies founded on the basis of a great idea can lead to focusing on the idea rather than laying the groundwork for building a great company. Sony's founder, for example, wrote a nine-page philosophical prospectus setting the stage for this great company, yet he had few product ideas in his firm's early days. Early products, such as a rice cooker, failed.

Great, visionary companies are rigid and unyielding when it comes to respecting their core ideologies and principles. On the other hand, such companies also tinker and experiment to stimulate positive change and innovation. And despite their often-stunning financial success, great companies usually have an aspiration higher than or equal to maximizing profits: fulfilling a purpose and being driven by values. This book is packed with insights, information, and examples, so don't expect to absorb all its contents in one reading.

Collins subsequently wrote another outstanding book, *Good to Great: Why Some Companies Make the Leap . . . And Others Don't* (HarperCollins), which he calls the prequel to *Built to Last.* In *Good to Great,* Collins presents the engaging and insightful results of another long-term study of numerous companies that over time moved from being average companies to outstanding companies. As with *Built to Last,* this newer book can assist readers not only with managing their own small businesses but also with selecting companies to invest in.

Mutual Funds For Dummies

The latest edition of my book *Mutual Funds For Dummies* (Wiley) complements this book because it details how to build and manage a stock and bond portfolio by using the best mutual funds and exchange-traded funds (ETFs). In the book, I discuss dozens of the best funds available and provide sample portfolios for investors in differing situations.

Chapter 19

Investigating Internet and Software Resources

Thousands of investing software packages, blogs, and websites claim to enable you to more easily make profitable investments. As with most other advertising claims, the reality of using your computer for investing and other tasks often falls short of the promises and the hype.

WARNING

In this chapter, I show you ways that your computer may help you with your investing challenges and chores. Throughout this discussion, however, remember the following important caveats:

>> Some highly successful investors don't use their computers, or they use them infrequently, to deal with their investments. (Warren Buffett comes to mind.)

>> You may subject yourself to information overload and spend a fair amount of money without seeing many benefits if you don't choose wisely.

Evaluating Investment Software

Good investment software should be user-friendly and provide quality information for making sound decisions. Software that helps you make personal investment decisions also needs to provide, if applicable, well-founded advice.

REMEMBER

The software that's best for you depends on what you're trying to accomplish as well as your level of investment knowledge and computer savvy. Software can help you with a variety of investment tasks, from tracking your investments to researching, planning, and placing trades through your computer (a topic that I discuss in Chapter 9). The following sections help you find the best software for your needs.

Taking a look at investment tracking software

Software that can help you with investment tracking falls into one of two main groups:

>> Personal finance software that also includes investment-tracking capabilities

>> Software that focuses exclusively on investment tracking

TIP

The broader personal finance packages, such as *Quicken*, are more user-friendly and probably more familiar if you already use these packages' other features (such as a bill-paying feature).

In the following sections, I outline what I see as the advantages and disadvantages of using tracking software based on your needs, and I offer a few alternative approaches to tracking your investments.

Reviewing the benefits

Investment tracking software offers a number of positive features that may appeal to you:

>> **Organization:** One of the best benefits of these packages is that using them can help you get organized. If you enter your investments into the program, the software can help you make sure you don't lose track of your holdings. The fact that investors lose billions of dollars annually to *escheatment* — a situation in which financial institutions turn money over to the state because the owner loses track of his investment (often because the investor moved or passed away) — is testimony to the disarray of some investors' tracking systems.

>> **At-a-glance access:** In addition to organizing all your investment information in one place, investment software allows you to track the original purchase price, current market values, and rates of return on your investments. If you have accounts at numerous investment firms, using software can reduce some of the complications involved in tracking your investing kingdom.

>> **Overall return data:** Investment software can be useful for helping you keep track of your returns. Monitoring all those numbers yourself isn't always easy. People usually know their CD and bond yields, but ask most people investing in individual stocks and bonds what the total return was on their entire portfolio, and, at best, you get a guess. It's the rare person who can quote you total returns or tell you whether her returns are on pace to reach her future financial goals. If an investor does know her investments' returns, she probably doesn't know whether that return is good or bad. For example, she may feel good having made 22 percent on her portfolio of stocks over the past year, but she shouldn't if an index of comparable stocks was up 35 percent over the same period.

Investment tracking software can be more useful for stock traders. In my experience, stock traders, the people who would most benefit from using these programs, often don't track their overall returns. If they did, they could calculate the benefit (or lack thereof) of all their trading. (I've never worked with a stock picker who completed this exercise with me and had return numbers that beat the market indexes over the long term.)

Surveying the drawbacks

My review of investment tracking packages suggests that you need to be prepared to make a substantial time commitment to find out how to use these programs and that you know that other, less high-tech alternatives may be more efficient and enlightening. Also know that a good portion of program users tire of entering all the required data and then feel guilty for falling behind.

If you want to see what your investment returns have been over the years, be aware that entering historic data from your account statements (if you can find them) is a time-consuming process, regardless of which package you use. To calculate your returns, you generally have to enter each new investment that you make as well as all your reinvestments of dividends, interest, and capital gains distributions (such as those made on mutual funds). Ugh! See the following section to discover some alternatives to using these time-consuming products.

Checking out some alternatives

TIP

If you're not into data entry, you have some alternative routes to consider. The following list shows you what to do if you want

>> **To organize:** Keeping a current copy of each of your investment statements in a binder or file folder can accomplish the same result as organizing all your holdings.

>> **At-a-glance access:** Investment software can track all the facts and figures for all your investments — purchase price, market value, rates of return, and so on. But you can accomplish the same things by consolidating your investments at one investment company. (See my discussion of discount brokers in Chapter 9.)

>> **To know your overall return data:** You can easily estimate the return of your overall portfolio using the old-fashioned paper-and-pencil method. Simply weight the return of each investment by the portion of your portfolio that's invested in it. For example, with a simple portfolio equally divided between two investments that returned 10 percent and 20 percent, respectively, your overall portfolio return would be 15 percent $\left(10 \times 0.50 + 20 \times 0.50 = 15\right)$. If you're not adding to or taking money from a portfolio, you can simply compare the portfolio's value at year end to the prior year end.

People who make investments at various times throughout the year and want to know what their actual returns were during the year can use software to get answers. However, unless you're a frequent trader trying to measure the success of your trading, knowing the exact returns based on the precise dates on which you fed money into investments has limited value. This fact is especially true if you're a regular, dollar-cost-averaging investor (see Chapter 3). In this situation, instead of opting for a software program, know that an increasing number of investment companies provide personal return data via their websites and/or on account statements.

And if you're a buy-and-hold mutual fund and exchange-traded fund investor, a path that I find great value in, tracking software gives you limited benefits because of the time required to enter your data. Funds and many other published resources tell you what a fund's total return was for the past year, so you don't need to enter every dividend and capital gain distribution.

Considering investment research software

Investment research software packages usually separate investment beginners (and others who don't want to spend a lot of their time managing their money) from those who enjoy wallowing in data and conducting primary research. If you already have a plan in mind and just want to get on with investing, then go to it! But even if you don't want to conduct more specific research, some of the packages that I discuss in this section can also help you conduct online investment transactions and track an investment's performance.

REMEMBER

When working with research software, you may have the problems of sifting through too much data and differentiating the best from the mediocre and downright awful. And unless cost is no object, you need to make sure you don't spend too much of your loot simply accessing the information.

Before you plunge in to the data jungle and try to become the next Peter Lynch or Warren Buffett by picking individual stocks, be honest about your reasons for wanting to research. Some investors fool themselves into believing that their research will help them beat the markets. However, few investors, even so-called professionals, ever succeed at that goal. Witness the fact that over long time periods (ten-plus years), mutual funds that invest in a fixed-market index, such as the Standard & Poor's 500, outperform about three-quarters of their actively managed peers thanks to the index fund's lower operating expenses (see Chapter 8 for more information on fund investing options).

The best software for researching individual securities

ERIC'S
PICKS

If you like to invest in individual securities, the *Value Line Investment Analyzer* helps you research individual stocks using the data that the *Value Line Investment Survey* provides (as I discuss in Chapter 6). This software package lets you sift through Value Line's data efficiently. You can also use it to track your stock portfolio.

A three-month introductory offer for Value Line's software costs $75, and an annual subscription costs $598 for monthly updates. The software is available from Value Line at 800-535-9648 or by visiting its website at www.valueline.com.

Morningstar, which is better known for its mutual fund information, has followed in Value Line's footsteps in providing lots of data on individual stocks and analyst reports. Morningstar.com's Premium Membership costs $199 per year. You can reach Morningstar at 866-486-9750 or visit its website at www.morningstar.com.

UNDERSTANDING HOW SOFTWARE CALCULATES RETURNS

Most software programs calculate returns in one of two ways:

- **The effective or internal rate of return method:** The programs calculate your effective or internal rate of return (IRR) by comparing your original amounts invested to the current market value. Of those programs I've tested that calculate IRR — and some don't — the results were accurate. After you calculate your returns, knowing how they compare with relevant market averages would be nice. Unfortunately, not all programs allow you to compare your performance to various market indexes.

- **The tax or cost basis method:** All the software packages I've reviewed calculate your cost basis for accounting purposes. Your cost basis is your original investment plus reinvested dividends and capital gains, for which you have already paid taxes in a non-retirement account. To get an accurate cost basis, you need to enter all your investments, including reinvested distributions. Time-starved investors can take solace in the fact that most investment companies, particularly larger mutual fund providers, provide cost basis information for you upon request or when you sell an investment.

Some packages provide only this cost basis information and don't report actual returns. Cost basis reports make your returns look less generous because reinvested distributions increase your original investment and seemingly reduce your returns. I know from experience with counseling clients and students who have taken my courses that investors often look at cost basis reports and assume that the reports tell them what their investment returns are. This happens partly because of the cost basis reports' misleading names, such as "investment performance" or "investment analysis."

The difference between the rate of return using the cost basis and IRR methods is generally substantial. For the data that I used in my research, the cost basis method software calculated a 2.7 percent annual return, and the IRR method software calculated a 13 percent annual return. The actual portfolio's total return was 13 percent, but an investor using a software package that calculates only cost basis is led to believe that her profit was just 2.7 percent (which is correct for tax purposes only for a non-retirement account).

Is all this calculation method mumbo jumbo too technical for your taste? I don't blame you. Luckily, because they already have the data on your accounts, some investment firms can produce your account's performance numbers. Still, surprisingly few investment firms provide personal investment returns. (See Chapter 9 for information regarding brokerage firms and the services they provide.)

The best software for researching funds

ERIC'S PICKS

For mutual funds and exchange-traded funds (ETFs), Morningstar offers subscription services for mutual fund and ETF investors. Value Line publishes a number of software packages, similar in price to the *Value Line Investment Survey.* These packages are geared toward more sophisticated investors who understand mutual funds and ETFs and how to select them. For details, pick up a copy of the latest edition of my book *Mutual Funds For Dummies* (Wiley).

Investigating Internet Resources

Because people interested in managing their money surf the Internet today more than ever, thousands of websites have sprung up to meet the demand. Although the low barriers to entry in the online world make it easy for scammers and incompetents to flog their wares and flawed advice, this medium can offer some helpful resources if you know where to look and how to discern the good from the not-so-good.

The Securities and Exchange Commission (SEC) shutters numerous online scams, such as the one that bilked investors out of millions of dollars by promising to double investors' money in four months in a fictitious security it called "prime bank."

WARNING

Although you may be smart enough to avoid offers that promise pie in the sky, you're far more likely to fall for unsound financial advice, which is abundant online. You can find plenty of self-serving advertorial content and bad advice online, so you should be wary and cautious. The next section offers tips for evaluating Internet resources.

Assessing online resources

Fraud and bad financial advice existed long before the Internet came around. The SEC describes online scams as "new medium, same message." But don't worry. The tips in the following sections can help you find the nuggets of helpful online advice and avoid the land mines.

Being aware of agendas

Get an idea of who's behind a site before you trust its information. Some sites go to extraordinary lengths — including providing lots of information and advice and attempting to conceal the identity of the company that runs the site — to disguise their agendas. Therefore, don't turn to the web for advice or opinions, because the advice and opinions you find usually aren't objective. Similarly, approach online financial calculators with skepticism; most are simplistic and biased.

INVESTIGATE

Many websites and blogs have icons (or About tabs) that you can click on to see some background regarding the site's sponsor and to find out whether the site solicits potential advertisers. With a simple click, you can quickly see that a site purporting to be a reference service of the best small-company stocks in which to invest may be nothing more than an online Yellow Pages of companies that paid the site an advertising fee. Look for sites that exercise quality control in what they post and that use sensible screening criteria for outside information or companies they list.

Just because every Tom, Dick, and Jane can easily and at a relatively low cost set up an Internet site or blog doesn't mean that their sites and advice are worthy of your time. Not surprisingly, the financial companies with reputations for integrity offline are the ones that offer some of the best integrity online. For example, as I discuss later in this chapter, the leading and most investor-friendly investment companies often have the best education-oriented websites.

Soliciting grassroots customer feedback

The Internet can be a useful place to do consumer research. The more enlightening message board conversations that I encounter usually start with someone asking what others thought about particular financial service firms, such as brokerage firms. If you're investigating a certain financial service, the Internet can be an efficient way to get feedback from other people who have experience dealing with that firm.

TIP

In order to find a dozen people offline who have done business with a given firm, you'd probably have to speak with hundreds of people. Online, finding customers is a snap. Those who feel wronged by a particular firm are more than willing to share their gripes through sites such as www.planetfeedback.com. As in the offline world, though, don't believe everything you hear, and watch out for employees of a given firm who post flattering comments about their firms and dis the competition.

Verifying online advice and information by fact checking

TIP

Enhance the value of the online information you gather by verifying it elsewhere. You can do some fact-checking both online and offline. For example, if you're contemplating the purchase of some stock based on financial data that you read on an investing site, first check out those numbers at the library or at one of the websites I recommend later in this chapter.

Lots of Internet investment advice (and most of the scams) focuses on smaller companies and investment startups; unfortunately, these are often the most difficult businesses to locate information about. The SEC requires companies that are raising less than $1 million to file a Form D, so you should check to see whether a small company that's soliciting you has filed one.

To inquire whether a company has filed Form D, call the SEC's Office of Investor Education and Advocacy at 202-551-8090, or send an email to publicinfo@sec.gov. Also check with your state securities regulator. For contact information for state regulators, call the North American Securities Administrators Association at 202-737-0900, or visit its website at www.nasaa.org.

REMEMBER

If something sounds too good to be true, check out and possibly report your concerns to Internet fraud-fighting organization sites. In addition to the SEC's website, check out the Financial Industry Regulatory Authority website (www.finra.org) and the National Consumers League's Fraud Information Center (www.fraud.org; 800-876-7060).

Picking the best investment websites

The quality of the investing information that's on the Internet is gradually improving, and a handful of sites are setting a high standard. The consumer advocacy sites that I recommend earlier in this chapter are a start. And in the following sections, I provide my top picks for those investing sites that are worthy of your online time. (Also, check out my website, www.erictyson.com, for updated analysis of investments, economic news, research, books worth reading, and more.)

CorporateInformation.com

ERIC'S
PICKS

CorporateInformation.com (http://corporateinformation.com) is owned and operated by Wright Investors' Services, which, in addition to managing money for affluent individuals, publishes comprehensive reports on thousands of companies around the globe. Those who are interested in web-based stock research will also enjoy the many links to other Internet-investing and research sites. This site also provides plenty of current business news.

Morningstar.com

The behemoth of the mutual fund data business, Morningstar.com, has a website (www.morningstar.com) that provides information and tools for mutual fund and stock research. The basic stuff is free, but you have to pay $199 per year to access the analyst reports, stock research reports, and other premium content. In addition to providing more data than you could ever possibly digest on funds and stocks, this site also includes short, insightful articles that are useful to more educated investors.

LOOK WHO'S TALKING

If you're at a cocktail party and you receive investing information and advice from someone you've just met, check him out to determine how much credence you should give to his words. And no matter how wise he seems, don't judge his investing savvy on just one conversation.

In the online world, you need to be just as cautious, but you may have greater difficulty determining who's doing the talking and why. Not only do some site owners conceal their identities, but on some sites, visitors may post comments and opinions (often anonymously) on message boards.

As the Financial Industry Regulatory Authority (FINRA) says on its website, "In most instances, there is simply no way to uncover someone's true identity. Are you getting information from a broker, short seller, corporate insider, amateur investor, or stock touter?" You have to use a little logic and a lot of intuition. Start by eliminating any advice from online posters who are totally anonymous. Pseudonyms are common online as well, and some salespeople use them to try to hide their true identities.

Among the more popular message boards on the Internet are those where people debate and discuss the prospects for individual stocks. The postings play fast and loose with the facts. "Investors need to understand that, although they may be reading honest conversations, they could just as easily be looking at the work of a corporate insider, stock promoter, or short seller using an alias to deceive the unsuspecting or to manipulate the market," says the FINRA Regulation unit.

St. Louis Federal Reserve

For those who enjoy analyzing economic data, the St. Louis Federal Reserve website (www.research.stlouisfed.org) is the place to be. In addition to sometimes heady articles, such as "Pandemic Economics: The 1918 Influenza and Its Modern-Day Implications," this site provides a treasure-trove of current economic data along with graphs. The long-term graphs are particularly useful in providing the often missing long-term perspective in your daily diet of news.

For example, I had to laugh the other day when I saw a headline online that screamed, "Dollar at Record Low." The article mentioned only the euro, and it never pointed out that the euro only came into existence in 1999!

In fact, when you compare the dollar to a broad basket of other currencies represented by U.S. trading partners, the U.S. dollar is still more than double the value it was a generation ago. You can see this fact for yourself by examining the *trade weighted exchange index* on the St. Louis Fed site. According to the St. Louis Fed site, the trade weighted exchange index is "A weighted average of the foreign exchange value of the U.S. dollar against the currencies of a broad group of major U.S. trading partners. Broad currency index includes the Euro Area, Canada, Japan, Mexico, China, United Kingdom, Taiwan, Korea, Singapore, Hong Kong, Malaysia, Brazil, Switzerland, Thailand, Philippines, Australia, Indonesia, India, Israel, Saudi Arabia, Russia, Sweden, Argentina, Venezuela, Chile, and Colombia."

Sec.gov

ERIC'S PICKS

All publicly held companies and mutual funds must file annual and quarterly reports and other documents electronically with the U.S. Securities and Exchange Commission. This information is easily accessible for free (paid for by tax dollars) on the SEC website (www.sec.gov).

If you're researching individual companies, you can find all the corporate reports — annual reports, 10-Ks, and the like — that I discuss in Chapter 6 through this website. Or you can call the individual companies that interest you and ask them to mail you the desired material.

The SEC site isn't pretty, and searching the Electronic Data Gathering, Analysis, and Retrieval system (EDGAR) database can be challenging, especially for the novice investor. But if you're tenacious, you may find something that's hard to come by on the web these days: cold, hard facts and no spin.

Vanguard.com

ERIC'S PICKS

Few sites run by investment companies are worth visiting unless you're an account holder at the firm and you want to review your accounts or conduct transactions online. Here's why: Much of the content is self-serving, biased, and advertorial in nature. However, the nation's second-largest mutual fund company, the Vanguard Group, operates a site (www.vanguard.com) that is the exception.

Of course, at its website, you can find details on Vanguard's fine family of funds, but you also find some useful educational materials. I'm not surprised — one reason that I've long liked the company is that it advocates for investors' best interests.

And if you're one of the millions of Vanguard shareholders, you can access your accounts and perform most transactions online. Vanguard's discount brokerage division, also accessible online, allows you to invest in many other fund companies' funds (as well as Vanguard's) through a single account. The company's website also enables you to link accounts that you may hold through most other financial institutions.

ONLINE INVESTING "GENIUSES"

Nowhere will you find more self-proclaimed investing geniuses than online (well, except maybe on cable). Here are some important perspectives and lessons to keep in mind as you surf the web:

- **Beware of promises of easy riches.** To deter investors from mutual funds, one website says of its stock picking, "We hope to have put you in position to nearly double the S&P 500 . . . . It'll demand little research per year, and present you little, if any, long-term risk." If investing were that easy, everyone would be rich! And as any professional money manager knows firsthand, successfully managing a portfolio of individual stocks takes a lot of time, not just a few hours per year.

- **Beware of bloated performance claims.** Not surprisingly, many online investing pundits hype claimed returns from their investment recommendations. If you can't independently verify a performance claim, don't believe it. Also, keep in mind that even if performance numbers are indeed accurate, calculated returns often overlook trading commissions and taxes (which can be especially high for sites that advocate selling investments after holding them for less than one year).

- **Successful investing doesn't require following the market closely.** Buying and holding index or other quality funds for many years doesn't take much review time — perhaps as little as a few hours per year to read the fund's annual reports. The daily and even minute-by-minute tracking of stock prices on many sites causes investors to lose sight of the long term and the big picture (although it draws more visitors to the site, which satisfies advertisers and enriches the site owners).

The bottom line? Be skeptical of financial prognosticators. Like politicians, they're out to make themselves look as good as possible, taking credit when things go well and blaming external forces when they don't. For more on popular investment and economic gurus, see the "Guru Watch" section of my website at www.erictyson.com. Also, see Chapter 17 for more about investment newsletters.

6

The Part of Tens

Get in the right mindset for investing success by facing some psychological traps and obstacles to overcome.

When you're considering selling an investment, be as informed as you are when you're thinking of buying.

Take advantage of a down market by protecting your existing investments and applying advice for adding some new ones to your portfolio.

Chapter 20

Ten Investing Obstacles to Conquer

Just as with raising children or as in one's career, "success" with personal investing is in the eye of the beholder. In my work as a financial counselor, instructor, and writer, I've come to define a successful investor as someone who, with a modest commitment of time, develops an investment plan to accomplish financial and personal goals and who earns competitive returns given the risk he's willing to accept.

In this chapter, I point out ten common obstacles that may keep you from being successful and fully realizing your financial goals. I also share tips and advice for overcoming those obstacles on the road to investing success.

Trusting Authority

Some investors assume that an advisor is competent and ethical if she has a lofty title (financial consultant, vice president, and so on), dresses well, and works in a snazzy office. Unfortunately, such accessories are often indicators of salespeople — not objective advisors — who recommend investments that will earn them big commissions that come out of your investment dollars.

If you overtrust an advisor, you may not research and monitor your investments as carefully as you should. Figuring that Mr. Vice President is an expert, some investors go along without ever questioning his advice or watching what's going on with their investments. Too many investors blindly follow analysts' stock recommendations without considering the many conflicts of interest that such brokerage firm employees have. Brokerage analysts are often cheerleaders for buying various companies' stock because their firms are courting the business of new stock and bond issuance of the same companies. And just because a big-name accounting firm has blessed a company's financial statements (Enron) or a company's CEO says everything is fine (Bear Stearns) doesn't make a firm's financial statements accurate or its conditions sound.

TIP

You can't possibly evaluate the competence and agenda of someone you hire until you understand the basics. Without mastering financial fundamentals, you can't know that an analyst's report or a professional service firm's recommendation or approval of a company is worth the paper it's printed on. Read good publications on the topic to master the jargon and figure out how to evaluate investments. Seek independent second opinions before you act on someone's recommendations. If you're in the market for a broker, be sure to read Chapter 9.

Getting Swept Up by Euphoria

Feeling strength and safety in numbers, some investors are lured into buying hot stocks and sectors (for example, industries like technology, healthcare, biotechnology, retail, and so on) after major price increases. Psychologically, it's reassuring to buy into something that's going up and gaining accolades. The obvious danger with this practice is buying into investments selling at inflated prices that will soon deflate.

By the late 1990s, investors in the U.S. stock market were being spoiled with gains year after year in excess of the historic average annual return of 9 to 10 percent. Numerous surveys conducted during this period showed that many investors expected to earn returns in the range of 15 to 20 percent annually, nearly double the historic average. As always happens, though, after a period of excessively high returns such as those of the 1990s, returns were below average in the subsequent period beginning in 2000 (and were quite negative in the early and late 2000s). During the market slump in the early 2000s, real estate–related stocks continued to do well; some folks mistakenly believed that the housing sector was immune to setbacks and were surprised by the slump in that sector in the late 2000s.

TIP

Develop an overall allocation among various investments (especially diversified mutual funds), and don't make knee-jerk decisions to change your allocation based on what the latest hot sectors are. If anything, de-emphasize or avoid stocks and sectors that are at the top of the performance charts. Think back to the last time you went bargain shopping for a consumer item — you looked for value, not high prices. See Chapter 5 to find out how to spot good values in the financial markets and which speculative bubbles to avoid.

Being Overconfident

As I discuss in Part 5, newsletters, books, blogs, and financial periodicals lead investors to believe that they can be the next Peter Lynch or Warren Buffett if they follow a simple stock-picking system. The advent of the Internet and online trading capabilities has spawned a whole new generation of short-term (sometimes even same-day) traders.

In my work as a financial counselor, I came across plenty of people who lost a lot of money after they had an early winner and had attributed that success to their investing genius. These folks usually landed on my doorstep after great and humbling losses woke them up.

TIP

If you have the speculative bug, earmark a small portion of your portfolio (no more than 10 to 20 percent) for more aggressive investments. See Chapter 5 for information to help you decide whether you or someone you know has a gambling problem.

Giving Up When Things Look Bleak

Inexperienced or nervous investors may be tempted to bail out when it appears that an investment isn't always profitable and enjoyable. Some investors dump falling investments precisely when they should be doing the reverse: buying more. Sharp stock market pullbacks attract a lot of attention, which leads to concern, anxiety, and, in some cases, panic. This situation occurred during the financial crisis of 2008. As layoffs mushroomed and stocks sank, fear and talk of another Great Depression took hold.

Investing always involves uncertainty. Many people forget this, especially during good economic times. I find that investors are more likely to feel comfortable with riskier investments, such as stocks, when they recognize that all investments carry uncertainty and risk — just in different forms.

History has repeatedly proved that continuing to buy stocks during down markets increases your long-term returns. The worst thing you can do in a slumping market is to throw in the towel. Folks who dumped their stocks in late 2008 and early 2009 missed out on the doubling in stock values over the subsequent two years.

Unfortunately, the short-term focus that the media so often takes causes some investors to worry that their investments are in shambles during the inevitable bumps in the road. As I discuss in Part 5, the media are often to blame because they hype short-term events and blow those events out of proportion to captivate viewers and listeners. History has shown that financial markets and economies generally recover. If you invest for the long term, then the last six weeks — or even the last couple of years — is a short period. Plus, countless studies demonstrate that no one can predict the future, so you gain little from trying to base your investment plans on predictions. In fact, you can lose more money by trying to time the markets.

Larger-than-normal market declines hold a significant danger for investors: They may encourage decision-making that's based on emotion rather than logic. Just ask anyone who sold *after* the stock market collapsed in 1987 — the U.S. stock market dropped 35 percent in a matter of weeks in the fall of that year. Since then, even with the significant declines in the early and late 2000s, the U.S. market has risen about tenfold!

Investors who can't withstand the volatility of riskier growth-oriented investments, such as stocks, may be better off not investing in such vehicles to begin with. Examining your returns over longer periods helps you keep the proper perspective. If a short-term downdraft in your investments depresses you, avoid tracking your investment values closely. Also, consider investing in highly diversified, less-volatile funds that hold stocks worldwide as well as bonds (see Chapter 8).

Refusing to Accept a Loss

Although some investors realize that they can't withstand losses and sell at the first signs of trouble, other investors find that selling a losing investment is so painful and unpleasant that they continue to hold a poorly performing investment despite the investment's poor future prospects. Psychological research backs these feelings — people find the pain of accepting a given loss twice as intense as the pleasure of accepting a gain of equal magnitude.

TIP

Analyze your lagging investments to identify why they perform poorly. If a given investment is down because similar ones are also in decline, hold on to it. However, if something is inherently wrong with the investment — such as high fees or poor management — you can make taking the loss more palatable:

>> Remember that if your investment is a non-retirement account investment, selling at a loss helps reduce your income taxes.

>> Consider the opportunity cost of continuing to keep your money in a lousy investment. In other words, what returns can you get in the future if you switch to a "better" investment?

Over-Monitoring Your Investments

The investment world seems so risky and fraught with pitfalls that some people believe that closely watching an investment can help alert them to impending danger. "The constant tracking is not unlike the attempt to relieve anxiety by fingering worry beads. Yet paradoxically, it can increase emotional distress because it requires a constant state of vigilance," says psychologist Dr. Paul Minsky.

In my work as a financial counselor, I noticed that investors who were the most anxious about their investments and most likely to make impulsive trading decisions were the ones who watched their holdings too closely, especially those who monitored prices daily. The proliferation of Internet sites and stock market cable television programs offering up-to-the-minute quotations gives these investors even more temptation to over-monitor investments.

TIP

Restrict your diet of financial information and advice. Quality is far more important than quantity. Watching the daily price gyrations of investments is akin to eating too much junk food: Doing so may satisfy your short-term cravings but at the cost of your long-term health. If you invest in diversified mutual funds and exchange-traded funds (see Chapter 8), you really don't need to examine your fund's performance more than twice per year. An ideal time to review your funds is when you receive their annual or semiannual reports. Although many investors track their funds daily or weekly, far fewer read their annual reports. Reading these reports can help you keep a long-term perspective and gain some understanding as to why your funds perform as they do and how they compare to major market averages.

Being Unclear about Your Goals

Investing is more complicated than simply setting your financial goals (see Chapter 3) and choosing solid investments to help you achieve them. Awareness and understanding of the less tangible issues can maximize your chances for investing success.

TIP

In addition to considering your goals in a traditional sense (when you want to retire and how much of your kids' college costs you want to pay, for example) before you invest, you should also consider what you want and don't want to get from the investment process. Do you treat investing as a hobby or simply as another one of life's tasks, such as maintaining your home? Do you enjoy the intellectual challenge of picking your own stocks? Don't just ponder these questions on your own; discuss them with family members, too — after all, you're all going to have to live with your decisions and the investment results.

Ignoring Your Real Financial Problems

I know plenty of high-income earners, including more than a few who earn six figures annually, who have little to invest. Some of these people have high-interest debt outstanding on credit cards and auto loans, yet they spend endless hours researching and tracking investments. I also know folks who built significant personal wealth despite having modest-paying jobs. The difference is the ability to live within their means.

REMEMBER

You may be tempted to think that you can't save if you don't earn a high income. Even if you're a high-income earner, you may think that you can hit an investment home run to accomplish your goals or that you can save more if you can bump up your income. This way of thinking justifies spending most of what you earn and saving little now. Investing is far more exciting than examining your spending and making cutbacks. If you need help coming up with more money to invest, see the latest edition of my book *Personal Finance For Dummies* (Wiley).

Overemphasizing Certain Risks

Saving money is only half the battle. The other half is making your money grow. Over long time periods, earning just a few percent more makes a big difference in the size of your nest egg. Earning inflation-beating returns is easy if you're willing to invest in stocks, real estate, and small businesses. Figure 20-1 shows you how much more money you'll have in 25 years if you earn investment returns that are greater than the rate of inflation (which historically has been about 3 percent).

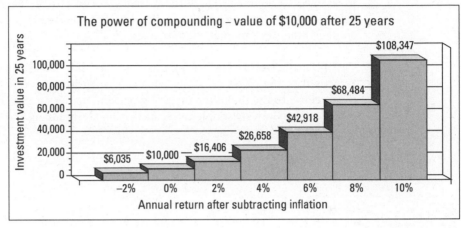

FIGURE 20-1: Slightly higher returns compound to really make your money grow.

As I discuss in Chapter 2, ownership investments (stocks, real estate, and small business) have historically generated returns that are 6 or more percent greater than the inflation rate, while lending investments (savings accounts and bonds) tend to generate returns of only 1 to 2 percent greater than inflation. However, some investors keep too much of their money in lending investments out of fear of holding an investment that can fall greatly in value. Although ownership investments can plunge in value, you need to keep in mind that inflation and taxes eat away at your lending investment balances.

Believing in Gurus

Stock market declines, like earthquakes, bring all sorts of prognosticators, soothsayers, and self-anointed gurus out of the woodwork, particularly among those in the investment community, such as newsletter writers, who have something to sell. The words may vary, but the underlying message doesn't: "If you had been following my sage advice, you'd be much better off now."

People spend far too much of their precious time and money in pursuit of a guru who can tell them when and what to buy and sell. Peter Lynch, the former manager of the Fidelity Magellan Fund, amassed one of the best long-term stock market investing track records. His stock-picking ability allowed him to beat the market averages by just a few percent per year. However, even he says (as does investment legend Warren Buffett) that you can't time the markets. He also acknowledges knowing many pundits who have correctly predicted the future course of the stock market "once in a row"!

Clearly, in the world of investing, the most successful investors earn much better returns than the worst ones. But what may surprise you is that you can end up much closer to the top of the investing performance heap than the bottom if you follow some relatively simple rules, such as regularly saving and investing in low-cost growth investments.

Chapter 21

Ten Things to Consider When Weighing an Investment Sale

You can and should hold good investments for years and decades. Each year, people sell trillions of dollars' worth of investments. My experience helping folks get a handle on their investments suggests that too many people sell for the wrong reasons (while other investors hold on to investments that they should sell for far too long). In this chapter, I highlight ten important issues to consider when you contemplate selling your investments.

Remembering Preferences and Goals

REMEMBER

If your life has changed (or you've inherited investments) since the last time you took a good look at your investment portfolio, you may discover that your current portfolio no longer makes sense for you. To avoid wasting time and money on investments that aren't good for you, be sure to review your holdings at least annually. But don't make quick decisions about selling. Instead, take your time and be sure that you understand tax consequences and other ramifications before you sell.

The time that it takes you to manage your portfolio is a vital matter if you're starved for time or weary of managing time-consuming investments. Leo, for example, loved to research, track, and trade individual stocks — until his daughter was born. Then Leo realized how many hours his hobby was taking away from his family. This realization put his priorities into perspective. Leo now invests in time-friendly mutual funds and exchange-traded funds and doesn't follow them like a hawk.

One of my clients, Mary, loves investing in real estate because she enjoys the challenge of researching, selecting, and managing her properties. She works in a job where she has to put up with lots of controlling, stressed-out bosses. For Mary, real estate isn't just a profitable investment; it's also a way of expressing herself and growing personally.

Maintaining Balance in Your Portfolio

A good reason to sell an investment is to allow yourself to better diversify your portfolio. Suppose, for example, that before reading this book, you purchased a restaurant stock every time you read about one. Now your portfolio resembles several strip malls, and restaurant stocks comprise 80 percent of your holdings. Or maybe, through your job, you've accumulated such a hefty chunk of stock in your employer that this stock now overwhelms the rest of your investments.

If your situation sounds anything like these, it's time for you to diversify. Sell off some of the holdings that you have too much of and invest the proceeds in some of the solid investments that I recommend in this book. If you think your employer's stock is going to be a superior investment, holding a big chunk is your gamble. At a minimum, review Chapter 6 to see how to evaluate a particular stock. But remember to consider the consequences if you're wrong about your employer's stock.

Conservative investors often keep too much of their money in bank accounts, Treasury bills, and the like. Read Chapter 3 to come up with an overall investment strategy that fits with your personal financial situation.

Deciding Which Ones Are Keepers

Often, people are tempted to sell an investment for the wrong reasons. One natural human tendency is to want to sell investments that have declined in value. Some people fear a further fall, and they don't want to be affiliated with a loser, especially when money is involved.

REMEMBER

Instead, step back, take some deep breaths, and examine the merits of the investment you're considering selling. If an investment is otherwise still sound, why bail out when prices are down and a sale is going on? What are you going to do with the money? If anything, you should be contemplating buying more of such an investment. Also, don't make a decision to sell based on your current emotional response, especially to recent news events. If bad news has recently hit, it's already old news. Don't base your investment holdings on such transitory events. Use the criteria in this book for finding good investments to evaluate the worthiness of your current holdings. If an investment is fundamentally sound, don't sell it.

A better reason to sell an investment is that it comes with high fees relative to comparable investments. For example, if you own a bond fund that is socking you with high fees, check out Chapter 8 to discover high-performing, lower-cost funds.

Tuning In to the Tax Consequences

When you sell investments that you hold outside a tax-sheltered retirement account, such as in an IRA or a 401(k), taxes should be one factor in your decision. (See Chapter 3 to find out about tax rates that apply to the sale of an investment as well as to the distributions that investments make.) If the investments are inside retirement accounts, taxes aren't an issue, because the accounts are sheltered from taxation until you withdraw funds from them.

REMEMBER

Just because you pay tax on a profit from selling a non-retirement account investment doesn't mean you should avoid selling. With real estate that you buy directly, as opposed to publicly held securities like REITs, you can often avoid paying taxes on the profit that you make (see Chapters 10 and 11 for details).

With stocks and mutual funds, you can specify which shares you want to sell. This option makes selling decisions more complicated, but you may want to consider specifying what shares you're selling because you may be able to save taxes. (Read the next section for more information on this option.) If you sell all your shares of a particular security that you own, you don't need to concern yourself with specifying which shares you're selling.

Figuring Out What Shares Cost

When you sell a portion of the shares of a security (for example, stock, bond, or mutual fund) that you own, specifying which shares you're selling may benefit you taxwise. Here's an example to show you why you may want to specify selling certain shares — especially those shares that cost you more to buy — so you can save on your taxes.

Suppose you own a total of 300 shares of a stock and you want to sell 100 shares to pay for a root canal. Suppose further that you bought 100 of these shares a long time ago at $10 per share, 100 shares two years ago at $16 per share, and the last 100 shares one year ago at $14 per share. Today the stock is at $20 per share.

The IRS allows you to choose which shares you want to sell. Electing to sell the 100 shares that you purchased at the highest price — those you bought for $16 per share two years ago — saves you in taxes. To comply with the tax laws, you must identify the shares that you want the broker to sell by the original date of purchase and/or the cost when you sell the shares. The brokerage firm through which you sell the stock should include this information on the confirmation slip that you receive for the sale.

The other method of accounting for which shares are sold is the method that the IRS forces you to use if you don't specify before the sale which shares you want to sell — the *first-in-first-out* (FIFO) method. FIFO means that the first shares that you sell are simply the first shares that you bought. Not surprisingly, because most stocks appreciate over time, the FIFO method usually leads to you paying more tax sooner. The FIFO accounting procedure leads to the conclusion that the 100 shares you sell are the 100 that you bought long, long ago at $10 per share. Thus, you owe a larger amount of taxes than if you sold the higher-cost shares under the specification method.

REMEMBER

Although you save taxes today if you specify selling the shares that you bought more recently at a higher price, remember that when you finally sell the other shares, you'll then owe taxes on the larger profit. The longer you expect to hold these other shares, the greater the value you'll likely derive from postponing, realizing the larger gains and paying more in taxes. If you expect your tax rate to decline in the future, you have another good reason to hold off selling the shares in which you have greater profit.

When you sell shares in a mutual fund, the IRS has yet another accounting method, known as the *average cost method,* for figuring your taxable profit or loss when you sell a portion of your holdings in a mutual fund. This method comes in handy if you bought shares in chunks over time or reinvested the fund payouts into purchasing more shares of the fund. As the name suggests, the average cost method allows you to take an average cost for all the shares you bought over time.

Selling Investments with Hefty Profits

Of course, no one likes to pay taxes, but if an investment you own has appreciated in value, someday you'll have to pay taxes on it when you sell — unless, of course, you plan to pass the investment to your heirs upon your death. The IRS wipes out the capital gains tax on appreciated assets at your death. Capital gains tax applies when you sell an investment at a higher price than you paid for it (see Chapter 3).

Odds are, the longer you've held securities such as stocks, the greater the capital gains you'll have, because stocks tend to appreciate over time. If all your assets have appreciated significantly, you may resist selling to avoid taxes. However, if you need money for a major purchase, sell what you need and pay the tax. Even if you have to pay state as well as federal taxes totaling some 35 percent of the profit, you'll have lots left. (For "longer-term" profits from investments held more than one year, your federal and state capital gains taxes would probably total less than 25 percent.)

REMEMBER

Before you sell, do some rough figuring to make sure you'll have enough money left to accomplish what you want. If you seek to sell one investment and reinvest in another, you'll owe tax on the profit unless you're selling and rebuying real estate (see Chapters 10 and 11).

If you hold a number of assets, in order to diversify and meet your other financial goals, give preference to selling your largest holdings with the smallest capital gains. If you have some securities that have profits and some that have losses, you can sell some of each to offset the profits with the losses.

Cutting Your (Securities) Losses

Perhaps you have some losers in your portfolio. If you need to raise cash for some particular reason, you may consider selling select securities at a loss. You can use losses to offset gains as long as you hold both offsetting securities for more than one year (long term) or you hold both for no more than one year (short term). The IRS makes this delineation because the IRS taxes long-term gains and losses on a different rate schedule than short-term gains and losses (see Chapter 3).

REMEMBER

If you need to sell securities at a loss, be advised that you can't claim more than $3,000 in net losses in any one year. If you sell securities with net losses totaling more than $3,000 in a year, you must carry the losses over to future tax years. This situation not only creates more tax paperwork but also delays realizing the value of deducting a tax loss. So try not to have *net losses* (losses + gains) that exceed $3,000 in a year.

Some tax advisors advocate doing year-end tax-loss selling with stocks, bonds, and mutual funds. The logic goes that if you hold a security at a loss, you should sell it, take the tax write-off, and then buy it (or something similar) back.

WARNING

When selling investments for tax-loss purposes, be careful of the so-called *wash sale* rules. The IRS doesn't allow the deduction of a loss for a security sale if you buy that same security back within 30 days. As long as you wait 31 or more days, you won't encounter any problems. If you're selling a mutual fund or exchange-traded fund, you can purchase a fund similar to the one you're selling to easily sidestep this rule.

Dealing with Unknown Costs

Sometimes you may not know what an investment originally cost you. Or you may have received some investments from another person, and you're not sure what he or she paid for them. If you don't have the original statement, start by calling the firm where the investment was purchased. Whether it's a brokerage firm or a mutual fund company, the company should be able to send you copies of old account statements, although you may have to pay a small fee for this service.

Also, increasing numbers of investment firms, especially mutual fund companies, can tell you upon the sale of an investment what its original cost was. The cost calculated is usually the average cost for the shares you purchased.

Recognizing Broker Differences

If you're selling securities such as stocks and bonds, you need to know that some brokers charge more — in some cases, lots more — to sell. Luckily, even if the securities that you want to sell currently reside at a high-cost brokerage firm, you can transfer them to a discount brokerage firm. Head to Chapter 9 to read about the different types of brokerage firms and how to select the best one for your situation.

Finding a Trustworthy Financial Advisor

If you delegate your investment decision-making to an advisor, you may be disappointed in your returns. Few financial advisors offer objective and knowledgeable advice. Unfortunately, if you're grappling with a selling decision, finding a competent and impartial financial advisor to help with the decision is about as difficult as finding a politician who doesn't accept special-interest money. Most financial consultants work on commission, and the promise of that commission can cloud their judgment. Among the minority of fee-based advisors, almost all manage money, which creates other conflicts of interest. The more money you give them to invest and manage, the more money these advisors make.

TIP

If you need advice about whether to sell some investments, turn to a tax or financial advisor who works on an hourly basis.

Chapter 22

Ten Tips for Investing in a Down Market

Unless a lot of other breaking news occurs on a particular day, sharp drops in the stock market make headlines — stock market gyrations are great media fodder. Every day the market environment is different, and new stocks are always plunging and rising. And now, with more individuals holding stocks (including mutual funds and exchange-traded funds) through company and personal retirement plans, most folks watch financial market movements. In this chapter, I discuss how to maximize your chances for investing success when stocks take an extended turn for the worse.

Don't Panic

No one enjoys turning on his car radio, clicking on his television set, or logging on to the Internet and getting this news: "Stocks plunge. The Dow Jones Industrial plummeted 400 points today." When you hear this news, don't panic — it's just one day's events. (In 2008, the market seemingly had day after day of such drops, and the events could accurately be described as a financial panic, the likes of which the nation hadn't experienced in generations. I describe this situation more in the later section "View Major Declines as Sales.")

Just because a home burned to the ground recently in your town and the news is being broadcast all over the local media, you probably wouldn't start living on the street out of fear of being at home during a fire. But you may take some sensible precautions, such as installing smoke alarms and repairing any malfunctioning appliances that may cause a fire, to ensure that your home isn't likely to become the next fire department statistic.

Likewise, don't shun stocks, which produce terrific long-term returns, just because of the down periods. As I discuss in Chapter 2, risk and return go hand in hand. If you want wealth-building investments that provide superior long-term returns, you must be willing to accept risk (that is, volatility and down periods). You should take sensible precautions — with diversification being the star of the show — to reduce your risk.

Although other wealth-building investments, such as real estate and small business, go through significant declines, you generally see few headlines on their daily price movements. A good reason for this lack of headlines is that no one reports on the pricing of real estate and small businesses minute by minute every business day, as is done with stock prices.

Keep Your Portfolio's Perspective in Mind

If you follow my advice, your portfolio will consist of diversified stock holdings, including some international stocks and some bonds. Having a diversified portfolio can help in a down market because some investments will increase as others decrease, thus balancing the losses.

One of my counseling clients called me when the stock market was dropping precipitously. "I just saw that the S&P 500 is now down 28 percent so far this year, and the NASDAQ is down 34 percent. Should I sell?"

He was quite surprised when I crunched some numbers and determined that *his* portfolio of stocks and bonds was down just 8 percent for the year. Now, mind you, I wasn't trying to minimize or trivialize the fact that he had lost money so far that year. However, he overlooked the fact that the bonds in his portfolio had actually increased in value, as had some of his stock funds that were invested in value-oriented stocks. See Chapter 8 for tips on how to build a diversified fund portfolio.

View Major Declines as Sales

REMEMBER

Unlike retail stores, which experience larger crowds when prices are cut, fewer investors, especially individual investors, want to buy stocks after they've suffered a sharp decline. However, when stock prices decline, don't get swept up in the pessimism. View declines as the financial markets having a sale on stocks. Stocks usually bottom when pessimism reaches a peak. Why? Those who were motivated to sell have done so, and the major selling has exhausted itself.

During the recession and stock market decline that reached a crescendo in 2008, negativity and pessimism were rampant. Global stock prices dropped by half in about one year's time. The banking and financial system was in crisis and governments were intervening. Talk of a depression became common as U.S. unemployment surged to 10 percent. After bottoming in early 2009, stocks went on an upward rampage that resulted in a doubling in value in just two years — a rare historic event.

Now, I'm not saying you should randomly buy just any stock after a decline. I'm not an advocate of buying individual stocks, especially a collection of stocks focused in the same industry (such as technology or auto manufacturing). When technology stocks started declining in 2000, some investors made the mistake of buying more of them after prices dropped 10 or 20 percent. What such "buy on the dip" investors didn't realize was that the technology stocks they were buying were still grossly overpriced when measured by price-earnings ratios and other valuation measures (see Chapter 5).

TIP

You're best off buying stocks gradually over time through well-managed, diversified mutual funds and exchange-traded funds (see Chapter 8). When the broad stock market suffers a substantial decline and stocks are at reduced prices — on sale — you can step up your buying.

Identify Your Portfolio's Problems

Stock market declines can be effective at quickly exposing problems with your portfolio, such as having too many investments from the same industry.

For example, when technology stocks tumbled in the early 2000s, I started getting lots of emails and letters from investors who had loaded up on these stocks and wanted my advice on what they should do with their holdings. Many of these investors kept thinking about how much more their technology stocks were worth at their peak before the decline set in. I urged such investors to acknowledge the huge risk they were taking by putting so many eggs in one basket. I also highlighted the dangers of chasing after a hot sector, and I pointed out that today's hot sector often becomes tomorrow's laggard.

In addition to revealing poorly diversified portfolios, a declining stock market can expose the high fees you may be paying on your investments. Fewer investors care about getting whacked with fees amounting to, say, 2 percent annually when they're making 20 percent yearly. But after a few years of low or negative returns, such high fees become quite painful and more obvious.

Avoid Growth Stocks If You Get Queasy Easily

In a sustained stock market slide *(bear market)*, the stocks that get clobbered the most tend to be the ones that were most overpriced from the period of the previous market rise *(bull market)*. Like fads such as hula hoops, pet rocks, and Cabbage Patch Kids, in each bull market, particular types of growth stocks, such as Internet companies or biotechnology companies, can be especially hot.

REMEMBER

Predicting the duration and magnitude of a bear market is nearly impossible. Consequently, it makes sense to focus your stock investing on those stocks that produce solid long-term returns and that tend to decline less in major market declines. For instance, so-called *value stocks* tend to be among the safer types of stocks to hold during a bear market. Value stocks generally have less downside risk because they have relatively greater underlying asset values in comparison to their stock valuations. (Value stocks also typically pay higher dividends.)

As has happened in some other past bear markets, numerous value-oriented stocks actually appreciated during the bear market in the early 2000s. (This didn't happen during the more severe, late-2000s bear market, however.) Check out Chapter 8 for my discussion of the different types of stocks and of funds that practice value stock investing.

Tune Out Negative, Hyped Media

When the stock market is crumbling, subjecting yourself to a daily diet of bad news and conflicting opinions about what to do next makes most investors do the wrong things. Just like a steady diet of junk food is bad for your physical health, a continuous stream of negative, hyped news is bad for your financial health. Dwelling on bad news doesn't do such great things for people's emotional health, either.

REMEMBER

The economy goes through periods of expansion and occasional periods of decline (with the former generally being longer and stronger than the latter). Conflict is always occurring somewhere in the world. The business world will always have some unethical and corrupt company executives. Holding stocks always carries risk. So those who see the glass as half full and who see the positive and not just the negative build wealth by holding stocks, real estate, and small business over the long term.

Ignore Large Point Declines But Consider the Percentages

It drives me crazy when the news media show a one-day chart of a major stock market index, such as the Dow Jones Industrial Average, on a day when the index drops a large number of points. In recent years, 200- and 300-point drops in the Dow happened fairly frequently.

REMEMBER

Look at an index's percentage decline rather than at its point decline. Although 200 to 300 points sounds like a horrendous drop, such a drop amounts to a move of about 1 to 2 percent for an index trading around 16,000. No one likes losing that portion of their wealth invested in stocks in one day, but the percentage of change sounds less horrifying than the point change.

Don't Believe You Need a Rich Dad to Be a Successful Investor

A young man wrote to me about something he'd read in an interview with Robert Kiyosaki, author of the *Rich Dad, Poor Dad* series. According to the interviewer, Kiyosaki said that the rich are different from the rest of the population because "They teach their children how to be rich. . . . These get-rich techniques include investing with leverage . . . and staying away from mutual funds and 401(k)s, which are way too risky."

The young man came from a humble background and had been salting money away in mutual funds through his company's retirement plan. But he thought that he may be doomed to a lifetime of poverty after reading what the *Rich Dad* guru had to say. Luckily, I was able to set the young man straight.

I've known plenty of people over the years who have come from nonwealthy families and have built substantial wealth by living within their means and investing in the three wealth-building assets that I focus on in this book: stocks, real estate, and small business.

In addition to saying that mutual funds and 401(k)s are way too risky, Kiyosaki said, "Those vehicles are only good for about 20 percent of the population, people making $100,000 or more." I couldn't disagree more. In fact, my experience is that mutual funds and exchange-traded funds are tailor-made for nonwealthy people who don't have the assets to properly create a diversified portfolio themselves.

Kiyosaki also said that he doesn't like mutual funds because "mutual funds have got no insurance from a stock market crash. To me, that's sad, and I am concerned." As I discuss in Parts 1 and 2 of this book, the best way to reduce the risk of investing in stocks is to diversify your holdings not only in a variety of stocks — which is precisely what good stock mutual funds do — but also in other investments that don't move in tandem with the stock market (such as bond funds).

Kiyosaki claimed that he invests with the benefit of insurance when investing in real estate. He said, "My banker requires me to have insurance from catastrophic losses." This comparison is nonsensical because such an insurance policy would cover losses from say, a fire, but not from a decline in market value of the real estate due to overall market conditions. Interestingly, Kiyosaki followers got clobbered by piling into real estate, which dropped sharply in most areas in the mid- to late-2000s.

Understand the Financial Markets

When the going gets tough in the stock market, you can easily lose perspective and start making rash decisions. Instead, you must have the long-term perspective you need to succeed with stock investing, and you really need to understand how the financial markets work. So, even if you've already read Chapters 4 and 5, go back and read them again. These chapters explain how the stock market works and what influences stock prices in the short term versus the longer term.

Talk to People Who Care about You

Life's challenging events can be humbling and sometimes depressing. Holding an investment that's dropped a lot in value — whether it's a stock, a mutual fund, real estate, or a small business — is one such event. But you don't have to carry the burden yourself. Talk about your feelings with someone who understands and cares about you. Be clear about and communicate what you're seeking — empathy, good listening, a sounding board, or advice.

Index

Numerics

A

V

vacancy rates, 231

value
  as benefit of real estate investing, 220
  compared with growth, 173–174
  determining for businesses, 333–334
  of property, 232–237
  of small business to purchase, 322

value averaging, 62

Value Line Investment Survey, 112–117, 367
  analyst assessment section, 114
  annual rates section, 117
  business section, 112–113
  capital structure section, 116
  current position section, 116
  historic financials section, 115
  Internet resources, 119
  quarterly financials section, 117
  ratings section, 114
  stock price performance section, 114–115
  websites, 119, 367

value stocks, 170–171, 396

Van Andel, Jay (Amway founder), 330

Vanguard, 189, 193, 198, 373

Vanguard funds, 177, 183, 184, 185, 186, 188, 189

variety of funds, as reason for investing in mutual funds, 160

W

Wal-Mart, 141

Warning! icon, 4

Wealth Without Risk (Givens), 349–350

websites
  bizbuysell, 323
  Cheat Sheet, 4
  CorporateInformation.com, 371
  credit reports, 247
  Department of Treasury, 150
  Dodge & Cox Funds, 189
  Dummies, 4
  E*Trade, 198
  Fairholme Funds, 189
  FDICs BankFind, 136
  Federal Trade Commission, 248
  FEMA (Federal Emergency Management Agency), 216
  Fidelity Funds, 189
  FINRA (Financial Industry Regulatory Authority), 371
  FPA Funds, 189
  Harbor Funds, 189
  IRS (Internal Revenue Service), 313
  Litman Gregory Masters Funds, 189
  Morningstar, 118, 371
  National Consumers League's Fraud Information Center, 371
  North American Securities Administrators Association, 371
  Oakmark, 189
  planetfeedback, 370
  researching, 119
  SBA (Small Business Administration), 323
  SCORE (Service Corps of Retired Executives), 300
  Scottrade, 198
  SEC (Securities and Exchange Commission), 371
  Sec.gov, 373
  Sequoia, 189

St. Louis Federal Reserve, 372–373

T. Rowe Price, 189, 198

TD Ameritrade, 198

Tweedy, Browne Funds, 189

Tyson, Eric, 108, 161, 295, 343, 371, 374

U.S. Bureau of Labor Statistics, 230

USAA Funds, 189

USGS (U.S. Geologic Survey), 216

Value Line Investment Survey, 118, 367

Vanguard, 189, 198, 373

The Whiz Kid of Wall Street's Investment Guide (Seto), 358

Williams, Richard E. (professor), 61

Wilshire 5000, 86

working from home, 310, 329

worldwide stock funds, 175–177

Wounded Warrior Project, 274

write-offs, 278

Y

Yahoo!, 94

Yellen, Janet (chairman of Federal Reserve Bank), 79

yield
  bond funds, 179–180
  defined, 33

yield curve, 143

Young, Owen D. (GE president), 99

Z

zero coupon bonds, 147

About the Author

Eric Tyson is an internationally acclaimed and best-selling personal finance author, lecturer, and advisor. Through his work, he is dedicated to teaching people to manage their money better and to successfully direct their own investments.

Eric is a former management consultant to businesses for which he helped improve operations and profitability. Before, during, and after this time of working crazy hours and traveling too much, he had the good sense to focus on financial matters.

He has been involved in the investing markets in many capacities for more than three decades. Eric first invested in mutual funds back in the mid-1970s, when he opened a mutual fund account at Fidelity. With the assistance of the late Dr. Martin Zweig, a famous investment market analyst, Eric won his high school's science fair for a project on what influences the stock market. In addition to investing in securities over the decades, Eric has also successfully invested in real estate and started and managed his own business. He has counseled thousands of clients on a variety of investment quandaries and questions.

He earned a bachelor's degree in economics at Yale and an MBA at the Stanford Graduate School of Business. Despite these impediments to lucid reasoning, he came to his senses and decided that life was too short to spend it working long hours and waiting in airports for the benefit of larger companies.

An accomplished freelance personal finance writer, Eric is the author of numerous best-selling books, including *For Dummies* books on personal finance, mutual funds, taxes (coauthor), and home buying (coauthor). He is also a syndicated columnist. His work has been featured and quoted in hundreds of national and local publications, including *Kiplinger's Personal Finance Magazine, Los Angeles Times, Chicago Tribune, The Wall Street Journal,* and *Bottom Line/Personal* and on NBC's *Today Show,* ABC, CNBC, PBS's *Nightly Business Report,* FOX, CNN, CBS national radio, Bloomberg Business Radio, National Public Radio, and Business Radio Network. He's also been a featured speaker at a White House conference on retirement planning.

To stay in tune with what real people care about and struggle with, Eric maintained a financial counseling practice for many years.

You can visit him on the web at www.erictyson.com.

Dedication

Actually, before I get to the thank-yous, please allow me a *really* major thank-you and dedication. This book is hereby and irrevocably dedicated to my family and friends, as well as to my counseling clients and customers, who ultimately have taught me everything I know about how to explain financial terms and strategies so that all of us may benefit.

Author's Acknowledgments

First, I'd like to thank Elizabeth Rea. Thanks also to Danielle Voirol for all of her fine editing and to all the fine folks involved in making this book and all my charts and graphs look great! Thanks also to everyone else who contributed to getting this book done well and on time.

And last but not least, a tip of my cap to the fine technical reviewer who helped to ensure that I didn't write something that wasn't quite right. For the seventh edition, this important job was well-handled by John Nelson.

Publisher's Acknowledgments

Acquisitions Editor: Stacy Kennedy

Project Editor: Elizabeth Rea

Senior Copy Editor: Danielle Voirol

Technical Editor: John Nelson, CFA

Project Coordinator: Patrick Redmond

Cover Image: Baevskiy Dmitry/Shutterstock